ADVANCE PRAISE

"Nothing is more practical that a good theory, and Stephen Porges's masterful theory of the nervous system is one of a handful of breakthroughs that define what our age has contributed to increasing our understanding of the mind-brain-body connection. That connection, so often, and rightly, talked about as the only sensible approach to understanding who we are, is nonetheless often discussed in only the vaguest of terms. Porges's triumph is to show these connections in the nervous system in specific detail, and to help us understand how its evolutionary history determines how it functions in use now, down to the minutest detail, gesture, facial expression, sigh. There's a reason that professionals from so many disciplines are using his work: it's one of the most detailed, true to life portraits of the embodied nervous system—something of which we only had glimpses of, because of some huge blind spots that Porges has remedied. This new book of seminal papers extends the range of a theory so important that it is painful to think what our understanding of the nervous system was like without it."

—**Norman Doidge, M.D.**, author of *The Brain That Changes Itself* and *The Brain's Way of Healing*

"Based in deep science, this groundbreaking book is full of practical and powerful tools to help people feel calmer, stronger, more connected, and more confident."

—**Rick Hanson, Ph.D.**, author of *Buddha's Brain: The Practical Neuroscience of Happiness, Love, and Wisdom*

"*Polyvagal Safety* updates Dr. Porges's *The Polyvagal Theory* and elaborates its contributions to understanding the present moment. The Polyvagal Theory is not a static theory, but a framework for understanding the human interface with the world. The theory emphasizes our need for safety and connection. Dr. Porges expands our concept of the mind and reminds us there is only one nervous system that integrates the regulation of the brain and body. His transdisciplinary theory provides a brain–body neuroscience that emphasizes the embodied nature of the mind and underscores the fact that the body plays a central role in how people regulate. This regulation relies on socioemotional exchanges embedded in bidirectional exchanges between autonomic nervous systems. *Polyvagal Safety* explores the application of the theory and potential insights from the theory across a broad range of topics."

—**Dr. Drew Pinsky**, Addiction Medicine Specialist

"This remarkable volume underscores the vast scope of Porges's Polyvagal Theory, interpreted and applied to a diversity of disciplines and conditions. Highlighting that our most basic human need—to feel safe—is conditional on our autonomic state, *Polyvagal Safety* is a deeply engaging, innovative, and satisfying read. Infused with both compassion and science, it offers unexpected insights relevant to daily life as well as to various therapeutic settings, leaving the reader with a profound sense of the overarching significance of safe human connectedness."

—**Pat Ogden**, Founder, Sensorimotor Psychotherapy Institute, and author of *The Pocket Guide to Sensorimotor Psychotherapy, Trauma and the Body*, and *Sensorimotor Psychotherapy* (with Janina Fisher)

"This indispensable volume presents the essentials of Stephen Porges's brilliant Polyvagal Theory as it applies to many clinical conditions as, indeed, to human life and development. Nuanced, richly detailed, and written with clarity, *Polyvagal Safety* is a matchless gift to physicians and therapists, and to all students of the body's inextricable unity with the psyche."

—**Gabor Maté, M.D.**, author of *When The Body Says No: Exploring the Stress-Disease Connection*

POLYVAGAL SAFETY
Attachment, Communication, Self-Regulation

The Norton Series on Interpersonal Neurobiology
Louis Cozolino, PhD, Series Editor
Allan N. Schore, PhD, Series Editor (2007–2014)
Daniel J. Siegel, MD, Founding Editor

The field of mental health is in a tremendously exciting period of growth and conceptual reorganization. Independent findings from a variety of scientific endeavors are converging in an interdisciplinary view of the mind and mental well-being. An interpersonal neurobiology of human development enables us to understand that the structure and function of the mind and brain are shaped by experiences, especially those involving emotional relationships.

The Norton Series on Interpersonal Neurobiology provides cutting-edge, multidisciplinary views that further our understanding of the complex neurobiology of the human mind. By drawing on a wide range of traditionally independent fields of research—such as neurobiology, genetics, memory, attachment, complex systems, anthropology, and evolutionary psychology—these texts offer mental health professionals a review and synthesis of scientific findings often inaccessible to clinicians. The books advance our understanding of human experience by finding the unity of knowledge, or consilience, that emerges with the translation of findings from numerous domains of study into a common language and conceptual framework. The series integrates the best of modern science with the healing art of psychotherapy.

A NORTON PROFESSIONAL BOOK

POLYVAGAL SAFETY

Attachment, Communication, Self-Regulation

STEPHEN W. PORGES

W. W. NORTON & COMPANY
Independent Publishers Since 1923

Note to Readers: Standards of clinical practice and protocol change over time, and no technique or recommendation is guaranteed to be safe or effective in all circumstances. This volume is intended as a general information resource for professionals practicing in the field of psychotherapy and mental health; it is not a substitute for appropriate training, peer review, and/or clinical supervision. Neither the publisher nor the author(s) can guarantee the complete accuracy, efficacy, or appropriateness of any particular recommendation in every respect. As of press time, the URLs displayed in this book link or refer to existing sites. The publisher and author are not responsible for any content that appears on third-party websites.

Certified by Polyvagal Institute as accurately representing the principles described in Polyvagal Theory.

For information about permission to reproduce selections from this book, write to Permissions, W. W. Norton & Company, Inc., 500 Fifth Avenue, New York, NY 10110

For information about special discounts for bulk purchases, please contact W. W. Norton Special Sales at specialsales@wwnorton.com or 800-233-4830

Manufacturing by Sheridan Books
Production manager: Gwen Cullen

Library of Congress Cataloging-in-Publication Data

Names: Porges, Stephen W., author.
Title: Polyvagal safety : attachment, communication, self-regulation / Stephen W. Porges.
Description: First edition. | New York : W.W. Norton & Company, [2021] | Series: The Norton series on interpersonal neurobiology | "A Norton professional book." | Includes bibliographical references and index.
Identifiers: LCCN 2021010000 | ISBN 9781324016274 (hardcover) | ISBN 9781324016281 (epub)
Subjects: LCSH: Autonomic nervous system. | Affective neuroscience. | Psychic trauma—Treatment.
Classification: LCC QP368 .P67 2021 | DDC 612.8/9—dc23
LC record available at https://lccn.loc.gov/2021010000

W. W. Norton & Company, Inc., 500 Fifth Avenue, New York, N.Y. 10110
www.wwnorton.com

W. W. Norton & Company Ltd., 15 Carlisle Street, London W1D 3BS

1 2 3 4 5 6 7 8 9 0

To the heroic survivors of trauma who have
taught me to cherish shared feelings of safety.

Contents

Acknowledgments

The past year has been challenging to all of humanity as we have been confronted with the global threat of the pandemic. During this period, we have witnessed and experienced how our nervous systems respond to cues of threat. These experiences remind us of the deep connection we have with others and our shared pain and grief when observing the impact of the virus.

In acknowledging those who have contributed to *Polyvagal Safety*, I first want to acknowledge the role the pandemic had on our lives and the help that many of us have received from the unnamed workforce that supported our ability to function. I want to express my gratitude and appreciation to those who have heroically served the community. I want to acknowledge both the heroic healthcare providers and the hardworking individuals who insured that the food supply chain was not disrupted and others who selflessly supported us, such as grocery store workers and the drivers for delivery services that provided contactless opportunities to order and deliver necessities and the products that we enjoy.

Polyvagal Safety and the pandemic are intertwined in terms of concepts, personal experiences, and timeframe. On March 3, 2020, just before New York City was recognized as the epicenter of the pandemic in the United States, I boarded a flight to New York. It is now mid-June 2021, and I have not been on a plane or been in an airport in more than 15 months. The trip to New York was eventful and transformative. It was the last time I talked in front of a live audience. I recall saying to participants that I would give hugs and shake hands at the meeting but might not in a month. Obviously, everything, including my capacity to be spontaneously sociable, changed within a week.

On March 4, 2020, we had an organizational meeting to create guidelines for the Polyvagal Institute (see polyvagalinstitute.org). Polyvagal Institute is now an active not-for-profit institute focused on developing and disseminating information on the Polyvagal Theory. The Institute will also be certifying programs, books, organizations, and products that accurately represent the principles embedded in Polyvagal Theory as *Polyvagal Informed.*

On March 5, I visited the Norton offices and met with my editor, Deborah Malmud. In our discussion we finalized *Polyvagal Safety.* Deborah suggested the title and conceptualized the volume as an update of the 2011 Norton volume. I am indebted to Deborah for helping me navigate from the world of an academic scientist to a broader clinically oriented audience. Her deep understanding of this helped shape the current volume, *Polyvagal Safety.*

During the pandemic, we have seen a remarkable adaptive shift in how society works. Many of us have been privileged with sufficient resources and access to healthcare services that enabled rapid identification of the virus, appropriate treatment, and effective mitigation through following public health guidelines. These successful strategies assumed that we were privileged to have sufficient financial and social resources or internet access to enable home schooling or work and the maintenance of social connections. With these resources we were able to remain healthy until the vaccines were available. Personally, my family and I were privileged to escape infection and not to be financially insecure. However, my nervous system has been greatly influenced by the isolation and minimal social interactions with a resulting shift in my neuroception towards caution. Having been fully vaccinated, I am not fearful of infection, yet I am cautious about interacting with others. Obviously, this reflects the consequences on my nervous system, which is now adaptively retuned to be threat biased. As I self-monitor during the transition back to a more normal social world, I continue to learn about the power of sociality as a neuromodulator of physiological state and how chronic threat narrows the window of social accessibility. This real-life experience shared with many reinforces the importance of connectedness and co-regulation in our lives and emphasizes the profound consequences of social isolation on mental and physical health.

Post-pandemic we need to be aware that a second pandemic is in our midst. This second pandemic is the consequence of the millions whose nervous systems have been retuned through the chronic threat of the pandemic; threat either of the virus or the impact of the virus on social and economic structures of our society. Note that not all family units are safe and that even in more optimal times abuse and neglect are prevalent. We need to be more aware of the vulnerable and how society—by marginalizing groups—retunes nervous systems, creating greater risks for mental and physical health problems. *Polyvagal Safety* is a timely volume in helping us understand how context (via neuroception) influences our physiological state, which in turn influences our behavior and the behaviors of others.

During the 15 months that we have been working on *Polyvagal Safety,* the lessons of the pandemic can be summarized as the theme and title of the book. Polyvagal Theory provides the perspective of understanding safety as a felt sense that fosters the necessary sociality leading to optimized mental and physical health. As you read the chapters, you will appreciate the influence of my co-authors as we collaborated, expanding the application of Polyvagal Theory while being true to the importance of feeling safe.

I want to acknowledge the support I have received from my family. My wife, Sue, who has patiently listened to my ideas as they transitioned from vague thoughts to a concrete expression in my talks and papers. Our sons, Eric and Seth, who have given me the greatest pleasures, the opportunity to watch them express their creativity and humanity. And, our granddaughter, Minna, whose smile and curiosity puts meaning into our lives.

Above all, I want to acknowledge the heroic survivors of trauma, who have shared their personal journeys. As I listened to their narratives, I felt a true sense of humility and experienced a deep sense of gratitude in knowing that my insights have been helpful.

Introduction: An Embedded History of a New Science

When the Polyvagal Theory was initially conceptualized, I did not consider it as an expansive paradigm-shifting model. In developing it, I thought it was consistent with antecedent research and theory. In a way, I thought it was the obvious next step. During the 25 years following the initial presentation of the Polyvagal Theory, through my experiences with the scientific community across many disciplines, I learned that the theory provides the framework for a new brain-body or mind-body science. Moreover, I learned that as health-related disciplines embraced the theory, a new polyvagal-informed strategy could be embedded in mental and physical health treatment models. This strategy would focus on recruiting the nervous system of the client or patient as a collaborator on a shared journey toward wellness. Embracing this strategy would emphasize that the body's quest for safety is embedded in the actions of the nervous system in promoting health. Thus, safety and threat are not only psychological constructs, but have parallels in the autonomic nervous system. When the autonomic nervous system is in a state of calmness and social accessibility, then treatments for both mental and physical disorders can be efficiently implemented. In contrast, when the autonomic nervous system is in a state of defense and vulnerability, then it is in an antagonistic state that blunts the effectiveness of treatment. Simply stated, the theory uncovered the structures and portals through which our neurobiological quest for safety through connectedness with others may be implemented.

When a new theory is presented, its intellectual accessibility is dependent on several complex and often not acknowledged historical features. Most importantly, there is a need to understand (1) antecedent theories, (2) the language used to describe the hypothetical constructs illustrating the functions described in the theory, and (3) questions that the theory proposes to answer. Since evolution is an organizing principle in Polyvagal Theory, in which neuroanatomical structures are proposed to facilitate specific adaptive functions, an understanding of vertebrate evolution and neuroanatomy of the neural regulation of the autonomic nervous system are required for a critical dialogue. In addition, since the theory leads to testable hypotheses based on dynamic adjustments in autonomic function, a sophisticated understanding of the metrics of measurement (e.g., time series analyses) is necessary.

Scientists are intellectually focused and affiliated with peer groups defined by a shared commitment to study common problems. They see the world through their research questions, explicit and implicit theories, and methodologies. My scientific origins are rooted in the world of psychophysiology, a science that emerged in the 1960s to study how physiological responses paralleled psychological phenomena such as mental effort, attention, expectancy, stimulus detection, decision making, truthfulness, and preference. At the time I first presented the Polyvagal Theory, arousal theory was prevalent in psychophysiology. Although arousal theory had a long, influential history in science, it had a relatively simplistic underlying model. Basically, arousal theory emphasized that arousal was a linear construct indexing a dimension from low to high levels of activation that could be measured or inferred from observing behavior or physiology. The relationship between arousal and performance was often portrayed as an inverted U-shaped function in which optimal performance occurred within a midlevel range, while poor performance was observed at low and high levels of arousal. This relationship was known as the Yerkes-Dodson law (Yerkes & Dodson, 1908). Metaphorically, arousal represented the energy of the human nervous system. Arousal was easily understood, since when it was reflected behaviorally it could be quantified as greater activity and when reflected autonomically it could be observed as increases in sweating and heart rate.

Early psychophysiological research assumed that peripheral autonomic measures provided sensitive indicators of arousal. This view was based on a rudimentary understanding of the autonomic nervous system in which changes in electrodermal activity (e.g., sweating) and heart rate were assumed to be accurate indicators of sympathetic activity. As the activation arousal theory developed, a continuity between peripheral autonomic responses and central mechanisms was assumed (see Darrow et al., 1942), and sympathetic activity was assumed to parallel activation of the brain. According to this assumption, organs influenced by sympathetic efferent fibers, such as the sweat glands, blood vessels, or the heart, were potential indicators of limbic or cortical activity (Duffy, 1957; Lindsley, 1951; Malmo, 1959).

Although the specific pathways relating these various levels were never outlined and are still sketchy, electrodermal (e.g., GSR) and heart rate became the primary focus of research during the early history of the Society for Psychophysiological Research. This was due to their presumed sympathetic innervation and, in part, to their measurement availability. By default, this emphasis created a research environment that neglected several important factors: (a) parasympathetic (e.g., vagal) influences, (b) interactions between sympathetic and para-sympathetic processes, (c) peripheral autonomic afferents, (d) central regulatory structures, (e) the adaptive and dynamic nature of the autonomic nervous system, and (f) phylogenetic and ontogenetic differences in structural organization and function.

Polyvagal Theory proposed a more complex nonlinear model of autonomic regulation that focused on identifiable and potentially measurable neural pathways that contribute to autonomic regulation through a definable feedback system that could promote homeostatic function. The theory required a conceptualization of autonomic regulation that was challenging to psychophysiologists. At the time, psychophysiology emphasized a top-down representation of central nervous system function in measurable peripheral physiology (e.g., autonomic response patterns). Thus, many psychophysiologists hypothesized that systematic quantification of peripheral autonomic responses would provide reliable information linked to brain function and mental processes. Prior to the Polyvagal Theory, my research was consistent with this top-down perspective. For example, I wrote an article titled "Heart Rate Patterns in Neonates: A Potential Diagnostic Window to the Brain" (Porges, 1983).

By 1994 when the Polyvagal Theory was introduced, my views about neural regulation of the autonomic nervous system had changed. At that time, I was working on what I called the vagal paradox. The neural pathways underlying the plausible solution to the paradox became the Polyvagal Theory. In contrast to the prevalent working models of my colleagues, Polyvagal Theory emphasized bidirectional communication between the brain and the visceral organs represented in the autonomic nervous system. Acknowledging the theory confronted scientists with the plausible possibility that peripheral visceral organs could influence brain processes, including the cognitive and emotional processes assumed to originate in the brain.

Polyvagal Theory did not fit well within the constraints of arousal theory, although Polyvagal Theory could provide a neural explanation of arousal theory. Arousal theory fit an outdated, but still taught, model of the autonomic nervous system that interpreted arousal as a competition between the sympathetic and parasympathetic nervous systems. However, it did not provide any explanation of how low arousal could occur with increases in parasympathetic nervous system activation.

Polyvagal Theory required a different quantification strategy, and a new family of metrics (e.g., respiratory sinus arrhythmia as an index of vagal regulation of the heart) was needed to be developed to accurately monitor the dynamic regulation of the autonomic nervous system. The theory encouraged scientists to look beyond mean levels of variables and to study the periodicities in the physiological signal that represented the features of the feedback system that evolved to optimize homeostasis. Time series methodologies complemented descriptive statistics, and new measures could describe the systematic perturbations around the set point. In my world, this was observed as periodic variations in heart rate around the mean or set point of the heart. For example, the periodic variations of heart rate at the frequency of spontaneous respiration define respiratory sinus arrhythmia and neurophysiologically reflect the feedback between the heart and the brainstem through the ventral vagus. The amplitude of this oscillation is a valid index of a component of cardiac vagal tone being mediated through the myelinated ventral vagal pathway to the sinoatrial node, the pacemaker of the heart. In preparation for, or while, moving, the amplitude of this oscillation is dampened to optimize the sympathetic nervous system's influence on the heart to increase cardiac output to support mobilization. The damping of this feedback loop also represents the dampening of the role the autonomic nervous system is playing in maintaining homeostasis. Conceptually, we can visualize the amplitude of respiratory sinus arrhythmia as an index of the degree that the autonomic nervous system is supporting either homeostasis or bodily movement, often in support of flight and fight behavioral reactions to threat. In addition, since the amplitude of respiratory sinus arrhythmia represents the strength of the vagal brake, by monitoring respiratory sinus arrhythmia we are functionally monitoring the homeostatic reserve of the autonomic nervous system to the challenges that we often label as stress. Thus, disruption of homeostasis would be an accurate measurable indicator of the impact of challenges and might be a more functional definition of stress than levels of adrenal hormones (e.g., cortisol).

Through the lens of the Polyvagal Theory, homeostasis has a more nuanced meaning involving the status of feedback circuits involving the bidirectional communication between organs and the brainstem. The traditional autonomic model assumed that homeostasis was relatively stable and was maintained by the competing inputs from the sympathetic and parasympathetic divisions of the autonomic nervous system, although the pathways involved in feedback circuits determining homeostasis were not elaborated. Polyvagal Theory, with its emphasis on bidirectional communication between brain structures and visceral organs, assumes that homeostasis is best described not solely by a static set point, but requires an additional assessment of the systematic perturbations around the set point.

Strikingly, there is little acknowledgment of the important role of visceral afferents that travel primarily through the vagus from each visceral organ to a brainstem center, providing the relevant information to ensure that the output to the organs supports homeostasis. Without sensitive metrics to assess the neural regulation supporting visceral organs, medicine is unable to detect the antecedent disruption in neural regulation that would precede organ damage. Although the sensory pathways of the vagus function as a surveillance system continuously updating brainstem regulatory centers on organ status, this conceptualization of dynamic feedback in the regulation of visceral organs has not been emphasized in the training of physicians. Although end-organ evaluation through biopsy and blood tests dominates the assessment models of visceral organs, tapping into the constant surveillance of visceral organs through vagal or other neural pathways has not been frequently acknowledged by physicians. If you are curious about this statement, just ask your internist what they have learned about the sensory fibers linking the brain with the organs they treat (e.g., heart, kidney, liver, lung).

Against the backdrop of arousal theory, a bias toward static metrics of autonomic function (e.g., resting heart rate, blood pressure), and a limited understanding of how the dynamic regulation of the autonomic nervous system could support or disrupt homeostasis, Polyvagal Theory emerged on an October morning in 1994. The initial framework of the theory was introduced during my presidential address at the annual meeting of the Society for Psychophysiological Research in Atlanta, Georgia. The presentation was formalized into a manuscript and published in the society's journal, Psychophysiology (Porges, 1995). At that time, my objective was to archive the extracted principles from my previous 25 years of research and to challenge my discipline to explore autonomic reactivity from a new perspective. Although several of the principles were novel, the general questions were familiar to psychophysiologists, who were vested in exploring the utility of monitoring heart rate patterns to gain additional information about mental and health-related processes. My address was well received by my colleagues, and I anticipated that formulation of the theory would drive research within psychophysiology by providing an alternative perspective of the role that the autonomic nervous system played in regulating mental processes, physiological state, and behavior. At that time, I had no expectation that Polyvagal Theory would lead to clinical insights, interventions, and new approaches to mental and physical health.

During the following 25 years, as the science of the neural regulation of the autonomic nervous system grew, our understanding of how the theory informs us about human behavior and health expanded. In parallel to the growth in scientific knowledge, the theory evolved to include new constructs that were proposed to integrate and translate this new knowledge into a better understanding of mental health. Four new constructs, briefly described in the following paragraphs, provided a language to communicate relevant features of the theory to therapists. The publications documenting the introduction of these constructs are listed in Table I.1 and are reprinted in *The Polyvagal Theory: Neurophysiological Foundations of Emotions, Attachment, Communication, Self-regulation* (Porges, 2011).

Vagal Brake

The vagal brake reflects the inhibitory influence of vagal pathways on the heart, which slow the intrinsic rate of the heart's pacemaker (Porges et al., 1996). If the vagus no longer influenced the heart, heart rate would spontaneously increase without any change in sympathetic excitation. The intrinsic heart rate of young, healthy adults is about 90 beats per minute. However, baseline heart rate is noticeably slower due to the influence of the vagus functioning as a vagal brake. The vagal brake represents the actions of engaging and disengaging the vagal influences on the heart's pacemaker. Tasks requiring the systematic engagement and disengagement of the vagal brake may be conceptualized as neural exercises that would enhance vagal brake function, including self-calming and self-regulation. It has been assumed that the vagal brake is mediated through the myelinated ventral vagus. Although the unmyelinated vagal fibers appear to mediate clinical bradycardia in preterm neonates, this process has not been conceptualized in the vagal brake construct. The functioning of the vagal brake is a core foundational construct in Polyvagal Theory and is involved in down-regulating defenses and promoting social accessibility that may evolve into coregulation.

Social Engagement System

The social engagement system consists of a somatomotor (i.e., neural control of striated muscles) component and a visceromotor (i.e., neural control of muscles of visceral organs) component (Porges, 1998). The somatomotor component involves special visceral efferent pathways that regulate the striated muscles of the face and head. The visceromotor component involves the ventral myelinated supradiaphragmatic vagus that regulates the heart and bronchi. Functionally, the social engagement system emerges from a heart-face connection that coordinates the heart with the muscles of the face and head. The initial function of the system is to coordinate sucking, swallowing, breathing, and vocalizing. Atypical coordination of this system early in life is an indicator of subsequent difficulties in social behavior and emotional regulation. It is through the social engagement system that individuals broadcast their physiological state in their voices and faces. Astute therapists intuitively detect these features and appropriately coregulate their clients into calmer and more accessible states.

Neuroception

Neuroception is the process through which the nervous system evaluates risk without requiring awareness (Porges, 2003). This automatic process involves brain areas that evaluate cues of safety, danger, and life threat. Once these are detected via neuroception, physiological state automatically shifts to optimize survival. Although we are usually not aware of cues that trigger neuroception, we tend to be aware of the physiological shift (i.e., interoception). Sometimes we experience this as feelings in our gut or heart or as an intuition that the context is dangerous. Alternatively, this system also triggers physiological states that support trust, social engagement behaviors, and the building of strong relationships. Neuroception is not always accurate. Faulty neuroception might be an adaptive survival reaction that biases neuroception toward detecting risk when there is no risk, or identifying cues of safety when there is risk. Individuals with a trauma history frequently experience such a biased neuroception.

The Frequency Band of Perceptual Advantage

The frequency band of perceptual advantage represents the acoustic frequency range in which conspecifics vocalize to communicate cues of safety and reciprocal positive social intentions (Porges & Lewis, 2010). This band, based on the physics of middle ear structures, determines the specific frequency ranges within which cues of safety are communicated. Vocalizations occurring within this frequency band signal safety and calm the listener's internal state, while vocalizations occurring outside this frequency signal danger and threat and disrupt the listener's internal state. These interpretations of acoustic features are based on the phylogenetic evolutionary history of vertebrates. At relatively high frequencies, vocalizations represent distress calls and likely signal nearby conspecifics of injury or threat. An example can be found in the infant cry, which occurs in a relatively high spectral range of human hearing and produces caregiver responses to reduce infant distress. Low-frequency sounds below the low end of a mammal's frequency band of perceptual advantage have an unlearned association with cues of life threat. Over the course of mammalian evolutionary history, vocalizations in a relatively low-frequency region were likely to be produced by larger predators. Thus, acoustic signals with high energy (louder) above or below a mammal's frequency band of perceptual advantage may trigger resource mobilization for fight-flight responses or the shutdown behaviors that define death feigning. The Safe and Sound Protocol is an acoustic intervention that functions as a neural exercise of the social engagement system by focusing on the frequency of perceptual advantage. For more information on the intervention, see Integrated Listening Systems (https://integratedlistening.com/porges/).

With these constructs, the theory could inform therapists and potentially change treatment strategies. With understanding of these constructs, therapists could more effectively recruit their client's nervous systems as collaborators on a shared journey to wellness. Therapists, by leveraging their own social engagement systems to project cues of safety, could lead their clients through sequential states of coregulation to self-regulation and resilience. As the theory transformed from foundational laboratory research to clinical and applied areas, a new language evolved to communicate the constructs of the theory to a broader audience, including clinicians and their clients.

In the 25 years following the presentation of the initial features of the theory, the theory has evolved and transformed. Much of this transformation has been driven through my experiences and collaborations in clinical fields. During the 25-year period since the inception of the theory, thousands of researchers have

TABLE I.1.

Construct	Citation
Vagal brake	Porges, S. W., Doussard-Roosevelt, J. A., Portales, A. L., & Greenspan, S. I. (1996). Infant regulation of the vagal "brake" predicts child behavior problems: A psychobiological model of social behavior. *Developmental Psychobiology*, 29(8), 697–712.
Social engagement system	Porges, S. W. (1998). Love: An emergent property of the mammalian autonomic nervous system. *Psychoneuroendocrinology*, 23(8), 837–861.
Neuroception	Porges, S. W. (2003). Social engagement and attachment: A phylogenetic perspective. *Annals of the New York Academy of Sciences*, 1008(1), 31–47.
Frequency band of perceptual advantage	Porges, S. W., & Lewis, G. F. (2010). The polyvagal hypothesis: Common mechanisms mediating autonomic regulation, vocalizations and listening. In S. M. Brudzynski (Ed.), *Handbook of behavioral neuroscience: Handbook of mammalian vocalization* (Vol. 19, pp. 255–264). New York: Elsevier.

cited the theory to explain their results, while tens of thousands of therapists and clients have used the theory to explain the impact of chronic stress and trauma on mental and physical health. The impact and application of the theory has crossed discipline boundaries.

Accessibility is critical in translating scientific knowledge into the therapeutic and the public consciousness. Most peer-reviewed journals have costly subscriptions that limit readership to those who have academic affiliations. Even if articles are published in open-access journals, they are not written for the public. As aspects of the theory have become more accessible through the internet and books, creative and intuitive scientists and clinicians have embedded themes from the theory in foundational research and therapeutic treatments. A cursory survey using Google Scholar identifies more than 10,000 citations in peer-reviewed papers, while a Google search identifies more than 500,000 webpages, and a YouTube search identifies a vast selection of videos with accumulated views well above a million.

Over time, the theory became embedded in clinical perspectives, and polyvagal-informed therapies emerged. In 2018, Deb Dana and I edited a volume titled *Clinical Applications of the Polyvagal Theory: The Emergence of Polyvagal-Informed Therapies* (Porges & Dana, 2018) in which independent and creative therapists across several disciplines wrote chapters illustrating how they embedded Polyvagal Theory into their practice. Editing the book was a transformative experience and left me with a sense of gratitude as I witnessed Polyvagal Theory being incorporate into the creative works of others.

Following more recent discussions with Deborah Malmud, the director of Norton Professional Books, we decided to create a book that contained relevant articles published primarily since the publication of *The Polyvagal Theory* (Porges, 2011). *Polyvagal Safety* is the product of those discussions. This book provides the opportunity to share our expanded understanding of the theory since the publication of the initial polyvagal book.

In reading this book, keep in mind that scientific knowledge upon which the theory is based has expanded since 1994. Basically, what is now known is not equivalent to the information available when the theory was developed. Also, consider the value of a theory in providing plausible explanations of clinical observations and how theory is tested. In general, theories explain phenomena and are seldom proven true or false. Rather, they are either updated by information derived from research or displaced by a competing theory that is more effective in explaining the phenomena. By tracking the publications following the disclosure of the theory, the reader can grasp the refinement of the theory as it has continued to focus on clinical features. The collective work continues to emphasize that our mental and physical health can thrive only when our autonomic nervous system is in a state of safety.

Polyvagal Theory is not a static theory, but a framework for organizing information and structuring hypotheses. It is a theory about our human interface with the world and our need for safety and connection through trusting relationships. Through a polyvagal perspective, there is only one nervous system that integrates the regulation of brain and body. Functionally, Polyvagal Theory provides a brain-body neuroscience that links social communication to the regulation of our autonomic nervous system. It is a theory that is agnostic about the causal direction of mental and physical comorbidities. It is a theory that emphasizes feedback systems that support homeostasis and focuses on operational definitions of stress (e.g., disruption of homeostasis) and emphasizes the role of autonomic state in creating both vulnerabilities for mental and physical health and opportunities for rehabilitation and healing. As you read the book, I welcome you to share my enthusiasm for discovery as we learn to appreciate the wonderful attributes of being a human mammal. The book contains 14 chapters that provide examples of recent theoretical, empirical, and applied elaborations of the theory. The appendix provides an additional chapter: a primer summarizing the theory.

REFERENCES

Darrow, C. W., Jost, H., Solomon, A. P., & Mergener, J. C. (1942). Autonomic indicators of excitatory and homeostatic effects on the electroencephalogram. *Journal of Psychology, 14,* 115–130.

Duffy, E. (1957). The psychological significance of the concept of "arousal" or "activation." *Psychological Review, 64*, 265–275.

Lindsley, D. (1951). Emotion. In S. S. Stevens (Ed.), *Handbook of experimental psychology* (pp. 473–516). New York: Wiley.

Malmo, R. B. (1959). Activation: A neurophysiological dimension. *Psychological Review, 66*, 367–386.

Porges, S. W. (1983). Heart rate patterns in neonates: A potential diagnostic window to the brain. In T. M. Field & A. M. Sostek (Eds.), *Infants born at risk: Physiological and perceptual responses* (pp. 3–22). New York: Grune and Stratton.

Porges, S. W. (1995). Orienting in a defensive world: Mammalian modifications of our evolutionary heritage. A Polyvagal Theory. *Psychophysiology, 32*(4), 301–318.

Porges, S. W. (1998). Love: An emergent property of the mammalian autonomic nervous system. *Psychoneuroendocrinology, 23*(8), 837–861.

Porges, S. W. (2003). Social engagement and attachment: A phylogenetic perspective. *Annals of the New York Academy of Sciences, 1008*(1), 31–47.

Porges, S. W. (2011). *The Polyvagal Theory: Neurophysiological foundation of emotions, attachment, communication, self-regulation*. New York: Norton.

Porges, S. W., & Dana, D. A. (2018). *Clinical applications of the Polyvagal Theory: The emergence of polyvagal-informed therapies*. New York: Norton.

Porges, S. W., Doussard-Roosevelt, J. A., Portales, A. L., & Greenspan, S. I. (1996). Infant regulation of the vagal "brake" predicts child behavior problems: A psychobiological model of social behavior. *Developmental Psychobiology, 29*(8), 697–712.

Porges, S. W., & Lewis, G. F. (2010). The polyvagal hypothesis: Common mechanisms mediating autonomic regulation, vocalizations and listening. In S. M. Brudzynski (Ed.), Handbook of behavioral neuroscience: *Handbook of mammalian vocalization* (Vol. 19, pp. 255–264). New York: Elsevier.

Yerkes, R. M., & Dodson, J. D. (1908). The relation of strength of stimulus to rapidity of habit-formation. *Journal of Comparative Neurology and Psychology, 18*(5), 459–482.

CHAPTER 1

Neurocardiology Through the Lens of the Polyvagal Theory

Stephen W. Porges and Jacek Kolacz

THE BRAIN-BODY CONNECTION IN MEDICINE

Knowledge and experience frame our perspective of how the brain and the autonomic nervous system interact. What we are taught influences how we form research questions and test hypotheses. As understanding of the neurophysiology of the autonomic nervous system expands, it changes the scope of inquiry. New knowledge slowly permeates medical education and even more slowly impacts how clinicians understand and treat conditions.

The conceptualization of the autonomic nervous system within medical education has not kept pace with the neurophysiological research expanding our understanding of bidirectional connections between the brain and visceral organs. Medical education provides few opportunities to learn how neural circuits in the brain regulate peripheral organs and even fewer opportunities to learn how peripheral organs influence brain function. This limited knowledge results in many physicians not understanding the potential pathways that would promote health or result in dysfunction. When diagnoses are negative and there is no measurable functional or structural manifestation in the organ, a lack of understanding the role of the bidirectional neural communication between the brain and visceral organs may result in the physician assuming that patient's symptoms are not credible.

Medical specialties are organ focused, resulting in disciplines that study the organ and not the neural regulation of the organ. In addition, when there is a more general system dysfunction in neural regulation, this strategy may result in the appearance of dysfunction in more than one organ (i.e., comorbidities). Frequently, the assessment of an organ, without a concrete metric of disruption of function, assumes that the disorder is not physiologically based and is solely psychological. This conclusion limits the support and treatment that the clinician can provide and places the patient at risk. Several disorders have been assumed to have psychological determinants, since the neural pathways are not known and the intensity of symptoms is frequently linked to stressful situations.

A primary objective for integrating disciplines, such as neurocardiology, is to objectively describe the relationship between the nervous system and visceral organs. However, for those who study the neural regulation of the heart and other visceral organs, there is a shared knowledge that brain structures and peripheral organs are interconnected through neural pathways that send signals from visceral organs to the brainstem and from the brainstem to the visceral organs. These bidirectional communication circuits provide dynamic regulatory mechanisms through which brain structures influence visceral organs and visceral organs inform and influence brain function. This premise is the basis of Polyvagal Theory and an important assumption in neurocardiology.

HISTORICAL PERSPECTIVES ON THE BRAIN-BODY CONNECTION

The contemporary conceptualization of bidirectional communication between visceral organs and the brain is rooted in the work of Walter Hess. In 1949 Hess was awarded the Nobel Prize in Physiology/Medicine for his paradigm-shifting work on the central control of visceral organs. His Nobel lecture discussing brain control of visceral organs was titled "The Central Control of the Activity of Internal Organs." The first paragraph of his Nobel Prize speech is both prescient and historical. It provides the context upon which development, application, and acceptance of neuro-autonomic disciplines, such as neurocardiology, have emerged. This context provides the contradictory values of encouraging a better understanding of the dynamics of neural regulation of an integrated nervous system, while being constrained by reductionistic experimental methods and limited paradigms.

> A recognized fact, which goes back to the earliest times, is that every living organism is not the sum of a multitude of unitary processes, but is, by virtue of interrelationships and of higher and lower levels of control, an unbroken unity. When research, in the efforts of bringing understanding, as a rule examines isolated processes and studies them, these must of necessity be removed from their context. In general, viewed biologically, this experimental separation involves a sac-

rifice. In fact, quantitative findings of any material and energy changes preserve their full context only through their being seen and understood as parts of a natural order. This implies that the laws governing organic cohesion, the organization leading from the part to the whole, represent a biological uncertainty, indeed an uncertainty of the first order. It becomes all the more acute, the more rapidly the advances of specialization develop and threaten the ability to grasp, or even to appreciate it. While this state of affairs has just been referred to, our subject is defined by its general content. In particular it deals with the neural mechanisms by which the activity of the internal organs is adapted to constantly changing conditions, and by which they are adjusted to one another, in the sense of interrelated systems of functions. It only remains to be added that broadening of our knowledge in these respects is of benefit not only with regard to the human compulsion to understand, but also to the practical healing art. For man also, in health and sickness, is not just the sum of his organs, but is indeed a human organism. (Hess, 1949)

Hess's view of an integrated nervous system involving the mutual and dynamic bidirectional interactions between the brain and visceral organs did not receive traction within traditional medical education. In contrast, medical education confirmed Hess's view that advances in specialization resulting in medical subdisciplines threaten the ability to appreciate the organization from an organ to the integrated organism.

Few physicians are familiar with Hess's landmark research and his warning against partitioning the body into central and peripheral nervous systems. From Hess's perspective there is only one integrated nervous system. Instead of incorporating Hess's prescient view, medical education remained dependent on an earlier and more limited view of the autonomic nervous system proposed by Langley in 1921, which has remained the predominant model taught in medical schools. If you doubt this, ask a cardiologist, a nephrologist, a hepatologist, a gastroenterologist, or even a more eclectic internist, if specific neural pathways could contribute to symptoms of dysfunction. If they are in agreement, ask them what neural test would confirm this speculation. In addition, ask the specialist if anxiety, depression, or chronic stress could be a function of or the cause of an organ dysfunction. Also inquire about the possibility that medical treatments to peripheral organs could, via afferent feedback from the organ to the brain, contribute to the specific symptoms experienced. These inquiries will provide an understanding of the massive gaps in our knowledge involving the role of the nervous system in health and illness.

Langley was a distinguished professor of physiology at the University of Cambridge. In 1898 he proposed the term autonomic nervous system "to describe the sympathetic system and the allied nervous system of the cranial and sacral nerves, and for the local nervous system of the gut" (Langley, 1898, p. 270). Collectively, the autonomic function of the cranial and sacral nerves defined the parasympathetic nervous system, and the nervous system of the gut became known as the enteric nervous system. In the first paragraph of his classic text, *The Autonomic Nervous System, Part I*, he clearly provided his definition of the autonomic nervous system (Langley, 1921). He stated that "the autonomic nervous system consists of the nerve cells and nerve fibres, by means of which efferent impulses pass to tissues other than multi-nuclear striated muscle."

Langley's view of the autonomic nervous system consists of efferent pathways and target organs in the viscera, a top-down model excluding both the brain structures involved in regulation and the afferent pathways communicating peripheral organ status back to the brain.

In fact, the Langley model does not include the requisite components of a system capable of regulation through feedback. Such a system would require a central regulator connected to a target structure via both motor and sensory pathways. The Langley model disrupted the expanding view of an integrated whole-body nervous system proposed by Bernard (1865) and described by Darwin (1872), characterized by bidirectional communication between the brain and the visceral organs.

A naive treatment of autonomic responses without the consequential influence of afferent feedback is consistent with Langley's (1921) definition of a limited autonomic nervous system excluding the influence of the sensory fibers that accompany most visceral motor fibers.

Although the definition is often expanded to include both visceral afferents and central structures (e.g., medulla, hypothalamus), contemporary textbooks focus on the motor components, minimizing in their description the important role of afferent and central contributions to the regulation of the peripheral autonomic organs. This bias, by ignoring the importance of the afferent pathways, neglects the feedback and central regulatory features of a functional system. Moreover, it limits the study of the dynamic regulatory function of the autonomic nervous system, since the regulation of visceral state and the maintenance of homeostasis implicitly assume a feedback system with the necessary constituent components of motor, sensory, and regulatory structures. Thus, from a systems perspective, the autonomic nervous system includes afferent pathways conveying information regarding the visceral organs and the brain areas that interpret the afferent feedback and exert control over the motor output back to the visceral organs.

Darwin (1872) provided historical insight into the potential importance of the vagus in bidirectional communication between the brain and the heart. Although Darwin focused on facial expressions in defining emotions, he acknowledged the dynamic relationship between the vagus and the central nervous system activity that accompanied the spontaneous expression of emotions. He speculated that there were identifiable neural pathways that provided the necessary communication between specific brain structures and peripheral organs to promote the unique pattern of autonomic activity associated with emotions. For example:

> When the mind is strongly excited, we might expect that it would instantly affect in a direct manner the heart; and this is universally acknowledged. . . . When the heart is affected it reacts on the brain; and the state of the brain again reacts through the pneumogastric [vagus] nerve on the heart; so that under any excitement there will be much mutual action and reaction between these, the two most important organs of the body. (Darwin, 1872, p. 69)

For Darwin, when an emotional state occurred, the beating of the heart changed instantly (i.e., via vagal efferents) and the change in cardiac activity influenced brain activity (i.e., via vagal afferents). He did not elucidate the neurophysiological mechanisms that translate the initial emotional expression to the heart. Our current knowledge of brainstem anatomy and the neurophysiology of the vagus were not available to Darwin. At that time, it was not known that vagal fibers originate in several medullary nuclei and that the branches of the vagus exert control over the periphery through different feedback systems. However, Darwin's statement is important, because it emphasizes the afferent feedback from the heart to the brain, independent of the spinal cord and the sympathetic nervous system, and the regulatory role of the pneumogastric nerve (renamed the vagus at the end of the 19th century) in the expression of emotions.

Darwin attributed these ideas to Claude Bernard as an example of nervous system regulation of le milieu interieur (the environment within). Consistent with more contemporary psychophysiology and neurocardiology, Claude Bernard viewed the heart as a primary response system capable of reacting to all forms of sensory stimulation. He explicitly emphasized the potency of central nervous system pathways to the heart (Cournand, 1979). These pathways may be assumed to travel through the vagus. These ideas are expressed in the following observation by Claude Bernard:

> In man the heart is not only the central organ of circulation of blood, it is a center influenced by all sensory influences. They may be transmitted from the periphery through the spinal cord, from the organs through the sympathetic nervous system, or from the central nervous system itself. In fact, the sensory stimuli coming from the brain exhibit their strongest effects on the heart. (Cournand, 1979, p. 118)

Bernard and Darwin, by appreciating the importance of afferent feedback in the neural regulation of the heart, may serve as historic founders of neurocardiology. Langley was not alone in minimizing the potential bidirectional communication between visceral organs and the brain. Walter Cannon (1927), another iconic physiologist, proposed that the autonomic responses associated with emotions were driven primarily by brain structures and transmitted through sympathetic-adrenal pathways to support fight-flight behaviors. Cannon's view contradicted William James (1884), who proposed that it was the afferent feedback from the body that framed the emotional experience. Cannon's view was readily accepted and merged with the views of Hans Selye (1936, 1956) to dominate contemporary views of stress physiology. Perhaps James's lack of physiological sophistication and an inability to describe the neural pathways through which the afferent feedback traveled from the periphery to the brain contributed to this bias. The generalized stress responses described by Cannon and Selye emphasized the sympathetic nervous system and the adrenals. These views minimized the role of the vagus and did not acknowledge the primary role of afferent vagal pathways as a surveillance system in physiological and emotional regulation, communicating organ status to brain structures.

As researchers attempt to communicate and translate findings and conceptualizations into clinical practice, they continue to be confronted with the products of a medical education that conceptualized the autonomic nervous system within the limitations of the Langley definition. This restricted model influenced physicians' general understanding and conceptualization of the communication between the brain and visceral organs. At best, physicians acknowledge the top-down communication from brain to organ, although virtually all physicians have limited knowledge about the afferents monitoring visceral organs and informing the brain centers that regulate the organs.

The Langley model, in part, has been misunderstood, since its contribution represented important progress by providing an organizing principle to the efferent regulation of visceral organs. It was not proposed as an alternative to the more integrative features of visceral regulation proposed 50 years earlier by Bernard. From a historical perspective, it is important to reconcile these discontinuities as the science and clinical practice become reintegrated into neuro-autonomic disciplines such as neurocardiology. It was in search of a more integrative model of the neural regulation of the autonomic nervous system that the Polyvagal Theory emerged (Porges, 1995, 1998, 2001b, 2007, 2009, 2011).

THE VAGAL PARADOX: ORIGIN OF THE POLYVAGAL THEORY

Polyvagal Theory emerged from a paradox observed while studying heart rate patterns in human fetuses and newborns. In obstetrics and neonatology, bradycardia is a clinical index of risk and assumed to be mediated by the vagus. In the same clinical populations, beat-to-beat heart rate variability is a clinical index of resilience and also is assumed to be mediated by the vagus. If cardiac vagal tone is a positive indicator of health of a fetus or neonate when monitored with heart rate variability, then how could vagal tone be a negative indicator of health when it is manifested as bradycardia? Animal research demonstrated that both signals could be disrupted by severing the vagal pathways to the heart or via pharmacological blockade (i.e., atropine) interfering with the inhibitory action of the vagus on the sinoatrial node (Porges, 1995).

The resolution to the paradox came from the observation that through the evolution of the vertebrate autonomic nervous system, mammals evolved with two vagal efferent pathways. One has a respiratory rhythm, is uniquely mammalian, is myelinated, originates in an area of the brainstem known as the nucleus ambiguus, travels primarily to organs above the diaphragm, and interacts within the brainstem with structures (i.e., ventral vagal complex) regulating the striated muscles of the face and head. The other does not have a respiratory rhythm, is observed in virtually all vertebrates, is unmyelinated, travels primarily to organs below the diaphragm, and originates in an area of the brainstem known as the dorsal nucleus of the vagus.

RESPIRATORY SINUS ARRHYTHMIA: AN INDEX OF CARDIAC VAGAL TONE

To explore the distinction between vagal-mediated bradycardia and vagal-mediated heart rate variability, we need to understand the neural mechanisms mediating both responses through the vagus. The mechanism producing massive bradycardia is well understood as a surge of vagal inhibition of the sinoatrial node and can be mimicked by electrical stimulation of the vagus directly or indirectly via brainstem areas. Validation experiments using similar protocols are unable to distinguish between the tonic background vagal activity and the vagal activity due to acute stimulation. Nor are the stimulation studies able to selectively distinguish between myelinated and unmyelinated vagal pathways. Moreover, the manipulation of acute changes in vagal efferent activity does not provide insight into the mechanisms that produce tonic variations in heart rate variability.

In healthy mammals, the heart does not beat at a constant rate. Although intrinsic firing rate of the sinoatrial node, the heart's pacemaker, may be relatively fixed, this rate is modulated by the transitory inhibition of the pacemaker by vagal pathways. When the spontaneous respiration rate is manifested in the heart rate pattern, it is called respiratory sinus arrhythmia (RSA).

References to RSA were made in the early 1900s. Wundt stated that "respiratory movements are . . . regularly accompanied by fluctuations of the pulse, whose rapidity increases in inspiration and decreases in expiration" (Wundt, 1902). Hering (1910) reported the functional relation between the amplitude of RSA and cardiac vagal tone. Hering reported that breathing provided a functional test of the vagal control of the heart. Hering stated, "It is known with breathing that a demonstrable lowering of heart rate is indicative of the function of the vagi." Contemporary neurophysiology supports these early reports (Dergacheva et al., 2010). Since the neural mechanisms mediating RSA are well understood as the functional output of myelinated efferent vagal pathways, our research has focused on RSA and not on other metrics of heart rate variability, the origins of which have yet to be clearly defined.

POLYVAGAL THEORY

Phylogenetic Shifts in Vertebrate Autonomic Nervous Systems

By tracking the evolutionary changes in vertebrates, a phylogenetic pattern emerges in which two vagal pathways to the heart evolved in mammals. This pattern could be described as three evolutionary stages during which neural circuits evolved to regulate the heart. During the first stage, vertebrates relied on an unmyelinated vagus with efferent pathways originating in an area of the brainstem resembling the dorsal vagal complex, containing the origin of efferent and the termination of afferent pathways. As vertebrates evolved, a spinal sympathetic nervous system developed. Finally, with the emergence of mammals, there was a transition in how the autonomic nervous system was regulated. During this transition, some of the cells of origin of the vagus migrated ventrally from the dorsal nucleus of the vagus to the nucleus ambiguus. During this evolutionary process, many of the vagal efferent fibers originating in the nucleus ambiguus became myelinated and integrated in the function of the brainstem regulation of special visceral efferent pathways, which regulated the striated muscles of the face and head. Interestingly, Langley (1921) hypothesized a phylogenetic shift in the vagal fibers consistent with this description in the Polyvagal Theory (Porges, 1995):

> The hypothesis I would suggest as to the proximate cause of the existence of the two kinds of nerve fibres is that cells with non-medullated [unmyelinated] fibres were the first in phylogeny to migrate from the central nervous system, a later migration occurring when a further specialisation of the central nervous cells had occurred, and that the cells of this migration gave rise to medullated [myelinated] fibres. On this hypothesis, the two forms of embryonic cells have persisted to a varying degree in different vertebrates, each form giving rise to its own kind of axon. (Langley, 1921, p. 25)

In mammals, the unmyelinated vagal pathways originating in the dorsal nucleus of the vagus primarily regulate the organs below the diaphragm, though some of these unmyelinated vagal fibers terminate on the sinoatrial node. Polyvagal Theory hypothesizes that these unmyelinated vagal fibers primarily remain dormant until life threat and are probably potentiated during hypoxia and states in which the influence of the myelinated vagal input to the heart is depressed. This sequence is observable in human fetal heart rate, when bradycardia is more likely to occur when the tonic influence of the myelinated vagal pathways, manifested in RSA, is low (Reed et al., 1999).

In ancient vertebrates, an unmyelinated vagal pathway emerging from the brainstem was a critical component of the neural regulation of the entire viscera. This bidirectional system reduced metabolic output when resources were low, such as times of reduced oxygen. The nervous systems of primitive vertebrates did not need much oxygen to survive and could lower heart rate and metabolic demands when oxygen levels dropped. Thus, this circuit provided a conservation system that in mammals was adapted as a primitive defense system manifested as death feigning and trauma-driven responses of syncope and dissociation. Because this defense system could be lethal in oxygen-demanding mammals, it functioned as the last option for survival. The phylogenetically older unmyelinated vagal motor pathways are shared with most vertebrates, and in mammals, when not recruited as a defense system, function to support health, growth, and restoration via neural regulation of subdiaphragmatic organs (i.e., internal organs below the diaphragm).

The myelinated vagal circuit with efferents originating in a brainstem area called the nucleus ambiguus is uniquely mammalian. The newer myelinated vagal motor pathways regulate the supradiaphragmatic organs (e.g., heart and lungs) and are integrated in the brainstem with structures that regulate the striated muscles of the face and head via special visceral efferent pathways, resulting in a functional social engagement system. This newer vagal circuit slows heart rate and supports states of calmness.

The Emergence of the Social Engagement System

The integration of the myelinated cardiac vagal pathways with the neural regulation of the face and head gave rise to the mammalian social engagement system. As illustrated in Figure 1.1, the outputs of the social engagement system consist of a somatomotor component and a visceromotor component. The somatomotor component involves special visceral efferent pathways that regulate the striated muscles of the face and head. The visceromotor component involves the myelinated supradiaphragmatic vagus that regulates the heart and bronchi.

Functionally, the social engagement system emerges from a heart-face connection that coordinates the heart with the muscles of the face and head. The initial function of the system is to coordinate sucking, swallowing, breathing, and vocalizing. Atypical coordination of this system early in life is an indicator of subsequent difficulties in social behavior and emotional regulation.

When fully engaged, two important biobehavioral features of this system are expressed. First, bodily state is regulated in an efficient manner to promote growth and restoration (e.g., visceral homeostasis). Functionally, this is accomplished through an increase in the influence of myelinated vagal motor pathways on the cardiac pacemaker to slow heart rate, inhibit the fight-or-flight mechanisms of the sympathetic nervous system, dampen the stress response

FIGURE 1.1.   The social engagement system consists of a somatomotor component (solid blocks) and a visceromotor component (dashed blocks). The somatomotor component involves special visceral efferent pathways that regulate the striated muscles of the face and head, while the visceromotor component involves the myelinated vagus that regulates the heart and bronchi.

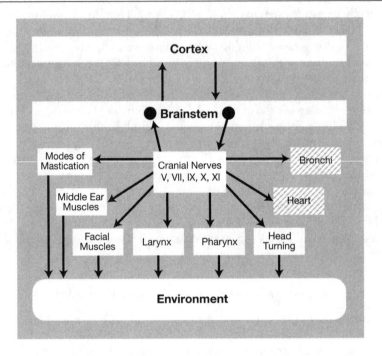

system of the hypothalamic-pituitary-adrenal (HPA) axis (responsible for cortisol release), and reduce inflammation by modulating immune reactions (e.g., cytokines; Porges, 2007). Second, the phylogenetically mammalian face-heart connection functions to convey physiological state via facial expression and prosody (intonation of voice) as well as regulate the middle ear muscles to regulate listening frequency response (Porges, 2007, 2009, 2011; Porges & Lewis, 2010; Kolacz et al., 2018).

The brainstem source nuclei of the social engagement system are influenced by higher brain structures (i.e., top-down influences) and by visceral afferents (i.e., bottom-up influences). Direct corticobulbar pathways reflect the influence of frontal areas of the cortex (i.e., upper motor neurons) on the medullary source nuclei of this system. Bottom-up influences occur via feedback through the afferent vagus (e.g., tractus solitarius), conveying information from visceral organs to medullary areas (e.g., nucleus of the solitary tract) and influencing both the source nuclei of this system and the forebrain areas that are assumed to be involved in several psychiatric disorders (Craig, 2005; Thayer & Lane, 2000, 2007). In addition, the anatomical structures involved in the social engagement system have neurophysiological interactions with the HPA axis, the social neuropeptides (e.g., oxytocin and vasopressin), and the immune system (Carter, 1998; Porges, 2001a).

Afferents from the target organs of the social engagement system, including the muscles of the face and head, also provide potent afferent input to the source nuclei regulating both the visceral and somatic components of the social engagement system. The source nucleus of the facial nerve forms the border of the nucleus ambiguus, and afferents from the trigeminal nerve provide a primary sensory input to the nucleus ambiguus. Thus, the ventral vagal complex, consisting of the nucleus ambiguus and the nuclei of the trigeminal and facial nerves, is functionally related to the expression and experience of emotion. Activation of the somatomotor component (e.g., listening, ingestion, lifting eyelids) could trigger visceral changes that would support social engagement, while modulation of the visceral state, depending on whether there is an increase or decrease in the influence of the myelinated vagal efferents on the sinoatrial node (i.e., increasing or decreasing the influence of the vagal brake), would either promote or impede social engagement behaviors (Porges, 1995, 2007). For example, stimulation of visceral states that would promote mobilization (i.e., fight-or-flight behaviors) would impede the ability to express social engagement behaviors.

The face-heart connection enabled mammals to detect whether a conspecific was in a calm physiological state and safe to approach, or in a highly mobilized and reactive physiological state, during which engagement would be dangerous. The face-heart connection concurrently enables an individual to signal safety through patterns of facial expression and vocal intonation, and potentially to calm an agitated conspecific to form a social relationship. When the newer mammalian vagus is optimally functioning in social interactions (i.e., inhibiting the sympathetic excitation that promotes fight-or-flight behaviors), emotions are well regulated, vocal prosody is rich, and the autonomic state supports calm, spontaneous social engagement behaviors. The face-heart system is bidirectional, with the newer myelinated vagal circuit influencing social interactions and positive social interactions influencing vagal function to optimize health, dampen stress-related physiological states, and support growth and restoration. Social communication and the ability to coregulate interactions, via reciprocal social engagement systems, lead to a sense of connectedness and is an important defining feature of the human experience.

Dissolution

The human nervous system, similar to that of other mammals, evolved not solely to survive in safe environments but also to promote survival in dangerous and life-threatening contexts. To accomplish this adaptive flexibility, the mammalian autonomic nervous system, in addition to the myelinated vagal pathway that is integrated into the social engagement system, retained two more primitive neural circuits to regulate defensive strategies (i.e., fight-flight and death-feigning behaviors). It is important to note that social behavior, social communication, and visceral homeostasis are incompatible with the neurophysiological states that support defense.

Polyvagal response strategies to challenge are phylogenetically ordered, with the newest components of the autonomic nervous system responding first. This model of autonomic reactivity is consistent with John Hughlings Jackson's (1884) construct of dissolution, in which he proposes that "the higher nervous arrangements inhibit (or control) the lower, and thus, when the higher are suddenly rendered functionless, the lower rise in activity." In this hierarchy of adaptive responses, the newest social engagement circuit is used first; if that circuit fails to provide safety, the older circuits are recruited sequentially.

Neuroception

Polyvagal Theory proposes that the neural evaluation of risk does not require conscious awareness and functions through neural circuits that are shared with our phylogenetic vertebrate ancestors. Thus, the term neuroception was introduced to emphasize a neural process, distinct from perception, capable of distinguishing environmental (and visceral) features that are safe, dangerous, or life threatening (Porges, 2003, 2004). In safe environments, the autonomic state is adaptively regulated to dampen sympathetic activation and to protect the oxygen-dependent central nervous system, especially the cortex, from the metabolically conservative reactions of the dorsal vagal complex (e.g., vasovagal syncope).

Neuroception is proposed as a reflexive mechanism capable of instantaneously shifting physiological state. Neuroception is a plausible mechanism mediating both the expression and the disruption of positive social behavior, emotion regulation, and visceral homeostasis.

Neuroception might be triggered by feature detectors involving areas of temporal cortex that communicate with the central nucleus of the amygdala and the periaqueductal gray, since limbic reactivity is modulated by temporal cortex responses to biological movements including voices, faces, and hand movements. Embedded in the construct of neuroception is the capacity of the nervous system to react to the intention of these movements. Neuroception functionally decodes and interprets the assumed goal of movements and sounds of inanimate and living objects. This process occurs without awareness. Although we are often unaware of the stimuli that trigger different neuroceptive responses, we are aware of our body's reactions. Thus, the neuroception of familiar individuals and individuals with appropriately prosodic voices and warm, expressive faces translates into a positive social interaction, promoting a sense of safety.

Autonomic State Is an Intervening Variable

The Polyvagal Theory proposes that physiological state is a fundamental part, and not a correlate, of emotion and mood. According to the theory, autonomic state functions as an intervening variable biasing our detection and evaluation of environmental cues. Depending on physiological state, the same cues will be reflexively evaluated as neutral, positive, or threatening. Functionally, a change in state will shift access to different structures in the brain and support either social communication or the defensive behaviors of fight-flight or shutdown. Contemporary research on the impact of vagal nerve stimulation on cognitive function and emotion regulation supports this model (Groves & Brown, 2005). The theory emphasizes a bidirectional link between brain and viscera, which would explain how thoughts change physiology, and how physiological state influences thoughts. As individuals change their facial expressions, the intonation of their voices, the pattern in which they are breathing, and their posture, they are also changing their physiology primarily through circuits involving myelinated vagal pathways to the heart.

The Role of Visceral Afferents in Regulating the Heart

The prevalent focus of research investigating the neural regulation of the heart has been efferent pathways emerging from brainstem nuclei and sympathetic ganglia. Limited research has been conducted on the influence of visceral afferents in the neural regulation of the heart and how these influences are manifested in the neural regulation of the heart and other visceral organs. This is, in part, due to the efferent bias in medical education that has resulted in a limited conceptualization of the neural regulation of the heart. However, this bias is rapidly changing due to research investigating the effects of vagal nerve stimulation, a bottom-up model that focuses on the vagus as an afferent nerve (approximately 80% of the vagal fibers are sensory). Interestingly, the side effects of vagal nerve stimulation are frequently due to the influence of vagal nerve stimulation on efferent pathways. These side effects are primarily noted on features of the social engagement system including changes in voice and difficulties swallowing (Ben-Menachem, 2001). However, in some cases the stimulation has been manifested, via stimulation of efferent pathways, in subdiaphragmatic organs, resulting in diarrhea (Sanossian & Haut, 2002). As vagal nerve stimulation becomes more commonly applied to medical disorders, there is an emerging awareness of the role of vagal afferent input on neurophysiological function (e.g., epilepsy), emotional state (e.g., depression), and cognition (e.g., learning and attention) (Howland, 2014; Sanossian & Haut, 2002).

According to the Polyvagal Theory, the source nuclei of the myelinated vagus are regulated by complex neural circuits, involving both visceral afferents (i.e., bottom-up) and higher brain structures (i.e., top-down) that influence the brainstem source nuclei controlling both the myelinated vagus and the striated muscles of the face and head (i.e., the social engagement system). As the function of the visceral afferents is incorporated into an understanding of the autonomic nervous system, clinicians and researchers begin to recognize manifestations in the vagal control of the heart in patients with a variety of disorders of peripheral organs. Rather than interpreting the atypical neural regulation of the heart, which may reflect forms of heart and cardiovascular disease, comorbidities become interpreted not as correlates but as manifestations of system dysfunction consistent with the prescient views of Walter Hess.

Several chronic diseases manifested in specific subdiaphragmatic organs (e.g., kidney, pancreas, liver, gut, genitals, etc.) have identifiable features that have led to treatments that target organs (e.g., medication, surgery). However, other disorders that impact quality of life, such as irritable bowel syndrome and fibromyalgia, are defined by nonspecific symptoms. The literature links these nonspecific chronic disorders with atypical vagal regulation of the heart, reflected in diminished heart rate variability (Mazurak et al., 2012; Staud, 2008). Consistent with these findings, heart rate variability has been proposed as a biomarker for these disorders.

Polyvagal Theory proposes an alternative interpretation of this covariation. Consistent with the integrated model of the autonomic nervous system described in the theory, atypical heart rate variability is not interpreted as a biomarker of any specific disease. Rather, depressed heart rate variability is proposed as a neurophysiological marker of a diffuse retuning of the autonomic nervous system following an adaptive complex autonomic reaction to threat.

Compatible with this interpretation, there are strong links between the prevalence of a history of abuse, especially sexual abuse in women, and the manifestations of nonspecific clinical disorders such as irritable bowel syndrome and fibromyalgia. In addition, emotional stress intensifies symptoms and hinders positive treatment outcomes, and trauma may trigger or aggravate symptoms (Clauw, 2014; Whitehead et al., 2007). We propose that an initially adaptive neural response to threat, via visceral afferent feedback from the visceral organs to the brainstem, may result in a chronic reorganization of the autonomic regulation observed in vagal regulation of the heart (i.e., depressed heart rate variability) in conjunction with altered subdiaphragmatic organ function and afferent pain signaling.

CONCLUSION

Neurocardiology defines an emergent discipline that provides an opportunity to study the bidirectional communication between the brain and the heart. By viewing living organisms as a collection of dynamic, adaptive, interactive, and interdependent physiological systems, it becomes apparent that the autonomic nervous system cannot be treated as functionally distinct from the central nervous system. Consistent with the Polyvagal Theory, the heart is not floating in a visceral sea, but is metaphorically anchored to central structures by efferent pathways and continuously signaling central regulatory structures via an abundance of afferent pathways. Thus, the treatment and assessment of cardiac function and the manifestation of autonomic dysfunction in the neural regulation of the heart should be based on bidirectional connections between autonomic and central brain structures. Such knowledge informs us about vulnerability to cardiac disease and dysfunction associated with triggering the autonomic nervous system into chronic states of defense as well as the resilience promoted by functional management by the social engagement system.

REFERENCES

Ben-Menachem, E. (2001). Vagus nerve stimulation, side effects, and long-term safety. *Journal of Clinical Neurophysiology, 18*(5), 415–418.

Bernard, C. (1865). *Introduction à l'étude de la médecine expérimentale* [Introduction to the study of experimental medicine]. New York: J.B. Ballierre.

Cannon, W. B. (1927). The James-Lange theory of emotions: A critical examination and an alternative theory. *American Journal of Psychology, 39*(1/4), 106–124.

Carter, C. S. (1998). Neuroendocrine perspectives on social attachment and love. *Psychoneuroendocrinology, 23*(8), 779–818.

Clauw, D. J. (2014). Fibromyalgia: A clinical review. *JAMA, 311*(15), 1547–1555.

Cournand, A. (1979). Claude Bernard's contributions to cardiac physiology. In E. D. Robin (Ed.), *Claude Bernard and the internal environment*. New York: Marcel Dekker.

Craig, A. D. (2005). Forebrain emotional asymmetry: A neuroanatomical basis? *Trends in Cognitive Sciences, 9*(12), 566–571.

Darwin, C. (1872). *The expression of emotions in man and animals*. New York: D. Appleton.

Dergacheva, O., Griffioen, K. J., Neff, R. A., & Mendelowitz, D. (2010). Respiratory modulation of premotor cardiac vagal neurons in the brainstem. *Respiratory Physiology and Neurobiology, 174*(1), 102–110.

Groves, D. A., & Brown, V. J. (2005). Vagal nerve stimulation: A review of its applications and potential mechanisms that mediate its clinical effects. *Neuroscience and Biobehavioral Reviews, 29*(3), 493–500.

Hering, H. (1910). A functional test of the heart vagi in man. *Menschen Munchen Medizinische Wochenschrift, 57*, 1931–1933.

Hess, W. (1949). The central control of the activity of internal organs. Nobel Lecture, December 12. Nobel Prize. https://www.nobelprize.org/nobel_prizes/medicine/laureates/1949/hess-lecture.html.

Howland, R. H. (2014). Vagus nerve stimulation. *Current Behavioral Neuroscience Reports, 1*(2), 64–73.

Jackson, J. H. (1884). The Croonian lectures on evolution and dissolution of the nervous system. *British Medical Journal, 1*(1215), 703–707.

James, W. (1884). What is an emotion? *Mind, 34*, 188–205.

Kolacz, J. K., Lewis, G. F., & Porges, S. W. (2018). The integration of vocal communication and biobehavioral state regulation in mammals: A polyvagal hypothesis. In S. M. Brudzynski (Ed.), *Handbook of ultrasonic vocalization: A window into the emotional brain*. London: Elsevier.

Langley, J. N. (1898). On the union of cranial autonomic (visceral) fibres with the nerve cells of the superior cervical ganglion. *Journal of Physiology, 23*(3), 240–270.

Langley, J. N. (1921). *The autonomic nervous system* (Part 1). Oxford, UK: Heffer.

Mazurak, N., Seredyuk, N., Sauer, H., Teufel, M., & Enck, P. (2012). Heart rate variability in the irritable bowel syndrome: A review of the literature. *Neurogastroenterology and Motility, 24*(3), 206–216.

Porges, S. W. (1995). Orienting in a defensive world: Mammalian modifications of our evolutionary heritage. A Polyvagal Theory. *Psychophysiology, 32*(4), 301–318.

Porges, S. W. (1998). Love: An emergent property of the mammalian autonomic nervous system. *Psychoneuroendocrinology, 23*(8), 837–861.

Porges, S. W. (2001a). Is there a major stress system at the periphery other than the adrenals? In D. M. Broom (Ed.), *Report of the 87th Dahlem Workshop on Coping with Challenge: Welfare in animals including humans* (pp. 135–149). Berlin: Dahlem University Press.

Porges, S. W. (2001b). The Polyvagal Theory: Phylogenetic substrates of a social nervous system. *International Journal of Psychophysiology, 42*(2), 123–146.

Porges, S. W. (2003). The Polyvagal Theory: Phylogenetic contributions to social behavior. *Physiology and Behavior, 79*(3), 503–513.

Porges, S. W. (2004). Neuroception: A subconscious system for detecting threats and safety. *Zero to Three, 24*(5), 19–24.

Porges, S. W. (2007). The polyvagal perspective. *Biological Psychology, 74*(2), 116–143.

Porges, S. W. (2009). The Polyvagal Theory: New insights into adaptive reactions of the autonomic nervous system. *Cleveland Clinic Journal of Medicine, 76*(Suppl. 2), S86.

Porges, S. W. (2011). *The Polyvagal Theory: Neurophysiological foundations of emotions, attachment, communication, and self-regulation.* New York: Norton.

Porges, S. W., & Lewis, G. F. (2010). The polyvagal hypothesis: Common mechanisms mediating autonomic regulation, vocalizations and listening. In S. M. Brudzynski Ed.), *Handbook of mammalian vocalization: An integrative neuroscience approach* (pp. 255–264). London: Elsevier.

Reed, S. F., Ohel, G., David, R., & Porges, S. W. (1999). A neural explanation of fetal heart rate patterns: A test of the Polyvagal Theory. *Developmental Psychobiology, 35*(2), 108–118.

Sanossian, N., & Haut, S. (2002). Chronic diarrhea associated with vagal nerve stimulation. *Neurology, 58*(2), 330.

Selye, H. (1936). A syndrome produced by diverse nocuous agents. *Nature, 138*(3479), 32.

Selye, H. (1956). *The stress of life.* New York: McGraw-Hill.

Staud, R. (2008). Heart rate variability as a biomarker of fibromyalgia syndrome. *Future Rheumatology, 3*(5), 475–483.

Thayer, J. F., & Lane, R. D. (2000). A model of neurovisceral integration in emotion regulation and dysregulation. *Journal of Affective Disorders, 61*(3), 201–216.

Thayer, J. F., & Lane, R. D. (2007). The role of vagal function in the risk for cardiovascular disease and mortality. *Biological Psychology, 74*(2), 224–242.

Whitehead, W. E., Palsson, O. S., Levy, R. R., Feld, A. D., Turner, M., & Von Korff, M. (2007). Comorbidity in irritable bowel syndrome. *American Journal of Gastroenterology, 102*(12), 2767–2776.

Wundt, W. (1902). *Outlines of psychology* (2nd ed.). Oxford, UK: Engelmann.

CHAPTER 2

Polyvagal Theory
A Biobehavioral Journey to Sociality

Stephen W. Porges

THE TRANSDISCIPLINARY ORIGINS AND
CORE OF POLYVAGAL THEORY

This chapter is designed to clarify what the Polyvagal Theory is and what it is not. Via evolutionary transition from reptiles to mammals, the autonomic nervous system was repurposed to suppress defensive strategies in order to support and express sociality. The product of this transition was an autonomic nervous system with capacities to self-calm, to spontaneously engage others socially, and to mitigate threat reactions in ourselves and others through social cues. Thus, social behavior became a neurobiological process with capabilities to support homeostatic processes that would lead to optimized health, growth, and restoration. Succinctly, Polyvagal Theory emphasizes sociality as the core process underlying mental and physical health.

To understand the origins of Polyvagal Theory, visualize a Rubik's cube with the surfaces representing different scientific disciplines moving in time as each science is selectively updated by new information. Metaphorically, Polyvagal Theory is the solution of a Rubik's puzzle, a solution to how evolution repurposed the mammalian autonomic nervous system to contain defensive reactions and enable sociality to thrive. This metaphor is helpful, since Polyvagal Theory is a product of an extraction of principles derived from the integration of several disciplines, each with its own history, research paradigms, literature, methodology, and theoretical context.

Through my personal and passionate intellectual journey, elements from several disciplines converged into the principles of the theory. The theory evolved to ask new questions and was not conceptualized to replace the predominant theories associated with these foundational disciplines. Thus, the solution to the puzzle produced a transdisciplinary theory that had a foundational basis but was not limited or biased by any specific discipline. The upside of this strategy is that the theory provides an opportunity to explain and conduct research investigating new questions linking neural regulation of autonomic state to health and behavior. However, the downside is that, since an understanding of the theory requires a degree of sophistication in several disciplines, it may provoke a defensiveness from researchers within its foundational disciplines. This may occur when these scientists are focused on the research questions that define their disciplines. However, they may lack sufficient knowledge of other disciplines and not understand or value research that addresses the role that regulation of autonomic state may play in behavior and health.

This chapter is intended to provide both the research and clinical communities with a better understanding of what Polyvagal Theory is and what it is not and thus dispel misunderstandings of the theory. By clarifying the theory, the chapter will contribute to two primary objectives: (1) to provide research scientists with a better understanding of the principles of the theory, which will enable them to conduct research testing relevant hypotheses derived from the theory; and (2) to provide clinicians and clinical researchers with plausible Polyvagal Theory–informed explanations of mental and physical health disorders that would stimulate research leading to improved assessments and treatment models.

The chapter is structured to introduce the reader to two disparate areas of science related to Polyvagal Theory. The first part explains how evolution and development of neuroanatomical structures and neurophysiological processes contribute to the theory. The second part introduces the reader to a methodology for extracting cardiac vagal tone that can be useful in testing polyvagal-informed hypotheses.

The initial assumptions of the Polyvagal Theory provided insights into deconstructing autonomic and behavioral reactions to threat consistent with the Jacksonian principle of dissolution, or evolution in reverse (Jackson, 1884). Thus, evolution became the initial organizing principle. As the theory developed, other disciplines provided convergent support of the hierarchy of autonomic states introduced in the initial publication of the Polyvagal Theory (Porges, 1995). The study of development and maturation paralleled the insights extracted from evolutionary biology (see Porges & Furman, 2011). In addition, the idea of dissolution of autonomic state converged with the personal narratives of trauma survivors. The theory gave voice and credibility to the immobilization shutdown responses documented by survivors.

All three pathways (i.e., evolution, development, clinical observation) help us understand the dependence of sociality on the neural regulation of the autonomic nervous system. From evolutionary biology, we see shifts in structure and function of the autonomic nervous system as vertebrates evolved into social mammals with a biological imperative to connect, nurse, cooperate, and trust select others. From developmental biology, we observe shifts in neural regulation of the autonomic nervous system starting during the last trimester that prepare the newborn to suckle, breathe, and to coregulate. From the study of trauma, we see the dissolution of many of these social systems, with profound consequences for mental and physical health. Similarly, during difficult deliveries, the neonate follows a predictable pattern of dissolution that is characterized by a sequence of loss of heart rate variability, metabolically costly tachycardia, and finally the shutting down of vital systems, as indexed by life-threatening bradycardia (Reed et al., 1999).

HISTORICAL CONTEXT

The early conceptualization of the vagus nerve in mammals focused on an undifferentiated efferent (motor) pathway that was assumed to modulate tone concurrently to several target organs. Little attention was directed to the afferent (sensory) limb of the vagus, which provides dynamic feedback to the brainstem structures regulating the efferent outflow. Thus, neural circuits regulating the supradiaphragmatic (e.g., myelinated vagal pathways originating in the nucleus ambiguus and terminating primarily above the diaphragm) were not functionally distinguished from the subdiaphragmatic (e.g., unmyelinated vagal pathways originating in the dorsal motor nucleus of the vagus and terminating primarily below the diaphragm). Without this distinction, research and theory focused on the paired antagonism between the parasympathetic and sympathetic innervation to target organs. The consequence of an emphasis on paired antagonism in physiology was an acceptance and use of global constructs such as autonomic balance, sympathetic tone, and vagal tone in psychophysiology and psychosomatic medicine.

About 70 years ago, W. Hess (1954) proposed that the "autonomic" nervous system was not solely "vegetative" and automatic but was an integrated system with both peripheral and central neurons. Hess demonstrated the influence of the hypothalamus on the autonomic nervous system. By emphasizing the central mechanisms that mediate the dynamic regulation of peripheral organs, Hess anticipated the need for methodologies and technologies to continuously monitor the neural circuits involving both defined brain structures and peripheral nerves in the regulation of visceral function and state. Consistent with these insights, the Polyvagal Theory was proposed and methods were suggested to extract the time course of the influence of two vagal circuits on the beat-to-beat heart rate pattern (Porges, 1995, 2007b) .

In 1949, Hess was awarded the Nobel Prize in Physiology or Medicine. The title of his Nobel lecture was "The Central Control of the Activity of Internal

Organs." The opening paragraph of his lecture provides a framework for evaluating subsequent progress in developing theory, describing neural circuits, providing measurement technologies, and understanding clinical conditions. The lecture provides a succinct statement: (1) to emphasize the importance of feedback circuits linking peripheral organs to brain structures and the bidirectionality of these feedback circuits; and (2) to acknowledge that, although much can be learned about neural structures and functions via traditional experimental paradigms (e.g., neural blockade, surgery, electrical stimulation), the dynamic feedback circuits cannot be adequately studied through these paradigms. This limits our understanding of how these circuits function in real time to support survival challenges, a limitation that still characterizes much of the research in contemporary neurophysiology.

In his Nobel lecture, Hess paid respects to Gaskell (1916), Langley (1921), and Meyer and Gottlieb (1926), scientists who contributed to the understanding of the paired antagonistic innervations of the internal organs and the definition of sympathetic and parasympathetic functions. Prior to Hess, the prevailing conceptualization of the neural regulation of visceral organs focused on vegetative and autonomic features. Hess (1949) notes, however, "In contrast to the exploration of the vegetative nervous system, which is very far-reaching (even if it is not still without certain inner contradictions), stands a relatively limited understanding of the central organization of the whole mechanism of control."

Hess was aware that, although the components of a feedback circuit might be identified and studied independently, the functioning of independent parts did not explain how the system, as a whole, functioned dynamically during the moment-to-moment challenges of life. This limitation was, in part, dependent on the methodologies of the day that required pharmacological, surgical, or electrical manipulations to block or stimulate global branches of the autonomic nervous system that shared either a specific neurotransmitter (e.g., acetylcholine) or an easily identifiable nerve (e.g., vagus) that could be cut or stimulated. Needed was a technology that would enable real-time dynamic monitoring of various limbs of the autonomic nervous system.

INTRODUCTION AND IMPACT OF POLYVAGAL THEORY

More than 25 years ago, Polyvagal Theory was introduced during my presidential address to the Society for Psychophysiological Research. The theory was an attempt to shift psychophysiology from a descriptive science conducting empirical studies and describing correlations between psychological and physiological processes to an inferential science generating and testing hypotheses related to common neural pathways involving both mental and physiological processes. Basically, it was the first volley in a conceptual dialogue challenging the questions and methods involved in psychophysiological research, especially in the subdomain of cardiovascular psychophysiology. Psychophysiology emerged in the 1960s, a relatively atheoretical empirical period of science. In the initial presentation of the theory (Porges, 1995), the historical context is described. Polyvagal Theory was an attempt to provide an integrated theory, based on the literatures of several disciplines, that would provide the basis for testable hypotheses relating autonomic function to sociality and health in humans and nonhuman mammals.

The extent to which the theory has been adopted and evaluated in contemporary experimental sciences can be documented by a Google Scholar search, which identifies thousands of peer-reviewed articles that cite articles and books describing the theory (see Table 2.1, listing the number of citations). It is important to note that the National Institutes of Health continuously funded the research developing and testing the theory from 1975 to 2013. One of the grants was a highly competitive 10-year career development award from the National Institute of Mental Health. This award paid my university salary to free my time from teaching and administrative responsibilities to conduct the research that led to Polyvagal Theory.

Recently, the theory has gained traction in cardiology and gastroenterology. An editorial in the American Journal of Gastroenterology focused on our article using Polyvagal Theory to understand and treat functional abdominal pain disorders (FAPD; Kovacic et al., 2020). The editorial stated that the article's "underlying premise . . . the polyvagal hypothesis, provides a fascinating explanatory model for FAPDs" (Leontiadis & Longstreth, 2020). In the area of cardiology, our chapter on neurocardiology (Porges & Kolacz, 2018; see Chapter 1, this volume) was highlighted in a book review as "a corollary worthy of the work [the entire book] since it exposes the future of Neurocardiology through the lens of the polyvagal theory" (Piñeiro, 2019).

The impact of Polyvagal Theory among mental health practitioners has been transformative in the treatment of trauma. By having a neurophysiological explanation for immobilization as an adaptive defensive reaction, many survivors of trauma have been given a rational voice to explain their inability to fight and flee from their abusers. For clinicians working with survivors of trauma, the theory provides a plausible narrative that can be shared with clients. The narrative enables clients to have a greater appreciation of their body's adaptive reactivity, often enabling them to survive severe adversity, including abuse, injury, and neglect. Functionally, the theory enables clients to shift their narrative from blame and shame to respecting the wisdom of their bodily adaptive, and often reflexive, physiological shifts, which optimized survival. This understanding of bodily responses to adversity may shift trauma survivors from feeling betrayed by their nervous systems into honoring their bodily reactions.

Several trauma therapists have told me that the first step in their treatment strategy is to share the basic principles of the theory with their clients. Specifically, the therapists explain that under severe threat there is a "dissolution" in which autonomic state shifts to progressively more primitive circuits (Jackson,

TABLE 2.1.   Citations of Primary Foundational Polyvagal Theory Publications

Citation	Cited by (as of 5/1/2021)
Porges, S. W. (1995). Orienting in a defensive world: Mammalian modifications of our evolutionary heritage. A polyvagal theory. *Psychophysiology*, 32(4), 301–318.	1,850
Porges, S. W., Doussard-Roosevelt, J. A., Portales, A. L., & Greenspan, S. I. (1996). Infant regulation of the vagal "brake" predicts child behavior problems: A psychobiological model of social behavior. *Developmental Psychobiology*, 29(8), 697–712.	686
Porges, S. W. (1998). Love: An emergent property of the mammalian autonomic nervous system. *Psychoneuroendocrinology*, 23(8), 837–861.	505
Porges, S. W. (2001). The polyvagal theory: Phylogenetic substrates of a social nervous system. *International Journal of Psychophysiology*, 42(2), 123–146.	1,887
Porges, S. W. (2003). The polyvagal theory: Phylogenetic contributions to social behavior. *Physiology and Behavior*, 79(3), 503–513.	882
Porges, S. W. (2007b). The polyvagal perspective. *Biological Psychology*, 74(2), 116–143.	3,029
Porges, S. W. (2009). The polyvagal theory: New insights into adaptive reactions of the autonomic nervous system. *Cleveland Clinic Journal of Medicine*, 76(Suppl. 2), S86.	699
Porges, S. W., & Furman, S. A. (2011). The early development of the autonomic nervous system provides a neural platform for social behaviour: A polyvagal perspective. *Infant and Child Development*, 20(1), 106–118.	446
Porges, S. W. (2011). *The polyvagal theory: Neurophysiological foundations of emotions, attachment, communication, and self-regulation* (Norton Series on Interpersonal Neurobiology). New York: Norton.	2,291
Porges, S. W. (2017). *The pocket guide to the polyvagal theory: The transformative power of feeling safe.* New York: Norton.	180
Porges, S. W., & Dana, D. A. (2018). *Clinical applications of the polyvagal theory: The emergence of polyvagal-informed therapies* (Norton Series on Interpersonal Neurobiology). New York: Norton.	67
Total citation of major articles and books	12,522

1884). This is experienced as moving from a calm state that supports social interactions (i.e., the ventral vagal circuit and the social engagement system) to a mobilized defensive fight-flight state (i.e., supported by a withdrawal of the ventral vagal circuit and an activation of the sympathetic nervous system), and finally to a state of motoric immobilization and behavioral shutdown that may be accompanied by fainting or dissociation (i.e., supported by a withdrawal of both the ventral vagal and sympathetic pathways and an activation of the dorsal vagal pathway). Consistent with the impact of the theory on the client's personal narrative, I have received numerous emails from trauma survivors expressing gratitude for the theory and explaining how it has helped them make sense of their experiences.

A search of Polyvagal Theory on YouTube identifies videos targeted to the clinical community that have had cumulatively well over a million hits. A search on Google identifies approximately 500,000 websites, many of which describe clinical applications within mental health. In fact, my research at the Traumatic Stress Research Consortium (Kinsey Institute, Indiana University Bloomington) has surveyed trauma therapists, and one of the most frequently endorsed therapeutic strategies for trauma treatment is "Polyvagal Informed," although there is not a specific polyvagal therapy.

WHAT THE POLYVAGAL THEORY IS AND IS NOT

As Polyvagal Theory becomes commonly identified, it is important to acknowledge what the theory is and what it is not; what the theory actually states and not what others assume the theory is stating. As part of this exercise, it is important to distinguish, within the presentation of the Polyvagal Theory, what is theory and what is based on an extraction from the scientific literature—in other words, which aspects of the theory are hypothetical and potentially testable and which aspects are evidenced based, less theoretical, and are a derived descriptive model based on scientific evidence extracted from the literature. These evidence-based principles embedded in Polyvagal Theory lead to testable hypotheses. This is not equivalent to stating that all hypotheses derived from the theory have been or will be confirmed. The steps involved in the extraction of principles from the literature are detailed in the primary foundational articles supporting and describing the theory (Porges, 1995, 1998, 2001, 2007b).

Polyvagal Theory was not developed as a static, dogmatic theory. It was developed to stimulate research questions. In its initial presentation (Porges, 1995) and subsequent elaborations (Porges, 1998, 2001, 2007b), every premise and hypothesis was supported by a detailed literature review. Often, preliminary data were presented to stimulate future research. This detailed literature review provided the basis for interpretation and extraction of principles. To contradict these conclusions, an appropriate criticism would require a detailed explanation of why a scientist would arrive at a different conclusion from the peer-reviewed research cited and described in the foundational articles upon which the theory is based. To this date, scholarship has not led to any major contradictions in the theory. This is not to say that there have not been criticisms, but the criticisms have been more about misunderstandings of the specifics and scope of the theory.

In general, the criticisms have focused on incorrectly assumed attributes of the theory. In some situations, criticisms of the theory have focused on new findings in comparative neurophysiology that are updating our understanding that myelinated vagal pathways and heart rate–respiratory interactions may be observed in primitive vertebrates that evolved long before mammals. Although these observations are interesting, they are unrelated to Polyvagal Theory. They are used as criticisms since the authors assume that the theory uniquely attributes to mammals myelinated vagal pathways and heart rate–respiratory interactions. This assumption is a misunderstanding of the theory, which uses evolution to emphasize the repurposing and modification of the neural regulation of the autonomic nervous system in mammals to actively support sociality by constraining autonomic states that support defense. The theory does specify that this function is supported by myelinated vagal fibers. However, the theory specifies that the myelinated fibers originate from the nucleus ambiguus, where interactions are occurring with the nerves that regulate the muscles of the face and head.

Consistent with this misunderstanding, there has been a criticism that there is no evidence that the dorsal vagal nucleus is an evolutionarily older brainstem parasympathetic source than the nucleus ambiguus. This faulty view is based on an assumption the occurrence of vagal preganglionic neurons ventrolateral to the dorsal vagal nucleus is tantamount to confirming the existence of the nucleus ambiguus. Neuroanatomical and neurophysiological research documents a phylogenetic trend toward a differentiation in the brainstem area, from which vagal preganglionic neurons originate, into a dorsal vagal nucleus and a discrete nucleus ambiguus. There is no question that both cardiac and noncardiac vagal neurons may be found outside the dorsal vagal nucleus in more primitive vertebrates. The phylogeny of the vagus illustrates, on a neuroanatomical level, differentiation of the visceral efferent column of the vagus into a dorsal motor nucleus and a ventrolateral motor nucleus (i.e., nucleus ambiguus), which is first seen in some reptiles. Thus, the neuroanatomical identification of a discrete nucleus ambiguus might be assumed to be limited to all mammals and select reptiles. However, this does not preclude the evolutionary trend of vagal preganglionic neurons being found ventrolateral to the dorsal vagal nucleus. Missing from the dialogue is the evolutionary progression in which the source nuclei of the special visceral efferent pathways in the glossopharyngeal, vagus, and accessory nerves migrate to form the nucleus ambiguus (a portion of the vagal preganglionic neurons that form the nucleus ambiguus in mammals and regulate striated muscles including the larynx and pharynx). This progression, when supplemented with the migration of vagal cardioinhibitory neurons into the nucleus ambiguus, provides the neuroanatomical pathways that support the mammalian agenda of sociality and coregulation.

Although not part of the theory, methodologies to measure vagal pathways are important in testing theory-informed hypotheses. Methods leading to metrics of cardiac tone or the impact of the myelinated vagal pathway originating from the nucleus ambiguus are important. The theory makes no statement or inference related to myelinated vagal fibers originating in the dorsal motor nucleus in mammals or in any other vertebrate. Similarly, the theory makes no statement or inference about the utility and interpretation of nonmammalian forms of respiratory–heart rate activity.

EVOLUTION INFORMS FOCUS ON BIOBEHAVIORAL ADAPTATIONS TO SUPPORT SOCIALITY

Evolution has informed the development of Polyvagal Theory to focus on how mammals adapted many of the phylogenetic ancestral structures that evolved to support survival in a hostile world. Note that the title of the initial publication presenting the theory (Porges, 1995) is actually a synopsis of the theory: "Orienting in a Defensive World: Mammalian Modifications of Our Evolutionary Heritage. A Polyvagal Theory." The title summarizes a phylogenetic narrative in which the survival of mammals was dependent on an ability to downregulate and modify the innate defensive systems that were inherited from their reptilian ancestors. These embedded vestigial circuits with their emergent adaptive strategies are embedded in genes of mammals. For mammals, whose survival is dependent on their sociality to cooperate, to connect, and to coregulate, the ancient defense programs had to be harnessed and repurposed to enable the expression of several defining features, including the ability to calm and to signal safety and calmness in proximity to another trusted mammal.

It is surprising that the primary criticisms of the theory have focused on neuroanatomical research on vertebrates that evolved prior to mammals. Obviously, the authors were unable to extract from the title that Polyvagal Theory was about a mammalian transition and have assumed that the theory was inclusive of the evolutionary changes in the neuroanatomy of vagal pathways across all vertebrates.

Misunderstandings are predictable responses to a transdisciplinary theory. However, across a broad range of scientific and clinical disciplines, the theory has stimulated research and provided new understandings. A careful reading of the theory's foundational articles provides sufficient evidence to document that the criticisms are either inaccurate or irrelevant to the theory. In general, the few criticisms in the literature have been focused on questions and hypotheses that are not related to the theory. In summary, there is no substitute for good scholarship. In the sections below, I give specifics to enable a better understanding of the principles embedded in the theory and to provide a basis for exploring the validity of speculations that may incorrectly be assumed to be part of the theory.

Evolution Repurposes the Ventral Vagal Complex to Support Sociality

Polyvagal Theory's interest in investigating mammalian autonomic regulation from a phylogenetic perspective does not focus on the obvious similarities with more ancient vertebrates. Rather, it focuses on the unique modifications that enabled mammals to optimize their survival. Consistent with this theme, Polyvagal Theory focuses on the evolved neural circuits that enabled mammals to downregulate defenses, to reduce psychological and physical distance with conspecifics, and to functionally coregulate physiological and behavioral states. The theory focuses on the transition from reptiles to mammals and emphasizes the neural adaptations that enable cues of safety to downregulate states of defense. Within Polyvagal Theory, the evolutionary trend has led to a conceptualization of an emergent and uniquely mammalian social engagement system in which a modified branch of the vagus is integral.

To survive, mammalian offspring must initially nurse as the primary mode of ingesting food. To nurse, the infant must suck, a process dependent on a brainstem circuit involving the ventral vagal complex. Survival is dependent on the infant's nervous system efficiently and effectively coordinating suck-swallow-breathe-vocalize behaviors with vagal regulation of the heart through the ventral vagal pathways originating in the nucleus ambiguus. Through maturation and socialization, this ingestive circuit provides the structural neural platform for sociality and coregulation as major mediators to optimize homeostatic function, leading to health, growth, and restoration. For mammals, the function of this circuit depends on reactions to contextual cues. Cues of threat may disrupt, while cues of safety may enhance function. The sensory branches of the facial and trigeminal nerves provide major input into the ventral vagal complex. Functionally, changes in the state of this circuit, through the process of dissolution, will either disinhibit phylogenetically older autonomic circuits to support defense (e.g., predator, disease, physical injury, etc.) or inform all aspects of the autonomic nervous system, including the enteric system (e.g., Kolacz & Porges, 2018; Kolacz et al., 2019) to optimize homeostatic function.

Mammals uniquely have detached middle ear bones, which heightens sensitivity to acoustic cues of safety. Middle ear bones are small bones that separate from the jawbone during gestational development and form an ossicle chain that connects the eardrum to the inner ear. Small muscles regulated by branches of the trigeminal and facial nerves regulate the transfer function of the middle ear and determine the frequencies of sounds transduced through middle ear structures by controlling the stiffness of the ossicle chain. When the chain is stiff, the eardrum is tighter, and low-frequency sounds are attenuated;

when the muscles relax, lower-frequency sounds pass into the inner ear. In all mammalian species, based on the physics of their middle ear structures, there is a frequency band of perceptual advantage that is expressed when the middle ear muscles contract. It is within this frequency band that social communication occurs. The low frequencies that through evolution have been associated with predators are attenuated (Porges & Lewis, 2010). Interestingly, the coordination of the contraction and relaxation of these small muscles is frequently coregulated with autonomic state, and thus they contract when there is strong ventral vagal tone to promote social communication and coregulation. In contrast, when the autonomic nervous system shifts to a state of defense, the muscles relax to detect low-frequency predator sounds, which support defense strategies with auditory cues. The link between behavioral and autonomic state and listening is obvious in the study of language delays and auditory processing problems in children. Many children with problems in auditory processing also have behavioral state regulation limitations. This neurophysiological link provides a portal to regulate autonomic state through acoustic stimulation, which is easily observable when a mother calms her infant using prosodic vocalization. Similarly, we can observe the potent calming influences when a pet is calmed by the voice of a human. In addition, clinicians frequently report that survivors of trauma experience an auditory hypersensitivity to background sounds and an auditory hyposensitivity to human voices.

Through the evolution of vertebrates there are strong trends in the structures involved in regulating autonomic function. These trends may be summarized as moving from chemical to neural, and then the neural structures evolving greater specificity, efficiency, and speed through feedback circuits involving myelinated pathways. Evolution is a process of modification in which existing structures and circuits are modified to serve adaptive functions. In mammals, three primary autonomic states with specific neural circuits are observable and emerge at different times within the evolutionary history of vertebrates. In polyvagal terms, the newest is labeled the ventral vagal complex, the oldest is the dorsal vagal complex, and in between a spinal sympathetic nervous system evolved. Thus, evolution informs us of the sequence through which three circuits regulate autonomic function.

Dissolution Predicts Symptoms Associated With Threat, Chronic Stress, and Illness

Polyvagal Theory, following the work of John Hughlyns Jackson (1884), assumes a phylogenetic hierarchy in which the newer circuits inhibit the older. Thus, when the ventral vagus and the social engagement system are dampened or go offline, the autonomic nervous system moves into a sympathetic state that supports mobilization. If this functional shift in state does not lead to a positive survival outcome, the autonomic nervous system may abruptly shut down via the dorsal vagal circuit. Jackson described this process of sequentially disinhibiting older structures as dissolution, or evolution in reverse. Jackson used dissolution to explain the consequences of brain damage and disease, while Polyvagal Theory applies the principle of dissolution to adaptive autonomic reactions to cues of threat, which optimistically are reversible by cues of safety.

Convergent parallels with the phylogenetic evidence come from anatomical studies investigating human embryological origins and development of the autonomic nervous system through anatomical research via human autopsy studies. Being informed by the autopsy studies provides an opportunity to link maturational landmarks from anatomical studies with research monitoring fetal and preterm heart rate patterns. The neuroanatomical literature documents a maturational trend of myelination of the ventral vagus during the last trimester, with notable changes occurring after 30 weeks gestational age (see Porges & Furman, 2011). In our research, we have been able to infer the maturation of the ventral vagal circuit by monitoring respiratory sinus arrhythmia in very high-risk preterm newborns (Doussard-Roosevelt et al., 1997; Portales et al., 1997; Porges, 1992; Porges et al., 2019).

In full-term newborns, it is possible to observe a predictable dissolution sequence during challenging deliveries. This sequence is initiated by a withdrawal of ventral vagal tone (i.e., depressed respiratory sinus arrhythmia), leading to tachycardia and finally to potentially lethal bradycardia (see Reed et al., 1999). The literature supporting this maturational trend is summarized in Porges and Furman (2011). This literature documents that high-risk preterm newborns enter the postpartum world unprepared to cope with environmental challenges. Because the high-risk newborn enters the world with an immature ventral vagal circuit, the neural circuits are prone to recruit the threat reactions of the functionally available sympathetic nervous system, which would produce the metabolic-costly tachycardia (i.e., increases in heart rate); or the dorsal vagal circuit, which would produce a potentially lethal bradycardia (i.e., rapid and massive decreases in heart rate). Both reactions disrupt homeostatic function and compromise the preterm neonate's viability.

The survival challenges of the high-risk preterm infant provide a real-life example validating several features of Polyvagal Theory. First, we observe the hierarchical organization of the mammalian autonomic nervous system in support of basic homeostatic processes that lead to optimized health, growth, and restoration. Juxtaposed to the traditional paired antagonism model of the autonomic nervous system, which would focus on a hypothetical autonomic balance, we are informed that homeostasis requires the ventral vagus to functionally calm the autonomic nervous system to enable resources to be diverted from defense and directed toward health, growth, and restoration. Second, under challenge, we observe the process of dissolution. Third, we observe the development and coordination of the social engagement system as the preterm infant develops the capacity to coordinate suck-swallow-breathe actions, which is followed by directed vocalizations and facial expressivity, leading to sending cues of calmness and distress. These examples provide an understanding that stress or threat reactions may be operationally defined as the shifting of neural regulation of the autonomic nervous system (i.e., withdrawal of ventral vagal tone) into a state that does not support homeostatic processes.

Metaphorically, the high-risk neonate comes into the world with an autonomic nervous system that is more reptilian than mammalian. An additional consequence of the infant's depressed social engagement system is the impact on caregivers, who are not receiving cues of social connection via facial expressivity and prosodic vocalizations. The result may be a parent who may articulate that they love their child, but also voice that they feel that their child does not love them. Similar disconnects have been felt, if not voiced, by parents who have children with dampened social engagement systems, such as children on the spectrum of autism.

POLYVAGAL THEORY: A TESTABLE MODEL SOLVING THE VAGAL PARADOX

Polyvagal Theory emerged from my research studying heart rate patterns in human fetuses and newborns. In obstetrics and neonatology, the massive slowing of heart rate known as bradycardia is a clinical index of risk, assumed to be mediated by the vagus. During bradycardia, heart rate is so slow that it no longer provides sufficient oxygenated blood to the brain. This type of vagal influence on the fetal and neonatal heart could potentially be lethal. However, with the same clinical populations, a different index of vagal function was assumed to be a measure of resilience (Porges, 1992). This measure was the respiratory oscillation in beat-to-beat heart rate variability (i.e., respiratory sinus arrhythmia), which was the focus of my research for several decades. Animal research demonstrated that both signals could be disrupted by severing the vagal pathways to the heart or via pharmacological blockade (e.g., atropine), interfering with the inhibitory action of the vagus on the sinoatrial node (for review, see Porges, 1995). These observations posed a paradox. How could cardiac vagal tone be both a positive indicator of health when monitored with heart rate variability and a negative indicator of health when it manifests as bradycardia?

The resolution to the paradox came from understanding how the neural regulation of the autonomic nervous system changed during evolution and that the sequence of these phylogenetic shifts in global autonomic regulation was mirrored in prenatal development. The study of comparative neuroanatomy identified a structural change in vagal regulation occurring during the transition from primitive extinct reptiles to mammals. During this transition, mammals evolved a functional diaphragm (also observed in some reptiles) and a second cardioinhibitory vagal motor pathway that originated in the ventral vagal nucleus (i.e., nucleus ambiguus). This vagal pathway provides the primary cardioinhibitory influences on the heart. The circuit originating in the ventral vagal complex selectively services organs above the diaphragm (e.g., heart, bronchi) and interacts with the regulation of the striated muscles of the face and head via special visceral efferent pathways. This uniquely mammalian ventral vagal pathway is myelinated and conveys a respiratory rhythm to the heart's pacemaker, resulting in a rhythmic oscillation in heart rate at the frequency of spontaneous breathing known as respiratory sinus arrhythmia.

Polyvagal Theory uses evolution to highlight neuroanatomical and functional changes in how the brainstem regulates physiological state in mammals. These changes resulted in two vagal pathways, with one pathway being protective and supporting homeostasis, while the other evolutionarily older pathway supports homeostasis, but only if the new protective vagus is functional (Kolacz & Porges, 2018). Other than this coordinating role, this more modern vagal pathway has other attributes that functionally constrain, inhibit, and dampen other components of the autonomic nervous system that can be recruited in defense—the sympathetic nervous system that supports fight and flight behaviors and the older vagal circuit that triggers immobilization, behavioral shutdown, defecation, and potentially lethal bradycardia. Thus, when the newer circuit is withdrawn (i.e., dissolution), there is a shift in physiological state (i.e., loss of ventral vagal tone) with major survival-related consequences, as the neural regulation of the autonomic nervous system shifts to defensive strategies from coordinating other attributes of the autonomic nervous system that optimize health, growth, restoration, and social behavior.

Polyvagal Theory extracts from contemporary neuroanatomy, neurophysiology, and evolutionary biology several basic uncontroversial conclusions: (1) mammals have two vagal pathways (i.e., supradiaphragmatic, subdiaphragmatic); and (2) evolution and development provide insight into the changes in brainstem structures that enable mammals to be physiologically calm and to interact socially. Functionally, mammals have neural attributes that act efficiently via rapidly responding cardioinhibitory fibers (e.g., ventral vagal pathways), capable of calming to promote social communication. The ventral vagal pathways also coordinate and repurpose circuits that evolved to support defense in socially relevant processes, such as play (i.e., ventral vagal influences on sympathetic reactivity) and intimacy (i.e., ventral vagal influences on dorsal vagal reactivity).

A CHANGING LITERATURE WITH NEW DISCOVERIES

In developing the Polyvagal Theory, I anticipated that the theory would need modification because the supporting science from which the theory was extracted was dynamically changing. For example, the theory cited literature on the differentiation between the preganglionic receptors of the two vagal pathways, one being muscarinic and the other nicotinic. If validated, it would be possible to use selective blockades to develop a metric that would measure the autonomic signature for each pathway. Unfortunately, the originally cited research was not replicated in other laboratories. Thus, it was not possible to develop a technology to selectively differentiate the vagal tone heart rate signature from each source nucleus (i.e., dorsal nucleus of the vagus, nucleus ambiguus). In addition, more recent research has identified myelinated vagal fibers originating from the dorsal vagal nucleus in vertebrates other than mammals (Sanches et al., 2019).

At the time when the major foundational articles supporting the theory were published, the literature supported a conclusion that only mammals had myelinated vagal fibers coming from the nucleus ambiguus to the heart. This conclusion is still valid. However, although not contradicting the initial assumption, it has recently been reported that a myelinated vagal pathway originating in the dorsal motor nucleus of the vagus has been identified in a very ancient vertebrate (Monteiro et al., 2018). This pathway is used to regulate an extraordinarily slow heart rate–respiration interaction. Since myelinated pathways have been assumed to have evolved for increased speed of neural transmission, this newly identified myelinated pathway does not appear to provide an adaptive function. The authors who conducted this research heralded their findings as empirical evidence to disprove the Polyvagal Theory. This is a surprising conclusion, since Polyvagal Theory focuses on the myelinated fibers originating in the nucleus ambiguus in mammals and not on the vagal fibers originating from the dorsal motor nucleus in an ancient vertebrate. Based on the current state of vertebrate neuroanatomy, it is generally accepted that in mammals all myelinated vagal fibers originate in the ventral vagal nucleus, the nucleus ambiguus. Thus, a hypothesized evolutionary trend observed in the phylogenetic transition from reptiles to mammals in which the primary control of cardioinhibitory vagal fibers moved from the dorsal to the ventral vagal nucleus is thus far supported.

POLYVAGAL MODEL OF THE MAMMALIAN AUTONOMIC NERVOUS SYSTEM LEADS TO SOCIALITY

The polyvagal model emphasizes the evolutionary transition from extinct reptiles to primitive mammals to modern mammals and humans. This transition resulted in the capacity to functionally retune the autonomic nervous system, thus fostering social engagement behaviors and permitting physiological state coregulation through social interactions. The theory also provides an understanding of mammals' increased metabolic demands compared to reptiles. The theory emphasizes the need for social interactions in regulating the human autonomic nervous system and in fostering homeostatic functions. The theory further emphasizes that the mammalian autonomic nervous system has unique attributes that differ from those of reptiles and other earlier vertebrates, including the integration of brainstem structures (i.e., ventral vagal complex) to coordinate the regulation of the ventral vagal nucleus (i.e., nucleus ambiguus) with special visceral efferent pathways emerging from cranial nerves V, VII, IX, X, and XI to form an initial survival-related suck-swallow-breathe-vocalize circuit. As these pathways mature, they form, as proposed by the Polyvagal Theory, a spontaneous social engagement system that supports homeostasis and coregulation.

This link between vagal activity and social engagement behaviors potentially can be monitored through the neural outflow of ventral vagal pathways on the heart, providing a diagnostic and prognostic index of cardiac vagal tone (i.e., respiratory sinus arrhythmia). It is important to emphasize that respiratory sinus arrhythmia, by providing a quantifiable portal of the vagal contribution to the social engagement system, enables the structuring of testable hypotheses related to Polyvagal Theory. However, the theory is not dependent on the attributes or even the evolutionary history of respiratory sinus arrhythmia. Thus, the theory links mental and physical health and well-being through the coregulation of autonomic state through social behavior. Since the model is based on a detailed literature review, the reader is encouraged to read the initial presentation of the theory (see Porges, 1995), and the subsequent updates (Porges, 1998, 2001, 2007b).

AUTONOMIC STATE AS AN INTERVENING VARIABLE

Central to Polyvagal Theory is the role that the autonomic nervous system plays as an intervening variable influencing mammalian behavioral and physiological reactions to challenges both in the body (e.g., illness and distress) and in the environment (e.g., cues of threat and safety). The theory encourages us to think of autonomic state as a functional neural platform from which different adaptive behaviors and reactions may spontaneously emerge. The theory embraces a stimulus-organism-response (S-O-R) model, with autonomic state being a measurable intervening variable, rather than a deterministic stimulus-response (S-R) model that has been prevalent in both behaviorally oriented psychology and mechanistic models of physiology. The theory proposed that there were three global autonomic states that functioned, in general, as a hierarchy that was phylogenetically ordered. In this model, the evolutionarily newest vertebrate autonomic modification was a mammalian ventral vagal circuit with features that supported the mammalian dependence on transporting oxygenated blood to the brain and visceral organs, as well as the need to regulate physiological state through sociality and ingestion.

POLYVAGAL THEORY LEADS TO TESTABLE
HYPOTHESES AND POTENTIAL INTERVENTIONS

Once the conceptualization of the vagal brake was introduced within the Polyvagal Theory (Porges, 1996), the commonly observed changes in global measures of heart rate variability and the more specific vagal component of respiratory sinus arrhythmia during psychological and physical challenges could be understood from a neurobiological perspective. This perspective has embraced technologies to quantify specific neural signals such as respiratory sinus arrhythmia as an accurate index of ventral vagal tone. Similarly, once the integrated social engagement system (Porges, 1998) was introduced into the theory, then the cues of safety and trust that are features of social support could be mechanistically understood as supporting greater vagal regulation and healthful homeostatic functions.

We currently are living in a culture that honors technologies as potential interventions to optimize mental and physical health. Various noninvasive trigeminal and vagal nerve stimulators work through feedback mechanisms described in the Polyvagal Theory. Consistent with polyvagal principles, these devices stimulate afferent pathways that go to the brainstem area that communicates with the ventral vagus, via the ventral vagal complex, increasing vagal outflow, and resulting in calming and optimized homeostatic function. Based on these principles, I developed an intervention called the Safe and Sound Protocol that uses acoustic stimulation to engage the ventral vagal complex and the emergent social engagement behaviors.

THE SAFE AND SOUND PROTOCOL:
AN INTERVENTION BASED ON POLYVAGAL THEORY

The Safe and Sound Protocol that uses computer-altered modulated vocal music to amplify prosodic cues of social communication (see Porges et al., 2013, 2014). The stiumlation is similar to the acoustic cues that human and other mammalian nervous systems interpret as cues of safety and trust. For example, a mother's vocal cues have the capacity to signal safety and calm her child (e.g., infant-directed speech), and vocal cues from adults can calm their children and pets. These acoustic cues increase neural tone to middle ear muscles, which are regulated by brainstem structures (see Chapters 12 and 13) involved in responding to threat and safety, similar to the vagal brake. Under threat, the middle ear muscles relax, and the eardrums become sensitive to low-frequency sounds to detect movements that are potentially dangerous. In this state, the ability to detect human speech may be compromised. When there are cues of safety, the body calms and the autonomic nervous system is in a state predominantly regulated by the ventral vagus. This ventral vagal state is also reflected in a more melodic or prosodic human voice via a noncardiac branch of the vagus, the recurrent laryngeal nerve. Thus, the auditory system is an important portal to our autonomic nervous system. When the initial patent (Porges, 2018) was awarded for the technologies embedded in the Safe and Sound Protocol, the claim that the acoustic stimulation described in the Safe and Sound Protocol functioned as an acoustic vagal nerve stimulator was accepted. The Safe and Sound Protocol is available to professionals only through Integrated Listening Systems (https://integratedlistening.com/porges/).

CRITICISMS MISREPRESENT THE POLYVAGAL THEORY

Criticisms of Polyvagal Theory mispresent the theory and fail to acknowledge the theory's focus on the evolved link between neural regulation of the autonomic nervous system and the unique sociality of mammals. Table 2.2 provides a succinct summary of the contrasts between what the theory states and what the criticisms related to neuroanatomy and evolution have assumed. First, it appears that the authors of these criticisms have not carefully read the theory or even acknowledged the title of its initial presentation. Typically, they have failed to acknowledge the focus of the theory on the evolutionary transitions from asocial reptiles to social mammals. From the initial presentation of the theory, there has been a focus on how the mammalian autonomic nervous system had the capacity to tame and to calm the autonomic circuits that supported defense, including the sympathetic nervous system's support of defensive fight-flight behaviors and the dorsal vagal support for immobilization reflected in death feigning. Using evolution and developmental maturation to map the hierarchy of autonomic circuits, we can detect a pattern, creating a vivid map of the response sequence through which mammals progress when under threat, including disease and injury. This sequence following evolution in reverse, or dissolution as succinctly described by John Hughlyns Jackson (1884), mirrors accounts frequently retold by survivors of trauma. Basically, the criticisms are not criticisms of the Polyvagal Theory. The criticisms are not about testing the documented constructs embedded in theory: dissolution, vagal brake, neuroception, or social engagement system. Nor are the criticisms linked to expanding our understanding of the mechanisms involved in recruiting or monitoring the dorsal vagal circuit in mammals. Rather, the criticisms are at best tangential to the theory and at worst inaccurate representations that lead to misunderstandings of the theory.

New findings in the literature on the phylogeny of the autonomic nervous system need not be central to Polyvagal Theory. For example, the identification of myelinated vagal fibers originating from the dorsal vagal nucleus in other vertebrates suggests a series of questions related to adaptive function and whether there are myelinated vagal fibers originating from the dorsal vagal nucleus in humans that have not yet been identified. If myelinated fibers originate from the dorsal vagal nucleus, then their identification would potentially provide a parsimonious mechanism for massive and potentially lethal bradycardia and even neurogenic (vagal) death. I would encourage research on similar clinically relevant questions that would be of greater benefit than assuming that their research was testing the validity of the Polyvagal Theory.

Table 2.2 summarizes criticisms of the Polyvagal Theory linked to inaccurate assumptions. Note that criticisms seem to reflect a misunderstanding of the scope of the theory. These criticisms have come from one comparative neurophysiology laboratory focused on the research of Taylor, an accomplished scientist, whose work provided foundational support for Polyvagal Theory. Taylor and his colleagues seem focused on assuming that Polyvagal Theory can be falsified by observations of respiratory–heart rate interactions and myelinated vagal fibers in vertebrates that evolved before mammals. When Grossman and Taylor (2007) published their article in a special issue of Biological Psychology, I was invited to write a commentary on the entire issue. In my commentary (Porges, 2007a, p. 304), I addressed Taylor's misunderstandings of the Polyvagal Theory:

> In a paper recently published by Taylor's group (Campbell, Taylor, and Egginton, 2005), an attempt was made to identify RSA [respiratory sinus arrhythmia] in fishes and thus, demonstrate that central control of heart rate was observable and "reject the hypothesis that centrally controlled cardiorespiratory coupling is restricted to mammals, as propounded by the Polyvagal Theory of Porges (1995)." This statement is perplexing, since the specific restriction of cardiorespiratory coupling to mammals was not stated in the Polyvagal Theory. Moreover, as discussed in the commentary, from the Polyvagal perspective, RSA is a uniquely mammalian cardiorespiratory interaction because it is dependent on the outflow of the myelinated vagus originating in the nucleus ambiguus. This does not preclude cardiorespiratory interactions involving the unmyelinated vagus originating in the dorsal motor nucleus of the vagus in other vertebrates.

These comments have not influenced Taylor's continued inaccurate comments about Polyvagal Theory. Nor have he and his colleagues incorporated the insights regarding the adaptive consequences of the mammalian repurposing of the autonomic nervous system to support social behavior and how for mammals social behavior becomes an efficient portal to regulate autonomic function. Since the Polyvagal Theory is focused on repurposing and modifying the autonomic nervous system that mammals inherited from an ancient common ancestor with reptiles to support sociality, it is hard to reconcile the continued inaccurate proclamations by Taylor's group that research irrelevant to Polyvagal Theory serves as evidence to falsify the theory. His research is addressing different questions that are not related to the important conceptualizations embedded in Polyvagal Theory focusing on the evolved links between autonomic function and sociality observed in mammals.

TABLE 2.2.

Polyvagal Theory states (Porges, 1995, 1998, 2007b)	Inaccurate attributions of Polyvagal Theory (e.g., Grossman & Taylor, 2007; Monteiro et al., 2018; Campbell et al., 2005)
1	Evolutionary focus *only* on the transition from reptiles to mammals when the autonomic nervous system is repurposed to support sociality, and through afferent feedback sociality can support autonomic regulation, leading to optimized health, growth, and restoration.	Evolutionary focus on the autonomic nervous system is inclusive of all vertebrates.
2	Mammals have a unique myelinated vagal pathway originating *only* in the ventral vagal nucleus (i.e., nucleus ambiguus) with capacity to downregulate autonomic defensive states to support both sociality and health, growth, and restoration (i.e., homeostasis).	Myelinated vagal pathways are uniquely mammalian. Therefore, observations of myelinated vagal fibers from dorsal vagal nucleus in vertebrates other than mammals disproves the Polyvagal Theory.
3	Respiratory sinus arrhythmia is a term used to define a uniquely mammalian respiratory–heart rate interaction involving the rhythmic modulation of heart rate via vagal pathways originating *solely* in the ventral vagal nucleus (i.e., nucleus ambiguus).	The term respiratory sinus arrhythmia is equivalent to any respiratory–heart rate interaction observed in vertebrates other than mammals. Thus, observations of respiratory–heart rate interactions in vertebrates other than mammals involving vagal influences originating in the dorsal vagal nucleus disprove the theory.

PERPETUATING A STRAW MAN ARGUMENT

These misrepresentations have continued. For example, Sanches et al. (2019) stated, "These findings do not provide support for Porges' so-called 'polyvagal theory,' in which the author claims respiratory sinus arrhythmia and its basis in parasympathetic control of the heart is solely mammalian (Porges, 2013)." Later in the same article, they state, "Nevertheless, the promotor of the polyvagal theory recently stated that: 'only mammals have a myelinated vagus' (Porges, 2013)."

Why do these statements criticizing the theory continue to be voiced? Similar to my comments in 2007a, I continue to be perplexed by these statements. My first response is that the authors had a misunderstanding that might have been due to a lack of clarity in how I presented the theory in the foundational articles. This led me to carefully reread my foundational articles (i.e., Porges, 1995, 2007b) in search of segments that might potentially have led to these misunderstandings. My reread of the original works confirmed that I did not make statements that could be interpreted as being consistent with the criticisms. My reread confirmed that I was cautious not to overstate the points made and to support each extracted principle with well-documented literature.

My rereading left me with the conclusion that Taylor and his group not only missed the innovative contributions of the theory but had interpreted it from a myopic perspective that focused on the phylogeny of the cardiac inhibitory pathways independent of other changes in neural regulation and behavioral adaptation. They focused on their research questions and literally superimposed their research agenda on what they assumed were attributes of the Polyvagal Theory. They missed the embryological and developmental literature that identifies a sequence convergent with the extracted phylogenetic principles of Polyvagal Theory. For example, as cited in Porges (1995):

> neuroanatomical studies performed on human embryos and fetuses suggest that these visceromotor neurons may have migrated from dorsal vagal nucleus (Brown, 1990). In addition, in the human fetus the functional significance of vagal fibers from the nucleus ambiguus depends heavily on myelination, which does not begin until 23 weeks of gestation, when near mature axon diameter is achieved (Woźniak & O'Rahilly, 1981). Myelination of NA [nucleus ambiguus] vagal fibers increases linearly from 24 to 40 weeks gestation and, again, continues actively during the first year postpartum (Pereyra et al., 1992; Sachis et al., 1982).

Briefly stated, it is a sequence in which vagal regulation of the heart evolves to support the sociality of mammals by downregulating defensive states and supporting social engagement behaviors. Moreover, they missed the important evolutionary innovations of a social engagement system in mammals, a system that initially originated as a uniquely mammalian suck-swallow-breathe circuit involved the mammalian ventral vagal complex incorporating the modified evolved mammalian nucleus ambiguus.

They missed the essence of the theory by missing the powerful phylogenetic shifts in how cardioinhibitory pathways were repurposed in a uniquely mammalian nucleus ambiguus to support behavioral calmness and social interactions by downregulating autonomic defensive states. They missed differences between the mammalian brainstem structures, collectively organized within the ventral vagal complex, and those of other vertebrates. They missed the importance of mammalian respiratory sinus arrhythmia as a portal to dynamically monitor this mammalian inhibitory system and its support for homeostatic functions, leading to more optimal mental and physical health. But, given that they missed the essence of the theory, a theory supporting the mammalian journey to sociality, why did they make inaccurate claims about the theory?

Perhaps their misunderstandings are due to their research agenda. Taylor and his colleagues are focused on the phylogeny of cardiac vagal preganglionic neurons. They appear in their publications not to be aware of or interested in the transition of mammals from asocial reptiles into social mammalian species. They also seem to be unaware of technologies that could monitor transitory reactions in vagal reactions to challenges. For example, although they are focused on identifying and documenting respiratory–heart rate interactions in nonmammalian vertebrates, they appear to have no interest in testing hypotheses related to the adaptive function of changes in the amplitude of these signals. For example, can their observations lead to a quantification of dorsal vagal tone that would further our understanding of how this system reacts to challenges in nonmammalian vertebrates?

As discussed in the methodology section below, methods for accurately extracting oscillatory processes in the beat-to-beat heart rate time series are complex, and misunderstandings of the methodology may lead to inaccurate attributions. The methods used by the Taylor group lack sophistication, especially in an understanding of the influence of nonstationarities on the methodologies that they have used.

These criticisms do not explain how they have missed the essence of the theory to make such blatantly incorrect assertions. Especially, after their assumptions were contradicted in my 2007 commentary (Porges, 2007a), why did they persist in aggressively publishing faulty assertions? Obviously, poor scholarship would contribute, but let's assume that they sincerely believe that their findings falsify the theory. What might lead them to make these inappropriate assertions?

The Rubik's cube metaphor is helpful in trying to understand their perspective. Let's start with their statement regarding respiratory sinus arrhythmia that assumes two points: one, that the theory states and is dependent on respiratory sinus arrhythmia being observed in mammals, and two, that respiratory–heart rate interactions observed in evolutionarily older vertebrates disprove the theory. From my perspective, both points are inaccurate attributions to my published statements.

Respiratory sinus arrhythmia has historically been used to describe a mammalian heart rate rhythm. It has a history of use that has been agnostic of the heart rate–respiratory patterns of other vertebrates. In fact, Taylor's earlier articles (i.e., prior to 2000) acknowledged that in the literature the term "respiratory-sinus arrhythmia" was limited to describing mammalian heart-rate respiratory interactions.

Perhaps Taylor's atheoretical agenda has contributed to overgeneralizing from the comparative neuroanatomical evidence that the evolutionary origins in vertebrates of various structures regulating the cardiac functions are highly preserved during evolution and even evidenced in mammals. Of course, this generalization has its limitations, since evolution continues to repurpose and modify both the structure and function of the mammalian autonomic nervous system. If we do not acknowledge the evolutionary repurposing of structures, we would be vulnerable to criticism for accepting recapitulation, a disproven theory which assumes that evolution preserved not only structure but also function.

Polyvagal Theory emphasizes the evolutionary modification of the vagal circuits, while Taylor's group emphasizes the features that are evolutionarily preserved. It appears that Taylor's bias is expressed in a myopic view of evolution that has resulted in his group focusing on two points that he incorrectly believes are critical to Polyvagal Theory: (1) only mammals have respiratory-heart rate interactions, and (2) only mammals have myelinated vagal fibers. Let me emphasize that **these strong statements are not inferred or embedded in Polyvagal Theory**; they are confabulations of what this research group believes is the basis of Polyvagal Theory, and they are using these statements as a straw man argument to foster support and interest in their findings.

To build this straw man argument, Taylor argues that features and structures involved in vagal regulation of the heart in early vertebrates are highly preserved during evolution. Polyvagal Theory acknowledges evolutionary continuity. However, unlike Taylor's emphasis on similarities, **Polyvagal Theory focuses on differences in the repurposing of structures that emerged in ancient vertebrates for different functions in mammals**. Unlike the ancestral vertebrates from which mammals evolved, mammals are social and are dependent on conspecifics to survive. Often this dependence is observed as maternal behavior, socially bonded pairs, or cooperative, hierarchically organized groups. For mammals, as Polyvagal Theory states, physiological state is a profound mediator of social behavior, and social behavior is an emergent behavior dependent on autonomic state not being actively engaged in supporting defensive behaviors or internal defense against illness or injury.

FALLACY OF EQUIVALENCE

If we focus on differences, rather than similarities, we see profound distinctions between the mammalian respiratory sinus arrhythmia and heart rate–respiratory interactions in other vertebrates. First, in mammals there is a well-defined common central respiratory oscillator that sends a respiratory rhythm from the brainstem to both the heart and the bronchi. This information flows through the vagal neurons originating in the nucleus ambiguus. In fact, the oscillator can be conceptualized as an emergent property of the interactions among structures regulated by the nucleus ambiguus, including the larynx and pharynx (see Porges, 1995). This, of course, is not consistent with the features of a primitive nucleus ambiguus that might be seen in vertebrates that preceded mammals. The observation of a common central oscillator is functionally unique to mammals and is the neurophysiological foundation enabling the quantification of respiratory sinus arrhythmia to function as a portal to measure ventral vagal tone. It is unclear what utility the amplitude of the heart rate oscillations provides in nonmammalian vertebrates. These points are not addressed by Taylor and his group.

By focusing on the phenomenon of respiratory–heart rate interactions and not on the uniqueness of the structures and adaptive functions, Taylor and his group assume that all phenomena are equivalent. This does not preclude that features in this system may be common to other vertebrates, but acknowledges the role of evolution in modifying (i.e., repurposing) structures to support other functions. But the defining feature of their assumption of equivalence leads to a circular argument that if respiratory–heart rate interactions are observed phenomeno-logically in several vertebrates, even if the neurophysiological mechanisms vary, the phenomenon reflects the same process. This statement is contradicted by research summarized in the following quote (Porges, 1995) that proposes that respiratory sinus arrhythmia in mammals is a product of modulation due to a common cardiorespiratory oscillator that is uniquely mammalian.

> After investigating the neuroanatomical centers associated with laryngeal, pul-monary, and cardiac function, Richter and Spyer (1990) arrived at a convergent conclusion that NA [nucleus ambiguus] was a contributor to a common respi-ratory rhythm. They also speculated that mammals, with their great need for oxygen, have a medullary center to regulate cardiopulmonary processes. They proposed that a common cardiorespiratory oscillator evolved to foster coordina-tion between cardiac and respiratory processes. In their model, the respiratory rhythm is dependent on the interaction between two groups of neurons, one in NTS [nucleus tractus solitarius], the brainstem source nucleus of the afferent vagus] and the other in NA. Accordingly, the "common" oscillator producing respiratory frequencies is a manifestation of a neural network comprised of inter-neurons between areas containing the motoneurons regulating respiratory, laryn-geal, and cardiac functions. The cardiorespiratory oscillator does not involve DMNX [dorsal nucleus of the vagus]. To support their hypotheses, Richter and Spyer (1990) reported cross-correlational studies of single units. Thus, NA is part of the cardiorespiratory oscillator network, and the period of the oscillations in heart rate (the period of RSA [respiratory sinus arrhythmia]) provides a valid index of the output frequency of the cardiopulmonary oscillator.

In contrast, it appears that in general the respiratory modulation of heart rate in other ancestral vertebrates involves the vagal efferent pathways originat-ing from the dorsal nucleus of vagus. This differentiation remains even with the Taylor group's discovery of myelinated pathways originating from the dorsal vagal nucleus in the ancient lungfish. This statement would argue that there are major distinctions between mammals and nonmammalian vertebrates in the underlying mechanisms involved in generating respiratory–heart rate relationships.

In reflecting on the continued disparaging statements that Polyvagal Theory was dependent on the assumption that only mammals have a myelinated vagus, I tried to infer how this group arrived at that conclusion. Reviewing my writings, I had an intent to create understandable language to convey the uniqueness of the mammalian myelinated vagus. It appears that Taylor's group misinterpreted the repeated and carefully qualified nature of the "mammalian myelinated vagus" as the efferent output of a circuit that originates in the nucleus ambiguus and provides the visceromotor vagal pathways via a vagal branch going to organs above the diaphragm. This qualification provides another phylogenetic distinction, since only mammals and some reptiles have a functional diaphragm. To support their straw man argument, they have reframed the statement to fit their agenda from a "mammalian myelinated vagus" to "only mammals have a myelinated vagus"—obviously, oblivious to the statements of the theory that repeatedly qualified that the myelinated fibers originate from the nucleus ambiguus. If publications related to the theory had not repeatedly made these qualifications, they could have "informed" the theory with their findings and suggested that the theory be adjusted to emphasize this distinction. However, the original statement of theory made this distinction, emphasizing the locus of myelinated vagal fibers from its onset (see Porges, 1995).

During the past few years, a discussion group on Research Gate hosted by Grossman has had the focused agenda of falsifying Polyvagal Theory. Grossman uses Taylor's research portfolio as the evidence that falsifies the theory. In addition to the points described above about respiratory sinus arrhythmia and myelinated vagal fibers, Grossman adds another. He argues that the theory inaccurately asserts that the nucleus ambiguus is evolutionarily newer than the dorsal vagal nucleus. This is another straw man argument that has its basis in Taylor's publications in which he blurs the distinction of the nucleus ambiguus with the identification of cardiac vagal preganglionic neurons that are ventral to the dorsal nucleus of the vagus. From an evolutionary perspective, neurons migrate to form the cardioinhibitory component of the nucleus ambiguus. However, the nucleus ambiguus is not solely a visceromotor nucleus but evolved to regulate striated muscles of structures that emerged from the ancient gill arches. In fact, in Taylor's own article he describes an evolutionary trajectory in which only some reptiles and all mammals have a distinct nucleus ambiguus. He reinforces this evolutionary trajectory by labeling the cardiac preganglionic neurons that are observed ventral lateral to the dorsal nucleus of the vagus as a primordial nucleus ambiguus. In these two documented statements he is emphasizing that the dorsal vagal nucleus is a neuroanatomical structure observed in vertebrates that may be assumed to have evolved several hundred million years prior to mammals.

Let's deconstruct this straw man argument using Taylor's own work. This argument is all based on how the nucleus ambiguus is defined. Again, we see this through Taylor's myopic perspective: based on his own articles, it appears that he is characterizing all cardiac preganglionic neurons that occur ventral to the dorsal nucleus as a "primordial" nucleus ambiguus (Monteiro et al., 2018). He also discusses that the formation of a distinct nucleus ambiguus is seen in some, but not all, reptiles. Even from his nonmammalian cardiac-centric perspective, his own statements support an evolutionary trend toward more modern vertebrates (i.e., mammals and some reptiles) as having a nucleus ambiguus. However, missing from his phylogenetic discussion is how the cardioinhibitory preganglionic neurons became integrated within the nucleus ambiguus, an anatomical structure also containing the source nuclei regulating the striated muscles of the face and head via special visceral efferent pathways. It is this integration that provides the structures and functions of the social engagement system and the reciprocal functional abilities to use social behavior to calm physiological state and to calm physiological state to foster emergent social behavior. It is important to note that the nucleus ambiguus is more than a visceromotor regulatory center, but also a center that regulates and coordinates ingestion, breathing, and vocalization. It is a center that has the capacity to downregulate defenses and to promote interpersonal accessibility, while supporting homeostatic functions that promote resilience and optimize health, growth, and restoration.

RESPIRATORY SINUS ARRHYTHMIA: A QUANTIFIABLE METRIC TO TEST POLYVAGAL-INFORMED HYPOTHESES

Historical Background

The influence in mammals of myelinated cardioinhibitory vagal fibers originating in the nucleus ambiguus is frequently discussed within the context of Polyvagal Theory for two related reasons: (1) the functional output of this neural circuit can be accurately and reliably measured by quantifying the amplitude of respiratory sinus arrhythmia to provide a metric of cardiac vagal tone, and (2) the metric enables testable hypotheses to be evaluated and to inform Polyvagal Theory. If there were no direct precise vagal indicators in the heart rate pattern driven by the outflow of the vagal fibers originating from the nucleus ambiguus, the theory would not be falsified. However, with respiratory sinus arrhythmia as an easily available index of ventral vagal tone, it is now possible to test polyvagal-derived hypotheses by monitoring heart rate patterns. However, the theory potentially could still be tested using noncardiac vagal indicators (e.g., gut responses, subjective scales).

Fortunately, there is no controversy about the prominence of the myelinated cardioinhibitory fibers originating in the nucleus ambiguus and the causal influence of these fibers on respiratory sinus arrhythmia observed in mammals. Note that if the selected metric of respiratory sinus arrhythmia provides a distorted estimate of ventral vagal tone (i.e., a disconnect between respiratory sinus arrhythmia and ventral vagal tone), then that metric may lead to inaccurate inferences when used to test polyvagal-informed hypotheses. A detailed discussion of the sensitivity of specific metrics of respiratory sinus arrhythmia to ventral vagal control is presented below.

Can Ventral Vagal Tone be Monitored by Quantifying Respiratory Sinus Arrhythmia?

The published standards for quantifying heart rate variability in cardiology (Camm et al., 1996) and psychophysiology (Berntson et al., 1997) have not provided evaluations or recommendations of the methods used to quantify respiratory sinus arrhythmia on either statistical or neurophysiological bases. My interest in heart rate variability is focused on respiratory sinus arrhythmia because, unlike other components of heart rate variability that are characterized by frequencies slower than breathing, the neural mechanisms underlying respiratory sinus arrhythmia are understood, and its periodic features reflect identifiable feedback pathways that foster quantification. In the absence of critical criteria to evaluate respiratory sinus arrhythmia metrics, researchers have assumed that since commonly used respiratory sinus arrhythmia metrics are highly correlated, they are equivalent (e.g., Grossman et al., 1990; Goedhart et al., 2007). As Lewis et al. (2012) have demonstrated, this is not the case, since correlation is a deficient methodology to establish statistical equivalence between measures.

Physiologists have hypothesized that the quantification of respiratory-related changes in heart rate variability may provide a sensitive metric of cardiac vagal tone. This implicit assumption was preceded by pioneering research by Hering (1910), who linked respiratory sinus arrhythmia to vagal function. Following Hering, other physiologists conducted systematic research connecting vagal function to the amplitude of respiratory sinus arrhythmia. These scientists elected a simple intuitive measure of respiratory sinus arrhythmia that quantified the difference in heart rate between the peak and the trough of the periodic signal that characterizes respiratory sinus arrhythmia (e.g., Eckberg, 1983; Fouad et al., 1984; Hirsch & Bishop, 1981; Katona & Jih, 1975; Grossman & Kollai, 1993). Following the lead of physiologists, psychophysiologists (e.g., Grossman et al., 1990) applied the peak-to-trough methodology, often with an added restriction that limited the quantification of respiratory sinus arrhythmia to specific features of the respiratory pattern (e.g., heart rate extremes associated with inspiration and expiration). Although uncertain of the most appropriate criterion variable, most autonomic physiologists share the assumption that respiratory sinus arrhythmia is a window to the vagal regulation of the heart.

Contemporary technologies pose the possibility that the quantification of respiratory sinus arrhythmia may provide a metric that would track the dynamic vagal influence on the heart. Paradoxically, these relatively new technologies are often validated with criterion variables operationally defined by limited methodologies that were developed 50 to 100 years ago during the early years of physiology as an experimental science. Moreover, the validation paradigms are often dependent on historic concepts of disruption of vagal function via pharmaceutical blockade or surgery (see Porges, 2007b). These strategies assume that the heart rate changes will provide an accurate metric of vagal influence to the heart.

Polyvagal Theory questions the assumption that change in heart rate is the gold standard for testing the validity of metrics assumed to measure ventral vagal tone. Polyvagal Theory questions this assumption by arguing that although heart rate changes are influenced by the vagus, there are other nonvagal influences on heart rate, such as sympathetic influences, that could disrupt the cardioinhibitory actions of the vagus via dynamic feedback to the brainstem from the cardiac, pulmonary, and vascular systems. Moreover, Polyvagal Theory brings attention to the different neural pathways embedded in the vagus. The theory describes differences in these pathways in terms of neuroanatomical origins within the brainstem, evolutionary history, and adaptive functions. This focus requires a reconceptualization of the construct of cardiac vagal tone as potentially being influenced by vagal pathways originating from both the dorsal (i.e., dorsal motor nucleus of the vagus) and the ventral (i.e., nucleus ambiguus) vagal nuclei.

The resulting product of this approach is an acknowledgment that virtually all cardioinhibitory vagal fibers in mammals that have a respiratory rhythm originate in the nucleus ambiguus, the nucleus of the ventral vagus. Thus, the neuroanatomical pathways underlying respiratory sinus arrhythmia provide a well-documented justification that an appropriately designed respiratory sinus arrhythmia metric potentially could monitor dynamic changes in these ventral vagal pathways in mammals. To reduce complexity, I refer to ventral vagal control of the heart as cardiac vagal tone in the remainder of this chapter.

In contrast to current knowledge about the ventral vagus, the systematic impact of the dorsal vagal pathways on the heart is less understood, appears to have little tonic influence on the heart, and has been hypothesized by physiologists and stated within the Polyvagal Theory (Porges, 1995, 2007b; Reed et al., 1999) to be activated under extreme challenges such as during life threat and/or hypoxia. This conceptualization leads us to reframe the select features of vagal regulation that can be monitored with respiratory sinus arrhythmia. Specifically, the Polyvagal Theory leads us to propose that a reliable metric of the ventral vagal circuit can be monitored by the amplitude of respiratory sinus arrhythmia.

Of great relevance to the survival of humans and other mammals is the documentation that the area of the brainstem regulating the ventral vagus is influenced by and coregulated with the circuits regulating the striated muscles of the face and head (i.e., via special visceral efferent nerves traveling through cranial nerves V, VII, IX, X, and XI), resulting in an integrated social engagement system that has enabled mammals to use social behavior to coregulate physiological state (discussed in other chapters). According to the Polyvagal Theory, it is this relationship with the muscles of the face and head that links visceral state, which could be monitored by quantifying respiratory sinus arrhythmia, with many human emotional and behavioral reactions, including threat reactions and nonspecific chronic stress. It is this social engagement system that enables the autonomic state to support sociality and sociality to support the homeostatic functions of the autonomic nervous system. Functionally, the integrated social engagement system forms the neurophysiological substrate for the attributes of connectedness and cooperation, to which Dobzhansky (1962) attributed the successful survival of mammals.

Consistent with Dobzhansky, this evolutionary journey toward sociality functionally defines a core uniquely mammalian biological imperative in which survival and health are dependent on social connectedness and the ability to trust and feel safe with another conspecific. As Dobzhansky emphasized, it was the capacity to form social bonds rather than physical strength that enabled the evolutionary success of mammals. Thus, Dobzhanky's (1962) statement that "the fittest may also be the gentlest, because survival often requires mutual help and cooperation" provides a more accurate understanding of the meaning of survival of the fittest for mammals.

How Should Respiratory Sinus Arrhythmia Be Measured?

Given the importance of respiratory sinus arrhythmia, how should it be measured? Are the methods used in publications equivalent? During my research career of more than 50 years, I have dedicated decades to developing, refining, and evaluating methods to quantify and evaluate the validity of various respiratory sinus arrhythmia metrics as an index of cardiac vagal tone. I have placed the highest priority in my research on developing a valid metric of ventral vagal tone that can be standardized across laboratories, easily applied to clinical research questions, and helpful in bridging domains studying mental and physical health with a more nuanced understanding of autonomic regulation. Attempts to reach this goal are dependent on the selection of the method used to quantify respiratory sinus arrhythmia, since the validity of the metric used in research could influence interpretation and inference.

Peak-to-Trough Method Provides an Inaccurate Metric of Cardiac Vagal Tone

We start our discussion of respiratory sinus arrhythmia with the peak-valley or peak-to-trough metric (PT_{RSA} in this chapter). This method identifies the highest and lowest heart rate associated with the periodic oscillation in heart rate occurring at the frequency of breathing. In general, heart rate increases during inhalation and decreases during exhalation. This pattern approximates a sine wave with features that can be quantified. Attempts have been made to canonize this historic straightforward and intuitive strategy.

Unfortunately, applying the peak-to-trough metric to quantify respiratory sinus arrhythmia is fraught with statistical problems (Byrne & Porges, 1993; Lewis et al., 2012). Specifically, although the method had been heralded as providing an accurate tracking of cardiac vagal tone (Grossman et al., 1990), the method distorts the actual respiratory sinus arrhythmia signal, especially when the amplitude of respiratory sinus arrhythmia is low relative to the variability of the heart rate trend and breathing is slow. These vulnerabilities were documented about 30 years ago (see Byrne & Porges, 1993), yet proponents of this metric (e.g., Grossman & Taylor, 2007) have not acknowledged that their research based on their metric, PT_{RSA}, has led to faulty inference and misunderstandings relating respiratory sinus arrhythmia to underlying neural pathways. For example, their work has led to an inappropriate assumption that there is a disconnect between respiratory sinus arrhythmia and cardiac vagal tone (see Grossman & Taylor, 2007). In reality, the disconnect is not between respiratory sinus arrhythmia and cardiac vagal tone but is due to the distortion in the relation caused by features of their respiratory sinus arrhythmia metric, PT_{RSA}.

The peak-to-trough method has limited applications. It is not appropriate for heart rate time series, since such series are composites containing dynamically changing trend, a respiratory component (i.e., respiratory sinus arrhythmia), and slower periodic and aperiodic oscillations potentially influenced by vasomotor and blood pressure regulation. If respiratory sinus arrhythmia were the only component of the beat-to-beat heart rate time series, which it is not, then the methodology would work fine.

Inherent in the peak-to-trough method application in quantifying respiratory sinus arrhythmia is a bias due to respiratory features. This point will become evident when data derived with PT_{RSA} are used to argue that respiratory sinus arrhythmia, as a metric of cardiac vagal tone, is distorted by breathing. Our work (see Byrne & Porges, 1993; Lewis et al., 2012) documents how PT_{RSA} can distort inference and mislead the consumers of research into believing that the relationship between respiratory sinus arrhythmia and cardiac vagal tone is not linear or even monotonic and that this bias can be mitigated by adjustments based on respiration rate and tidal volume (see Grossman & Taylor, 2007). Unfortunately, Grossman and Taylor (2007) do not provide data documenting that their fix works in improving the relationship between cardiac vagal tone and their modified metric. Without evidence supporting their claims, either as data or simulations, Grossman and Taylor recommend that researchers perform these corrections.

Porges-Bohrer Method for Quantifying Respiratory Sinus Arrhythmia Provides an Accurate Index of Cardiac Vagal Tone

Fortunately, there are clearly defined steps to develop a sensitive index of cardiac vagal tone from the respiration-related oscillations that Hering observed more than 100 years ago. Basic to good scientific methodology are two obvious steps that need to be acknowledged and respected in developing a respiratory sinus arrhythmia metric that accurately monitors vagal regulation of the heart. **First, the method needs to be informed by the neurophysiology underlying respiratory sinus arrhythmia (i.e., signal), and second, the method needs to apply the appropriate statistical tools to accurately quantify the signal.** Neurophysiology and neuroanatomy inform us, as they did for Hering a century ago, that the amplitude of respiratory sinus arrhythmia is an observable index of the functional output of vagal outflow to the heart's pacemaker. This understanding of the source and impact of vagal outflow on heart rate provides the motivation to develop a technology that can accurately quantify respiratory sinus arrhythmia.

In 1985, based on years (i.e., 1967–1985) of conducting research quantifying heart rate variability, I was awarded a patent that provided the technology to extract accurately the amplitude of respiratory sinus arrhythmia, even when the oscillatory signal representing respiratory sinus arrhythmia had a low amplitude relative to the variance associated with slower frequency oscillations and baseline trend (Porges, 1985). This technology removed complex trends and slower processes from the heart rate pattern with an adaptive moving polynomial filter. The technique is frequently described as the Porges-Bohrer method (Porges & Bohrer, 1990), and the technique has been used and cited in approximately 500 peer-reviewed articles.

In this chapter, the Porges-Bohrer method is abbreviated PB_{RSA}. Further elaborations of this methodology enable the extraction of multiple rhythmic metrics from a single physiological signal. The strategy assumes that oscillatory characteristics of respiratory sinus arrhythmia reflect a dynamically adaptive neural feedback loop characterized by amplitude (i.e., respiratory sinus arrhythmia), frequency (respiratory sinus arrhythmia frequency provides an estimate of spontaneous breathing), and slope. This methodology has been expanded and generalized to include neural components at different frequencies that may be embedded in other physiological signals. The methodology has been awarded a patent that describes the extraction of neural components from physiological signals and the use of the neural components in feedback applications (see Porges, 2020).

More than 30 years ago (see Porges, 1986), I published a chapter that challenged the assumed superiority of changes in heart rate following cholinergic (e.g., atropine) blockade as the gold standard for cardiac vagal tone. The chapter documented that PB_{RSA} was more sensitive than heart rate to blockade using several doses of atropine. Ironically, the chapter was published in a volume edited by Grossman et al. (1986). In a more recent study (see Lewis et al., 2012) with more sophisticated statistics, we documented the superiority of PB_{RSA} as an index of cardiac vagal tone in response to partial vagal blockade by measuring effect size.

Contrasts Between Metrics of Respiratory Sinus Arrhythmia

Effect size is a statistic that quantifies the strength of the relationship in contrast to a significance test that informs the researcher if the observed effect is reliable. The effect size of the change of PB_{RSA} in response to partial vagal blockade was approximately 180% the effect size of changes in heart rate and about 250% greater than the effect size of changes in the PT_{RSA}. These findings provide the documentation to infer that PB_{RSA} is an extremely strong index of cardiac vagal tone by being more sensitive to vagal blockade than heart rate and that PT_{RSA} is a weak index.

Because both respiration and respiratory sinus arrhythmia involve common brainstem circuits, no measure of respiratory sinus arrhythmia is free from covariation with respiratory activity. Covariation does not imply distortion of an inferred relationship between respiratory sinus arrhythmia and cardiac vagal tone, although this has been proposed by Grossman and Taylor (2007). Neurophysiology provides a basis consistent with the intuition underlying several therapeutic strategies that attempt to manipulate breathing patterns to calm disruptions in the autonomic nervous system caused by chronic stress. Manipulating respiratory parameters is an efficient method to calm or activate the autonomic nervous system by changing the impact of the vagal brake. These respiratory strategies have a scientific basis. Since Hering's observations, it has been well accepted that there is a general inhibition of cardioinhibitory influence on the heart during inhalation and a general increase during exhalation (Eckberg, 2003). Thus, it would be anticipated that changes in depth and rate of breathing would influence the gating mechanisms of respiration on the vagal activity and thus cardiac vagal tone.

My research assumes that if respiratory sinus arrhythmia is appropriately quantified, it will reflect the dynamic changes in cardiac vagal tone regardless of the breathing parameters. Thus, my research does not view breathing as a confound that needs to be removed, since the criterion measure of cardiac vagal tone is the amplitude of respiratory sinus arrhythmia. However, if respiration parameters differentially influence the covariation of a respiratory sinus arrhythmia metric with a criterion variable of cardiac vagal tone, then specific respiratory patterns (e.g., breathing slowly or rapidly, breathing deeply or shallowly) may potentially improve or worsen the sensitivity to vagal influences. We will approach this question with moderation analysis.

With moderation analysis, we can evaluate whether breathing parameters distort the covariation between a respiratory sinus arrhythmia metric and a criterion measure of cardiac vagal tone. Moderation analysis statistically defines under which conditions two variables are associated with one another as a function of a third variable (Kraemer et al., 2002). Thus, moderation analysis can be used to define the nature of a significant interaction effect on the influence of changes in respiratory parameters or nonstationarity (i.e., trend) on the association between changes between the two respiratory sinus arrhythmia metrics or between changes in each metric and heart rate.

Using moderation analysis, Lewis et al. (2012) documented that the relationship between changes in heart rate and changes in PB_{RSA} were not qualified by changes in either respiration rate or tidal volume. In contrast, for PT_{RSA} the relations with heart rate were moderated by both respiration frequency and tidal volume. Given that PB_{RSA} was noticeably more sensitive to partial vagal blockade than heart rate, we used PB_{RSA} as the criterion measure of cardiac vagal tone and evaluated whether the relationship between PT_{RSA} and PB_{RSA} was moderated by either respiration rate or tidal volume. If it is, it might explain the apparently faulty assumption that there is a disconnect between respiratory sinus arrhythmia and cardiac vagal tone (see Grossman & Taylor, 2007).

Moderation analysis confirmed that the relationship between the two respiratory sinus arrhythmia metrics was moderated by both breathing rate and tidal volume. For the fast-breathing subjects, PT_{RSA} was significantly related to PB_{RSA}, while for the slow- breathing subjects it was poorly related. Given the relationship between spontaneous breathing rate and tidal volume, in which fast breathing is usually shallower and slower breathing is usually deeper, the moderation analyses for tidal volume yielded similar results. For deeper-breathing individuals, PT_{RSA} was a poor predictor of PB_{RSA}. Lewis et al. (2012) further documented that trend and the degree of violation of stationarity also moderated the relation between PT_{RSA} and PB_{RSA}. With greater background trend and more severe violations of stationarity, PT_{RSA} became progressively a poorer estimate of PB_{RSA}. These analyses confirm that unlike PB_{RSA}, the PT_{RSA} metric is greatly influenced by breathing rate, tidal volume, and trend.

These analyses inform us that the Grossman and Taylor (2007) argument to statistically adjust the respiratory sinus arrhythmia metric by respiratory parameters is dependent on the inadequacy of their methodology to provide a robust indicator of cardiac vagal tone. Moreover, the inference they have drawn from their biased metric-dependent findings, which they have generalized to all metrics of respiratory sinus arrhythmia, has influenced their theoretical arguments that center on the faulty conclusion that there is a disconnect between respiratory sinus arrhythmia and cardiac vagal tone. **Simply stated, their metric, PT_{RSA}, does a poor job in capturing vagal influence on the heart, and they have built a theoretical argument based on a metric that is inadequate for testing their hypotheses.**

In contrast to documented statistical arguments about the problems inherent in the PT_{RSA} metric, Grossman (1992) argued that the PT_{RSA} is "robust and relatively unaffected by various types of nonstationarity" and has continued to encourage the application of this methodology because it is easy to calculate and provides an estimate of respiratory sinus arrhythmia on a breath-by-breath basis regardless of the breathing rate (Grossman et al., 2004). The data in Lewis et al. (2012) contradict these assumptions. This pattern of representation without supporting documentation is consistent with an earlier publication in which Grossman argued that assigning zeros, when a peak-to-trough cannot be identified, is helpful when extracting respiratory sinus arrhythmia in nonstationary data (Grossman & Svebak, 1987). Rigorous analyses confirmed that adding zeros had no benefit (see Lewis et al., 2012). Regardless of these vulnerabilities, PT_{RSA} continues to be used, and arguments based on this faulty metric continue to be used to criticize Polyvagal Theory. Although hypotheses based on Polyvagal Theory can be tested using the Porges-Bohrer metric of RSA, PB_{RSA}, as a valid index of cardiac vagal tone, the theory is not based on the assumption that the metric is valid. However, with a validated metric of ventral vagal tone, polyvagal-informed hypotheses can be tested.

Designing a Metric That Extracts Neural Influences

The quantitative steps embedded in the PB_{RSA} metric are an example of how knowledge of neurophysiology can inform quantitative procedures to extract a signal from the heart rate pattern that behaves consistently and robustly as a dynamic index of regulation of the heart via vagal pathways originating in the nucleus ambiguus. Neurophysiology informs us that the functional output of the myelinated vagus originating from the nucleus ambiguus has a respiratory rhythm. Thus, there would be a temporal relation between the respiratory rhythm being expressed in the firing of these efferent pathways and the functional effect on the heart rate rhythm manifested as respiratory sinus arrhythmia. **From a signal-processing perspective, there are two tasks: (1) defining the frequency band to extract the periodic signal, and (2) removing all sources of variance that might influence the ability to accurately describe the extracted variance in the designated frequency band associated with spontaneous breathing.** In the case of the heart period time series, the variance not associated with the periodic signal defined by breathing frequencies would be manifested as a complex trend with slower periodic or quasi-periodic components. The PB_{RSA} method was designed to perform these two tasks.

When the above steps are not effectively implemented, even if the distributions still conform to parametric assumptions (e.g., via logarithmic transformations), respiratory sinus arrhythmia metrics, such as PT_{RSA}, may provide poor estimates of cardiac vagal tone that may be distorted by trend and respiratory parameters.

Methodology Summary

Analyses demonstrate that although metrics of respiratory sinus arrhythmia may be highly correlated, the metrics may also differ in terms of statistical features, moderation by respiration, distortion due to nonstationarities, and sensitivity to vagal manipulations (Lewis et al., 2012). Thus, the analyses confirm that the metrics are not equivalent and that PB_{RSA} is currently the only respiratory sinus arrhythmia metric adhering to the steps outlined above. This ensures that PB_{RSA} is sensitive to vagal influences, even more sensitive than the assumed gold standard (i.e., changes in heart rate in response to vagal blockade). The net result of these findings is that the literature reported during the past 30 years needs to be revisited if PT_{RSA} was used, since it does not incorporate appropriate transformations and effective detrending procedures. Lewis et al. (2012) report that spectral and time domain methods defining respiratory sinus arrhythmia have similar vulnerabilities if the heart rate time series is not detrended with a filter, such as the moving polynomial filter embedded in PB_{RSA} that dynamically adjusts the aperiodic features of the heart rate trend upon which the signal representing respiratory sinus arrhythmia is superimposed.

Even with the published peer-reviewed evidence that the peak-to-trough metric is biased and results in a disconnect between respiratory sinus arrhythmia and cardiac vagal tone, it continues to be used. For example, I recently reviewed an article for a peer-reviewed journal that used a metric of respiratory sinus arrhythmia based on Grossman's methodology to test hypotheses based on the Polyvagal Theory. The software generating the metric was marketed by James Long Company (Caroga Lake, NY, USA). This illustrates that a method known to distort the relationship between respiratory sinus arrhythmia and cardiac vagal tone is still being used (and marketed to researchers) and in this case is being used to test hypotheses dependent on an accurate monitoring of cardiac vagal tone.

Table 2.3 summarizes the main points about the quantification of respiratory sinus arrhythmia. Specifically, the argument of a disconnect between respiratory sinus arrhythmia and cardiac vagal tone is faulty and due to poor methodology. Information on the precision and accuracy of the Porges-Bohrer methodology and the inadequacy of the methods proposed by Grossman has been known and documented for almost 30 years. The paragraphs above reiterate the features of this argument to ensure that consumers of heart rate variability metrics are not misled or influenced by the faulty assumption of disconnect between respiratory sinus and vagal tone that continues to be expressed on social media as a fatal flaw in Polyvagal Theory (e.g., Research Gate) by Grossman.

CONCLUDING COMMENTS: WHAT IS POLYVAGAL THEORY?

From my perspective, Polyvagal Theory has two components: (1) a descriptive model, and (2) a series of hypotheses related to explanations and applications. The first component is a model of the mammalian autonomic nervous system. The second component is hypothesis driven and future oriented, which could potentially lead to enhancements of mental and physical health. This chapter was written to help researchers distinguish between the interdisciplinary literature that supports the principles of the theory and the testing of hypotheses

TABLE 2.3.

Polyvagal Theory states (Byrne & Porges, 1993; Lewis et al., 2012; Porges, 1995, 1998, 2007b)	Inaccurate attributions of Polyvagal Theory (e.g., Grossman & Taylor, 2007)
1. Respiratory sinus arrhythmia accurately reflects cardiac vagal tone via myelinated cardioinhibitory vagal fibers originating in nucleus ambiguus.	Disconnect between respiratory sinus arrhythmia and cardiac vagal tone.
2. Polyvagal Theory is not based on respiratory-heart rate interactions being uniquely mammalian.	Polyvagal Theory is based on respiratory-heart rate interactions being uniquely mammalian.
Polyvagal Theory is not based on respiratory sinus arrhythmia being an accurate index of cardiac vagal tone.	Polyvagal Theory can be disproved by observing respiratory-heart rate interactions in other vertebrates.
3. Respiratory sinus arrhythmia is an accurate index of cardiac vagal tone and reports of a disconnect between respiratory sinus arrhythmia and cardiac vagal tone is dependent on the methodology used.	Polyvagal Theory can be disproved by documenting a disconnect between respiratory sinus arrhythmia and cardiac vagal tone.
4. Respiratory sinus arrhythmia accurately indexes cardiac vagal tone only if the signal processing techniques and transformations similar to those incorporated in the PB_{RSA} metric are implemented.	Several methods of respiratory sinus arrhythmia are highly correlated and functionally equivalent, including those applying peak-to-trough methodologies.
5. The PT_{RSA} metric (Grossman & Taylor, 2007) distorts the relationship between respiratory sinus arrhythmia and cardiac vagal tone and cannot be statistically improved with linear adjustment based on respiratory parameters.	The relationship between respiratory sinus arrhythmia measured with the PT_{RSA} metric and cardiac vagal tone improves with linear corrections of respiratory parameters.
6. Polyvagal-related hypotheses can be tested with respiratory sinus arrhythmia only if the metric provides an accurate index of cardiac vagal tone originating in the nucleus ambiguus.	

derived from the theory. The interdisciplinary literature supports a convergence among sources of evidence, including the literatures describing: (1) the development of the neural structures regulating the autonomic nervous system, (2) the insights derived from studying the phylogeny and development of the autonomic nervous system, (3) research evaluating autonomic reactions to threat, and (4) clinical observations illustrating the principle of dissolution in physical and mental illness, especially in studying both high-risk preterm infants and the personal histories of individuals who have survived trauma.

As our science evolves, hopefully new technologies will be developed to measure the dynamic regulation of the dorsal vagus. When this is accomplished, then a polyvagal-informed autonomic mapping of an individual could potentially evaluate the function of each pathway. Currently, although dependent on an accurate metric of the ventral vagal tone, we have discovered a new dimension of this system that reflects "vagal efficiency," a metric that evaluates the effectiveness of dynamic change in the vagal brake (i.e., changes in the amplitude of respiratory sinus arrhythmia) on dynamic heart rate. In our initial published research, we identified sleep state differences in vagal efficiency in newborns (Porges et al., 1999), a maturational influence on vagal efficiency in high-risk preterm infants (Porges et al., 2019), and the utility of vagal efficiency in predicting pain reduction during noninvasive vagal stimulation in adolescents with functional abdominal pain disorders (Kovacic et al., 2020). In our ongoing research, we are observing that individuals with features of dysautonomia had noticeable low vagal efficiency. In addition, in another study we noted low vagal efficiency in survivors of trauma and maltreatment. Within the concept of dissolution, a reduction in vagal efficiency may reflect a dampening of feedback involved in regulating autonomic function that may precede end organ dysfunction.

What is the theory in general terms? The Polyvagal Theory emphasizes the role of autonomic state as an intervening variable in how we respond to internal and external cues. The theory changes the personal narrative from a documentary of events to a personalized narrative of feelings (i.e., autonomic state). Applications of Polyvagal Theory in the clinical world focus on autonomic state as a mediator of mental and physical health problems. For example, trauma retunes the autonomic nervous system from calmness and spontaneous social engagement to defense, thus interfering with the ability to socially engage, communicate, and connect. By placing autonomic state in the model as an intervening variable, it becomes both an assessment of neural state that would promote safety or defense and a portal for intervention. Functionally, **calm the physiological state and aberrant behaviors become less prevalent.**

The theory was not proposed to be either proven or falsified, but rather to be informed by research and modified. Claims of falsification would argue that the evolved changes in the autonomic nervous system would not support a social engagement system and that socially delivered cues of safety would not calm the autonomic nervous system and consequently would enhance social behavior. The theory is dependent on evolution and development to structure a hierarchical model of autonomic function inclusive of the Jacksonian principle of dissolution. This model could explain how coregulatory social interactions are not merely social behaviors but neurobiological regulators of autonomic state via an integrated social engagement system that is capable of either supporting or disrupting homeostatic functions. Thus, aspects of social behavior can functionally support or disrupt health. The theory uses evolution to extract a phylogenetic sequence of autonomic regulation. This sequence identifies stages during vertebrate evolution when a spinal sympathetic nervous system and the two vagal pathways emerged and became functional via maturation in mammals. It would be difficult to argue that the sequence does not occur, although it would be possible to identify antecedent similarities in most vertebrates regardless of class or group. **The question is not whether there are similarities in ancestral vertebrates, but rather how these circuits have been adapted to provide a unique mammalian autonomic nervous system that is intimately intertwined with coregulatory social behavior.**

There are many examples of the unique type of sociality expressed in mammals, which differentiates mammals from their reptilian ancestors. Polyvagal Theory is dependent on the processes that evolutionary theorists describe as ex-adaptation and co-opting. These processes involve modifications that shift in the function of a structure during evolution. For example, a structure can evolve because it served one particular function, but subsequently it may come to serve another. Exadaptation and co-opting are common strategies of repurposing vestigial structures in both anatomy and behavior. Polyvagal Theory is agnostic about the evolutionary pressures that result in the selection of specific changes. In contrast, the theory is more phylogenetically descriptive and more focused on the functional outcome of repurposing. More specifically, the theory is interested in how the structures regulated by the ventral vagal complex were repurposed to regulate an integrated social engagement system that provided the primary portal to socially engage and communicate, ingest, and calm. Current neuroanatomical knowledge documents the refinement of the ventral vagal complex in mammals. Thus, although the ventral vagus (i.e., nucleus ambiguus) may have an origin in reptiles (Taylor et al., 2014), it appears that it is only in mammals that this pathway has been repurposed to convey and respond to social cues, while modulating autonomic state.

Evolution transformed attributes of the autonomic nervous system into an integrated social engagement system that incorporated a brainstem communication area (i.e., the ventral vagal complex) that regulated, via special visceral efferent pathways, the striated muscles of the face and head and coordinated these processes with the vagal regulation of the heart and the bronchi. In mammals, the ventral vagal complex enables the coordination of a suck-swallow-breathe-vocalize system with the vagal regulation of the heart. As the neuroanatomy of this ingestive circuit matures, the circuit becomes a functional social engagement system that enables physiological state to be communicated to conspecifics via facial expression and vocalizations. This does not preclude the validity of observations that document in earlier vertebrates links between the brainstem regulation of the special visceral efferent and the source nuclei of the vagus. For example, in more primitive vertebrates the special visceral efferent pathways regulate structures that evolved from ancient gill arches. Thus, in fish there is often a synchrony between gill movements and heart rate, although the regulation of heart rate is mediated through the dorsal vagal nucleus. However, in mammals these structures and their neural regulation have been modified via evolution to support functions unique to the survival of mammals such as nursing and social communication via an integrated social engagement system dependent on the ventral vagal complex.

In retrospect, challenging a theory is like a card game. There is a time when the players need to show their cards. The criticisms of Polyvagal Theory have been relatively simple and do not address features of the theory. When these criticisms were initially voiced, I provided feedback through appropriate mainstream peer-reviewed journals. My feedback focused on correcting misconceptions of the theory and the methodology used to ensure that an accurate estimate of ventral vagal tone could be monitored in humans. This information has been available through a variety of responses in mainstream peer-reviewed journals, including clearly articulated emphases of the focus of the theory on mammalian autonomic function (see Porges, 2007b) and repeated documentations, via simulations and empirical data, confirming the vulnerability of the PT_{RSA} (Byrne & Porges, 1993; Lewis et al., 2012) and the superiority of the PB_{RSA} methodology in extracting a sensitive estimate of ventral vagal tone (Porges, 1986, 2007b; Lewis et al., 2012).

However, the scientists who have generated the criticisms have elected to ignore the feedback, and their arguments have migrated to social media, where these invalid assumptions regarding the theory thrive without oversight. Since I have provided succinct feedback on the scope of the theory (e.g., Porges, 2007b) and for about 35 years have provided feedback on the inadequacies of PT_{RSA} relative to PB_{RSA} (Porges, 1986, 2007; Byrne & Porges, 1993; Lewis et al., 2012), I am skeptical that additional feedback to these individuals via peer-reviewed journals will shift their agenda.

Deconstructing the specific criticisms has had benefits. The criticisms have stimulated the writing of this chapter, with two important consequences. First, the response to criticisms has resulted in parsimonious statements clarifying the theory. Succinct statements of what the theory is and what it is not are now formulated. Second, it forced clarity in the importance of the availability of a neural metric of ventral vagal tone in testing hypotheses related to the Polyvagal Theory. Interestingly, both sources of criticism have made faulty assumptions regarding equivalence: one case focusing on equivalence of respiratory–heart rate relationships across vertebrates, and the other focusing on equivalence of methods. Both investigators, by promoting asymmetrical arguments that emphasized similarities and not differences, have obfuscated unique findings that have potential to further our understanding of humans as social mammals.

The scientific method always seeks to distinguish valid points from conjectures. Theories that are useful in explaining phenomena inform future investigations. Of course, theories must be modified and informed by empirical research and when necessary replaced by alternative theories that are more effective in explaining naturally occurring phenomena. If we use this as an acceptable metric, Polyvagal Theory has provided a testable model of how the autonomic nervous system reacts to threat and safety. It is also providing insights into the consequences of autonomic state for mental and physical health. Perhaps most importantly, the theory gives a voice to the personal experiences of individuals who have experienced chronic threat (i.e., trauma and abuse) and structures an optimistic journey toward more optimal mental and physical health. The theory provides an understanding of the core features of mammalian nervous systems needed to coregulate and trust others. It is this core, described by the Polyvagal Theory, that links our biological imperative to connect with others to neural pathways that calm our autonomic nervous system. These systems, in the context of mammalian physiology, are foundational processes through which behavioral experiences can lead to sociality and optimal health, growth, and restoration.

REFERENCES

Berntson, G. G., Bigger Jr, J. T., Eckberg, D. L., Grossman, P., Kaufmann, P. G., Malik, M., Nagaraja, H. N., Porges, S. W., Saul, J. P., Stone, P. H., & van der Molen, M. W. (1997). Heart rate variability: Origins, methods, and interpretive caveats. *Psychophysiology*, 34(6), 623–648.

Brown, J. W. (1990). Prenatal development of the human nucleus ambiguus during the embryonic and early fetal periods. *American Journal of Anatomy*, 189, 267–283.

Byrne, E. A., & Porges, S. W. (1993). Data-dependent filter characteristics of peak-valley respiratory sinus arrhythmia estimation: A cautionary note. *Psychophysiology* 30, 397–404.

Camm, A. J., Malik, M., Bigger, J. T., Breithardt, G., Cerutti, S., Cohen, R. J., . . . & Lombardi, F. (1996). Heart rate variability: Standards of measurement, physiological interpretation and clinical use. Task Force of the European Society of Cardiology and the North American Society of Pacing and Electrophysiology. *Circulation*, 93(5).

Campbell, H. A., Taylor, E. W., & Egginton, S. (2005). Does respiratory sinus arrhythmia occur in fishes? Biology Letters, 1, 484–487.

Diamond, L. M. (2001). Contributions of psychophysiology to research on adult attachment: Review and recommendations. *Personality and Social Psychology Review*, 5(4), 276–295.

Dobzhansky, T. G. (1962). Mankind evolving: The evolution of the human species. *Eugenics Review, 54*(3), 168–169.

Doussard-Roosevelt, J. A., Porges, S. W., Scanlon, J. W., Alemi, B., & Scanlon, K. B. (1997). Vagal regulation of heart rate in the prediction of developmental outcome for very low birth weight preterm infants. *Child Development, 68*(2), 173–186.

Eckberg, D. L. (1983). Human sinus arrhythmia as an index of vagal cardiac outflow. *Journal of Applied Physiology, 54*, 961–966.

Eckberg, D. L. (2003). The human respiratory gate. *Journal of Physiology, 548*, 339–352.

Fouad, F. M., Tarazi, R. C., Ferrario, C. M., Fighaly, S., & Alicandri, C. (1984). Assessment of parasympathetic control of heart rate by a noninvasive method. *American Journal of Physiology, 246*, H838–H842.

Gaskell, W. H. (1916). *The involuntary nervous system.* London: Longmans Green.

Goedhart, A. D., van der Sluis, S., Houtveen, J. H., Willemsen, G., & De Geus, E. J. (2007). Comparison of time and frequency domain measures of RSA in ambulatory recordings. *Psychophysiology, 44*(2), 203–215.

Grossman, P. (1992). Breathing rhythms of the heart in a world of no steady state: A comment on Weber, Molenaar, and van der Molen. *Psychophysiology, 29*(1), 66–72.

Grossman P., Janssen K.H.L., Vaitl D. (1986). Cardiorespiratory and Cardiosomatic Psychophysiology. (Eds.) NATO ASI Series (Series A: Life Sciences), vol 114. Springer, Boston, MA. https://doi.org/10.1007/978-1-4757-0360-3_7

Grossman, P., & Kollai, M. (1993). Respiratory sinus arrhythmia, cardiac vagal tone, and respiration: Within- and between-individual relations. *Psychophysiology, 30*(5), 486–495.

Grossman, P., & Svebak, S. (1987). Respiratory sinus arrhythmia as an index of parasympathetic cardiac control during active coping. *Psychophysiology, 24*(2), 228–235.

Grossman, P., & Taylor, E. W. (2007). Toward understanding respiratory sinus arrhythmia: Relations to cardiac vagal tone, evolution and biobehavioral functions. *Biological Psychology, 74*(2), 263–285.

Grossman, P., van Beek, J., & Wientjes, C. (1990). A comparison of three quantification methods for estimation of respiratory sinus arrhythmia. *Psychophysiology, 27*(6), 702–714.

Grossman, P., Wilhelm, F. H., & Spoerle, M. (2004). Respiratory sinus arrhythmia, cardiac vagal control, and daily activity. *American Journal of Physiology: Heart and Circulatory Physiology, 287*, H728–H734.

Hering, H. (1910). A functional test of the heart vagi in man. *Munch Med Wochenschr., 57*, 1931–1933.

Hess, W. R. (1949). The central control of the activity of internal organs. *Nobel Lectures, Physiology or Medicine* (1942–1962). https://www.nobelprize.org/nobel_prizes/medicine/laureates/1949/hess-lecture.html

Hess, W. R. (1954). *Diencephalon, autonomic and extrapyramidal functions.* New York: Grune and Stratton.

Hirsch, J. A., & Bishop, B. (1981). Respiratory sinus arrhythmia in humans: How breathing pattern modulates heart rate. *American Journal of Physiology: Heart and Circulatory Physiology, 241*, H620–H629.

Jackson, J. H. (1884). The Croonian lectures on evolution and dissolution of the nervous system. *British Medical Journal, 1*(1215), 703–707.

Katona, P. G., & Jih, F. (1975). Respiratory sinus arrhythmia: Noninvasive measure of parasympathetic cardiac control. *Journal of Applied Physiology, 39*(5), 801–805.

Kolacz, J., Kovacic, K. K., & Porges, S. W. (2019). Traumatic stress and the autonomic brain-gut connection in development: Polyvagal theory as an integrative framework for psychosocial and gastrointestinal pathology. *Developmental Psychobiology, 61*(5), 796–809.

Kolacz, J., & Porges, S. W. (2018). Chronic diffuse pain and functional gastrointestinal disorders after traumatic stress: Pathophysiology through a polyvagal perspective. *Frontiers in Medicine, 5,* 145.

Kovacic, K., Kolacz, J., Lewis, G. F., & Porges, S. W. (2020). Impaired vagal efficiency predicts auricular neurostimulation response in adolescent functional abdominal pain disorders. *American Journal of Gastroenterology, 115*(9), 1534–1538.

Kraemer, H. C., Wilson, G. T., Fairburn, C. G., & Agras, W. S. (2002). Mediators and moderators of treatment effects in randomized clinical trials. *Archives of General Psychiatry, 59*(10), 877–883.

Langley, J. N. (1921). *The autonomic nervous system.* Cambridge: Heffer and Sons.

Leontiadis, G. I., & Longstreth, G. F. (2020). An evolutionary medicine perspective on treatment of pediatric functional abdominal pain. *American Journal of Gastroenterology, 115*(12), 1979–1980.

Lewis, G. F., Furman, S. A., McCool, M. F., & Porges, S. W. (2012). Statistical strategies to quantify respiratory sinus arrhythmia: Are commonly used metrics equivalent? *Biological Psychology, 89*(2), 349–364.

Meyer, H. H., & Gottlieb, R. (1926). *Experimental pharmacology as a basis for therapeutics.* Philadelphia: Lippincott.

Monteiro, D. A., Taylor, E. W., Sartori, M. R., Cruz, A. L., Rantin, F. T., & Leite, C. A. (2018). Cardiorespiratory interactions previously identified as mammalian are present in the primitive lungfish. *Science Advances, 4*(2), eaaq0800.

Piñeiro, D. (2019). Neurocardiology: Physiopathological aspects and clinical implications. *Argentine Journal of Cardiology, 87*(1).

Porges, S. W. (1985). *Method and apparatus for evaluating rhythmic oscillations in aperiodic physiological response systems* (U.S. Patent No. 4,510,944). U.S. Patent and Trademark Office.

Porges, S. W. (1986). Respiratory sinus arrhythmia: Physiological basis, quantitative methods, and clinical implications. In P. Grossman, K. Janssen, & D. Vaitl (Eds.), *Cardiorespiratory and cardiosomatic psychophysiology* (pp. 101–115). New York: Plenum.

Porges, S. W. (1992). Vagal tone: A physiologic marker of stress vulnerability. *Pediatrics, 90*(3, Pt. 2), 498–504.

Porges, S. W. (1995). Orienting in a defensive world: Mammalian modifications of our evolutionary heritage. A polyvagal theory. *Psychophysiology, 32*(4), 301–318.

Porges, S. W. (1998). Love: An emergent property of the mammalian autonomic nervous system. *Psychoneuroendocrinology, 23*(8), 837–861.

Porges, S. W. (2001). The polyvagal theory: Phylogenetic substrates of a social nervous system. *International Journal of Psychophysiology, 42*(2), 123–146.

Porges, S. W. (2007a). A phylogenetic journey through the vague and ambiguous Xth cranial nerve: A commentary on contemporary heart rate variability research. *Biological Psychology, 74*(2), 301–307.

Porges, S. W. (2007b). The polyvagal perspective. *Biological Psychology, 74*(2), 116–143.

Porges, S. W. (2018). *Methods and systems for reducing sound sensitivities and improving auditory processing, behavioral state regulation and social engagement behaviors* (U.S. Patent No. 10,029,068). U.S. Patent and Trademark Office.

Porges, S. W. (2020). *Systems and methods for modulating physiological state* (U.S. Patent No. 10,702,154 B2). U.S. Patent and Trademark Office.

Porges, S. W., Bazhenova, O. V., Bal, E., Carlson, N., Sorokin, Y., Heilman, K. J., Cook, E. H., & Lewis, G. F. (2014). Reducing auditory hypersensitivities in autistic spectrum disorder: Preliminary findings evaluating the listening project protocol. *Frontiers in Pediatrics, 2*, 80.

Porges, S. W., & Bohrer, R. E. (1990). Analyses of periodic processes in psychophysiological research. In J. T. Cacioppo & L. G. Tassinary (Eds.), *Principles of psychophysiology: Physical, social, and inferential elements* (pp. 708–753). New York: Cambridge University Press.

Porges, S. W., Davila, M. I., Lewis, G. F., Kolacz, J., Okonmah-Obazee, S., Hane, A. A., Kwon, K. Y., Ludwig, R. J., Myers, M. M., & Welch, M. G. (2019). Autonomic regulation of preterm infants is enhanced by family nurture intervention. *Developmental Psychobiology, 61*(6), 942–952.

Porges, S. W., Doussard-Roosevelt, J. A., Portales, A. L., & Greenspan, S. I. (1996). Infant regulation of the vagal "brake" predicts child behavior problems: A psychobiological model of social behavior. *Developmental Psychobiology, 29*(8), 697–712.

Porges, S. W., Doussard-Roosevelt, J. A., Stifter, C. A., McClenny, B. D., & Riniolo, T. C. (1999). Sleep state and vagal regulation of heart period patterns in the human newborn: An extension of the polyvagal theory. *Psychophysiology, 36*(1), 14–21.

Porges, S. W., & Furman, S. A. (2011). The early development of the autonomic nervous system provides a neural platform for social behaviour: A polyvagal perspective. *Infant and Child Development, 20*(1), 106–118.

Porges, S. W., & Kolacz, J. (2018). Neurocardiology through the lens of the Polyvagal Theory. In R. J. Gelpi & B. Buchholz (Eds.), *Neurocardiology: Pathophysiological Aspects and Clinical Implications.* Amsterdam: Elsevier.

Porges, S. W., & Lewis, G. F. (2010). The polyvagal hypothesis: common mechanisms mediating autonomic regulation, vocalizations and listening. *Handbook of Behavioral Neuroscience, 19*, 255 –264.

Porges, S. W., Macellaio, M., Stanfill, S. D., McCue, K., Lewis, G. F., Harden, E. R., Handelman, M., Denver, J., Bazhenova, O. V., & Heilman, K. J. (2013). Respiratory sinus arrhythmia and auditory processing in autism: Modifiable deficits of an integrated social engagement system? *International Journal of Psychophysiology, 88*(3), 261–270.

Portales, A. L., Porges, S. W., Doussard-Roosevelt, J. A., Abedin, M., Lopez, R., Young, M. A., Beeram, M. R., & Baker, M. (1997). Vagal regulation during bottle feeding in low-birthweight neonates: Support for the gustatory-vagal hypothesis. *Developmental Psychobiology, 30*(3), 225–233.

Reed, S. F., Ohel, G., David, R., & Porges, S. W. (1999). A neural explanation of fetal heart rate patterns: A test of the polyvagal theory. *Developmental Psychobiology,* 35(2), 108–118.

Sanches, P. V., Taylor, E. W., Duran, L. M., Cruz, A. L., Dias, D. P., & Leite, C. A. (2019). Respiratory sinus arrhythmia is a major component of heart rate variability in undisturbed, remotely monitored rattlesnakes, Crotalus durissus. *Journal of Experimental Biology,* 222(9).

Taylor, E. W., Leite, C. A., Sartori, M. R., Wang, T., Abe, A. S., & Crossley, D. A. (2014). The phylogeny and ontogeny of autonomic control of the heart and cardiorespiratory interactions in vertebrates. *Journal of Experimental Biology,* 217(5), 690–703.

Woźniak, W., & O'Rahilly, R. (1981). Fine structure and myelination of the human vagus nerve. *Acta Anatomica,* 109, 118–130.

CHAPTER 3

Play as a Neural Exercise
Insights From the Polyvagal Theory

Stephen W. Porges

We often think of play as an amusement or a diversion from the real work in our lives. When we observe children playing, we might judge the time engaged in play as a distraction from opportunities to learn. This view, denigrating play and revering classroom learning opportunities, is consistent with our cultural view of education. Educational systems attempt to maximize opportunities for classroom instruction and to minimize opportunities for social interactions available during recess and other interactive forums such as team sports, music, and theater. From an educator's perspective, play is the antithesis of learning; play steals the precious time that could be dedicated to learning. This perspective is based on assumptions derived from learning theories that were outlined by behaviorists about 100 years ago. What if this perspective, prevalent in our society, is outdated? What if play, rather than displacing learning experiences, actually provides a neural exercise that would facilitate learning?

Is our conceptualization of play inadequate? Are our views of play restricted interpretations dependent on a limited understanding of learning embedded in our educational institutions, parenting styles, and expectations of socialization? Can we take a different perspective and emphasize that play provides opportunities to exercise features of our nervous system that would foster learning and social behavior? If play were perceived from this perspective, then play, as a neural exercise, might foster state regulation, enabling individuals to transition efficiently from active to calm states. Consistent with this perspective, the ability to move rapidly into a calm state would facilitate efficient learning and optimize spontaneous and reciprocal social behavior.

The importance of play is dismissed in the cognitive-centric world of education. Within theoretical models of learning, little importance is placed on how bodily feelings, as an intervening variable, influence the ability to learn. Although we may want to sit and attend, at times our body may want to run, fight, or hide. Calmly sitting enables us to attend and to efficiently learn. However, when our body wants to run, fight, and hide, we are in a physiological state that supports defense. During these physiological states, neural feedback from our body to the higher brain structures will interfere with cognition and learning. Missing from the cognitive-centric perspective is the role that play may have in strengthening the neural circuits that can rapidly downregulate defense systems to foster learning by enabling us to sit calmly and attend.

The roots of play are linked to the evolution of a neural mechanism that enables mammals to shift between mobilized fight-flight and calm, socially engaging states. From an evolutionary perspective, mammals had to rapidly detect whether a conspecific was safe or dangerous. If the interaction was dangerous, they needed to be in a physiological state that would produce sufficient energy to defend (fight) or facilitate an instantaneous escape (flight). If the interaction had cues of safety, then the physical distance could be reduced and physical contact might ensue and terminate with mating behaviors.

To mate or to be in close contact with a conspecific, defense reactions have to be inhibited before cues of aggression or fear are expressed. An immediate decision has to be made to distinguish potential mate from potent threat. This process was so important to survival of both the individual and the species that the neural mechanisms were subjugated to brain processes outside the realm of conscious awareness.

Within the context of the Polyvagal Theory, the instantaneous process of evaluating risk outside the realm of awareness is called neuroception. Neuroception is the neural process through which our body reacts to features in the environment and shifts physiological state to deal with potential risk. Neuroception is not perception, because the process does not require awareness. If the cues trigger a neuroception of safety, our physiological state calms immediately, then we can easily socially engage or attend. If the cues trigger a neuroception of danger, our body prepares for movement. If the cues trigger life threat, then we lose social contact and immobilize. Although we are not aware of the stimuli that trigger our sense of danger or safety, we can become aware of our bodily responses triggered by neuroception. Thus, the cues from our body influence our personal comfort, which will vary as contexts and interactions with people change.

Functionally, play is a neural exercise in which cues triggering neuroception alternate between danger and safety. As an example, we can think of the simple game of peek-a-boo that a mother may play with her infant. By hiding her face and removing the cues of safety normally generated by the social engagement system (prosodic voice, facial expressions), the mother is creating a state of uncertainty in the infant. This state of uncertainty is followed by the mother startling the infant by showing her face and saying "peek-a-boo!" The sequence of the peek-a-boo game is ended, when the mother uses a prosodic voice with warm facial expressions to calm the startled infant.

Deconstructing the behavioral sequence involved in peek-a-boo, we see the neural exercise embedded in this play behavior. First, the initial hiding of the mother's face elicits a state of uncertainty and vigilance. This state is associated with a depression of the infant's social engagement system, including a withdrawal of the myelinated vagal pathways to the heart. This puts the infant in a vulnerable state in which a startle stimulus could easily recruit sympathetic activity to support mobilization (i.e., fight-flight behaviors). The mother provides the startle stimulus by showing her face and saying "boo" in a relatively loud and monotonic voice. The acoustic features of the mother's vocalizations support the unpredictable presentation of the mother's face, since the vocalizations of "boo" have acoustic features that are associated with danger and lack the prosodic features that would be calming. The cues of this sequence trigger a neuroception of danger, which recruits increased sympathetic activation. The next step in the sequence of this game provides the opportunity for a neural exercise that promotes resilience and enhances the infant's ability to calm.

After the infant is motorically and autonomically activated by the "boo" sound, the mother needs to calm the infant with her social engagement system by using a prosodic voice with warm facial expressions. The prosodic voice and warm facial expressions trigger a neuroception of safety, and the infant calms as the social engagement system comes back online, and the myelinated vagal pathways downregulate the sympathetic activity. When effectively implemented, peek-a-boo provides opportunities for the infant to neurally navigate through a sequence of states (i.e., from calm, to vigilant, to startle, and back to calm). Repeating this game provides opportunities for the social engagement system to efficiently downregulate, via social interactions and sympathetic activation. The child will need this neural skill to adapt in the classroom. In fact, the ability to use neural resources to regulate biobehavioral state is as important as IQ and motivation in predicting classroom performance.

Kittens playing provide a relevant example. I recall what I was taught about the play of cats and other mammals in graduate school. In courses in comparative psychology and animal behavior, we were taught that kittens were practicing their hunting and aggressive skills. However, when I revisited these images from a polyvagal perspective, I saw that the behaviors may have served another purpose. Visualize kittens in bouts of rough-and-tumble play. They are using their claws and teeth, but rarely injure each other. In fact, if you have a kitten, you may be surprised that they know when to retract their claws and relax their jaws once they make a gentle bite. However, an extremely important feature often goes unnoticed. The kittens maintain face-to-face interactions during most of the play. If a bite hurts, there is an immediate face-to-face interaction of their social engagement systems, and they cue each other that there was no intention to injure. But kittens, like children, vary in their ability to be aware of each other in a play scenario. If awareness of the other is poor, then injury may occur. In primate social groups, the juveniles who enthusiastically engage but, due to a lack of awareness of others, may injure peers are ostracized and marginalized from social groups.

Dogs have similar play sequences. Dogs will play a structured game of chase. One dog runs and is chased by another. When the dog chasing catches the other dog, the dog may bite the rear leg to inform the dog being chased that it is caught. The caught dog turns toward the other dog to initiate a face-to-face interaction to determine whether the bite was aggressive or play. If it is play, the two dogs interact via their social engagement systems (i.e., face to face), and then the game continues with a role reversal. If the bite is aggressive, then face-to-face is replaced with a face-to-neck attack.

We can observe similar situations on the playground. For example, when playing basketball, players are often shoved and fall. If the social engagement system is employed following this event, aggressive behaviors will be dampened. For example, aggression is defused if the person who did the shoving makes eye contact with the person on the floor, helps the other person off the floor, and asks if the person is okay. However, a fight might be triggered if the person who did the shoving just walks away. In my talks, I use an example from a professional basketball game in which this sequence results in a fight between Larry Bird and Julius Irving (Dr. J.).

By deconstructing the play of mammals, whether we are observing kittens, dogs, or children on the playground, we see a common feature of behaviors that simulate features of fight-flight that are actively inhibited by social engagement behaviors (e.g., facial expressions, head gestures, prosodic vocalizations). In the examples above, we can see that play transitions into aggressive behaviors, if the social engagement systems are not employed to downregulate any potential neuroception of danger.

The process of play is about active inhibition of the neural circuit that promotes fight-flight behaviors. Play functions as a neural exercise that improves the efficiency of the neural circuit that can instantaneously downregulate fight/flight behaviors. If we translate this into the classroom, we can identify children with difficulties in downregulating the neural circuits that promote fight-flight behaviors. These children have difficulties in sitting, in attending, in listening, and in socializing. If we watch these children on the playground, we might see deficits in their ability to play with others. They may not accurately anticipate the behaviors of others and, instead of a reciprocal interaction that inhibits fight-flight behaviors, they may functionally be physically bouncing off their peers.

When we are in neurophysiological states supporting mobilization and shutdown, our cognitive processes are greatly compromised. However, we have a neural circuit that can rapidly downregulate mobilization behaviors to foster the calm states that optimize learning and social behavior. Although play is frequently characterized by movement and often recruits many of the neural circuits involved in fight-flight behaviors, it may be operationally distinguished from defense, since it is easily downregulated by the social engagement system. However, the effectiveness of the social engagement system to downregulate fight-flight behaviors requires practice. This practice may start early in a child's development through play.

In this chapter, the definition of play, similar to other forms of co-regulation, requires reciprocal and synchronous interactions between mammals while using the social engagement system as a regulator of mobilization behavior (e.g., fight-flight). This definition of "play" may differ from the use of the term to describe interactions between an individual and a toy or computer. Play with a toy or computer lacks face-to-face interaction and will not exercise the social engagement system as a regulator of the neural circuits that foster fight-flight behaviors. Thus, as mammals, we need to respect our phylogenetic heritage and appreciate the importance of synchronous face-to-face interactions as an opportunity to exercise our social engagement systems. As the neural regulation of our social engagement system improves, we gain resilience in dealing with disruptions in our lives. Many of the features of play are shared with psychotherapy. A deconstruction of a therapeutic session will find the client (and often the therapist) shifting states from calm to defense and back to calm. Fortunately, we as mammals have a social engagement system that evolved to employ cues from face-to-face interactions to efficiently calm our physiological state and shift our fight-flight behaviors to trusting relationships.

CHAPTER 4

Vagal Pathways
Portals to Compassion

Stephen W. Porges

As contemplative neuroscience emerges as a discipline, research is being conducted to identify the neural pathways that contribute to compassion. Paralleling these scientific explorations, clinicians in mental health disciplines are developing interventions designed to enhance compassion toward others and self (Gilbert, 2009). Limiting these investigations and applications is the lack of a consensus definition of compassion. This ambiguity limits both scientific investigations of the neural pathways determining compassion and the evaluation of compassion-based therapies.

Definitions of compassion and the tools used to assess it vary within the literature (see Strauss et al., 2016). Compassion has been viewed as an action, a feeling, an emotion, a motivation, and a temperament. Although common themes may be extracted from the literature, no assessment tool conforms to the standards commonly employed in scientific research (Strauss et al., 2016). Without a consensus definition, researchers investigating compassion lack a toolkit that would foster scientific inquiry, and clinicians lack a metric to assess the outcome of compassion-based therapies.

In contrast to the frequent definitions of compassion as a psychological construct, this chapter proposes that compassion is an emergent process dependent on one's neurophysiological state. Consistent with this perspective, compassion cannot be investigated as a voluntary behavior or a psychological process independent of the physiological state. Thus, compassion cannot be taught through classic rules of learning, nor can it be indexed by specific neurophysiological processes, behavioral actions, or subjective experiences independent of the bidirectional communication between peripheral physiological state and brain function. In the proposed model of compassion, physiological state functions as an intervening variable between the person who is suffering and the responses to the person, which are manifested as the subjective experiences and behavioral actions that form operational definitions of compassion.

This chapter proposes that a physiological state mediated via vagal pathways is a necessary, but not sufficient, condition for an individual to experience compassion. The vagus is a cranial nerve, which provides the major bidirectional (motor and sensory) communication between the brain and the body. The vagus is a major component of the parasympathetic branch of the autonomic nervous system. Functionally, specific vagal motor pathways are able to inhibit the reactivity of the sympathetic branch of the autonomic nervous system, while vagal sensory pathways provide a major surveillance portal between the body and the brain. I propose a model that emphasizes the dependence of compassion on a vagal-mediated state that supports feelings of safety, which enables feeling one's own bodily responses at a given time while acknowledging the bodily experiences of another person. The emphasis on shifting physiological state via vagal mechanisms to experience compassion is consistent with the historic use of rituals in contemplative training.

Since compassion depends on a vagal-mediated physiological state, it may be separated from other subjective experiences that have a different physiological substrate. For example, although empathy is frequently assumed to be interchangeable with compassion, the physiological state associated with empathy may differ from the physiological state associated with compassion. Empathy is frequently operationally defined as feeling someone else's pain or negative emotion (e.g., Decety & Ickes, 2009). If we deconstruct empathy from a neurobiological perspective, empathy should be associated with the activation of the sympathetic nervous system. This would occur because the autonomic response to pain is characterized by a withdrawal of vagal influences and an activation of the sympathetic nervous system. Thus, from a neurobiological perspective, compassion is not equivalent to empathy, given that compassion engages vagal pathways.

If compassion is associated with a calm vagal state, it would promote a physiological state associated with safety of self that projects calmness and acceptance toward the other. Functionally, the vagal pathways are a major component of a branch of the autonomic nervous system, historically labeled the parasympathetic nervous system. A linguistic cue for the function of the parasympathetic system is in the use of *para* in its name. *Para* is derived from the ancient Greek παρά, meaning "contrary" or "against." Thus, the parasympathetic nervous system, as suggested by its name, provides an implicit understanding of the containment of the defensive reactivity associated with the sympathetic nervous system. Consistent with this view of the containment of defensive reactions, the critical portal to express compassion would be dependent on the capacity to recruit the vagal pathways that actively inhibit sympathetic reactivity and promote a calm physiological state that projects safety and acceptance to others.

The physiological state mediated by vagal pathways is not equivalent to compassion. Rather, it is a state that promotes or facilitates feelings of safety, positive feelings toward others (e.g., Stellar et al., 2015), connectedness, and the potential to respect both the suffering and joy of others (e.g., Kok & Fredrickson, 2010).

It is through the vagal inhibition of the neurophysiological defenses (hypothalamic-pituitary-adrenal–sympathetic responses) that the vagal state functionally contains the behavioral and physiological reactivity to suffering. This containment provides opportunities to witness without judgment and to subsequently be helpful in alleviating the suffering of self or other. Brain-imaging studies attempting to distinguish between empathy and compassion are consistent with the proposed state differences associated with empathy and compassion. Klimecki et al. (2014) suggest that the excessive sharing of others' negative emotions (i.e., empathy) may be maladaptive, and that compassion training dampens empathic distress and strengthens resilience. Similarly, it has been suggested that empathy involves resonating with or mirroring another's emotion in neurophysiological, peripheral physiological, and behavioral domains (for an overview, see Decety & Ickes, 2009).

A cornerstone to compassion is respecting the individual's capacity to experience their own pain. By respecting the individual's capacity to experience pain, compassion functionally allows the individual to have their experiences witnessed by another without hurting the other, by empathically sharing their pain and activating the defensive sympathetic nervous system in the other. This allows the pain to be expressed without fear of negative evaluation or the potential shame that emerges from evaluation. Compassion allows and respects the other's right to own their experiences. This respect of the other in itself contributes to the healing process by empowering the other and not subjugating or diminishing the value of the person's experiences of pain or loss. Compassion functionally allows one who has lost or is suffering not to be defensive about the loss and not to experience shame for the loss. If we attempt to fix the problem without successfully expressing compassion, the intervention will disrupt the individual's process of expression by triggering behavioral and physiological defense strategies associated with a shift in physiological state, which is characterized by a withdrawal of vagal influences and activation of the sympathetic nervous system. Thus, compassion relies on a neural platform that enables an individual to maintain and express a physiological state of safety when confronted with the pain and suffering of others.

VAGAL STATES ARE INTERTWINED WITHIN THE HISTORY OF CONTEMPLATIVE PRACTICES

Throughout the history of humanity, rituals such as chants, prayers, meditation, dance, and posture have provided the behavioral platform for contemplative practices. A careful investigation of many rituals results in the discovery that the rituals are functional exercises of vagal pathways (see Table 4.1). Although chants, prayers, and meditation have been incorporated into formal religions, the function of these rituals may be different from that of the narratives upon which religions are based. The narratives are attempts to fulfill the human need to create meaning out of uncertainty and to understand the unknowable mysteries of the human experience in a dynamically changing and challenging world. While this assumption may be consistent with the history of the narratives that form the corpus of formalized religions, the function of rituals may be more closely related to health and personal subjective feelings of connectedness to others, and feelings of connectedness to both others and a deity.

The documented positive effects of meditation on mental and physical health (Bohlmeijer et al., 2010; Chiesa & Serretti, 2009; Davidson et al., 2003) have stimulated an interest in contemplative practices as health-related interventions, such as mindfulness-based stress reduction (e.g., Kabat-Zinn, 2003). Science is now interfacing with insights derived from historical and often ancient contemplative practices. The accumulated knowledge suggests that meditative practices not only lead to a different perspective of reality that fosters a connectedness with others expressed through feelings of compassion, but also may have positive influences on health. These observations have led to a new discipline of contemplative neuroscience that attempts to document the shift in neural regulation that occurs during contemplative practices such as meditation.

Contemplative neuroscience has focused on documenting the mechanisms through which meditation heals. Thus, contemplative neuroscience assumes directional causality, in which mental processes can influence and potentially optimize bodily function. This top-down model emphasizes mind in the mind-body relationship and assumes that thought is the driving force through which meditation functions effectively. Functionally, the research has emphasized the investigation of mind-brain relationships through imaging and electrophysi-

TABLE 4.1. The Physiology of Rituals

Ritual	Vagal Mechanism
Chant (vocalization)	Laryngeal nerves Pharyngeal nerves Respiration (long exhalation and deep abdominal inhalation enhance vagal brake)
Meditation (breath)	Respiration (long exhalation and deep abdominal inhalation enhance vagal brake)
Prayer (posture)	Carotid baroreceptors (vagal contribution to blood pressure regulation)

ological studies of brain circuits of expert meditators (e.g., Lutz et al., 2013). Within contemplative neuroscience, investigations of the influences of meditation on the neural regulation of visceral organs have not been emphasized.

The predominant model within contemplative neuroscience, including the study of neural pathways associated with compassion, assumes a directional causality in which mental activity drives brain function. Although this directional causality has been reliably documented (i.e., mental processes reliably influence neural activity), the model is limited because it does not incorporate two intervening variables that may mediate the effectiveness and efficiency of contemplative practices. First, the model does not acknowledge the influence of context on the nervous system. Second, the model does not acknowledge the influence of peripheral physiological state on brain function. Without detailed attention to these two variables, the functional impact of contemplative practices on mental and physical health will be unpredictable. In addition, the efficiency of contemplative practices in increasing a sense of connectedness and an ability to express compassion may be compromised.

This chapter presents a model in which contemplative practices are conceptualized as methods that require, as a prerequisite, enhanced vagal regulation of biobehavioral states. Functionally, by enhancing vagal regulation, these methods efficiently promote health and may enable expansive subjective experiences related to compassion and a universal connectedness. The model proposes that specific voluntary behaviors (e.g., breath, vocalization, and posture), which characterize ancient rituals and form the core of contemplative practices, have the potential to trigger a physiological state that fosters health and enables subjective experiences that have been the objective of contemplative practices.

The model emphasizes that two well-defined and sequential antecedent conditions are necessary for the beneficial properties of contemplative practices to be experienced. First, the environment in which contemplative practices are performed needs to have physical features that are calming and soothing. Across history and cultures, contemplative practices have been performed in quiet and safe environments. There are specific neurophysiological reasons for this consistency. To survive, humans needed to identify danger and therefore detect environments and others who were either safe or dangerous. Thus, the human nervous system needed to be sensitive to features that define physical spaces, which may either trigger or dampen defensive physiological reactivity. Second, rituals of chants, prayers, meditation, dance, and posture provide potent stimuli to our nervous system to exercise the vagal pathways. These pathways downregulate defense and promote states of calmness and stillness.

In a safe environment, when a person no longer needs to be vigilant in anticipation of danger, the nervous system tends to shift into a qualitatively and measurably different physiological safe state. This safe state may function as a neural catalyst for subjective feelings of social connectedness and compassion. Without the appropriate contextual cues of safety, and without the body shifting into a safe physiological state, attempts at contemplative practices may be ineffective, and may even promote defensive feelings focused on self-survival that promote hypervigilance and hyperreactivity. Consistent with this premise, via personal communications, clinicians treating veterans with post-traumatic stress disorder (PTSD) have reported situations in which mindfulness techniques have triggered defensiveness.

POLYVAGAL THEORY: DECONSTRUCTING ANCIENT RITUALS FROM A POLYVAGAL PERSPECTIVE

Polyvagal Theory (Porges, 1995, 2011) explains how rituals associated with contemplative practices contribute to bodily feelings of safety, trust, and connectedness. Polyvagal Theory holds that cues of risk and safety, which are continuously monitored by the nervous system, promote either states of safety and calmness or states of vigilance toward sources of potential threat and defense. The theory assumes that mammals are searching for safety, which, when obtained, facilitates health and social connectedness. The theory explains how the rituals associated with contemplative practices trigger physiological states that calm neural defense systems and promote feelings of safety that may lead to expressing and feeling compassion.

The human nervous system provides two paths to trigger the neural mechanisms capable of downregulating defensiveness to enable states of calmness that support health and connectedness. One path is passive and does not require conscious awareness (see the section Neuroception in this chapter), while the other requires conscious volitional behaviors that trigger specific neural mechanisms that, in turn, change one's physiological state. Spontaneous positive social behavior expressed in facial expressions and vocal intonation is dependent on the former, and optimal outcomes of contemplative practices such as meditation and chants are dependent on the latter. Features of voice (e.g., prosody, voice intonation) and facial expression, which characterize the interactions of positive social behavior, provide potent cues to ways the nervous system downregulates defense circuits. In contrast to the passive pathway of calming through affiliative social engagement, contemplative training is usually conducted within the context of a spiritual space (e.g., quiet space with calming music) that triggers the passive pathway to promote the physiological state associated with feeling safe. Once in a safe state, the individual is instructed to perform voluntary behaviors such as breathing, posture shifts, and vocalizations that functionally exercise the vagal circuit and that further promote, reinforce, and strengthen states of calmness. These voluntary behaviors, which we observe as rituals, directly tap into and engage vagal circuits that efficiently manipulate one's physiological state. This enables rituals to function as neural exercises of vagal pathways.

THE ROLE OF THE VAGUS IN
BIDIRECTIONAL COMMUNICATION

During the phylogenetic transition from ancient reptiles to mammals, the autonomic nervous system changed. In ancient reptiles, the autonomic nervous system regulated bodily organs via two subsystems: the sympathetic nervous system and the parasympathetic nervous system. Modern reptiles share these global features. The sympathetic nervous system provided the neural pathways for visceral changes that support defensive fight-and-flight behaviors. This physiological adjustment to support mobilization for self-preservation was associated with increases in heart rate and an inhibition of digestive processes, which required suppression of parasympathetic (i.e., vagal) influences to the heart and the gut.

In ancient reptiles, the parasympathetic nervous system complemented the function of the sympathetic nervous system by providing reciprocal influences on visceral organs. The reptilian parasympathetic nervous system served two primary adaptive functions: (1) when not recruited as a defense system, it supported processes of health, growth, and restoration; and (2) when recruited as a defense system, it reduced metabolic activity by dampening heart rate and respiration, enabling the immobilized reptiles to appear inanimate to potential predators (i.e., a death feigning response). When not under threat, the sympathetic and parasympathetic branches of the autonomic nervous system in reptiles function reciprocally (and frequently antagonistically) to simultaneously innervate the visceral organs that support bodily functions. This synergy between the two branches of the autonomic nervous systems in support of health (not defense) is maintained in mammals, but only when mammals are safe. In this safe state, the potential of the autonomic nervous system to be recruited in support of defense is greatly reduced.

Most of the neural pathways of the parasympathetic nervous system travel through the vagus nerve. The vagus is a large cranial nerve that originates in the brainstem and connects visceral organs throughout the body with the brain. In contrast to the nerves that emerge from the spinal cord, the vagus connects the brain directly to bodily organs. The vagus contains both motor fibers to influence the function of visceral organs and sensory fibers to provide the brain with continuous information about the status of these organs. The flow of information between body and brain informs specific brain circuits that regulate target organs. Bidirectional communication provides a neural basis for a mind-body science, or a brain-body medicine, by providing plausible portals of intervention to correct brain dysfunction via peripheral vagal stimulation (e.g., vagal nerve stimulation for epilepsy, depression, and PTSD) and plausible explanations for exacerbation of clinical symptoms by psychological stressors, such as stress-related episodes of irritable bowel syndrome. In addition, bidirectional communication between the brain and specific visceral organs provides an anatomical basis for historical concepts of the optimal balance among physiological systems, such as Walter Cannon's homeostasis (Cannon, 1932) and Claude Bernard's internal milieu (Bernard, 1872).

POLYVAGAL THEORY: OVERVIEW

Polyvagal Theory provides a reconceptualization of how autonomic state and behavior interface. The theory emphasizes a hierarchical relationship among components of the autonomic nervous system that evolved to support adaptive behaviors in response to the particular environmental features of safety, danger, and life threat (Porges, 2011). The theory is named "polyvagal" to emphasize that there are two vagal circuits: an ancient vagal circuit associated with immobilization defense strategies (e.g., freeze, death feigning) and a phylogenetically newer circuit related to feeling safe and displaying spontaneous affiliative social behavior. The theory articulates two defense systems: (1) the commonly known fight-or-flight system that is associated with activation of the sympathetic nervous system, and (2) a less-known system of immobilization and dissociation that is associated with activation of a phylogenetically more ancient vagal pathway.

The Polyvagal Theory describes the neural mechanisms through which physiological states communicate the experience of safety and contribute to an individual's capacity: (a) to feel safe and spontaneously approach or engage cooperatively with others, (b) to feel threatened and recruit defensive strategies, or (c) to become socially invisible by feigning death. The theory articulates how each of three phylogenetic stages, in the development of the vertebrate autonomic nervous system, is associated with a distinct and measurable autonomic subsystem. In humans, each of these three subsystems becomes activated and is expressed physiologically under specific conditions (Porges, 2009). The three autonomic subsystems are phylogenetically ordered and behaviorally linked to three general adaptive domains of behavior: (a) social communication (e.g., facial expression, vocalization, listening); (b) defensive strategies associated with mobilization (e.g., fight-or-flight behaviors); and (c) defensive immobilization (e.g., feigning death, vasovagal syncope, behavioral shutdown, and dissociation). Based on their phylogenetic emergence during the evolution of the vertebrate autonomic nervous system, these neuroanatomically based subsystems form a response hierarchy.

The Polyvagal Theory emphasizes the roles of two distinct vagal motor pathways identified in the mammalian autonomic nervous system. The vagus conveys (and monitors) the primary parasympathetic influence to the viscera. Most of the neural fibers in the vagus are sensory (approximately 80%). However, most interest has been directed to the motor fibers that regulate the visceral organs, including the heart and the gut. Of these motor fibers, approximately only 15% are myelinated (i.e., approximately 3% of the total vagal fibers). Myelin, a fatty coating over the neural fiber, enables faster and more tightly regulated neural control circuits. The myelinated vagal pathway to the heart is a rapidly responding component of a neural feedback system, involving the brain and heart, which rapidly adjusts the heart rate to meet challenges.

Humans, as well as other mammals, have two functionally distinct vagal circuits. One vagal circuit is phylogenetically older and unmyelinated. It originates in a brainstem area called the dorsal motor nucleus of the vagus. The other vagal circuit is uniquely mammalian and myelinated. The myelinated vagal circuit originates in a brainstem area called the nucleus ambiguus. The phylogenetically older unmyelinated vagal motor pathways are shared with most vertebrates, and, in mammals, when not recruited as a defense system, these pathways function to support health, growth, and restoration via neural regulation of subdiaphragmatic organs (i.e., internal organs below the diaphragm). The phylogenetically newer myelinated vagal motor pathways, which are observed in mammals, regulate the supradiaphragmatic organs (e.g., heart and lungs). This newer vagal circuit slows the heart rate and supports states of calmness. It is this newer vagal circuit that both mediates the physiological state necessary for compassion and is functionally exercised during rituals associated with contemplative practices.

VAGAL BRAKE: A MECHANISM TO CONTAIN EMOTIONAL REACTIVITY

When mammals evolved, the primary vagal regulation of the heart shifted from the unmyelinated pathways originating in the dorsal motor nucleus of the vagus to include myelinated pathways originating in the nucleus ambiguus. The myelinated vagus provided a mechanism to rapidly and efficiently regulate visceral organs to foster calm prosocial behaviors and psychological and physical health. For example, the myelinated vagus functions as an active, efficient brake (see Porges et al., 1996), in which rapid inhibition and disinhibition of vagal tone to the heart can rapidly calm or mobilize an individual. Moreover, the myelinated vagus actively counteracts the sympathetic nervous system's influences on the heart and dampens hypothalamic-pituitary-adrenal (HPA) axis activity (see Porges, 2001). The vagal brake can modulate visceral state, especially the sympathetic nervous system reactions that frequently accompany empathy. Functionally, regulation of the vagal brake keeps autonomic reactivity from moving into a range that supports defensive behaviors. Thus, the vagal brake enables the individual to rapidly engage and disengage with objects and other individuals, while maintaining a physiological resource that is capable of promoting self-soothing behaviors and calm states. Ancient rituals, employing breathing, posture, and vocalizations, actively recruit and exercise the vagal brake to downregulate defensive biases and to enhance positive engagement with others with feelings of compassion.

THE FACE-HEART CONNECTION: THE EMERGENCE OF THE SOCIAL ENGAGEMENT SYSTEM

When an individual feels safe, two important features are expressed. First, the bodily state is regulated in an efficient manner to promote growth and restoration (e.g., visceral homeostasis). This is accomplished through an increase in the influence of myelinated vagal motor pathways on the cardiac pacemaker (sinoatrial node) to slow heart rate and inhibit the fight-or-flight mechanisms of the sympathetic nervous system. In addition, the myelinated vagal pathways dampen the stress response system of the HPA axis (e.g., cortisol) and reduce inflammation by modulating immune reactions (e.g., cytokines). Second, through the process of evolution, the brainstem nuclei that regulate the myelinated vagus became integrated with the nuclei that regulate the muscles of the face and head via special visceral efferent (motor) pathways. These emergent changes in neuroanatomy provided a face-heart connection in which there are mutual interactions between the vagal influences to the heart and the neural regulation of the striated muscles of the face and head. The phylogenetically novel face-heart connection provided mammals with an ability to convey their physiological state via facial expression and prosody (intonation of voice), enabling facial expression and voice to calm physiological state (Porges, 2011; Porges & Lewis, 2010; Stewart et al., 2013).

The face-heart connection enables mammals to detect whether a conspecific is in a calm physiological state and safe to approach, or is in a highly mobilized and reactive physiological state during which engagement would be dangerous. The face-heart connection concurrently enables an individual to signal safety through patterns of facial expression and vocal intonation, and potentially calm an agitated conspecific to form a social relationship. When the newer mammalian vagus is functioning optimally in social interactions (i.e., inhibiting and containing the sympathetic excitation that promotes fight-or-flight behaviors), emotions are well regulated, vocal prosody is rich, and the autonomic state supports calm, spontaneous social engagement behaviors. The face-heart system is bidirectional, with the newer myelinated vagal circuit influencing social interactions and positive social interactions influencing vagal functions to optimize health, dampen stress-related physiological states, and support growth and restoration. Social communication and the ability to coregulate another person, via reciprocal social engagement systems, leads to a sense of connectedness, which is a defining feature of the human experience.

Polyvagal Theory proposes that physiological state is a fundamental part, and not a correlate, of emotion and mood. The theory emphasizes a bidirectional link between brain and viscera, which would explain both how thoughts can change our physiology and how our physiological state influences our thoughts. Thus, the initiation of contemplative practices is dependent on physiological state, and through the mental process defining contemplative practices, it influences our physiological state. As individuals change their facial expressions, the intonation of their voices, the pattern in which they are breathing, and their posture, they are also changing their physiology, primarily through manipulating the function of the myelinated vagus to the heart.

Regulating the physiological state through the myelinated vagus is an implicit underlying principle of contemplative practices. However, contemplative practices, by directly exercising the vagal regulation of state, co-opt the need for social interactions to reflexively calm the practitioner (see section on neuroception) and expand the sense of connectedness from a proximal social network to an unbounded sense of oneness. Neurophysiologically, the rituals involved in contemplative practices elicit the same neural circuits that evolved with mammals to signal safety. Through our phylogenetic history, these signals were usually emitted by the mother to calm her vulnerable infant. Thus, the metaphor of the mother calming the child is neurophysiologically embedded in contemplative training and practices and is frequently used in various spiritual narratives. As we learn more about the face-heart connection, we are informed that contemplative practices may recruit this system to obtain states of calmness. This is initially accomplished sequentially, first through the passive pathway detecting features of safety in the context in which contemplative practices are typically experienced, and then through a voluntary pathway (i.e., neural exercises) that uses efficient and reliable behavioral manipulations (e.g., breathing, vocalization, posture) that we know as rituals.

THE SOCIAL ENGAGEMENT SYSTEM: A SYSTEM THAT EXPRESSES AND ACKNOWLEDGES EMOTION

The phylogenetic origin of the behaviors associated with the social engagement system is intertwined with the phylogeny of the autonomic nervous system. As the muscles of the face and head emerged as social engagement structures, a new component of the autonomic nervous system (i.e., a myelinated vagus) evolved that was regulated by the nucleus ambiguus. This convergence of neural mechanisms produced an integrated social engagement system with synergistic behavioral (i.e., somatomotor) and visceral components, as well as interactions among ingestion, state regulation, and social engagement processes. The neural pathways originating in several cranial nerves that regulate the striated muscles of the face and head (i.e., special visceral efferent pathways) and the myelinated vagal fibers formed the neural substrate of the social engagement system (see Porges, 1998, 2001, 2003a).

As illustrated in Figure 4.1, the somatomotor component includes the neural structures involved in social and emotional behaviors. Special visceral efferent nerves innervate striated muscles, which regulate the structures derived during

FIGURE 4.1. The social engagement system consists of a somatomotor component (i.e., special visceral efferent pathways that regulate the striated muscles of the face and head) and a visceromotor component (i.e., the myelinated vagus that regulates the heart and bronchi). Solid blocks indicate the somatomotor component. Dashed blocks indicate the visceromotor component.

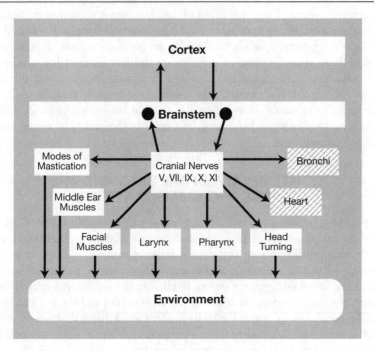

embryology from the ancient gill arches (Truex & Carpenter, 1969). The social engagement system has a control component in the cortex (i.e., upper motor neurons) that regulates brainstem nuclei (i.e., lower motor neurons) to control eyelid opening (i.e., looking), facial muscles (e.g., emotional expression), middle ear muscles (e.g., extracting human voice from background noise), muscles of mastication (e.g., ingestion), laryngeal and pharyngeal muscles (e.g., prosody and intonation), and head-turning muscles (e.g., social gesture and orientation). Collectively, these muscles function both as determinants of engagement with the social environment and as filters that limit social stimuli. The neural pathway involved in raising the eyelids (i.e., facial nerve) also tenses the stapedius muscle in the middle ear, which facilitates hearing human voices. Thus, the neural mechanisms for making eye contact are shared with those needed to listen to human voices. As a cluster, poor eye gaze, difficulties with extracting the human voice from background sounds, blunted facial expression, minimal head gestures, limited vocal prosody, and poor state regulation are common features of individuals with autism and other psychiatric disorders.

Afferents from the target organs of the social engagement system, including the muscles of the face and head, provide potent input to the source nuclei in the brainstem regulating both the visceral and somatic components of the social engagement system. Thus, activation of the somatomotor component (e.g., listening, ingestion, lifting eyelids) could trigger visceral changes that would support social engagement, while modulation of the visceral state, depending on whether there is an increase or decrease in the influence of the myelinated vagal efferents on the sinoatrial node (i.e., increasing or decreasing the influence of the vagal brake), would either promote or impede social engagement behaviors. For example, stimulating the visceral states that promote mobilization (i.e., fight-or-flight behaviors) will impede the ability to express social engagement behaviors.

CONTEMPLATIVE PRACTICES AND THE SOCIAL ENGAGEMENT SYSTEM

The pathways defining the social engagement system enable many of the processes associated with contemplative practices (e.g., listening, chanting, breathing, shifting posture during prayer, and facial expressivity) to influence one's physiological state via a myelinated branch of the vagus. The passive pathway recruits the social engagement system (including the myelinated ventral vagus) through the cues of safety, such as a quiet environment and the presentation of prosodic vocalizations (e.g., chants) in the frequency band that would overlap with the vocal signals of safety that a mother uses to signal safety to her infant. In male-dominated religious practices, where females are not available to provide the vocal signals of safety, female-like voices are produced by boy choirs and, historically, by castrato soloists to promote feelings of spirituality.

Shifts in breathing patterns are perhaps the most accessible potent manipulations of the output of the myelinated vagus. Research documents that respiration modulates the influence of the vagus on the heart (see Eckberg, 2003). The vagal inhibition of the heart's pacemaker is potentiated during exhalation and dampened during inhalation. Thus, both the duration of exhalation and the inhalation/exhalation ratio are critical in manipulating the functional calming effect of the vagus on the heart. Rituals such as chants require extending the duration of the exhalation relative to the inhalation. Moreover, as the phrases of the chants become longer, the parameters of breathing spontaneously adjust to provide a sufficient volume of air, and breathing movements expand from the chest toward the abdomen. With abdominal or belly breathing, the diaphragm is actively pushed downward. This action stimulates vagal afferents, which functionally influence the vagal outflow to the heart. As described below in Table 4.2, the manipulation of breathing during chants and meditation provides a potent mechanism to regulate vagal efferent activity. Thus, in these rituals, breathing strategies optimize and exercise the vagal influence on the heart.

Chants and other forms of vocalizations are frequent features of contemplative practices. These processes not only require active manipulation of breathing but also recruit additional components of the social engagement system. For example, chants require the production and the monitoring of sounds while regulating one's breath. The modulation of vocalizations requires the active involvement of neural regulation of laryngeal and pharyngeal muscles (see Figure 4.1) to change pitch and to regulate resonance. Breath is critical, since the acoustic features of vocalizations are a product of a controlled expiration, which passes air at a sufficient velocity across structures in the larynx to produce sounds.

Successful social communication via vocalizations requires rapid adjustments in both the production and detection of vocalizations. This process requires a complex feedback loop that informs brain areas of acoustic properties conveying cues of safety or danger (see Neuroception section). The cues result in dynamic adjustments in the transfer function of middle ear structures via cranial nerves to enhance or dampen the loudness of sounds within the frequency band in which social communication occurs. Without sufficient neural tone to the middle ear muscles, the sounds of human vocalizations will be lost in the low-frequency background noise that characterizes our environment.

Virtually all the neural pathways involved in the social engagement system (see Figure 4.1) are recruited and coordinated while chanting. This would include the regulation of muscles of the mouth, face, neck, middle ear, larynx, and pharynx. Thus, chanting may provide an efficient active pathway to recruit and exercise several features of the social engagement system, while promoting a calm state through the myelinated ventral vagal pathway.

Rituals often involve voluntary posture shifts. Posture shifts influence blood pressure receptors known as baroreceptors. Baroreceptors send signals to the brainstem that will either increase heart rate by downregulating vagal efferent output (and often stimulate sympathetic output), or decrease heart rate by increasing vagal efferent output. Manipulating posture functions as an efficient voluntary method to shift one's physiological state, often enabling a visceral feeling of activation (due to a transitory withdrawal of the myelinated ventral vagus) that is rapidly followed by calming (due to a reengagement of the myelinated ventral vagus).

Functionally, rituals provide a complementary alternative to social engagement behaviors, an opportunity to use voluntary behaviors to regulate and exercise several neural pathways involved in the social engagement system. As an individual becomes more proficient with the rituals, the autonomic nervous system becomes more resilient and exhibits a greater capacity to downregulate defense and to support states that promote health, social behavior, and compassion.

Consistent with the Polyvagal Theory, effective contemplative practices can only occur during states experienced as safe. Only in safe states are neurobiological defense strategies inhibited and emotional reactivity contained. Thus, a key to successful contemplative training would be to conduct contemplative exercises in an environment that supports feelings of safety. This step is mediated through the passive pathway, which simultaneously downregulates the involuntary defense subsystems and potentiates the physiological state associated with the evolutionarily newer social engagement system. Functionally, during contemplative training, rituals involving breath, posture, and vocalizations provide, through an active pathway, neural exercises of circuits involving structures described in the social engagement system. As these neural exercises enhance the efficiency and reliability of the neural pathways inhibiting defense systems, the individual acquires greater access to feelings of safety, openness, and connectedness, which are explored during contemplative practices and are antecedent states for compassion.

The processes and mechanisms involved in exercising the active pathway have been explained. To understand how the passive pathway is recruited, it is necessary to understand two additional features of the Polyvagal Theory: dissolution and neuroception. First, through the process of dissolution (see Dissolution section), the theory describes autonomic reactivity as a phylogenetically organized response hierarchy in which evolutionarily newer circuits inhibit older circuits. Dissolution explains how specific autonomic states can support either defensive or calm behaviors. Moreover, the autonomic state that supports calm behavior also has the capacity to actively downregulate reactivity and defense. Thus, it is insufficient for an individual solely to abstain from defensive behaviors. The individual must also be in an autonomic state that is incompatible with defensive behaviors. Second, through the process of neuroception (see Neuroception section), context can influence one's autonomic state. Neuroception is a complex neural process that evaluates risk in the environment independently of cognitive awareness. Neuroception detects risk from sensory patterns in the environment and reflexively shifts a person's autonomic state to support either defense or safe interactions. Neuroception provides the clues to understanding how the passive pathway is elicited. Dissolution provides an understanding of the emergent hierarchical relationship among the components of the autonomic nervous system that are related to resilience and vulnerability.

DISSOLUTION

The three circuits defined by the Polyvagal Theory are organized and respond to challenges in a phylogenetically determined hierarchy consistent with the Jacksonian principle of dissolution. Jackson proposed that in the brain, higher (i.e., phylogenetically newer) neural circuits inhibit lower (i.e., phylogenetically older) neural circuits and "when the higher are suddenly rendered functionless, the lower rise in activity" (Jackson, 1882, p. 412). Although Jackson proposed dissolution to explain changes in brain function due to damage and illness,

Polyvagal Theory proposes a similar phylogenetically ordered hierarchical model to describe the sequence of autonomic response strategies to challenges.

The human nervous system, like those of other mammals, evolved not solely to survive in safe environments, but also to promote survival in dangerous and life-threatening contexts. To accomplish this adaptive flexibility, the mammalian autonomic nervous system, in addition to the myelinated vagal pathway that is integrated into the social engagement system, retained two more primitive neural circuits to regulate defensive strategies (i.e., fight-flight and death-feigning behaviors). It is important to note that social behavior, social communication, and visceral homeostasis are incompatible with the neurophysiological states that support defense. Thus, via evolution, the human nervous system retains three neural circuits, consistent with the Jacksonian principle of dissolution, that are in a phylogenetically organized hierarchy. In this hierarchy of adaptive responses, the newest circuit is used first; if that circuit fails to provide safety, the older circuits are recruited sequentially. From a contemplative practice perspective, it is necessary to recruit the phylogenetically newest circuit that downregulates defense and involves the social engagement system and the myelinated vagus.

As we have described, via the active pathway, rituals exercise the integrated social engagement system, including the myelinated vagus. However, before rituals can function as efficient neural exercises, the individual must be in a calm and safe physiological state. Only in this state is the active pathway available and not in conflict with adaptive defense reactions. Thus, an understanding of how to regulate the passive pathway to maintain a calm physiological state is the initial and most critical step leading to subjective experiences related to compassion and a universal connectedness. Neuroception provides the insight into the mechanisms that enable or disable the passive pathway.

NEUROCEPTION

To effectively switch from defensive to social engagement strategies, the mammalian nervous system needs to perform two important adaptive tasks: (1) assess risk, and (2) if the environment is safe, inhibit the more primitive limbic structures involved in fight, flight, or immobilization (e.g., death-feigning) behaviors. Any stimulus that has the potential for signaling cues of safety also has the potential to recruit an evolutionarily more advanced neural circuit that promotes calm behavioral states and supports the prosocial behaviors of the social engagement system.

The nervous system, through the processing of sensory information from the environment and from the viscera, continuously evaluates risk. Polyvagal Theory proposes that the neural evaluation of risk does not require conscious awareness but functions through neural circuits that are shared with our phylogenetic ancestors. Thus, the term *neuroception* (Porges, 2003b, 2004) was introduced to emphasize a neural process, distinct from perception, that is capable of distinguishing environmental (and visceral) features that are safe, dangerous, or life threatening. In safe environments, our autonomic state is adaptively regulated to dampen sympathetic activation and to protect the oxygen-dependent central nervous system, especially the cortex, from the metabolically conservative reactions of the dorsal vagal complex (e.g., fainting).

Neuroception mediates both the expression and the disruption of positive social behavior, emotion regulation, and visceral homeostasis (Porges, 2004, 2007). Neuroception might be triggered by feature detectors involving areas of temporal cortex that communicate with the central nucleus of the amygdala and the periaqueductal gray, since limbic reactivity is modulated by temporal cortex responses to biological movements, including voices, faces, and hand gestures (Ghazanfar et al., 2005; Pelphrey et al., 2005). Embedded in the construct of neuroception is the capacity of the nervous system to react to the intention behind these movements and sounds. Neuroception functionally decodes and interprets the assumed goal of movements and sounds of animate and inanimate objects. This process occurs without our awareness. Although we are often unaware of the stimuli that trigger different neuroceptive responses, we are aware of our body's reactions. Thus, the neuroception of familiar individuals and individuals with appropriately prosodic voices and warm, expressive faces translates into a positive social interaction, promoting a sense of safety.

In most situations, the passive pathway is activated during social interactions by identifiable social engagement features, including prosodic vocalizations, gestures, and facial expressions. However, within the proposed model, the passive pathway is recruited via exposure to the physical characteristics of the context in which contemplative training will occur. History helps us identify and describe optimal contexts. Contemplative training and practice often occur in structures with physical features that functionally remove background sounds. This contextual feature is similar to silent retreats, in which the passive triggering of safety is shifted from social interactions to context. In the silent retreat, the removal of distracters, including the inhibition of potential social engagement via voice, enables the body to move from either a state of hypervigilance or a state of reciprocal interaction to a state of calmness.

Historically, structures subjectively experienced as safe were often constructed with heavy, durable materials such as stone (e.g., ancient temples). The fortress attribute supports contemplative practices through two domains: (1) protection from others when in the physically vulnerable state associated with contemplative practices; and (2) reduction of sensory cues of danger by attenuating low-frequency sounds associated with predators and limiting distracting visual cues. In addition, the stone surfaces provided an acoustic environment in which vocalizations could be heard without effort and the acoustic characteristics were enhanced by echoes that might resonate with parts of the body. As vocalizations became ritual chants (e.g., Gregorian and Buddhist chants), the harmonics of the chants would echo through the space, and the acoustic energy would be interpreted as spiritual and healing. Physical features of these sanctuaries promoted, through a passive pathway, feelings of safety and were often the contexts in which contemplative practices were taught and expressed. Thus, contemplative practices, to be functional and to have positive outcomes, must be conducted during physiological states in which the autonomic nervous system is not supporting defense and in a context that does not elicit a neuroception of danger or life threat.

REGULATING AUTONOMIC STATE THROUGH PASSIVE AND ACTIVE PATHWAYS

Within Polyvagal Theory, social safety depends on recruiting the ventral vagal pathways to foster a calm physiological state and maintain physiological and behavioral resilience. Consistent with compassion-focused therapy (Gilbert, 2009), the recruitment of a social safety system is a prerequisite for experiencing or expressing compassion. Neuroception describes the passive pathway to recruit this state. Neuroception is the initial step to feeling safe in a safe environment. A neuroception of safety shifts our biobehavioral state by increasing the influence of both the ventral vagus of the heart and the special visceral efferent pathways regulating the striated muscles of the face and head described in the social engagement system.

To experience a state of safety, the contextual cues in the environment have to elicit, via neuroception, the ventral vagal pathways that actively downregulate autonomic defense systems mediated by the sympathetic nervous system and the dorsal vagus. Feeling safe requires two complementary features. First, states of hypervigilance are reduced by removing cues of distraction and potential predators. In general, the focus is on auditory and visual cues, since our nervous system is hardwired to interpret the intentionality of movements and sounds. Low-frequency sounds are hardwired cues of predators and potential life threats. High-frequency sounds are also hardwired cues of danger (see Porges & Lewis, 2010). Since our nervous system continuously attempts to interpret the intention of movements, removal of visual distracters enables individuals to shift from hypervigilance to calmness.

Removal of cues of danger is not sufficient for everyone to feel safe. Some people experience a quiet space as restful and spiritual, while others become anxious and hypervigilant. To ensure a neuroception of safety, the individual must process additional sensory features in the environment. This is most reliably accomplished through the use of acoustic stimulation that is modulated in the frequency band of a mother's lullaby. Functionally, humans are hardwired to be calmed by the modulation of the human voice (Porges & Lewis, 2010).

The acoustic features for calming infants are universal and have been repurposed by classical composers in music (Porges, 2008). Composers implicitly understood that they could lull the audience into a state of safety (i.e., via neuroception) by constructing melodic themes that duplicated the vocal range of a mother soothing her infant, while limiting the contribution of instruments that contributed low-frequency sounds. The acoustical structure of liturgical vocal music follows a similar convention by minimizing low-frequency sounds and emphasizing voices in the range of the nurturing mother calming her infant.

A large pipe organ, generating low-frequency tones, triggers a feeling of awe, not safety. The low tones of an organ have acoustical features that overlap with our hardwired reactions of immobilization in the face of a predator. Thus, loud, low tones from a pipe organ could potentially disrupt the passive pathway and interfere with the state of safety required to experience compassion and connectedness with another. However, the presentation of low-frequency tones within a confined environment may trigger a sense of submission that could be associated with psychological feelings of surrendering to a deity.

Once the passive pathway effectively shifts our physiological state, the second step can be initiated. The second step, exercising the vagal brake, recruits the active (voluntary) pathway through rituals requiring manipulations of breath, posture, and vocalization. These manipulations of the vagal brake exercise the inhibitory influence of the vagus on the heart as an efficient calming mechanism. Neurophysiologically, the vagus functions as a brake on the heart's pacemaker, resulting in the heart beating at a rate substantially slower than the intrinsic rate of the pacemaker.

Breathing is an efficient and easily accessible voluntary behavior to systematically reduce and increase the influence of the vagus on the heart. More than a hundred years ago, Hering (1910) reported that the cardio-inhibitory vagal pathways had a respiratory rhythm that reflected the dynamic adjustment of the vagal control of the heart. Further articulation of this phenomenon was summarized as a "respiratory gate" by Eckberg (2003), who emphasized the enhancement of the vagal influences on the heart during exhalation, and the dampening of vagal influences on the heart during inhalation. Many rituals require breathing pattern shifts. Perhaps the most obvious are chants and other forms of vocalization, which manipulate the respiratory gate by expanding the duration of exhalation and reducing the duration of inspiration. Other rituals involving prayer and meditation may also influence vagal regulation through posture shifts, which trigger baroreceptors (blood pressure receptors) to adjust blood flow to the brain. This process involves systematic changes in vagal regulation of the heart to avoid dizziness and fainting (e.g., vasovagal syncope).

As described in Table 4.2, Polyvagal Theory explains how the manipulation of vagal pathways is involved in the foundational processes upon which contemplative training and practice are based. These processes require two pathways (passive and active) to regulate the autonomic state and lead to a physiological state, which would enable feelings of safety and compassion to be felt and expressed. Involving the two pathways to regulate the physiological state is a

TABLE 4.2. Steps to Compassion

Step	Polyvagal Process
1. Experience safe context (recruit passive pathway)	• Neuroception of safety • Remove predator cues • Add acoustic cues of a loving mother
2. Perform rituals (recruit active pathway)	• Exercise vagal brake to enhance autonomic flexibility and resilience
3. Contemplative training (e.g., meditation)	• Mental exercises involving brain functions that are dependent on maintaining ventral vagal state
4. Experiencing compassion and a sense of oneness	• Emergent property of higher brain processes, while maintaining a ventral vagal state

prerequisite for effective contemplative practices (e.g., meditation). The two pathways function sequentially. Thus, once one is in a physiological state that supports feelings of safety, successful training would result in a resilient autonomic nervous system that would acknowledge, without mirroring, the emotional reactivity and pain often expressed by those who are suffering.

If the passive pathway does not enable the person to be in a calm ventral vagal state, then the active pathway, rather than being an enabler of compassion, may trigger defensiveness. If an individual engages in the active pathway in a vulnerable physiological state (during either downregulated ventral vagal influences or upregulated sympathetic influences), then exercising the vagal brake may create a transitory state of vulnerability. This would occur when the neural exercises associated with the active pathway withdraw the vagal brake (e.g., during inspiration while meditating or chanting) and trigger a sympathetic excitation sufficient to support fight-flight behaviors.

CONCLUSION

In this chapter, a multistep sequential model is proposed that would optimize the effects of contemplative training, leading to a greater capacity to feel and express compassion. The model includes

1. a passive pathway that is elicited by feeling safe in an environment that provides sensory cues that, via neuroception, downregulate defense;
2. an active pathway that is implemented via voluntary behaviors (i.e., neural

exercises and features of the social engagement system to shift autonomic state sufficiently to facilitate the effectiveness of rituals, as neural exercises, in enhancing autonomic regulation;

3. the active pathway, through the efficient use of rituals, exercises vagal regulation of autonomic state to optimize health and resilience; and
4. the efficient use of rituals promotes a physiological state in which the outcomes of contemplative training are optimized.

Thus, an appreciation of the physiological state as an important prerequisite for compassion may result in more efficient and positive outcomes of practices, including compassion-focused therapy, leading to enhanced compassion.

REFERENCES

Bernard, C. (1872). *De la physiologie générale*. Paris: Hachette.

Bohlmeijer, E., Prenger, R., Taal, E., & Cuijpers, P. (2010). The effects of mindfulness-based stress reduction therapy on mental health of adults with a chronic medical disease: A metaanalysis. *Journal of Psychosomatic Research, 68*(6), 539–544.

Cannon, W. B. (1932). *The wisdom of the body*. New York: Norton.

Chiesa, A., & Serretti, A. (2009). Mindfulness-based stress reduction for stress management in healthy people: A review and meta-analysis. *Journal of Alternative and Complementary Medicine, 15*(5), 593–600.

Davidson, R. J., Kabat-Zinn, J., Schumacher, J., Rosenkranz, M., Muller, D., Santorelli, S. F., Urbanowski, F., Harrington, A., Bonus, K., & Sheridan, J. F. (2003). Alterations in brain and immune function produced by mindfulness meditation. *Psychosomatic Medicine, 65*(4), 564–570.

Decety, J., & Ickes, W. J. (Eds.). (2009). *The social neuroscience of empathy*. Cambridge, MA: MIT Press.

Eckberg, D. L. (2003). The human respiratory gate. *Journal of Physiology, 548*(Pt 2), 339.

Ghazanfar, A. A., Maier, J. X., Hoffman, K. L., & Logothetis, N. K. (2005). Multisensory integration of dynamic faces and voices in rhesus monkey auditory cortex. *Journal of Neuroscience, 25*(20), 5004–5012.

Gilbert, P. (2009). Introducing compassion-focused therapy. *Advances in Psychiatric Treatment, 15*(3), 199–208.

Hering, H. E. (1910). A functional test of heart vagi in man. *Menschen Munchen Medizinische Wochenschrift, 57*, 1931–1933.

Jackson, J. H. (1882). On some implications of dissolution of the nervous system. *Medical Press and Circular, 2*, 411–414.

Kabat-Zinn, J. (2003). Mindfulness-based interventions in context: Past, present, and future. *Clinical Psychology: Science and Practice, 10*(2), 144–156.

Klimecki, O. M., Leiberg, S., Ricard, M., & Singer, T. (2014). Differential pattern of functional brain plasticity after compassion and empathy training. *Social Cognitive and Affective Neuroscience, 9*, 873–879.

Kok, B. E., & Fredrickson, B. L. (2010). Upward spirals of the heart: Autonomic flexibility, as indexed by vagal tone, reciprocally and prospectively predicts positive emotions and social connectedness. *Biological Psychology, 85*(3), 432–436.

Lutz, A., McFarlin, D. R., Perlman, D. M., Salomons, T. V., & Davidson, R. J. (2013). Altered anterior insula activation during anticipation and experience of painful stimuli in expert meditators. *Neuroimage, 64*, 538–546.

Pelphrey, K. A., Morris, J. P., Michelich, C. R., Allison, T., & McCarthy, G. (2005). Functional anatomy of biological motion perception in posterior temporal cortex: An fMRI study of eye, mouth and hand movements. *Cerebral Cortex, 15*(12), 1866–1876.

Porges, S. W. (1995). Orienting in a defensive world: Mammalian modifications of our evolutionary heritage. A Polyvagal Theory. *Psychophysiology, 32*(4), 301–318.

Porges, S. W. (1998). Love: An emergent property of the mammalian autonomic nervous system. *Psychoneuroendocrinology, 23*(8), 837–861.

Porges, S. W. (2001). The Polyvagal Theory: Phylogenetic substrates of a social nervous system. *International Journal of Psychophysiology, 42*(2), 123–146.

Porges, S. W. (2003a). The Polyvagal Theory: Phylogenetic contributions to social behavior. *Physiology and Behavior, 79*(3), 503–513.

Porges, S. W. (2003b). Social engagement and attachment: A phylogenetic perspective. Roots of mental illness in children. *Annals of the New York Academy of Sciences, 1008*(1), 31–47.

Porges, S. W. (2004). Neuroception: A subconscious system for detecting threats and safety. *Zero to Three (J), 24*(5), 19–24.

Porges, S. W. (2007). The polyvagal perspective. *Biological Psychology, 74*(2), 116–143.

Porges, S. W. (2008). Music therapy and trauma: Insights from the Polyvagal Theory. In K. Stewart (Ed.), *Music therapy and trauma: Bridging theory and clinical practice.* New York: Satchnote Press.

Porges, S. W. (2009). The Polyvagal Theory: New insights into adaptive reactions of the autonomic nervous system. *Cleveland Clinic Journal of Medicine, 76*, S86–S90.

Porges, S. W. (2011). *The Polyvagal Theory: Neurophysiological foundations of emotions, attachment, communication, and self-regulation.* Norton Series on Interpersonal Neurobiology. New York: Norton.

Porges, S. W., Doussard-Roosevelt, J. A., Portales, A. L., & Greenspan, S. I. (1996). Infant regulation of the vagal "brake" predicts child behavior problems: A psychobiological model of social behavior. *Developmental Psychobiology, 29*(8), 697–712.

Porges, S. W., & Lewis, G. F. (2010). The polyvagal hypothesis: Common mechanisms mediating autonomic regulation, vocalizations and listening. *Handbook of Behavioral Neuroscience, 19*, 255–264.

Stellar, J. E., Cohen, A., Oveis, C., & Keltner, D. (2015). Affective and physiological responses to the suffering of others: Compassion and vagal activity. *Journal of Personality and Social Psychology, 108*(4), 572–585.

Stewart, A. M., Lewis, G. F., Heilman, K. J., Davila, M. I., Coleman, D. D., Aylward, S. A., & Porges, S. W. (2013). The covariation of acoustic features of infant cries and autonomic state. *Physiology and Behavior, 120*, 203–210.

Strauss, C., Taylor, B. L., Gu, J., Kuyken, W., Baer, R., Jones, F., & Cavanagh, K. (2016). What is compassion and how can we measure it? A review of definitions and measures. *Clinical Psychology Review, 47*, 15–27.

Truex, R. C., & Carpenter, M. B. (1969). *Human neuroanatomy.* Baltimore, MD: Williams and Wilkins.

CHAPTER 5

Yoga Therapy and Polyvagal Theory

The Convergence of Traditional Wisdom and Contemporary Neuroscience for Self-Regulation and Resilience

Marlysa B. Sullivan, Matt Erb, Laura Schmalzl, Steffany
Moonaz, Jessica Noggle Taylor, and Stephen W. Porges

INTRODUCTION

Mind-body therapies, including yoga therapy, are proposed to benefit health and well-being through an integration of top-down and bottom-up processes facilitating bidirectional communication between the brain and body (Muehsam et al., 2017; Taylor et al., 2010). Top-down processes, such as the regulation of attention and setting of intention, have been shown to decrease psychological stress as well as hypothalamic-pituitary-adrenal (HPA) axis and sympathetic nervous system (SNS) activity, and in turn modulate immune function and inflammation (Muehsam et al., 2017; Taylor et al., 2010). Bottom-up processes, promoted by breathing techniques and movement practices, have been shown to influence musculoskeletal, cardiovascular, and nervous system function and also affect HPA and SNS activity, with concomitant changes in immune function and emotional well-being (Muehsam et al., 2017; Taylor et al., 2010).

The top-down and bottom-up processes employed in mind-body therapies may regulate autonomic, neuroendocrine, emotional, and behavioral activation and support an individual's response to challenges (Taylor et al., 2010). Self-regulation, a conscious ability to maintain stability of the system by managing or altering responses to threat or adversity, may reduce symptoms of diverse conditions such as irritable bowel syndrome, neurodegenerative conditions, chronic pain, depression, and PTSD through the mitigation of allostatic load, with an accompanying shift in autonomic state (Gard et al., 2014; Muehsam et al., 2017; Schmalzl et al., 2015; Streeter et al., 2012; Taylor et al., 2010). Gard et al. (2014) have proposed such a model of top-down and bottom-up self-regulatory mechanisms of yoga for psychological health.

Resilience may provide another benefit of mind-body therapies, as it includes the ability of an individual to bounce back and adapt in response to adversity and/ or stressful circumstances in a timely way such that psychophysiological resources are conserved (Haase et al., 2016; Resnick et al., 2011; Tugade & Fredrickson, 2004; Whitson et al., 2016). High resilience is correlated with quicker cardiovascular recovery following subjective emotional experiences (Tugade & Fredrickson, 2007), less perceived stress, greater recovery from illness or trauma, and better management of dementia and chronic pain (Resnick et al., 2011). Compromised resilience is linked to dysregulation of the autonomic nervous system (ANS) through measures of vagal regulation (respiratory sinus arrhythmia) (Dale et al., 2009). Yoga is correlated with improvement in both measures of psychological resilience (Dale et al., 2011) and vagal regulation (Chu et al., 2017; Khattab et al., 2007; Sarang & Telles, 2006; Telles et al., 2016; Tyagi & Cohen, 2016).

This chapter explores the integration of top-down and bottom-up processes for self-regulation and resilience through both Polyvagal Theory (Porges, 2011) and yoga therapy. Polyvagal Theory is described in relation to contemporary understandings of interoception as well as the biobehavioral theory of the preparatory set, which is defined later. This will help to lay out an integrated systems view from which mind-body therapies facilitate the emergence of physiological, emotional, and behavioral characteristics for the promotion of self-regulation and resilience.

We will examine the convergence of the neural platforms, described in Polyvagal Theory, with the three gunas, a foundational concept of yogic philosophy that describes the qualities of material nature. Both Polyvagal Theory and yoga provide frameworks for understanding how underlying neural platforms (Polyvagal Theory) and gunas (yoga) link emergence and connectivity between physiological, psychological, and behavioral attributes. By affecting the neural platform, or guna predominance, as well as one's relationship to the continual shifting of these neural platforms, or gunas, the individual learns skills for self-regulation and resilience. Moreover, these frameworks share characteristics that parallel one another, where the neural platform reflects the guna predominance, and the guna predominance reflects the neural platform (see Figure 5.1).

This exploration is intended to be a comparative and translatory approach aimed at enabling the complexity of the yoga tradition to be understood for its benefits and application into modern health care contexts, while still rooted in its own traditional wisdom and explanatory framework. A model through which self-regulation and resilience occurs is described from a yoga foundational framework, which converges with current ideas in neurophysiology and biobehavioral regulation (see Figure 5.1).

FIGURE 5.1. The central eye represents the body, mind, and environmental context (BME), and the peripheral eye represents the context of an observer/experiencer of that content. Within prakriti, resilience is represented by the capacity to recognize and shift states, as well as changing the relationship to the fluctuations of the gunas (rajas/tamas/sattva) and neural platforms (sympathetic nervous system, SNS; dorsal vagal complex, DVC; ventral vagal complex, VVC). Yoga aims to facilitate the emergence of qualities such as eudaemonia by strengthening the experience of sattva and VVC as well as developing facility in moving between gunas and neural platforms and changing the relationship and response to the inherent changing nature of the body, mind, and environment reflected in gunas and neural platforms.

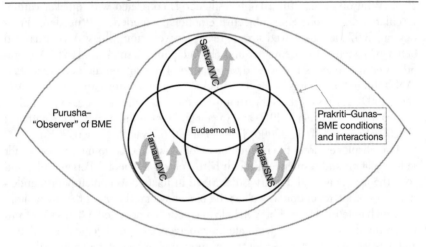

POLYVAGAL THEORY

Polyvagal Theory and other emerging theories such as neurovisceral integration (Smith et al., 2017; Thayer & Lane, 2000), help elucidate connections between the systems of the body, the brain, and the processes of the mind, offering increased insight into complex patterns of integrated top-down and bottom-up processes that are inherent to mind-body therapies. Polyvagal Theory delineates three distinct neural platforms in response to perceived risk (i.e., safety, danger, life threat) in the environment that operate in a phylogenetically determined hierarchy consistent with the Jacksonian principle of dissolution (Jackson, 1884; Porges, 2001, 2003). Polyvagal Theory introduces the concept of neuroception to describe the subconscious detection of safety or danger in the environment reflected in bottom-up processes involving vagal afferents, sensory input related to external challenges and endocrine mechanisms that are the consequences of reflexive top-down mechanisms evaluating environmental risk prior to conscious elaboration by higher brain centers (Porges, 2003).

The three polyvagal neural platforms, as described below, are linked to the behaviors of social communication, defensive strategy of mobilization, and defensive immobilization (Porges, 1995, 1998, 2001, 2003, 2007, 2009, 2011).

1. The ventral vagal complex (VVC) provides the neural structures that mediate the social engagement system. When safety is detected in the internal and external environment, the VVC provides a neural platform to support prosocial behavior and social connection by linking the neural regulation of visceral states, supporting homeostasis and restoration to facial expressivity and the receptive and expressive domains of communication (e.g., prosodic vocalizations and enhanced ability to listen to voices). The motor component of the VVC, which originates in the nucleus ambiguus (NA), regulates and coordinates the muscles of the face and head with the bronchi and heart. These connections help orient the person toward human connection and engagement in prosocial interactions and provide more flexible and adaptive responses to environmental challenges, including social interactions (Porges, 2011, 2017; Porges & Carter, 2017).

2. The SNS is frequently associated with fight-flight behaviors. Fight-flight behaviors require activation of the SNS and are the initial and primary defense strategies recruited by mammals. This defense strategy requires increased metabolic output to support mobilization behaviors. Within Polyvagal Theory, the recruitment of the SNS in defense follows the Jacksonian principle of dissolution and reflects the adaptive reactions of a phylogenetically ordered response hierarchy in which the VVC is inadequate to mitigate threat. When the SNS circuit is recruited, there are massive physiological changes, including an increase in muscle tone, shunting of blood from the periphery, inhibition of gastrointestinal function, a dilation of the bronchi, increases in heart rate and respiratory rate, and a release of catecholamines. This mobilization of physiological resources sets the stage for responding to real or assumed danger in the environment and toward the end goals of safety and survival. When the SNS becomes the dominant neural platform, the VVC influence may be inhibited in favor of mobilizing resources for rapid action. Whereas prosocial behaviors and social connection are associated with the VVC, in the absence of VVC influences, the SNS is associated with behaviors and emotions such as fear or anger that help to orient to the environment for protection or safety.

3. The dorsal vagal complex (DVC) arises from the dorsal nucleus of the vagus and provides the primary vagal motor fibers to organs located below the diaphragm. In the absence of cues of safety, this circuit evolved to adaptably respond to immense danger or terror and is the most primitive (i.e., evolutionarily oldest) response to stress. Activation of the DVC in

defense results in a passive response characterized by decreased muscle tone, dramatic reduction of cardiac output to reserve metabolic resources, and alteration in bowel and bladder function via reflexive defecation and urination to reduce metabolic demands of digestion and other bodily processes. This inhibition of viscera reflects an attempt to reduce metabolic and oxygen demands to the smallest amount necessary for survival. Behaviorally, this is often referred to as immobilization or shutdown associated with feigning death, behavioral shutdown, collapse, or freeze responses, and may be experienced in humans as a disembodied dissociative state that may include loss of consciousness.

Polyvagal Theory posits that through these neural platforms, particular physiological states, psychological attributes, and social processes are connected, emerge, and are made accessible to the individual (Porges, 1998, 2003, 2011, 2017; Porges & Carter, 2017). The physiological state established by these neural platforms in response to threat or safety (as determined via the integrated processes of neuroception) allows for or limits the range of emotional and behavioral characteristics that are accessible to the individual (Porges, 2003).

A core aspect of Polyvagal Theory is that patterns of physiological state, emotion, and behavior are particular to each neural platform (for a detailed review of the neurophysiological, neuroanatomical, and evolutionary biological bases of Polyvagal Theory, see Porges [1995, 1998, 2001, 2007, 2009, 2011]). For example, the neural platform of the VVC is proposed to connect visceral homeostasis with emotional characteristics and prosocial behaviors that are incompatible with the neurophysiological states, emotional characteristics, or social behaviors that manifest in the neural platforms of defensive strategies seen in SNS or DVC activation. When the VVC is dominant, the vagal brake is implemented, and prosocial behaviors and emotional states such as connection and love have increased potential to emerge. When the SNS is the primary defensive strategy, the NA turns off the inhibitory action of the ventral vagal pathway to the heart to enable sympathetic activation, and behavioral and emotional strategies of mobilization are supported. If the DVC immobility response is the defensive strategy, the dorsal motor nucleus is activated as a protective mechanism from pain or potential death, and active response strategies are not available (Porges, 1998, 2003, 2009, 2011; Porges et al., 2008; Porges & Carter, 2017). It is important to note that the VVC has other attributes that enable blended states with the SNS (e.g., play) or with the DVC (e.g., intimacy). However, in these examples of blended states, the VVC remains easily accessible and functionally contains the subordinate circuits. When the VVC is functionally withdrawn, it promotes accessibility of the SNS as a defense fight-flight system. Similarly, the SNS functionally inhibits access to the DVC immobilization shutdown response. Thus, the profound shutdown reactions that may lead to death become neurophysiologically accessible only when the SNS is reflexively inhibited.

VAGAL ACTIVITY, INTEROCEPTION, REGULATION, AND RESILIENCE

Vagal activity, via ventral vagal pathways, is suggested to be reflective of regulation and resilience of the system, where high cardiac vagal tone correlates with more adaptive top-down and bottom-up processes such as attention regulation, affective processing, and flexibility of physiological systems to adapt and respond to the environment (Park & Thayer, 2014; Porges, 2011; Streeter et al., 2012; Strigo & Craig, 2016; Thayer & Lane, 2000). Vagal control has also been shown to correlate with differential activation in brain regions that regulate responses to threat appraisal, interoception, emotion regulation, and the promotion of greater flexibility in response to challenge (Park & Thayer, 2014; Streeter et al., 2012). Conversely, low vagal regulation has been associated with maladaptive bottom-up and top-down processing, resulting in poor self-regulation, less behavioral flexibility, depression, generalized anxiety disorder, and adverse health outcomes including increased mortality in conditions such as lupus, rheumatoid arthritis, and trauma (Muehsam et al., 2017; Park & Thayer, 2014; Thayer & Lane, 2000; Tsuji et al., 1994).

The vagus nerve is composed of 80% afferent fibers and serves as an important conduit for interoceptive communication about the state of the viscera and internal milieu to brain structures (Porges, 2004, 2011). Interoception has been explored as essential to the bridging of top-down and bottom-up processing and in the investigation of the relationships between sensations, emotions, feelings, and sympathovagal balance (Craig, 2015; Farb et al., 2015; Porges, 1993; Strigo & Craig, 2016). Support has been found for the integration of interoceptive input, emotion, and regulation of sympathovagal balance in the insular and cingulate cortices, facilitating a unified response of the individual to body, mind, or environmental (BME) phenomena (Craig, 2015; Strigo & Craig, 2016).

Self-regulation is proposed to be dependent on the accuracy with which we interpret and respond to interoceptive information, with greater accuracy leading to enhanced adaptability and self-regulation (Farb et al., 2015). As such, interoception is considered to be important in pain, addiction, emotional regulation, and healthy adaptive behaviors including social engagement (Ceunen et al., 2016; Farb et al., 2015; Porges, 2011). In addition, interoception has been proposed as key to resilience, as the accurate processing of internal bodily states promotes a quick restoration of homeostatic balance (Haase et al., 2016).

It has been proposed that mind-body therapies are an effective tool for the regulation of vagal function, with consequent fostering of adaptive functions including the mitigation of adverse effects associated with social adversity (Black et al., 2013; Bower et al., 2014; Cole, 2013), the reduction of allostatic load, and the facilitation of self-regulatory skills and resilience of the ANS across various patient populations and conditions (Muehsam et al., 2017; Porges, 2017; Porges & Carter, 2017; Schmalzl et al., 2015; Streeter et al., 2012).

POLYVAGAL THEORY AND MIND-BODY THERAPIES
FOR REGULATION AND RESILIENCE

Mind-body therapies emphasize the cultivation of somatic awareness, including both interoception and proprioception, combined with the mindfulness-based qualities of nonjudgment, nonreactivity, curiosity, or acceptance in order to engage in a process of reappraisal of stimuli (Farb et al., 2015; Mehling et al., 2011). While being encouraged to cultivate awareness of BME phenomena and stimuli, the individual is supported in a process of reinterpretation or reorientation to such stimuli so that insight may occur and adaptability, regulation, and resilience may be fostered (Farb et al., 2015; Mehling et al., 2011). This capacity to alter the relationship and reaction to BME phenomena is thought to be essential for self-regulation and well-being (Farb et al., 2015). It has been shown that patients utilizing mind-body therapies for healing reported a shift in both their experience of and response to negative emotions and sensations as well as the development of self-regulatory skills in dealing with pain, emotional regulation, and reappraisal of life situations (Mehling et al., 2011).

Polyvagal Theory offers insight into how learning to recognize and shift the underlying neural platform of any given psychophysiological state may directly affect physiology, emotion, and behavior, thus helping the individual cultivate adaptive strategies for regulation and resilience to benefit physical, mental, and social health (Porges, 2011). As mind-body therapies affect the vagal pathways, they are suggested to form a means of exercising these neural platforms to foster self-regulation and resilience of physiological function, emotion regulation, and prosocial behaviors (Gard et al., 2014; Porges, 2017; Porges & Carter, 2017; Schmalzl et al., 2015).

Optimal neural regulation of the ANS and the related endocrine and immune systems is fostered through active engagement of the VVC by utilizing specific movements or positions, breathing practices, chanting, or meditation, which affect both top-down and bottom-up processes (Cottingham, Porges, & Lyon, 1988; Cottingham, Porges, & Richmond, 1988; Eckberg, 2003; Hayano & Yasuma, 2003; Porges, 2017; Porges & Carter, 2017). Resilience is proposed to be fostered by both downregulating defensive states and supporting more flexibility and adaptability in relationship to various phenomena of the BME to promote physiological restoration as well as positive psychological and social states (Porges, 2017; Porges & Carter, 2017). The individual can learn to improve activation of the VVC with its homeostatic influence on the organism, as well as increase the facility to move in and out of other neural platforms such as the SNS or DVC when real or perceived stress is encountered.

In sum, mind-body practices can teach the individual to make the VVC more accessible, widen the threshold of tolerance to other neural platforms, change the relationship and response to SNS and DVC neural platforms that occur as natural fluctuations of the BME, and become more skilled at moving in and out of these neural platforms (Porges, 2017; Porges & Carter, 2017). Breathing maneuvers within yoga often facilitate similar shifts in autonomic state, with convergent psychological and health consequences (e.g., Brown & Gerbarg, 2005a, 2005b, 2012; Brown et al., 2013). These practices may also contribute to our potential to experience connection beyond social interactions or networks and to a more universal and unbounded sense of oneness and connection (Porges, 2017).

FIVE GLOBAL STATES AND PREPARATORY SETS

Polyvagal Theory further proposes that the three neural circuits of SNS, VVC, and DVC are not mutually exclusive nor antagonistic; rather, these three circuits co-arise, co-exist, and co-mingle to create the complex array of human physiological, emotional, and behavioral states (Porges, 1998, 2011). Berntson elucidated coactivation and complexity in SNS and parasympathetic nervous system interactions in the doctrine of autonomic space (Berntson et al., 1991). This complexity allows for response to threat to start with a withdrawal of cardiac vagal tone before SNS activation as well as greater flexibility and precision to adjust to circumstances.

The Polyvagal Theory defines five global states based on the neural platform(s) that are predominant or active (Porges, 1998, 2011). The VVC, SNS, and DVC circuits, as just described, represent three of the global states, and the other two arise from their coactivation.

When the VVC and SNS circuits coarise, there is a fourth state of safe mobilization. The VVC enables the experience of safety and connection, while the SNS supports the mobilization of the body's resources for dexterity, movement, and the quick or creative thinking needed for activities such as dance, play, artistic expression, or writing. Mind-body practices such as the postural practice of hatha yoga or tai chi are examples where the body can be mobilized for action, but the mind and breath provide the stimulus for calmness, safety, and connection.

The fifth state arises from the coactivation of the VVC and DVC. These two circuits working together facilitate the state of safe immobilization. Immobilization without fear allows for the emergence of social bonds to be formed through prosocial activities such as childbirth, conception, and nursing.

The concept of preparatory sets provides for a dynamic understanding of the relationship between physical posture and muscle tone, visceral state/ ANS, affective state, arousal and attention, and cognitive expectation (Payne & Crane-Godreau, 2015). A change to any one of these components will result in shifts throughout the preparatory set, leading to an integrated reaction by the human system in response to the needs of the environment or situation.

The five global states of the Polyvagal Theory reflect a complexity of interactions throughout the preparatory set by way of the portal of the ANS, resulting in corresponding changes along somatomotor, affective, and cognitive levels (Payne & Crane-Godreau, 2015). In other words, impacting the neural platforms from which an individual is operating has concomitant effects on muscle tone, visceral state, attention, affect, and cognition.

Significant to this is the possibility that prolonged time in any Polyvagal Theory-defined maladaptive threat state may contribute to disorders or conditions that manifest with a combined disturbance of physiology, emotion, and behavior (Porges & Kolacz, 2018, Chapter 1). Porges and Kolacz (2018) have suggested the plausibility of autonomic dysregulation as a causative factor in irritable bowel syndrome and fibromyalgia, both of which are characterized by altered physiology, including decreased cardiac vagal tone inferred from a lack of heart rate variability (HRV), absence of obvious tissue pathology, and oftentimes associated with a history of trauma (Kolacz & Porges, 2018). This view is consistent with the expanding body of research linked to the original CDC-Kaiser Adverse Childhood Experiences Study demonstrating strong correlation of stress and trauma history to various pathologies later in life (Felitti et al., 1998).

An important insight that comes from an integrated understanding of Polyvagal Theory and preparatory sets is the necessity to investigate mind-body therapies as they were originally intended to be practiced, as integrative methodologies affecting simultaneous components of the individual's experience (Payne & Crane-Godreau, 2015). Many mind-body therapies, including yoga, call for simultaneous attention to the body, breathing, attentional and affective regulation, and cognition, thereby representing a comprehensive methodology and set of practices integrating both top-down and bottom-up processes in response to BME phenomena. It is imperative to realize that when these mind-body systems are reduced to investigate just one component, they are being taken outside the original context of their cohesive practice, thereby likely diminishing the intended combined effect.

Mind-body practices teach the individual to become aware of their preparatory set, to effectively shift unhealthy patterns of response to BME stimuli within their preparatory set, and to learn healthier and more adaptive preparatory set patterns in response to BME phenomena through various techniques (Payne & Crane-Godreau, 2015). Tools for self-regulation and the cultivation of resilience may develop as the individual learns the state of safe mobilization such that activation of the system does not drive out positive affective states or prosocial behavior and connection.

YOGA AND YOGA THERAPY

Payne and Crane-Godreau (2015) suggest yoga as one mind-body practice that can shift the preparatory set. Yoga consists of a variety of practices that may serve to affect one or more components of the preparatory set by influencing muscle tone/posture, the ANS, attention, affect, or cognition (Payne & Crane-

Godreau, 2015). Yoga practices can be utilized to affect the ANS and to both manipulate and change the relationship to these shifting neural platforms described in Polyvagal Theory.

While much of modern yoga practice focuses primarily on physical postures and movement sequences, the traditional roots are centered on a philosophical path toward understanding the causes of suffering and its alleviation (Easwaran, 2007; Mallinson & Singleton, 2017; Miller, 2012; Singleton, 2010; Stoler-Miller, 1998, 2004). To this point, work by Mallinson and Singleton (2017) highlights the variable meaning of yoga throughout the ancient texts. Historically the word *yoga* has been used to describe both the method of prescribed sets of practices (yoga as methodology) and the aim or goal of these practices (yoga as a state of being; Mallinson & Singleton, 2017). Yoga as a state of being includes the definition as "union," which can mean union with one's own essential nature or a supreme Self (Mallinson & Singleton, 2017). Other definitions of yoga include equanimity and "skill in action" (Mallinson & Singleton, 2017). Due to the variable definitions of yoga and in an effort to be nonbiased toward any one perspective, we will utilize concepts common throughout yogic texts such as the Upanishads (Easwaran, 2007), the Bhagavad Gita (Stoler-Miller, 2004), Samkhya Karika (Miller, 2012), and the Yoga Sutras (Stoler-Miller, 1998). By using concepts central to each of these texts, we will propose a framework that traverses individual lineages and helps create a shared language and understanding for yoga including relationship to current contexts.

Yoga therapy is an evolving practice in complementary and integrative health care (CIH), now with accreditation for schools and credentialing of yoga therapists (see International Association of Yoga Therapists, https://www.iayt.org/default.aspx). Yoga therapy is grounded in the ancient wisdom and practices of yoga, integrated with scientific knowledge for application in current health care contexts. There are a multiplicity of ways to define what constitutes a yoga practice. As such, the heterogeneity of the practices and poor research reporting have been reported as an obstacle to the professionalization of yoga therapy (Jeter et al., 2015). An explanatory framework for yoga therapy is therefore key to the understanding and utilization of yoga therapy as a unique and distinct CIH profession.

EXPLANATORY FRAMEWORK FOR YOGA THERAPY

Work has begun to define and establish an explanatory framework for yoga therapy and to suggest theoretical frameworks outlining the mechanisms underlying yoga-based practices from both neurophysiological and psychological perspectives (Gard et al., 2014; Schmalzl et al., 2015; Streeter et al., 2012; Sullivan et al., 2018). An explanatory model based on the philosophical and ethical foundations of yoga explored yoga therapy as a methodology for alleviating suffering by transforming an individual's relationship to BME phenomena and catalyzing the emergence of eudaemonic well-being (Sullivan et al., 2018).

Eudaemonia represents a state of human flourishing or sense of well-being that is nontransitory and is often connected to a sense of meaning, purpose, or self-realization (Keyes and Simoes, 2012; Ostwald, 1962). Eudaemonic well-being is linked to many health benefits such as the mitigation of gene expression changes in response to social adversity; reduction in perceived loneliness; decreased inflammation; improved immune regulation; mental flourishing; and decreased all-cause mortality independent of other variables (Cole et al., 2015; Fredrickson et al., 2013; Keyes & Simoes, 2012). Yoga has been correlated with both eudaemonia (Ivtzan & Papantoniou, 2014) and related gene expression changes found in the mitigation of the response to social adversity, resulting in decreased inflammation and improved immune regulation (Black et al., 2013; Bower et al., 2014). As such, it could be hypothesized that yoga facilitates its many positive physiological, mental, and social health benefits through its capacity to facilitate eudaemonic well-being. An explanatory framework of yoga therapy focused on its intention to promote the emergence of eudaemonic well-being with its concomitant physiological and mental health benefits is significant for both research and expanded integration into modern health care contexts for a wide variety of patient populations and conditions.

YOGA'S PHILOSOPHICAL FOUNDATION: PRAKRITI AND PURUSHA

Yoga teaches that suffering arises from the individual's relationship, reaction to, and misidentification with the various phenomena of the BME (Miller, 2012; Stoler-Miller, 1998, 2004). Yoga practices are intended to teach a method of discrimination to facilitate a change in the relationship to BME phenomena and ultimately in the experience of suffering itself (Bawra, 2012; Miller, 2012; Stoler-Miller, 1998, 2004). Through yoga, the individual learns the patterns of both behavior and actions that may perpetuate their suffering as well as a path toward a shift in those patterns for the potential alleviation of suffering.

This process of discernment to move from suffering to a change in identification with such suffering and possibly its alleviation is taught through inquiry into the difference between material nature, termed *prakriti*, and spirit, termed *purusha* (Bawra, 2012; Miller, 2012). Purusha can be defined as spirit, the indweller, the observer, the seer, or that which sees, and is said to be the experiencer of material nature (Bawra, 2012; Miller, 2012). Prakriti is the term given to all of material nature, or all that is seen, changes, and is made manifest (Bawra, 2012; Mallinson & Singleton, 2017; Miller, 2012). The clarity that arises from this discrimination and realization of the difference between purusha and prakriti shifts the yoga practitioner's relationship to BME phenomena such that suffering is eased and the experience of steadfast joy, or eudaemonia, may potentially emerge (Bawra, 2012; Easwaran, 2007; Miller, 2012; Stoler-Miller, 1998, 2004).

THE GUNAS, QUALITIES OF MATERIAL NATURE

Prakriti is said to be composed of three qualities. These three qualities, named the gunas, are said to underlie and shape the characteristics of everything that is of material nature, including the BME (Bawra, 2012; Miller, 2012). The gunas enable and support a dynamism in the BME, in which the fluctuations and differing proportions of these qualities give everything in the BME their unique and varied characteristics (Bawra, 2012; Miller, 2012; Stoler-Miller, 2004). As mentioned earlier, the root of suffering is said to arise from the misidentification of purusha with the various phenomena of the BME, or prakriti, and more specifically with the gunas (Bawra, 2012; Miller, 2012; Stoler-Miller, 1998, 2004). The knowledge and practices of yoga are intended to assist the individual in the realization that they may be experiencing the gunas, versus *being* the gunas. The apprehension and discernment of these three gunas is key to the realization of the difference between purusha and prakriti, thereby offering insight into the causes of suffering as well as its alleviation.

The Samkhya Karika, a text representing a seminal philosophy found across the yoga tradition, as well as the Bhagavad Gita and the Yoga Sutras of Patanjali, describes the gunas and their emergent physical, mental, and behavioral attributes as follows (Bawra, 2012; Larson & Isvarakrsna, 2014; Miller, 2012; Stoler-Miller, 1998, 2004).

Sattva is the quality of pleasure, calmness, and tranquility that serves the function of illumination. Sattva is described as lightness, clarity, harmony, buoyance, illumination, lucidity, joy, and understanding (Bawra, 2012; Miller, 2012; Stoler-Miller, 2004). The Bhagavad Gita highlights the importance of cultivating sattva as it is the foundation from which wisdom, discrimination, and clear seeing arise (Stoler-Miller, 2004). While sattva forms the base for many positive attributes, maladaptive states can also arise if one becomes overly attached to or dependent upon the quality of joy, as is briefly described in the Bhagavad Gita. In contemporary terminology, words such as avoidance, unhealthy attachment, psychospiritual crisis, or indifference have been used to describe this attempt to hold on to or maintain a static experience of sattva at the expense of allowing for the natural unfolding of the movement of the gunas within all BME and life experiences.

Rajas is the quality of energy, turbulence, and pain that serves to activate. The quality of rajas is given a spectrum of emergent attributes that comes from this underlying capacity to mobilize and activate. On one end, rajas is said to support movement, creativity, motivation, and activity. However, rajas can also underlie pain, anger, greed and agitation. The Bhagavad Gita explains that because rajas obscures knowledge and clear seeing, it impedes the yogi's capacity to discern the difference between prakriti and purusha. Rajas balanced with sattva and tamas creates the motivation and creativity for inspiring change, movement, and right action. Conversely, its preponderance may increase anger, agitation, or anxiety (Bawra, 2012; Miller, 2012).

Tamas is the quality of inertia, delusion, and indifference that serves to restrain or limit. Tamas is explained through a spectrum of emergent attributes from this underlying capacity to restrain or limit. Theoretically, tamas may provide support for experiences such as stillness, stability, or groundedness. However, it may also foster dullness, inertia, obscuration, delusion, heaviness, negligence, or ignorance. Tamas balanced with sattva and rajas may provide form and stability, whereas an overpredominance of tamas may give rise to delusion, inertia, or obscuration (Bawra, 2012; Miller, 2012).

The Samkhya Karika offers the metaphor of a lamp to illustrate that all three gunas work together. Just as the wick, oil, and flame work together for the purpose of illumination, the three gunas work together to reveal to the individual the difference between purusha and prakriti (Bawra, 2012; Larson & Isvarakrsna, 2014; Miller, 2012).

The three gunas are in constant movement and coexistence as they commingle to create the various manifestations of BME phenomena (Bawra, 2012; Miller, 2012). The different proportions of sattva, rajas, and tamas in each object of material nature, including the subtle mental components of personality, cognition, emotions, and identity, give them their unique attributes (Bawra, 2012; Miller, 2012; Stoler-Miller, 2004). The movement and shifting nature of the gunas are intrinsic to life as they continually rise and fall, grow and diminish. Suffering arises from either trying to stop the movement of the gunas or from our relationship with each guna—not from the guna itself. Each of these qualities can hold positive attributes in their capacity to illuminate, activate, or restrain. However, our relationship to these qualities of material nature, and any attempt to maintain one at the expense of the others, may lead to imbalance, pain, or suffering.

Yoga teaches a methodology to nonjudgmentally and compassionately observe and experience the movement of the gunas such that the relationship and response to the changing phenomena of the BME is altered. The individual learns how to welcome and explore the BME in a way that facilitates eudaemonic well-being in the face of stressors or adversity.

CONVERGENCE OF POLYVAGAL THEORY WITH THE GUNAS

Both Polyvagal Theory and the gunas provide a perspective to understand underlying foundations from which physical, psychological, and behavioral attributes emerge. Polyvagal Theory provides insight into how underlying neural platforms are activated in response to perceived threat or safety in the presence of BME phenomena. Yoga suggests that physical, psychological, and behavioral attributes emerge from and are influenced by the underlying interplay of the gunas.

Both frameworks discuss the coexistence and comingling of neural platforms

(Polyvagal Theory) or gunas (yoga) and attempt to convey complexity amid an inherent tendency toward reductionism within traditional academic disciplines. In Polyvagal Theory, the coexistence of neural platforms gives way to the varied experiences of play (safe mobilization) and intimacy (safe immobilization). In yoga, the coexistence of the gunas creates the varied phenomena of BME and influences the relationship and reaction to such stimuli. Both theories teach that it is from the surfacing of the neural platform of Polyvagal Theory or the guna of yoga that BME states are made manifest and established.

The gunas of yoga and neural platforms of Polyvagal Theory are also reflected in one another in a convergent and analogous manner. This relationship between the two models can be seen through the comparable descriptions of attributes. When the ANS comes under the influence of one of the gunas, a distinct neural platform of the Polyvagal Theory may be activated, supporting shared characteristics between the two. Likewise, when a neural platform is activated, it supports the predominance of a guna, and the shared characteristics between them emerge. For example, when sattva reflects through the nervous system, the physiological, mental, and behavioral characteristics of the VVC manifest, or when the VVC is activated, the attributes of sattva manifest, as is described in more detail below. This discussion explores the relationship between the two models in how they relate to and affect one another for the emergence of physical, mental, and behavioral attributes. Ultimately, this relationship is meant to foster an understanding that yoga therapy may affect both underlying neural platforms and gunas, resulting in improved self-regulation and resilience for the well-being of the individual.

COMPARATIVE LOOK AT NEURAL PLATFORMS, GLOBAL STATES, AND GUNAS

Both Polyvagal Theory and yoga describe three primary and combinable neural platforms or qualities from which specific physical, psychological, and behavioral attributes emerge.

1. Sattva and the VVC: Similar emergent attributes are found in descriptions of both sattva predominance and VVC activation. From sattva comes the realization of the connection between all beings. Sattvic joy is similar to eudaemonia with its more steadfast and everlasting quality and stems from calmness, tranquility, and understanding of the "Self" as in Stoler-Miller (2004). These attributes of connection, equanimity, and eudaemonia are proposed to be dependent on a neurophysiological foundation for their emergence. Halifax (2012) proposed a model where qualities such as equanimity and eudaemonia emerge only when the system is sufficiently primed and includes an axis titled "embodied/engaged" in which interoception is essential. The VVC neural platform provides

support for interoception, connection, equanimity, and eudaemonia as it links awareness of bodily sensations with self-regulatory capacity; the use of facial cues and vocal prosody to communicate safety and connect to others; tuning into human vocalizations to connect with others; and the inhibition of defensive states to support equanimity, eudaemonia, and connection through the capacity to nonjudgmentally listen, observe, and be in relationship with others (Porges, 2011, 2017). In sum, through sattvic predominance and/or VVC activation, the promotion of interoceptivity, connection, equanimity, and eudaemonia may emerge. This state is well adapted for restoration, relaxation, and connection and can be maladaptive when the individual is not able to adequately respond to the needs of the environment (including threat) as described within the other neural platforms and guna states.

2. Rajas and the SNS: The attributes that emerge from rajas and the SNS are shared in their spectrum from mobilization and activation to anger or fear. The guna of rajas and the neural platform of SNS provide a common foundation for activating and motivating forces. Similar to the state of safe mobilization and play that comes when the VVC and SNS synergistically work together, when rajas co-arises with a balance of the other gunas, attributes such as creativity, motivation, optimal action, and change emerge. When rajas becomes predominant and is not balanced by the other two gunas, similar to the SNS, it provides the base for mobilization and movement in response to any demand for psychophysiological resources. This includes a spectrum from eustress to real or perceived threat in the environment, with the emergence of behavioral attributes such as fear, anger, or aggression. This continuum of mobilization includes the well-adapted response to immediate threat, or may become maladaptive, contributing to excessive allostatic load.

3. Tamas and the DVC: The attributes that emerge from tamas and the DVC provide a spectrum of experiences from stability and restraint to immobilization. In the same way the VVC and DVC partner to create internal conditions for the emergence of social bonding and intimacy, tamas can co-arise with a balance of the other gunas to manifest as stability and form. When tamas predominates, similar to the DVC neural platform, it provides the base for the emergence of obscuration, dullness, immobilization, inertia, or dissociation. This spectrum includes well-adapted responses to extreme threat or may become maladaptive and contribute to chronic disease states, which has been proposed (Kolacz & Porges, 2018).

The parallels between Polyvagal Theory and gunas are further elucidated through the idea of the preparatory set. Five distinct preparatory sets stemming from Polyvagal Theory and the gunas are proposed, with their integrated patterns of muscle tone/posture, autonomic state, affect, attention, and expectation. As mentioned previously, if the underlying autonomic state is altered, there are concomitant changes throughout the preparatory set. Analogously, an alteration in the predominance of a guna from which an individual is operating may create changes in the layers of the preparatory set including muscle tone/posture, autonomic state, affect, attention, and expectation. This is congruent with the yoga therapy perspective, which utilizes an approach to evaluation and intervention that acknowledges the influence of the gunas on the physical, energetic, mental, and behavioral aspects of the individual.

By including and emphasizing these underlying gunas and their effect on physical, psychological, and behavioral attributes, yoga therapy can retain its integrated and comprehensive methodology based on its foundational teachings. The outcome of this understanding is a movement away from breaking apart the practices, where asanas (postures) are directed to musculoskeletal imbalances, pranayama (breathing practices) are directed to autonomic state, and meditation or yama and niyama (intentional ethical principles) are directed to attentional, affective, and cognitive states. A more cohesive approach can be implemented for both research and clinical applications where the evaluation, assessment, and direction of intervention is toward affecting the underlying guna. The result would be an intervention consisting of yama/niyama, asana, pranayama, and meditation intended to influence the gunas and their correlated physical, mental, and behavioral states. The resultant change in gunas would have concurrent effects on all layers of the preparatory set and on physical, psychological, and behavioral well-being.

In sum, both Polyvagal Theory and gunas play a vital role in understanding how yoga may help diverse conditions and patient populations by affecting the underlying gunas and correlated neural platforms. Given the complexity of living systems, this integrative yogic approach to the whole person, while still necessarily reduced for explanatory purposes, has high potential for an effect on the emergence of integrated physical, mental, social, and spiritual attributes and behaviors that facilitate well-being. These concepts also support the yoga therapist in developing evaluation, assessment, and intervention tools that are authentic to the foundations of yoga and the provision of its practices in a cohesive and comprehensive format while simultaneously assisting translation for researchers, the public, and health care contexts.

THE APPLICATION OF YOGA'S MODEL AND PRACTICES FOR SELF-REGULATION AND RESILIENCE

Yoga practices, when provided as a comprehensive methodology, are proposed to integrate autonomic, cognitive, affective, and behavioral processes for regulation across physical, psychological, and behavioral domains. Through both top-down and bottom-up practices, yoga may be effective at downregulating the system toward parasympathetic, ventral vagal dominance (Gard et al., 2014; Schmalzl et al., 2015; Streeter et al., 2012). In addition, the application of yoga practices for resilience of the system is discussed, as they may support the individual's capacity to work with shifting neural platforms and gunas.

Research has supported yoga's benefits for diverse conditions such as depression, epilepsy, PTSD, and chronic pain through its influence on the autonomic nervous system and other interrelated systemic mind-body mechanisms that contribute to improved physical and mental regulation and decreased reactivity to stressful stimuli (Streeter et al., 2012). Research has also corroborated yoga's effect on promoting vagal tone in diverse patient populations and its associated effects in decreasing allostatic load and enhancing self-regulation (Chu et al., 2017; Khattab et al., 2007; Sarang & Telles, 2006; Taylor et al., 2010; Telles et al., 2016; Tyagi & Cohen, 2016). In addition, yoga has demonstrated effects beyond physical exercise as it also concurrently benefits autonomic regulation, attention, and affect (Mackenzie et al., 2014). Furthermore, research has supported yoga's relationship to greater body awareness, compassion, and eudaemonic well-being (Fiori et al., 2017; Ivtzan & Papantoniou, 2014). A program developed for adolescent depression included the goals of autonomic regulation, the practice of attentional and interoceptive awareness, and identification of intrinsic values to promote prosocial behavior based on yoga's cohesive and integrative methodology and effect for regulation and resilience (Henje Blom et al., 2014).

Yoga is proposed to offer methods for regulation and resilience through the integrated practice of yamas and niyamas (ethical/intentional principles), asanas (physical exercises), pranayama (breathing techniques), and meditation (Gard et al., 2014; Schmalzl et al., 2015; Streeter et al., 2012). Ethical intention setting (yama and niyama) informs and directs the meeting of physical and mental sensations, such as from interoception or emotions, for the promotion of positive physiological and affective states and prosocial behavioral responses (Gard et al., 2014). The ethical principles provided by yoga may help to guide the reaction, relationship, and action of the individual in response to phenomena of the BME. For example, by meeting stimuli of the BME from a perspective of nonharming, nonattachment or contentment, the individual alters the way they pay attention to such stimuli, potentially facilitating an emergence of compassion, nonjudgment, or acceptance (Gard et al., 2014). Just as Aristotle taught that virtue ethics provided guideposts for eudaemonia (Ostwald, 1962), the ethical principles of yoga elucidate a process to meet BME phenomena to facilitate the emergence of such qualities as eudaemonia. Asanas or physical postures may serve as a bottom-up regulatory tool to help regulate and promote resilience by altering the state of the autonomic nervous system (Cottingham, Porges, & Lyon, 1988; Cottingham, Porges, & Richmond, 1988; Schmalzl et al., 2015). Breathing techniques are known to directly affect cardiac vagal tone and the initiation of the vagal brake to move the system toward the VVC platform

TABLE 5.1. Characteristics and Emergent Properties of Global States Based on Comparative Neural Platforms of Polyvagal Theory and Gunas of Yoga

Global State	Neural Platform	Guna	Emergent Properties
Social engagement	VVC	Sattva	Safety, connection, clarity, eudaemonia, calmness, tranquility, equanimity
Play/dance	VVC and SNS	Rajas with sattva and tamas	Activity, creativity, motivation, capacity for change
Fight or flight	SNS	Predominance of rajas	Fear, anger, greed
Intimacy	DVC with VVC	Tamas with sattva and rajas	Stability, form, restraint, social bonding
Shutdown/ immobilization	DVC	Predominance of tamas	Obscuration, inertia, dullness, ignorance, delusion, dissociation

and provide another bottom-up regulatory practice of yoga (Brown & Gerbarg, 2005a, 2005b; Porges, 2017; Porges & Carter, 2017). Finally, the yoga tradition offers an array of mind-training practices for regulation, such as focused attention and open monitoring meditation (Cramer et al., 2017; Gard et al., 2014; Hofmann et al., 2016; Pascoe & Bauer, 2015; Schmalzl et al., 2015).

YOGA PRACTICES FOR SELF-REGULATION: FACILITATING THE VVC NEURAL PLATFORM AND SATTVA

As many of the beneficial characteristics of physical and mental health as well as prosocial behavioral attributes are shared by sattva and VVC, it is proposed that yoga practices may be utilized to strengthen one to affect the other. The VVC neural platform may be activated or made more accessible through practices that cultivate sattva, and sattva may become more accessible or predominant through practices that activate the VVC neural platform.

The Samkhya Karika emphasizes the importance of fostering the quality of sattva through one's habits, environment, and behavior to realize the difference between purusha and prakriti and for the alleviation of suffering (Miller, 2012). This sattvic state is taught as being essential for the clarity needed to gather insight into the individual's relationship to various phenomena of the BME, which may lead to healthy or unhealthy responses to stressors or stimuli (Bawra, 2012; Miller, 2012; Stoler-Miller, 2004). Through the clarity of the *sattva guna*, the relationship to BME phenomena can be explored, and healthy relationships to both interoceptive and outer stimuli can be cultivated.

Yoga therapy often first focuses on building a strong foundation of the sattva guna to strengthen discriminative wisdom, developmental clarity, and systemic adaptability and resilience. Being established in the sattva guna enables the opportunity to build positive internal relationships with interoceptive sensations, memories, emotions, thoughts, and beliefs, which may in turn support positive relationships with others. These features of sattva all benefit the self-regulatory capacity of the individual. From this sattva guna base, the individual may experience the fluctuations of rajas and tamas and change their relationship and response to these qualities of material nature, potentially facilitating resilience of the system.

The VVC is a neural platform that supports physiological restoration, mental regulation, and prosocial behavioral attributes. The VVC also provides a key anchor to build the critical self-regulatory skills that lead to greater systemic adaptability and resilience. Enhancing the individual's ability to activate the VVC is proposed as a method to retune the autonomic nervous system in disorders with a combination of diminished HRV and physical, mental, and social health deterioration, such as irritable bowel syndrome and fibromyalgia (Kolacz & Porges, 2018; Porges & Kolacz, 2018).

Both the VVC neural platform and the sattva guna correlate with the emergence of such qualities as connection, tranquility, equanimity, and eudaemonia. We propose that sattva shares neurophysiological features with VVC-mediated states, during which cardiac vagal tone is increased, and the expanded integrated social engagement system is expressed. Both sattva and the VVC may be related to states of self-restoration, interoceptivity, and the emergence of prosocial emotions and behaviors such as connection and eudaemonia.

As noted previously, yoga therapy's explanatory framework can be described as the priming of the system for the emergence of eudaemonia, with its concomitant physiological and mental health benefits (Sullivan et al., 2018). It is through the potential for eudaemonic well-being and shifts in relationship to BME phenomena that yoga therapy is proposed to help with diverse clinical conditions and patient populations. Therefore, the reciprocal relationship between the VVC and sattva, which facilitates the emergence of eudaemonic well-being, is important to the yoga therapeutic process and application of yoga practices. Building the individual's facility in accessing and promoting the sattva guna and the VVC neural platform is proposed to be a crucial and foundational step in learning self-regulatory skills from which resilience will emerge. Through self-regulation processes, the nervous system enables healthy and more adaptive physiological, psychological, and behavioral responses and provides opportunities for greater insight into the relationship to BME phenomena to lessen and alleviate personal suffering. Healthy, adaptive physiological, psychological, and prosocial states of eudaemonia, connectedness, and equanimity may emerge when sattva and the VVC predominate. The practices of yama/niyama, asanas, pranayama, and meditation may enhance the function of the specific vagal pathways that optimize the neural platform of the VVC, and/or to strengthen the quality of sattva (Chu et al., 2017; Sarang & Telles, 2006; Telles et al., 2016; Tsuji et al., 1994; Tyagi & Cohen, 2016).

YOGA'S PRACTICES TO CULTIVATE RESILIENCE

Promoting practices that increase sattva or activation of the VVC can create a therapeutic container to safely challenge the building of resilience. Within Polyvagal Theory, these challenges would be conceptualized as neural exercises expanding the capacity of the VVC to regulate state and to promote resilience. Yoga also includes various practices that achieve similar effects in optimizing autonomic control, providing greater physiological and psychological adaptability and resilience through reducing emotional reactivity, and lowering the physiological set point of reactivity (Gard et al., 2014). In addition to developing downregulating capacity, we believe meeting the needs of the environment requires the healthy navigation of VVC, SNS, and DVC neural platforms and their combinations.

From a yoga perspective, the importance of resilience is also reflected in the model of the gunas. Just as the Bhagavad Gita elucidates the benefits of sattva, it also provides the ultimate aim of transcending the gunas through nonattachment, disidentification, and recognition of impermanence (Stoler-Miller, 2004). It is emphasized that this fluctuation and movement between clarity (sattva), activation (rajas), and restraint (tamas) is an intrinsic trait of all material nature (prakriti).

Since all behaviors and neurophysiological functions are dependent on movement of the gunas, the practice of yoga is not about staying in sattva or limiting the movement of the gunas. Rather, yoga teaches a methodology to create a different relationship to the continual mixing and movement of these qualities. This underlying objective is shared with the neural exercise model of Polyvagal Theory. It is important to note that this state of discrimination between purusha and prakriti, or the gunas, is not one of nonparticipation or detachment from life. Instead, it is a state whereby the individual experiences the movement of the gunas, but the "world does not flee from him, nor does he flee from the world" (Stoler-Miller, 2004, p. 113). In other words, through yoga the individual learns not to ignore the movement inherent to BME phenomena, but to change the relationship to the movement of such phenomena. The practice is not meant to subjectively isolate oneself from the world but provides a methodology and technology to experience the world such that suffering is lessened. Polyvagal Theory provides a neurophysiological explanation of the methods and techniques embedded in yoga.

Understanding and discriminating between this movement of the gunas that make up the BME and awareness, or purusha, an individual is able to experience deep equanimity, inexhaustible joy, and a sense of pure calmness even when the movement of the gunas continues (Stoler-Miller, 2004). When one learns to nonjudgmentally observe and experience this movement of the gunas, an unwavering and profound capacity for equanimity and eudaemonic joy emerges (Figure 5.1). The individual changes their relationship with the fluctuations of the BME and learns to respond and receive the changing phenomena of life differently.

The practices of yoga may serve this development of resilience through the idea of safe mobilization and safe immobilization. In the state of safe mobilization, there is activation of the SNS within a container of the VVC for safe activation of the system. Similarly, within a foundational platform of sattva, the individual is able to utilize the rising of rajas for creativity, motivation or change, rather than rajas becoming a negative force. By developing an improved ability to recruit and engage the neural platform of VVC or sattva, there is greater resilience when confronted with disturbances. For example, the individual can learn techniques of setting ethical intentions, attentional control, various other types of meditation, breath, and movement to cultivate sattva and maintain the neural platform regulated by the VVC. Then the individual can assume challenging or activating postures or breath techniques that mimic the activation of the system. Resilience is cultivated by maintaining or building the facility to find calm mental or physiological states while activated. The individual is able to learn to move between guna states and neural platforms and/or to experience the combined state of sattva with rajas, or neurophysiologically promoting a neural platform that integrates VVC with SNS.

By working with the qualities of rajas and tamas while maintaining access to sattva, the window of tolerance for sensation may be widened and resilience facilitated. Through maintaining the neural platform of the VVC while activating the system, as well as alternating between relaxing and activating practices, the individual may foster both regulation and resilience of the system. Thus, through the maintenance of the foundation of sattva, which provides clarity and insight while experiencing activation, the individual may find ways to change the relationship to BME, thereby learning tools of self-regulation that enhance resilience. The capacity to discern, alter reactivity, and even to hold a positive attitude in the presence of activation offers an important resource in promoting self-regulation, which may be utilized in response to stressors in the BME, including the experience of pain, illness, or disability and thereby also improving resilience both physiologically and psychologically.

The yoga therapy process encourages a foundation of safety/VVC from which rajas/SNS and tamas/DVC can be experienced with greater adaptability and resilience in the broad relationship to BME phenomena (Figure 5.1).

DISCUSSION

This chapter offers a theoretical model based on a convergent view of yoga and Polyvagal Theory, two analogous explanatory systems for understanding the function and interplay of underlying neural platforms (Polyvagal Theory) and gunas (yoga), and their role in manifesting physiological, psychological, and behavioral attributes. By affecting the neural platform or guna predominance and one's relationship to these shifting neural platforms, or qualities, the preparatory set of the individual is altered. The development of interoceptive awareness and sensitivity fosters regulation and resilience to these shifting neural platforms and gunas in response to phenomena of the BME. In addition, the gunas of yoga and the neural platforms of Polyvagal Theory share characteristics that parallel one another where the neural platform reflects the guna predominance and the guna predominance reflects the neural platform.

Yoga is suggested to provide a form of neural exercise and a methodology of working with the gunas for the regulation and resilience of the system. Through altering and/or changing the conscious relationship to the underlying state of the gunas and neural platforms described by Polyvagal Theory, the preparatory set is affected and physiological, psychological, and behavioral processes are reciprocally influenced (Payne & Crane-Godreau, 2015; Porges & Carter, 2017). Yoga practices may promote the accessibility of the VVC and the relative balance of sattva to the other gunas to assist processes of physiological restoration and positive psychological and behavioral states. Yoga practices may also be seen as helping develop facility with moving in and out of relative dominance of these theoretical neural platforms and guna states such that resilience of the system is cultivated. As an individual learns tools for self-regulation to explore and potentially alter the relationship to BME phenomena, the relationship to suffering may be improved (Figure 5.1).

While we do not wish to convey that the end goal is cultivation of sattva, the theoretical correlation to the neural platform of the VVC may be seen as a neurophysiological substrate or stepping-stone toward the emergence of such states as eudaemonia, connection, or tranquility. Similarly, we are not suggesting that the other gunas and neural platforms are bad, as these energies and states are inseparable and adaptive in understanding the complexity of human experience and behavior, and thus the potential influence of a yoga therapy framework for well-being. The capacity to cultivate eudaemonic well-being is significant to yoga therapy's explanatory framework in benefiting diverse patient populations and conditions for physical, mental, and behavioral health and well-being. The states of eudaemonia, calm, or tranquility that may emerge from the cultivation of yoga practices influences the preparatory set such that a healthier relationship to BME conditions may be learned and self-regulatory skills can be built.

From a strengthened foundation of the neural platform of VVC, and the guna of sattva, the individual has the resources to move through states of dominant rajas and tamas or SNS and DVC such that adaptability, flexibility, and resilience of the system are cultivated. The practices of yoga that engage both top-down and bottom-up processes may be utilized for the cultivation of resilience by moving between neural platforms and gunas (Figure 5.1).

This model may be utilized in several ways. In one practice of this model, sattva and the VVC serve as methods for self-regulation, and the practices of yoga build the tools to return to and strengthen these restorative and calm states. This is a useful practice if an individual experiences maladaptive or overwhelming states of rajas and SNS, or of tamas and DVC, and can learn to utilize yoga therapy techniques to return to sattva or VVC for clarity and calm. In another practice of this model, the individual learns to change the relationship with and widen their threshold of tolerance to both rajas and tamas, and SNS and DVC, thereby increasing the experience of safe mobilization and safe immobilization. This means that the individual learns how to find support in an underlying sattva or VVC state while other platforms or qualities of rajas and SNS, or tamas and DVC, are activated. An example is the utilization of postures or breath techniques that activate the system, while simultaneously engaging in practices of intention, meditation, and breath technique to facilitate the underlying sense of connection, calm, or tranquility.

The parallel between affecting the underlying neural platform or guna state is significant in enabling yoga therapy to be practiced in a manner consistent with its philosophical foundations while being translatable to current neurophysiological thinking. The ability to utilize the existing explanatory framework provided by yoga and the gunas combined with the biobehavioral model established by Polyvagal Theory enables the translation of yoga therapy into health care and research without the need to adopt an outside neurophysiological model and attempt to fit yoga into that model.

This work will contribute to yoga therapy being understood as a distinct health care profession that benefits physiological, psychological, and behavioral well-being for diverse patient populations through the cultivation of self-regulatory skills, resilience, and eudaemonic well-being. This model provides support for the creation of yoga therapy assessment tools to identify underlying guna predominance. In addition, it supports the yoga therapist in evaluating, assessing, and creating interventions aimed at working with underlying guna predominance and identifiable and measurable neural platforms toward these goals. Rather than creating protocols for allopathic conditions, the yoga therapist influences these underlying guna states and neural platforms to target the unique needs of each individual. Bridge-building efforts such as this work would support yoga therapists, who work with clients in a manner that is simultaneously based on yoga foundational theory and offers additional translatory language for research, the public, and integration into health care.

IMPLICATIONS AND FUTURE DIRECTIONS

The theoretical model proposed in this chapter points to several implications and future directions.

It is suggested that yoga therapy research include the comprehensive system of yoga in intervention protocols, including yama and niyama (ethical intentional practices), asanas (postures), pranayama (breathing practices), and meditation.

In order to reflect the intention of yoga, the application and research on yoga for diverse populations would benefit from being directed toward such ideas as facilitating eudaemonic well-being. In addition, the targeting of yoga therapy interventions to underlying guna states or neural platforms to enhance self-regulation and resilience and their relationship to the cultivation of eudaemonic well-being is proposed, yielding several directions of future study.

1. Examining eudaemonic well-being, interoception, and indices of HRV (e.g., respiratory sinus arrhythmia) as underlying mechanisms through which yoga therapy improves outcome measures such as improved quality of life, self-regulation, and resilience, and decreased pain, inflammation, perceived loneliness, anxiety, and depression in diverse patient populations and conditions.
2. Exploring the relationship between indices of HRV, measures of interoception, and eudaemonic well-being, and their connection to physical, psychological, and behavioral health and well-being, both quantitatively and qualitatively.
3. Testing the hypothesis of the convergence of neural platforms and gunas. It would be of particular interest to investigate whether the physiological states identified by Polyvagal Theory parallel the states and processes described in yoga. For example, is the VVC state, expressed as increased respiratory sinus arrhythmia, decreased blood pressure, and decreased catecholamines, associated with subjective experiences such as calm, equanimity, and connection that practitioners describe as sattva? Is the SNS state, expressed as decreased respiratory sinus arrhythmia, increased blood pressure, and increased catecholamines, associated with subjective experiences such as anxiety, fear, or worry that practitioners describe as rajas? Is the DVC state, expressed as decreased activity, decreased heart rate, and decreased blood pressure, associated with subjective experiences such as a disconnection from the world that practitioners describe as tamas?
4. Continued definition of the gunas and their relationship to the neural platforms and the utilization of their assessment, evaluation, and targeted intervention to facilitate regulation, resilience, and physiological, psychological, and behavioral health and well-being in diverse client populations and conditions.

CONCLUSION

Yoga therapy is proposed to facilitate eudaemonic well-being with its many effects for physical, mental, and behavioral health for diverse populations through the building of self-regulatory skills and cultivating resilience of the system (Figure 5.1). The attributes of the gunas of yoga and the neural platforms of the Polyvagal Theory, while not the same, are reflected in one another. As such, working with gunas and neural platforms that underlie physical, psychological, and behavioral attributes provides a methodology for the application of yoga practices for facilitating systemic regulation and resilience.

Yoga therapy builds a strong foundation in sattva and the neural platform of the VVC for the emergence of connection, tranquility, and eudaemonia with resulting benefits to physiological, psychological, and behavioral health and well-being. In addition, resilience is facilitated through changing the relationship to the natural fluctuations of the gunas of rajas and tamas, and their counterpart neural platforms of the SNS and DVC, such that the individual learns to effectively bounce back to states of restoration and to build resilience (Figure 5.1).

It is when yoga is practiced and understood as a cohesive and comprehensive system that the benefits for self-regulation and resilience may be realized. As one learns new responses to potential BME stressors, one may experience greater physiological, psychological, and behavioral health and well-being. The convergence of Polyvagal Theory and the gunas may help frame yoga therapy as a method that supports self-regulation and resilience, and lessens allostatic load through building healthy relationships to BME phenomena. When yoga therapy is applied through this perspective of shifting underlying guna states and neural platforms, the integrated nature of the practice can be understood as distinct from other CIH practices. It is hoped that this helps inform both research and health care contexts interested in integrating yoga interventions for various patient populations and conditions.

ACKNOWLEDGMENTS

We would like to thank Richard Miller, Neil Pearson, Erin Byron, and Peter Payne for fruitful discussions on the topics discussed in this chapter.

REFERENCES

Bawra, B. V. (2012). *Samkhya Karika*. Ravenna, OH: Brahmrishi Yoga.
Berntson, G. G., Cacioppo, J. T., & Quigley, K. S. (1991). Autonomic determinism: The modes of autonomic control, the doctrine of autonomic space and the laws of autonomic constraint. *Psychological Review, 98*, 459–487. doi:10.1037/0033-295x.98.4.459

Black, D. S., Cole, S. W., Irwin, M. R., Breen, E., St. Cyr, N. M., Nazarian, N., Khalsa, D. S., & Lavretsky, H. (2013). Yogic meditation reverses NF-κB and IRF-related transcriptome dynamics in leukocytes of family dementia caregivers in a randomized controlled trial. *Psychoneuroendocrinology, 38,* 348–355. doi:10.1016/j.psyneuen.2012.06.011

Bower, J. E., Greendale, G., Crosswell, A. D., Garet, D., Sternlieb, B., Ganz, P. A., Irwin, M. R., Olmstead, R., Arevalo, J., & Cole, S. W. (2014). Yoga reduces inflammatory signaling in fatigued breast cancer survivors: A randomized controlled trial. *Psychoneuroendocrinology, 43,* 20–29. doi:10.1016/j.psyneuen.2014.01.019

Brown, R. P., & Gerbarg, P. L. (2005a). Sudarshan Kriya yogic breathing in the treatment of stress, anxiety, and depression: Part II—clinical applications and guidelines. *Journal of Alternative and Complementary Medicine, 11,* 711–717. doi:10.1089/acm.2005.11.711

Brown, R. P., & Gerbarg, P. L. (2005b). Sudarshan Kriya yogic breathing in the treatment of stress, anxiety, and depression: Part I—neurophysiologic model. *Journal of Alternative and Complementary Medicine, 11,* 189–201. doi:10.1089/acm.2005.11.189

Brown, R. P., & Gerbarg, P. L. (2012). *The healing power of the breath: Simple techniques to reduce stress and anxiety, enhance concentration and balance your emotions.* Boston, MA: Trumpeter.

Brown, R. P., Gerbarg, P. L., & Muench, F. (2013). Breathing practices for treatment of psychiatric and stress-related medical conditions. *Psychiatric Clinics of North America, 36,* 121–140. doi:10.1016/j.psc.2013.01.001

Ceunen, E., Vlaeyen, J. W., & Van Diest, I. (2016). On the origin of interoception. *Frontiers in Psychology, 7,* 743. doi:10.3389/fpsyg.2016.00743

Chu, I.-H., Wu, W.-L., Lin, I.-M., Chang, Y.-K., Lin, Y.-J., & Yang, P.-C. (2017). Effects of yoga on heart rate variability and depressive symptoms in women: A randomized controlled trial. *Journal of Alternative and Complementary Medicine, 23,* 310–316. doi:10.1089/acm.2016.0135

Cole, S. W. (2013). Social regulation of human gene expression: Mechanisms and implications for public health. *American Journal of Public Health, 103,* S84–S92. doi:10.2105/ajph.2012.301183

Cole, S. W., Levine, M. E., Arevalo, J. M., Ma, J., Weir, D. R., & Crimmins, E. M. (2015). Loneliness, eudaimonia and the human conserved transcriptional response to adversity. *Psychoneuroendocrinology, 62,* 11–17. doi:10.1016/j.psyneuen.2015.07.001

Cottingham, J. T., Porges, S. W., & Lyon, T. (1988). Effects of soft tissue mobilization (Rolfing pelvic lift) on parasympathetic tone in two age groups. *Physical Therapy, 68,* 352–356. doi:10.1093/ptj/68.3.352

Cottingham, J. T., Porges, S. W., & Richmond, K. (1988). Shifts in pelvic inclination angle and parasympathetic tone produced by rolfing soft tissue manipulation. *Physical Therapy, 68,* 1364–1370. doi:10.1093/ptj/68.9.1364

Craig, A. D. (2015). *How do you feel? An interoceptive moment with your neurobiological self.* Princeton, NJ: Princeton University Press.

Cramer, H., Anheyer, D., Lauche, R., & Dobos, G. (2017). A systematic review of yoga for major depressive disorder. *Journal of Affective Disorders, 213,* 70–77. doi:10.1016/j.jad.2017.02.006

Dale, L. P., Carroll, L. E., Galen, G., Hayes, J. A., Webb, K. W., & Porges, S. W. (2009). Abuse history is related to autonomic regulation to mild exercise and psychological wellbeing. *Applied Psychophysiology and Biofeedback, 34,* 299–308. doi:10.1007/s10484-009-9111-4

Dale, L. P., Carroll, L. E., Galen, G. C., Schein, R., Bliss, A., Mattison, A. M., & Neace, W. (2011). Yoga practice may buffer the deleterious effects of abuse on women's self-concept and dysfunctional coping. *Journal of Aggression, Maltreatment, and Trauma, 20,* 90–102. doi:10.1080/10926771.2011.538005

Easwaran, E. (Trans.). (2007). *The Upanishads.* Tomales, CA: Blue Mountain Center of Meditation.

Eckberg, D. L. (2003). The human respiratory gate. *Journal of Physiology, 548,* 339–352. doi:10.1113/jphysiol.2002.037192

Farb, N., Daubenmier, J., Price, C. J., Gard, T., Kerr, C., Dunn, B. D., Klein, A. C., Paulus, M. P., & Mehling, W. E. (2015). Interoception, contemplative practice and health. *Frontiers in Psychology, 6,* 763. doi:10.3389/fpsyg.2015.00763

Felitti, V. J., Anda, R. F., Nordenberg, D., Williamson, D. F., Spitz, A. M., Edwards, V.,Koss, M. P., & Marks, J. S. (1998). Relationship of childhood abuse and household dysfunction to many of the leading causes of death in adults. *American Journal of Preventive Medicine, 14,* 245–258. doi:10.1016/s0749-3797(98)00017-8

Fiori, F., Aglioti, S. M., & David, N. (2017). Interactions between body and social awareness in yoga. *Journal of Alternative and Complementary Medicine, 23,* 227–233. doi:10.1089/acm.2016.0169

Fredrickson, B. L., Grewen, K. M., Coffey, K. A., Algoe, S. B., Firestine, A. M., Arevalo, J. M., Ma, J., & Cole, S. W. (2013). A functional genomic perspective on human well-being. *Proceedings of the National Academy of Sciences USA, 110,* 13684–13689. doi:10.1073/pnas.1305419110

Gard, T., Noggle, J. J., Park, C. L., Vago, D. R., & Wilson, A. (2014). Potential self-regulatory mechanisms of yoga for psychological health. *Frontiers in Human Neuroscience, 8,* 770. doi:10.3389/fnhum.2014.00770

Haase, L., Stewart, J. L., Youssef, B., May, A. C., Isakovic, S., Simmons, A. N., Johnson, D. C., Potterat, E. G., & Paulus, M. P. (2016). When the brain does not adequately feel the body: Links between low resilience and interoception. *Biological Psychology, 113,* 37–45. doi:10.1016/j.biopsycho.2015.11.004

Halifax, J. (2012). A heuristic model of enactive compassion. *Current Opinion in Supportive and Palliative Care, 6,* 228–235. doi:10.1097/spc.0b013e3283530fbe

Hayano, J., & Yasuma, F. (2003). Hypothesis: Respiratory sinus arrhythmia is an intrinsic resting function of cardiopulmonary system. *Cardiovascular Research, 58,* 1–9. doi:10.1016/s0008-6363(02)00851-9

Henje Blom, E., Duncan, L. G., Ho, T. C., Connolly, C. G., LeWinn, K. Z., Chesney, M., Hecht, F. M., & Yang, T. T. (2014). The development of an RDoC-based treatment program for adolescent depression: "Training for Awareness, Resilience, and Action" (TARA). *Frontiers in Human Neuroscience, 8,* 630. doi:10.3389/fnhum.2014.00630

Hofmann, S. G., Andreoli, G., Carpenter, J. K., & Curtiss, J. (2016). Effect of hatha yoga on anxiety: A meta-analysis: Yoga for anxiety. *Journal of Evidence-Based Medicine, 9,* 116–124. doi:10.1111/jebm.12204

Ivtzan, I., & Papantoniou, A. (2014). Yoga meets positive psychology: Examining the integration of hedonic (gratitude) and eudaimonic (meaning) wellbeing in relation to the extent of yoga practice. *Journal of Bodywork and Movement Therapy, 18,* 183–189. doi:10.1016/j.jbmt.2013.11.005

Jackson, J. H. (1884). The Croonian lectures on evolution and dissolution of the nervous system. *British Medical Journal, 1,* 703–707. doi:10.1016/s0140-6736(02)23422-4

Jeter, P. E., Slutsky, J., Singh, N., & Khalsa, S. B. S. (2015). Yoga as a therapeutic intervention: A bibliometric analysis of published research studies from 1967 to 2013. *Journal of Alternative and Complementary Medicine, 21,* 586–592. doi:10.1089/acm.2015.0057

Keyes, C. L., & Simoes, E. J. (2012). To flourish or not: Positive mental health and all-cause mortality. *American Journal of Public Health, 102,* 2164–2172. doi:10.2105/ajph.2012.300918

Khattab, K., Khattab, A. A., Ortak, J., Richardt, G., & Bonnemeier, H. (2007). Iyengar yoga increases cardiac parasympathetic nervous modulation among healthy yoga practitioners. *Evidence-Based Complementary and Alternative Medicine, 4,* 511–517. doi:10.1093/ecam/nem087

Kolacz, J., & Porges, S. W. (2018). Chronic diffuse pain and functional gastrointestinal disorders after traumatic stress: Pathophysiology through a polyvagal perspective. *Frontiers in Medicine, 5,* 145.

Larson, G. J., & Isvarakrsna. (2014). *Classical Samkhya: An interpretation of its history and meaning.* Delhi: Motilal Banarsidass.

Mackenzie, M. J., Carlson, L. E., Paskevich, D. M., Ekkekakis, P., Wurz, A. J., Wytsma, K., Krenz, K. A., McAuley, E., & Culos-Reed, S. N. (2014). Associations between attention, affect, and cardiac activity in a single yoga session for female cancer survivors: An enactive neurophenomenology-based approach. *Consciousness and Cognition, 27,* 129–146. doi:10.1016/j.concog.2014.04.005

Mallinson, J., & Singleton, M. (2017). *Roots of yoga.* London: Penguin.

Mehling, W. E., Wrubel, J., Daubenmier, J. J., Price, C. J., Kerr, C. E., Silow, T., Gopisetty, V., & Stewart, A. L. (2011). Body awareness: A phenomenological inquiry into the common ground of mind-body therapies. *Philosophy, Ethics, and Humanities in Medicine, 6,* 6. doi:10.1186/17475341-6-6

Miller, R. (2012). *The Samkhya Karika.* San Rafael, CA: Integrative Restoration Institute.

Muehsam, D., Lutgendorf, S., Mills, P. J., Rickhi, B., Chevalier, G., Bat, N., Chopra, D., & Gurfein, B. (2017). The embodied mind: A review on functional genomic and neurological correlates of mind-body therapies. *Neuroscience and Biobehavioral Reviews, 73,* 165–181. doi:10.1016/j.neubiorev.2016.12.027

Ostwald, M. (1962). *Aristotle: Nicomachean ethics.* Indianapolis: Library of Liberal Arts.

Park, G., & Thayer, J. F. (2014). From the heart to the mind: Cardiac vagal tone modulates top-down and bottom-up visual perception and attention to emotional stimuli. *Frontiers in Psychology, 5,* 278. doi:10.3389/fpsyg.2014.00278

Pascoe, M. C., & Bauer, I. E. (2015). A systematic review of randomised control trials on the effects of yoga on stress measures and mood. *Journal of Psychiatric Research, 68,* 270–282. doi:10.1016/j.jpsychires.2015.07.013

Payne, P., & Crane-Godreau, M. A. (2015). The preparatory set: A novel approach to understanding stress, trauma and the bodymind therapies. *Frontiers in Human Neuroscience, 9,* 178. doi:10.3389/fnhum.2015.00178

Porges, S. W. (1993). The infant's sixth sense: Awareness and regulation of bodily processes. *Zero to Three, 14,* 12–16.

Porges, S. W. (1995). Orienting in a defensive world: Mammalian modifications of our evolutionary heritage. A Polyvagal Theory. *Psychophysiology, 32,* 301–318. doi:10.1111/j.1469-8986.1995.tb01213.x

Porges, S. W. (1998). Love: An emergent property of the mammalian autonomic nervous system. *Psychoneuroendocrinology, 23,* 837–861. doi:10.1016/s03064530(98)00057-2

Porges, S. W. (2001). The Polyvagal Theory: Phylogenetic substrates of a social nervous system. *International Journal of Psychophysiology, 42,* 123–146. doi:10.1016/s01678760(01)00162-3

Porges, S. W. (2003). The Polyvagal Theory: Phylogenetic contributions to social behavior. *Physiology and Behavior, 79,* 503–513. doi:10.1016/s0031-9384(03)00156-2

Porges, S. W. (2004). Neuroception: A subconscious system for detecting threats and safety. *Zero to Three, 24,* 19–24.

Porges, S. W. (2007). The polyvagal perspective. *Biological Psychology, 74,* 116–143. doi:10.1016/j.biopsycho.2006.06.009

Porges, S. W. (2009). The Polyvagal Theory: New insights into adaptive reactions of the autonomic nervous system. *Cleveland Clinic Journal of Medicine, 76,* S86–S90. doi:10.3949/ccjm.76.s2.17

Porges, S. W. (2011). *The Polyvagal Theory: Neurophysiological foundations of emotions, attachment, communication, and self-regulation.* New York: Norton.

Porges, S. W. (2017). Vagal pathways: Portals to compassion. In E. M. Seppala (Ed.), *The Oxford handbook of compassion science* (pp. 189–202). New York: Oxford University Press.

Porges, S. W., & Carter, C. S. (2017). Polyvagal Theory and the social engagement system: Neurophysiological bridge between connectedness and health. In P. L. Gerbarg, P. R. Muskin, & R. P. Brown (Eds.), *Complementary and integrative treatments in psychiatric practice* (pp. 221–240). Arlington, VA: American Psychiatric Association.

Porges, S. W., Doussard-Roosevelt, J. A., & Maiti, A. K. (2008). Vagal tone and the physiological regulation of emotion. *Monographs of the Society for Research in Child Development, 59,* 167–186. doi:10.1111/j.1540-5834.1994.tb01283.x

Porges, S. W., & Kolacz, J. (2018). Neurocardiology through the lens of the Polyvagal Theory. In R. J. Gelpi & B. Buchholz (Eds.), *Neurocardiology: Pathophysiological aspects and* clinical implications (pp. 343-351). Amsterdam: Elsevier.

Resnick, B., Galik, E., Dorsey, S., Scheve, A., & Gutkin, S. (2011). Reliability and validity testing of the physical resilience measure. *Gerontologist, 51,* 643–652. doi:10.1093/geront/gnr016

Sarang, P., & Telles, S. (2006). Effects of two yoga based relaxation techniques on heart rate variability (HRV). *International Journal of Stress Management, 13,* 460–475.

Schmalzl, L., Powers, C., & Henje Blom, E. (2015). Neurophysiological and neurocognitive mechanisms underlying the effects of yoga-based practices: Towards a comprehensive theoretical framework. *Frontiers in Human Neuroscience, 9,* 235. doi:10.3389/fnhum.2015.00235

Singleton, M. (2010). *Yoga body: The origins of modern posture practice.* New York: Oxford University Press.

Smith, R., Thayer, J. F., Khalsa, S. S., & Lane, R. D. (2017). The hierarchical basis of neurovisceral integration. *Neuroscience and Biobehavioral Reviews, 75,* 274–296. doi:10.1016/j.neubiorev.2017.02.003

Stoler-Miller, B. (1998). *Yoga: Discipline of freedom.* New York: Bantam.

Stoler-Miller, B. (Trans.). (2004). *The Bhagavad-Gita.* New York: Bantam Classics.

Streeter, C. C., Gerbarg, P. L., Saper, R. B., Ciraulo, D. A., & Brown, R. P. (2012). Effects of yoga on the autonomic nervous system, gamma-aminobutyric-acid and allostasis in epilepsy, depression and post-traumatic stress disorder. *Medical Hypotheses, 78,* 571–579. doi:10.1016/j.mehy.2012.01.021

Strigo, I. A., & Craig, A. D. (2016). Interoception, homeostatic emotions and sympathovagal balance. *Philosophical Transactions of the Royal Society of London, B: Biological Sciences, 371,* 20160010. doi:10.1098/rstb.2016.0010

Sullivan, M. B., Moonaz, S., Weber, K., Taylor, J. N., & Schmalzl, L. (2018). Toward an explanatory framework for yoga therapy informed by philosophical and ethical perspectives. *Alternative Therapies in Health and Medicine, 24,* 38–47.

Taylor, A. G., Goehler, L. E., Galper, D. I., Innes, K. E., & Bourguignon, C. (2010). Top-down and bottom-up mechanisms in mind-body medicine: Development of an integrative framework for psychophysiological research. *Explore, 6,* 29–41. doi:10.1016/j.explore.2009.10.004

Telles, S., Sharma, S. K., Gupta, R. K., Bhardwaj, A. K., & Balkrishna, A. (2016). Heart rate variability in chronic low back pain patients randomized to yoga or standard care. *BMC Complementary and Alternative Medicine, 16,* 279. doi:10.1186/s12906016-1271-1

Thayer, J. F., & Lane, R. D. (2000). A model of neurovisceral integration in emotion regulation and dysregulation. *Journal of Affective Disorders, 61* 201–216. doi:10.1016/s0165-0327(00)00338-4

Tsuji, H., Venditti, F. J., Jr., Manders, E. S., Evans, J. C., Larson, M. G., Feldman, C. L., & Levy, D. (1994). Reduced heart rate variability and mortality risk in an elderly cohort. The Framingham Heart Study. *Circulation, 90,* 878–883. doi:10.1161/01.cir.90.2.878

Tugade, M. M., & Fredrickson, B. L. (2004). Resilient individuals use positive emotions to bounce back from negative emotional experiences. *Journal of Personality and Social Psychology, 86,* 320–333. doi:10.1037/0022-3514.86.2.320

Tugade, M. M., & Fredrickson, B. L. (2007). Regulation of positive emotions: Emotion regulation strategies that promote resilience. *Journal of Happiness Studies, 8,* 311–333. doi:10.1007/s10902-006-9015-4

Tyagi, A., & Cohen, M. (2016). Yoga and heart rate variability: A comprehensive review of the literature. *International Journal of Yoga, 9,* 97–113. doi:10.4103/0973-6131.183712

Whitson, H. E., Duan-Porter, W., Schmader, K. E., Morey, M. C., Cohen, H. J., & Colón-Emeric, C. S. (2016). Physical resilience in older adults: Systematic review and development of an emerging construct. *Journals of Gerontology, A: Biological Sciences and Medical Sciences, 71,* 489–495. doi:10.1093/gerona/glv202

CHAPTER 6

Mindfulness-Based Movement
A Polyvagal Perspective

Alexander R. Lucas, Heidi D. Klepin, Stephen W. Porges, and W. Jack Rejeski

Exercise Is Medicine is a global health initiative managed by the American College of Sports Medicine, which encourages primary care physicians and other health care providers to include exercise in the treatment plan for patients. Although there is strong empirical support for the health benefits of exercise, rates of recidivism are high, and the thought of exercise does not resonate well with many patients who are frequently overweight and burdened by physical symptoms, and often have limitations in physical capacities. Also, exercise does not negate the ill effects of excessive sedentary behavior. In this chapter, we focus on cancer, introducing the concept of mindfulness-based movement (MBM), a novel intervention that cuts across the continuum of physical activity.

There are three fundamental tenets that serve as the scaffolding for this intervention. First, MBM is conceptually rooted in Polyvagal Theory (Porges, 2007). Second, it is important to move and to move often, no matter how simple or limited the movement may be. Third, all movement—simple or complex, low demand or high demand—deserves participants' full attention. This orientation creates opportunities for embodied and relational experience; movement becomes a state of being rather than doing (Kabat-Zinn, 1994). And fourth, as symptoms and conditions permit, patients should experiment with and have goals for both decreasing sedentary behavior and increasing moderate to vigorous levels of physical activity.

As a brief overview for the reader, MBM represents an intervention for promoting a broad range of physical activity behaviors both during and following cancer treatment. It acknowledges the substantial health benefits that can be derived from both reducing sedentary behavior and increasing moderate to vigorous forms of physical activity. MBM is delivered as a group-mediated intervention, fostering positive emotions as well as the relational and playful nature of various forms of movement. Consistent with the view of Porges (2015, Chapter 3), play-oriented forms of physical activity that involve engagement with others constitute a neural exercise, helping patients transition from aroused motoric states associated with physical movements to calm states. Polyvagal Theory, which serves as the foundation for MBM, posits that recruiting and exercising the social engagement system is the go-to default activity that humans use to modulate stress. This capacity resides within the social engagement system because positive face-to-face interactions activate neural pathways through the vagus nerve that downregulate the sympathetic activation associated with both exercise and stress.

From the perspective of Polyvagal Theory, MBM functions as a neural exercise in which physiological state is manipulated by exercise, social engagement, and mindful focused attention. During calm states in which the social engagement system is functioning, the social cues from voice and face maintain a physiology of safety characterized by a strong vagal influence to the heart that supports health, growth, and restoration. Exercise requires an increase in cardiac output through both a removal of vagal inhibition and an increase in sympathetic influences on the heart. The time course of alternating physical activity and social engagement behaviors provides opportunities to exercise the neural regulation of the autonomic nervous system. Through repeated withdrawal of vagal inhibition to support movement and the recovery of vagal inhibition, the autonomic nervous system develops and promotes a more efficient shift from a physiological state of arousal to calm. Opportunities to enhance neural regulation of the autonomic nervous system are becoming relevant in the treatment of cancer, with findings linking autonomic nervous system function to outcomes in prostate and breast cancer (Couck et al., 2016; Magnon et al., 2013).

The chapter is divided into four sections. First, we briefly overview the field of physical activity in the context of cancer care and control. Second, we examine the concept of mindfulness as applied to cancer, emphasizing how it relates to embodiment and human relationships. Third, we discuss in detail the value of MBM, laying the groundwork for the fourth and final section, which details MBM from the perspective of Polyvagal Theory.

THE ROLE OF PHYSICAL ACTIVITY IN CANCER CARE AND CONTROL

Physical activity has received increasing attention in the context of cancer care and control. A key feature of MBM is that it encompasses the entire continuum

FIGURE 6.1.   Physical activity continuum.

of physical activity. The rationale for this decision is developed and reinforced throughout the chapter. Briefly, as shown in Figure 6.1, movement is inherent in a range of activities, from postural shifts to activities of daily living, and in leisure pursuits that involve light to vigorous exercise. Of particular importance is both reducing time spent in sedentary behavior to the left and increasing time in light- and higher-intensity activities in the middle and to the right of the continuum.

Some of the first studies to examine physical activity with cancer patients were performed in the 1980s by MacVicar, Winningham, and colleagues (MacVicar et al., 1989; Winningham & MacVicar, 1988; Winningham et al., 1989). A total of 45 breast cancer patients receiving adjuvant chemotherapy were randomized to one of three conditions: (a) 10 weeks of high-intensity aerobic exercise, (b) stretching/flexibility, or (c) a control group. The exercise intervention was found to be safe and resulted in positive changes in aerobic capacity, body composition, and self-reported nausea. Since then, there has been a significant increase in physical activity research from prediagnosis to palliative care. The physical exercise across the cancer experience (PEACE) framework is a conceptual model that is useful in identifying specific time points, prediagnosis and postdiagnosis or during and following treatment, when physical activity may be of most benefit (Figure 6.2) (Courneya & Friedenreich, 2001, 2007). In the current chapter, we use the term *survivors* to refer to persons in long-term care toward the right of the cancer continuum, whereas patients are those in active treatments closer to diagnosis.

Courneya (2014) has argued that, for cancer research involving physical activity to flourish, investigators need to specify how physical activity may be linked to cancer variables. Cancer variables can be either disease or treatment related. How these variables interact with one another and with various types of movement across the physical activity continuum (Figure 6.1) will shape each individual's response and ultimately health outcomes. There are four main types of relationships in this framework: cancer variables can be (a) outcomes of physical activity such as mortality, (b) moderators of health outcomes associated with physical activity, (c) determinants of adherence to physical activity, and (d) moderators of the known determinants of physical activity. It is important to recognize that whereas moderate to vigorous physical activity is important, reduction of sedentary behavior is an independent predictor of adverse health

FIGURE 6.2. PEACE Framework (adapted from Courneya & Friedenreich, 2001, p. 243). Reprinted from *Seminars in Oncology Nursing*, 23(4), Kerry S. Courneya and Christine M. Friedenreich, "Physical Activity and Cancer Control," 242–252, © 2007, with permission from Elsevier.

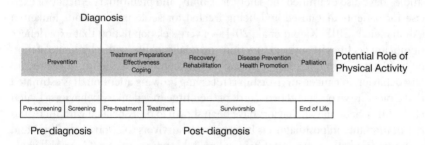

outcomes (Healy et al., 2008; Lynch, 2010; Seguin et al., 2012). Furthermore, for some patients or at a particular stage of cancer, the only reasonable goal may be reducing sedentary behavior.

To date, physical activity research on cancer has focused primarily on exercise for survivors of breast, prostate, and colorectal cancer. More recently, research has expanded to include a variety of disease subtypes and has also included patients who are undergoing treatment (Schmitz et al., 2005; Speck et al., 2010). For example, a question of interest is whether physical activity can reduce the adverse effects of primary cancer therapies because, for certain cancers, these therapies are known to be cardiotoxic (Jones et al., 2007, 2009). There is also a growing understanding of the negative effects of high levels of sedentary behavior, independent of time spent in higher-intensity activities, on morbidity and mortality. However, it is not yet clear how much or what type of physical activity is necessary in these circumstances and whether the effects are uniform or moderated by factors such as demographics, medical history, or genetic profiles.

A systematic review and meta-analysis of 82 randomized controlled trials of physical activity interventions both during and following treatment, including 66 high-quality studies, found that exercise resulted in large effects on muscular strength, moderate effects on fatigue and breast cancer–specific concerns, and small to moderate effects on physical activity level, cardiovascular fitness, and quality of life during treatment. Overall physical activity was found to be safe, feasible, and efficacious for patients undergoing a variety of treatment modalities (Speck et al., 2010). Prostate cancer patients who receive treatment with androgen deprivation therapy are prone to experience a loss of muscle mass and increases in adipose tissue deposition, potentially leading to functional decline, disability, and loss of independence (Boxer et al., 2005; Bylow et al., 2007, 2008). Evidence suggests that engaging in physical activity from the onset of androgen deprivation therapy may offer one way of offsetting these musculoskeletal changes and protecting against functional decline (Bourke et al., 2016; Segal et al., 2003). Recent studies have also examined the safety, feasibility, and preliminary efficacy of exercise for patients diagnosed and being treated for acute myelogenous leukemia (Alibhai et al., 2012; Klepin et al., 2011)—a very sick population that experiences significant declines in physical function and quality of life, with a high rate of mortality. On the other end of the physical activity continuum, the impact of sedentary behavior on cancer survivorship is receiving growing attention. It is estimated that cancer survivors spend two-thirds of their time in sedentary behaviors (Lynch et al., 2010). Sedentary behaviors have been shown to be associated with increased risk of mortality in postdiagnosis breast cancer survivors (Nelson et al., 2016) and with increased all-cause mortality in colorectal cancer survivors (Campbell et al., 2013). A harmonized analysis with data from three large breast cancer cohorts found that there was a 22% (hazard ratio = 1.22; 95% CI = 1.05, 1.42) increased risk of breast cancer mortality for women considered to be sedentary, even when controlling for the effects of comorbidities (Nelson et al., 2016). The high levels of sedentary behavior among cancer survivors and a lack of data on the biological mechanisms through which increased sedentary behavior affects health makes this a significant topic for future scientific inquiry (Lynch et al., 2013).

Despite the merits of physical activity for cancer patients and survivors, adherence to guidelines has been disappointing (Bellizzi et al., 2005; Mowls et al., 2016). Of note, breast cancer survivors have been found to engage in higher levels of moderate to vigorous physical activity compared with healthy women, yet they also have much higher levels of sedentary behavior (Phillips et al., 2015), a finding that supports the focus both for reducing sedentary behavior and increasing moderate to vigorous physical activity (Nicklas et al., 2014). In addition, for cancer patients undergoing active therapies, focusing on sedentary behavior allows for greater flexibility in patient-centered goals and increases the likelihood that patients will remain active beyond the supervised care setting. High competing care demands, symptoms, and functional decline are all barriers to cancer patients being physically active. If we further burden patients with a single-minded approach of increasing moderate to vigorous physical activity, we may well be setting patients up for failure.

MINDFULNESS AND MINDFULNESS-BASED INTERVENTIONS FOR CANCER

Over the past 20 years, a growing body of literature has supported the therapeutic value of mindfulness-based interventions (MBIs) in the treatment of cancer patients (Baer et al., 2004; Shennan et al., 2011; Smith et al., 2005; Zainal et al., 2013). In brief, meta-analytic studies of MBIs and cancer have reported moderate effect sizes on anxiety and somewhat smaller but significant effect sizes on depression (Cramer et al., 2012; Piet et al., 2012; Zainal et al., 2013). Positive effects have also been reported for enhanced well-being (Branstrom et al., 2012; Hoffman et al., 2012) and improved quality of life (McNeely et al., 2006); there is some evidence that MBIs have favorable effects on biomarkers of health and aging, including more favorable slopes for daily cortisol levels (Carlson et al., 2013) and improved telomere length (Carlson et al., 2015). In an article from the *Annals of the New York Academy of Sciences*, Carlson (2016) stated that support for the efficacy of MBIs in cancer is unequivocal.

As we demonstrate throughout this chapter, a working definition of the mind is critical to the concept of mindfulness and to the structure of MBM. As defined by Siegel, "The human mind is a relational and embodied process that regulates the flow of energy and information" (2010, p. 52). That is, one can view the mind as a process that establishes a network to support the flow of energy and information between the body, brain, and relationships (see Figure 6.3). As emphasized in our own work, the relational nature of the mind enables important connections not only with other people, but with the surrounding environment as well (Rejeski & Gauvin, 2013). The embodied nature of the mind underscores the fact that the body plays a central role in how people regulate energy and information flow that is then processed by the brain. A well-known example is the effect of different types of breathing techniques on anxiety (Chen et al., 2017). Further evidence comes from the role that intestinal microbes play in shaping both mood and behavior (Friedrich, 2015). It is also important to emphasize that the embodied and relational mind are interdependent; synergy between the two is essential to human thriving, a proposition that is central to Polyvagal Theory (Porges, 2007). Specifically, in early infancy, a secure attachment relationship between mother and child affects the flow of

FIGURE 6.3.   The mind: an embodied and relational process.

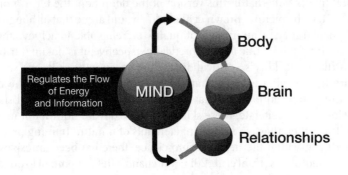

information to skeletal muscles and to the heart in a manner that downregu-lates states of defense by increasing cardiac vagal tone and promoting feelings of safety and human connection—the body has direct effects on shaping the brain but, in this case, in collaboration with interpersonal connection.

So what is mindfulness? In 2007, Brown and colleagues published a sem-inal article arguing that, as a psychological construct, mindfulness is "recep-tive attention to and conscious awareness of present events and experience" (p. 212), a definition that reflected early ideas articulated by Kabat-Zinn, who in 1990 suggested that "simply put, mindfulness is moment-to-moment awareness. It is cultivated by purposefully paying attention to things we ordinarily never give a moment's thought to" (p. 2). Brown et al. (2007) pointed out that aware-ness involves the conscious registration of events and experience—that it is our most proximal contact with reality. Particularly important to understanding the boundaries of this construct is the following passage from their article:

> Commonly, sensory objects are held in focal awareness only briefly, if at all, before some cognitive and emotional reaction to them is made. These rapid per-ceptual reactions have several characteristics of relevance to subjective experi-ence and functioning: First, they are often of a discriminative nature, in which a primary appraisal of the object is made as, most basically, "good," "bad," or "neu-tral," usually in reference to the self. Second, they are usually conditioned by past experience of the sensory object or other objects of sufficient similarity to evoke an association in memory. Third, perceptual experience is easily assimilated or, through further cognitive operations upon the object made to assimilate into existing cognitive schemas. The consequence of such processing is that concepts, labels, and judgments are often imposed, often automatically, on everything that is encountered. (Brown et al., 2007, p. 212)

Prior to this publication and subsequent to it, a number of authors expanded on the definition of mindfulness that was offered by Kabat-Zinn in 1990. In fact, in 1994, Kabat-Zinn himself stated that mindfulness involved "paying attention in a particular way; that is, on purpose, in the present moment, and nonjudg-mentally" (p. 4). Note that in this version of the definition, the term "nonjudg-mental" enters the picture. Brown et al. (2007) would argue that although being nonjudgmental may be an important quality of being able to achieve mindful awareness, from a scientific and theoretical perspective, it is not an attribute of the construct itself. This is a critical distinction because the skills and strategies necessary to achieving mindful states of awareness are central to the design of behavioral interventions that have the goal of promoting mindful states of being. However, to reiterate, these skills and strategies are not what it means to be mindful; rather, they are important elements of mindful training programs.

Interestingly, within the field of neuroscience, there has been an explosion of interest in mindfulness (Dahl et al., 2015; Marchand, 2014). Important to our discussion is the position espoused by Siegel (2007) that the mindful brain is an embodied, nonconceptual state of consciousness that has a strong relational orientation. In fact, the conceptual self, which is largely a product of the left hemisphere, can be a barrier to achieving mindful awareness (McGilchrist, 2009) because, as emphasized by Brown et al. (2007), the conceptual self filters and spins the raw experience of awareness for its own self-interest or protection. Porges (2007) also argues, as have others, that the brain has an evolutionary bias to protect humans from harm; thus, it expends a great deal of time as a watchtower for threat. However, according to Porges, Polyvagal Theory provides an understanding of the cues of safety that are embedded in positive social engagement behaviors, including prosodic voice, endearing facial expressions, and welcoming gestures that are capable of reflexively turning off vigilance and enable an individual to feel safe. Fredrickson (2001) posits that this evolutionary bias of the brain can be countered by the intentional experience of positive emotion, moving one toward brain states that promote openness, curiosity, and creativity—the "broaden and build" theory of positive emotion.

The theories posited by Porges (2007) and Fredrickson (2001) are particularly relevant to the design of MBIs from two perspectives. First, both emphasize the critical role of relationships to human thriving. In fact, the fundamental tenet of Polyvagal Theory is that the brain is a social organ that does not require conscious awareness to respond appropriately and reciprocally to cues of social engagement. And second, as shown by Fredrickson and colleagues, repeated conscious awareness of positive affect from relational experience enhances vagal tone and is a powerful enabling force in promoting positive well-being (Kok & Fredrickson, 2010) and the experience of embodied, nonconceptual self-awareness (Fogel, 2009).

Despite the value of being mindful in daily life (Brown et al., 2007), even under the best of circumstances, mindfulness can be difficult to achieve given our production-oriented society and its ever-increasing dependence on technology. For cancer patients, whose lives become fragmented by the disease and its treatment, the norm is to become preoccupied with the threat of physical symptoms and existential concerns, to get stuck in destructive modes of thinking and feeling about the conceptual self. As described by Carlson (2016), cancer results in most people experiencing significant fear, anxiety, and depression—life is no longer predictable or controllable. These emotional experiences are associated with an activation of the sympathetic nervous system, producing physiological states that support defense and are incompatible with mindfulness. Moreover, current research suggests chronic sympathetic activation without being constrained and regulated by vagal circuit is linked to poor outcomes following cancer diagnoses (Couck et al., 2016; Magnon et al., 2013). However, it is also important to recognize that despite the challenges of achieving mindful awareness in the face of cancer, most people do experience such states. This can occur when listening to a piece of music, gazing upon a scene in nature, or thinking about a loved one. The goal in MBIs is to help people access these states more readily and frequently.

Humans are relational beings and will engage readily in social interactions when they feel safe from harm (Porges, 2007). A diagnosis of cancer can disrupt the balance in people's lives and can serve to disconnect patients from their own bodies. Ongoing treatments can lead to physical deconditioning that places patients at risk of losing their independence (Hewitt et al., 2003). The ability to function independently is critical to feeling autonomous, and cancer can easily morph into a traumatic experience. The question is, how can people who are dealing with a diagnosis and treatment for cancer be supported in returning to a more self-determined life? What does MBM offer beyond the current available options for lifestyle interventions in these populations?

BENEFITS OF AN MBM INTERVENTION FOR CANCER

To date, most research on MBIs in cancer has been modeled after Mindfulness-Based Stress Reduction (MBSR), developed by Kabat-Zinn (1990); however, a program known as Mindfulness-Based Cancer Recovery includes material specific to coping with cancer, fear of recurrence, management of physical symptoms, and key principles related to cognitive coping strategies adapted from cognitive-behavioral therapy (Carlson et al., 2013, 2015). These modifications to MBSR are important because promoting mindful states of being requires intervening on factors that derail cancer patients and survivors from achieving such states. In this section, we discuss three distinct structural and conceptual innovations of an MBM intervention.

Whereas physical activity has favorable effects on the heart and improves metabolic, autonomic, inflammatory, and immune function, the ability of physical activity to rebuild the physical self for cancer patients and its potential to reestablish functioning in both social and physical roles are clear priorities as patient-centered outcomes. Additionally, cancer treatment has deleterious effects on the brain; physical activity may prove to be a viable antidote to declining brain health and associated cognitive decline (Cormie et al., 2015; Li et al., 2016). Whereas previous MBIs utilize gentle yoga and/or walking meditation, there is not an explicit focus on the benefits of physical activity per se. Of interest are reports that cancer patients express an interest in alternative therapies such as yoga and tai chi. As Porges (2007) has reported, when the autonomic nervous system is out of balance, people have a tendency to unconsciously self-select, engaging in such activities in an attempt to counter their discomfort. Hence, there is a strong conceptual rationale for the integration of mindfulness-based skills with exercise therapy.

Other innovations of MBM include the following: (a) promoting movement across a broad range of activities, (b) fostering the mindset that physical activity can be used to cultivate a sense of "being" rather than "doing" (Kabat-Zinn, 1994), and (c) using the power of a group-mediated approach to treatment. Let us first consider promoting a range of activities as opposed to an exclusive focus on moderate to vigorous physical activity. The advantages of such a perspective are considerable because sedentary behavior is an independent risk factor for compromised health and functional fitness beyond the effects of moderate to vigorous physical activity (Edwardson et al., 2012; Healy et al., 2011; Santos et al., 2012; Wilmot et al., 2012). Also, we have found that sedentary behavior interventions are well tolerated and valued by sedentary populations (Nicklas et al., 2014). Ultimately, what we seek to achieve with MBM is acceptance of the highs and lows of life—a central tenet of mindfulness (Kabat-Zinn, 1990)—and developing an understanding and awareness of the role that even simple movements play in our physical and emotional lives. A greater awareness of moment-to-moment movement is a cornerstone of MBM and of mindful awareness (Kabat-Zinn, 1990, 1994).

Second, MBM focuses on using movement as a time of being rather than doing (Kabat-Zinn, 1990). Too often, exercise is approached as an additional chore or commitment to add to daily life—something else to do. This orientation can be daunting for people with a chronic disease who are already overwhelmed by treatment regimens. In addition, this mindset risks fragmenting from movement the embodied and relational value of such experience. This is unfortunate because both theory (Rothman, 2000) and research (Falk et al., 2015) underscore the important role that value has in the promotion and maintenance of health behavior. In contrast, MBM promotes active living as an opportunity to consciously connect with the body—the embodied mind—in moment-to-moment movements throughout the day. MBM is also used to promote the relational mind both with others and in conjunction with the physical environment. Part of this experience is rediscovering the value inherent in movement and how it affects our lives. Positive emotion promotes an increase in cardiac vagal tone (Fredrickson, 2001), enhances resilience, and helps people navigate painful life experience (Tugade et al., 2004), which are important steps in coping with loss.

And third, MBM is based on a model of group-mediated lifestyle behavior change that we developed and tested over the past 20 years on a variety of aging patient populations (Brawley et al., 2000; McDermott et al., 2012; Rejeski et al., 2003, 2009, 2011). Originally, we successfully used the group as a means of increasing motivation and developing self-regulatory skills; however, in our more recent trials, we have expanded the scope of treatment to focus more on the relational value of the group experience (Marsh et al., 2013). By creating and fostering a safe and supportive environment for participants, MBM provides an opportunity for participants to develop a heartfelt connection with one another. A critical part of this process is the shared challenge that patients face with the cancer experience and, in particular, the feeling of common humanity. As Neff and colleagues have shown (Neff, 2003; Neff et al., 2007), a sense of common humanity—seeing one's experience as shared by others—is a core feature of developing self-compassion, which is central to psychological well-being. In

fact, we have shown that a group-mediated exercise intervention for patients
with peripheral artery disease substantially increased patients' social resources
as compared with those in a health education control group (Rejeski et al.,
2014). We have also applied this group-based approach to promoting adop-
tion and adherence to physical activity and dietary behavior in prostate cancer
patients undergoing androgen deprivation therapy (Focht et al., 2014).

MBM AND CANCER: A POLYVAGAL PERSPECTIVE

As noted in the introduction to this chapter, the conceptual model (Figure 6.4)
for MBM has its foundation in Polyvagal Theory (Porges, 2007). A central tenet
of this theory, rooted in evolution, is that the most basic human need or motive
is safety. From a developmental perspective, it is no accident that safety is first
secured through a successful infant-mother attachment relationship, making
the social engagement system described in Polyvagal Theory a key feature of
managing threat. The social engagement system involves the regulation of the
muscles of the face and head and the heart through motor fibers of five cranial
nerves (i.e., special visceral efferent pathways) that originate in the brainstem.
This system enables emotional communication through facial expressions and
prosodic vocalizations, enhances listening to voices, and calms the physiological and behavioral state by increasing vagal influence to the heart through
a branch of the vagus originating in the nucleus ambiguus. Functionally, the
social engagement system can be collectively described as the ventral vagal
complex. In fact, in the absence of safety, the second most basic human need
is to reduce threat; however, the removal of threat is not sufficient to trigger the
neural circuits that support connectedness and health, growth, and restoration.

The relevance of Polyvagal Theory in the management of cancer is that,
as mentioned earlier, the disease and its treatment constitute a traumatic
experience—whether real or imagined, cancer is often life-threatening. However, even if one's life is not threatened, the cancer experience strikes at the very
fabric of patients' day-to-day lives. For example, in prostate and breast cancer,
the effects of surgeries and radiation therapy can be devastating to the self-
image and sexuality of survivors. The ability to interact in intimate and mean-
ingful ways with partners and significant others as well as to perform social roles
can be compromised, and valued leisure activities may be lost.

When threatening events occur, particularly severe threat, Polyvagal Theory (Porges, 2007) proposes that one of three phylogenetically ordered networks
is innervated. The networks range from newer, highly developed responses to
primitive, survival-mode reactions. The latter occur only when more highly
developed networks are rendered ineffective. First, it is possible that people find
safety through attuned social interaction and that the threat is neutralized or
becomes manageable. According to Polyvagal Theory, interpersonal attunement
involves a heartfelt connection with another human being that is manifested

FIGURE 6.4.   The polyvagal perspective of mindfulness-based movement.

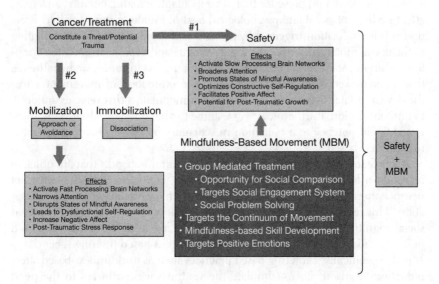

in the behavioral features of the social engagement system and an increase in cardiac vagal tone mediated through the ventral vagal complex. This hypothesis is supported in the findings of a study focused on autonomic flexibility, where it was shown that cardiac vagal tone was associated with the degree to which people felt connected and socially engaged over a nine-week period (Kok & Fredrickson, 2010). Individuals with higher initial levels of cardiac vagal tone experienced greater self-reported social connectivity and social engagement. Interestingly, those people who also reported an increase in their social connection and engagement also had greater increases in cardiac vagal tone, independent of levels at baseline. The work of Cozolino (2010) has also explored the neurobiology of attachment and how it has shaped the social and cultural evolution of humans and their communities. It is this experience of interpersonal attachment that provides theoretical support for the group-mediated approach of MBM. A second possible reaction is activation of the sympathetic nervous system and the hypothalamic-pituitary-adrenal (HPA) axis, preparing the individual for mobilization. However, there are actually two directions mobilization can take: (a) It can result in direct action to neutralize the threat, or (b) it may invoke psychological defenses such as avoidance. Whereas mobilization through direct action is functional in the face of acute stressors, chronic activation of the HPA axis leads to systemwide dysregulation and is known to have adverse effects on the hippocampus (Sapolsky et al., 1985). Additionally, although avoiding threat may seem adaptive at a conscious level, avoidance results in threat having a chronic unconscious presence that disrupts adaptive neural circuitry adversely, affecting both physical and psychological health. Finally, a third possible direction is immobilization triggered by activation of vagal motor fibers originating in the dorsal motor nucleus of the vagus. Fatigue and depression are often symptoms of an immobilization response to trauma. In this instance, we hypothesize that reducing sedentary behavior through the promotion of movement across the day stimulates dopamine and other neuromodulators that serve as antidotes to immobilization. Furthermore, as we argue further on in our discussion, there is additional potency to a reduction in sedentary behavior when movement is mindfulness based.

A key feature of threat is that it mobilizes neural networks that are quick to respond—a fast circuit (Ledoux, 1994)—which, consistent with the construct neuroception, bypass brain structures involved in conscious cognitive deliberation. This reduces the utility of conscious models of behavior change such as social cognitive theory (Bandura, 1991) until such time as the threat has passed or is neutralized. This is precisely why mindfulness-based training is central to MBM. Specifically, centering-based practices such as mindfulness-based stress reduction (Carlson, 2012) stimulate the ventral vagal pathways to the heart (Tang et al., 2009; Wu & Lo, 2008) and encourage the activation of the slow brain circuit (Ledoux, 1994). This slow circuit potentiates processes such as conscious self-regulation of behavior, self-reflection, and the opportunity for posttraumatic growth that has been a reported consequence of cancer and other chronic diseases (Danhauer et al., 2015; Morris et al., 2012).

What do we actually mean by mindful movement? And why is movement, particularly mindful movement, a viable intervention from the perspective of Polyvagal Theory? First, it is important to note that humans can be characterized as having the capacity for two distinct forms of movement: (a) movement of the body in space, activities that are supported by the spinal nerves; and (b) movement of the muscles of the face and middle ear, controlled by the cranial nerves. As a central feature of Polyvagal Theory (Porges, 2007), movement of the muscles of the face and middle ear facilitate reciprocal social interactions and the experience of attachment—interpersonal attunement. Indeed, as mentioned previously, research by Fredrickson and colleagues (Fredrickson, 2001; Kok & Fredrickson, 2010) has shown that social connection facilitates positive affect, which increases the calming effect of the vagus on the heart. Additionally, however, being attuned with another person is an experience in mindful awareness, as is attunement with our bodies as we move, or attunement with physical environments in which our lives are embedded. In essence, our hypothesis is that mindful awareness is mediated by regulating the ventral vagus as one totally embraces the present moment through movement in both physical and psychological space. There is a coherent integration between the spinal and cranial nerves that support human movement. Within this context, MBM is an active neural exercise that promotes resilience and improves the efficiency and effectiveness of engaging and disengaging the calming ventral vagal pathways to adjust the cardiac output necessary for movement. MBM promotes the experience of a heartfelt connection between participants by (a) providing a safe and supportive environment where (b) cancer survivors can share their experiences with others who can relate to and empathize with one another, and by (c) providing a specific set of tools and techniques for breaking up periods of immobilization, thereby engaging in opportunities to move within a social and physical environment. Finally, MBM aims to teach participants how to self-regulate their own behavior by first developing an awareness of their experience and then applying the skills learned though the MBM program. As we noted in the previous section of this chapter, too often, physical activity and engagement with life are experienced as a series of exercises—things to do on the treadmill of living productively—rather than an experience of being a part of life, fully engaged and playfully connected in an embodied and relational manner in moment-to-moment existence.

SUMMARY

In summary, there are significant health benefits to a lifestyle that includes physical activity, especially for people living with cancer. However, cancer patients and survivors face challenges in either returning to activity or beginning an active lifestyle following the disease and its treatment. As we have argued in our presentation of MBM, there is an advantage in promoting activity across the continuum of physical activity, teaching patients and survivors to appreciate the continuous flow of movement across the day and being mindfully aware as they do so. Polyvagal Theory offers a sound conceptual perspective for delivering MBM. The theory posits that for people to engage in approach behaviors that help foster social engagement and human development, they first need to feel safe. The theory also posits that when the social engagement system with the ventral vagal complex is functioning optimally, the older components of the autonomic nervous system (i.e., sympathetic nervous system, dorsal vagal complex) support health, growth, and restoration. In contrast, when the social engagement system is not functioning optimally, the older components assume control, with the main goal of activating cognitive and behavioral defensive strategies. Consistent with this model, research illustrates that the older components of the autonomic nervous system are involved in the initiation and proliferation of prostate cancer (Magnon et al., 2013), whereas greater ventral vagal regulation (indexed by heart rate variability) increased postdiagnosis survival duration in metastatic pancreatic cancer (Couck et al., 2016). The structure of social groups and communities can be one way of providing this safety and support, helping people identify opportunities for positive affective experience and reinforce relationships through movement and social connection—the core of MBM. Finally, we believe that MBM provides a vehicle to experience the embodied and relational nature of the mind, reconnecting people with the meaning and value inherent in being active rather than viewing physical activity as just another thing to do in the context of the challenges posed by cancer and its treatment.

REFERENCES

Alibhai, S. M. H., O'Neill, S., Fisher-Schlombs, K., Breunis, H., Brandwein, J. M., Timilshina, N., Tomlinson, G. A., Klepin, H. D., & Culos-Reed, S. N. (2012). A clinical trial of supervised exercise for adult inpatients with acute myeloid leukemia (AML) undergoing induction chemotherapy. *Leukemia Research, 36*, 1255–1261.

Baer, R. A., Smith, G. T., & Allen, K. B. (2004). Assessment of mindfulness by self-report: The Kentucky inventory of mindfulness skills. *Assessment, 11*, 191–206.

Bandura, A. (1991). Self-efficacy mechanism in physiological activation and health-promoting behavior. In J. Madden (Ed.), *Neurobiology of learning, emotion, and affect* (pp. 229–269). New York: Raven.

Bellizzi, K. M., Rowland, J. H., Jeffery, D. D., & McNeel, T. (2005). Health behaviors of cancer survivors: Examining opportunities for cancer control intervention. *Journal of Clinical Oncology, 23*, 8884–8893.

Bourke, L., Smith, D., Steed, L., Hooper, R., Carter, A., Catto, J., Albertsen, P. C., Tombal, B., Payne, H. A., & Rosario, D. J. (2016). Exercise for men with prostate cancer: A systematic review and meta-analysis. *European Urology, 69*, 693–703.

Boxer, R. S., Kenny, A. M., Dowsett, R., & Taxel, P. (2005). The effect of 6 months of androgen deprivation therapy on muscle and fat mass in older men with localized prostate cancer. *Aging Male, 8*, 207–212.

Branstrom, R., Kvillemo, P., & Moskowitz, J. T. (2012). A randomized study of the effects of mindfulness training on psychological well-being and symptoms of stress in patients treated for cancer at 6-month follow-up. *International Journal of Behavioral Medicine, 19*, 535–542.

Brawley, L. R., Rejeski, W. J., & Lutes, L. (2000). A group-mediated cognitive-behavioral intervention for increasing adherence to physical activity in older adults. *Journal of Applied Biobehavioral Research, 5*, 47–65.

Brown, K. W., Ryan, R. A., & Creswell, J. D. (2007). Mindfulness: Theoretical foundations and evidence for its salutary effects. *Psychological Inquiry, 18*, 211–237.

Bylow, K., Dale, W., Mustian, K., Stadler, W. M., Rodin, M., Hall, W., Lachs, L., & Mohile, S. G. (2008). Falls and physical performance deficits in older patients with prostate cancer undergoing androgen deprivation therapy. *Urology, 72*, 422–427.

Bylow, K., Mohile, S. G., Stadler, W. M., & Dale, W. (2007). Does androgen-deprivation therapy accelerate the development of frailty in older men with prostate cancer? A conceptual review. *Cancer, 110*, 2604–2613.

Campbell, P. T., Patel, A. V., Newton, C. C., Jacobs, E. J., & Gapstur, S. M. (2013). Associations of recreational physical activity and leisure time spent sitting with colorectal cancer survival. *Journal of Clinical Oncology, 31*, 876–885.

Carlson, L. E. (2012). Mindfulness-based interventions for physical conditions: A narrative review evaluating levels of evidence. *ISRN Psychiatry, 2012*, 651583.

Carlson, L. E. (2016). Mindfulness-based interventions for coping with cancer. *Annals of the New York Academy of Sciences, 1373,* 5–12.

Carlson, L. E., Beattie, T. L., Giese-Davis, J., Faris, P., Tamagawa, R., Fick, L. J., Degelman, E. S., & Speca, M. (2015). Mindfulness-based cancer recovery and supportive-expressive therapy maintain telomere length relative to controls in distressed breast cancer survivors. *Cancer, 121,* 476–484.

Carlson, L. E., Doll, R., Stephen, J., Faris, P., Tamagawa, R., Drysdale, E., & Speca, M. (2013). Randomized controlled trial of mindfulness-based cancer recovery versus supportive expressive group therapy for distressed survivors of breast cancer. *Journal of Clinical Oncology, 31,* 3119–3126.

Chen, Y. F., Huang, X. Y., Chien, C. H., & Cheng, J. F. (2017). The effectiveness of diaphragmatic breathing relaxation training for reducing anxiety. *Perspectives in Psychiatric Care, 53,* 329–336.

Cormie, P., Nowak, A. K., Chambers, S. K., Galvao, D. A., & Newton, R. U. (2015). The potential role of exercise in neuro-oncology. *Frontiers in Oncology, 5,* 85.

Couck, M. D., Marechal, R., Moorthamers, S., Laethem, J. L., & Gidron, Y. (2016). Vagal nerve activity predicts overall survival in metastatic pancreatic cancer, mediated by inflammation. *Cancer Epidemiology, 40,* 47–51.

Courneya, K. S. (2014). Physical activity and cancer survivorship: A simple framework for a complex field. *Exercise and Sport Sciences Reviews, 42,* 102–109.

Courneya, K. S., & Friedenreich, C. M. (2001). Framework PEACE: An organizational model for examining physical exercise across the cancer experience. *Annals of Behavioral Medicine, 23,* 263–272.

Courneya, K. S., & Friedenreich, C. M. (2007). Physical activity and cancer control. *Seminars in Oncology Nursing, 23,* 242–252.

Cozolino, L. (2010). *The neuroscience of psychotherapy: Healing the social brain.* Norton Series on Interpersonal Neurobiology. New York: Norton.

Cramer, H., Lauche, R., Paul, A., & Dobos, G. (2012). Mindfulness-based stress reduction for breast cancer: A systematic review and meta-analysis. *Current Oncology, 19,* e343–e352.

Dahl, C. J., Lutz, A., & Davidson, R. J. (2015). Reconstructing and deconstructing the self: Cognitive mechanisms in meditation practice. *Trends in Cognitive Science, 19,* 515–523.

Danhauer, S. C., Russell, G., Case, L. D., Sohl, S. J., Tedeschi, R. G., Addington, E. L., Triplett, K., Van Zee, K. J., Naftalis, E. Z., Levine, B., & Avis, N. E. (2015). Trajectories of posttraumatic growth and associated characteristics in women with breast cancer. *Annals of Behavioral Medicine 49,* 650–659.

Edwardson, C. L., Gorely, T., Davies, M. J., Gray, L. J., Khunti, K., Wilmot, E. G., Yates, T., & Biddle, S. J. H. (2012). Association of sedentary behaviour with metabolic syndrome: A meta-analysis. *PLoS One, 7,* e34916.

Falk, E. B., O'Donnell, M. B., Cascio, C. N., Tinney, F., Kang, Y., Lieberman, M. D., Taylor, S. E., An, L., Resnicow, K., & Strecher, V. J. (2015). Self-affirmation alters the brain's response to health messages and subsequent behavior change. *Proceedings of the National Academy of Sciences USA, 112,* 1977–1982.

Focht, B. C., Lucas, A. R., Grainger, E., Simpson, C., Thomas-Ahner, J.M., & Clinton, S. K. (2014). The Individualized Diet and Exercise Adherence Pilot Trial (IDEA-P) in prostate cancer patients undergoing androgen deprivation therapy: Study protocol for a randomized controlled trial. *Trials, 15,* 354.

Fogel, A. (2009). *The psychophysiology of self-awareness.* New York: Norton.

Fredrickson, B. L. (2001). The role of positive emotions in positive psychology: The broaden-and-build theory of positive emotions. *American Psychology, 56,* 218–226.

Friedrich, M. J. (2015). Unraveling the influence of gut microbes on the mind. *JAMA, 313,* 1699–1701.

Healy, G. N., Dunstan, D. W., Salmon, J., Shaw, J. E., Zimmet, P. Z., & Owen, N. (2008). Television time and continuous metabolic risk in physically active adults. *Medicine and Science in Sports and Exercise, 40,* 639–645.

Healy, G. N., Matthews, C. E., Dunstan, D. W., Winkler, E. A., & Owen, N. (2011). Sedentary time and cardio-metabolic biomarkers in US adults: NHANES 2003-06. *European Heart Journal, 32,* 590–597.

Hewitt, M., Rowland, J. H., & Yancik, R. (2003). Cancer survivors in the United States: Age, health, and disability. *Journal of Gerontology, A: Biological Science and Medical Science, 58,* 82–91.

Hoffman, C. J., Ersser, S. J., Hopkinson, J. B., Nicholls, P. G., Harrington, J. E., & Thomas, P. W. (2012). Effectiveness of mindfulness-based stress reduction in mood, breast- and endocrine-related quality of life, and well-being in stage 0 to III breast cancer: A randomized, controlled trial. *Journal of Clinical Oncology, 30,* 1335–1342.

Jones, L. W., Eves, N. D., Haykowsky, M., Freedland, S. J., & Mackey, J. R. (2009). Exercise intolerance in cancer and the role of exercise therapy to reverse dysfunction. *Lancet Oncology, 10,* 598–605.

Jones, L. W., Haykowsky, M. J., Swartz, J. J., Douglas, P. S., & Mackey, J. R. (2007). Early breast cancer therapy and cardiovascular injury. *Journal of the American College of Cardiology, 50,* 1435–1441.

Kabat-Zinn, J. (1990). *Full catastrophe living.* New York: Dell.

Kabat-Zinn, J. (1994). *Wherever you go, there you are: Mindfulness meditation in everyday life.* New York: Hyperion.

Klepin, H. D., Danhauer, S. C., Tooze, J. A., & Stott, K. (2011). Exercise for older adult inpatients with acute myelogenous leukemia: A pilot study. *Journal of Geriatric Oncology, 2,* 11–17.

Kok, B. E., & Fredrickson, B. L. (2010). Upward spirals of the heart: Autonomic flexibility, as indexed by vagal tone, reciprocally and prospectively predicts positive emotions and social connectedness. *Biological Psychology, 85,* 432–436.

Ledoux, J. E. (1994). Emotion, memory and the brain. *Scientific American, 270*(6), 50–57.

Li, C., Zhou, C., & Li, R. (2016). Can exercise ameliorate aromatase inhibitor-induced cognitive decline in breast cancer patients? *Molecular Neurobiology, 53,* 4238–4246.

Lynch, B. M. (2010). Sedentary behavior and cancer: A systematic review of the literature and proposed biological mechanisms. *Cancer Epidemiology, Biomarkers and Prevention, 19,* 2691–2709.

Lynch, B. M., Dunstan, D. W., Healy, G. N., Winkler, E., Eakin, E., & Owen, N. (2010). Objectively measured physical activity and sedentary time of breast cancer survivors, and associations with adiposity: Findings from NHANES (2003-2006). *Cancer Causes and Control, 21,* 283–288.

Lynch, B. M., Dunstan, D. W., Vallance, J. K., & Owen, N. (2013). Don't take cancer sitting down. *Cancer, 119,* 1928–1935.

MacVicar, M. G., Winningham, M. L., & Nickel, J. L. (1989). Effects of aerobic inter-val training on cancer patients' functional capacity. *Nursing Research, 38*, 348–351.

Magnon, C., Hall, S. J., Lin, J., Xue, X., Gerber, L., Freedland, S. J., & Fren-ette, P. S. (2013). Autonomic nerve development contributes to prostate cancer pro-gression. *Science, 341*, 1236361.

Marchand, W. R. (2014). Neural mechanisms of mindfulness and meditation: Evidence from neuroimaging studies. *World Journal of Radiology, 6*, 471–479.

Marsh, A. P., Janssen, J. A., Ambrosius, W. T., Burdette, J. H., Gaukstern, J. E., Morgan, A. R., Nesbit, B. A., Paolini, J. B., Sheedy, J. L., & Rejeski, W. J. (2013). The Cooper-ative Lifestyle Intervention Program-II (CLIP-II): Design and methods. *Contempo-rary Clinical Trials, 36*, 382–393.

McDermott, M. M., Domanchuk, K., Liu, K., Guralnik, J. M., Tian, L., Criqui, M. H., Ferrucci, L., Kibbe, M., Jones, D. L., Pearce, W. H., Zhao, L., Spring, B., & Rejeski, W. J. (2012). The Group Oriented Arterial Leg Study (GOALS) to improve walking performance in patients with peripheral arterial disease. *Contemporary Clinical Trials, 33*, 1311–1320.

McGilchrist, I. (2009). *The master and his emissary: The divided brain and the making of the Western world*. New Haven, CT: Yale University Press.

McNeely, M. L., Campbell, K. L., Rowe, B. H., Klassen, T. P., Mackey, J. R., & Cour-neya, K. S. (2006). Effects of exercise on breast cancer patients and survivors: A systematic review and meta-analysis. *Canadian Medical Association Journal, 175*, 34–41.

Morris, B. A., Shakespeare-Finch, J., & Scott, J. L. (2012). Posttraumatic growth after cancer: The importance of health-related benefits and newfound compassion for others. *Supportive Care in Cancer, 20*, 749–756.

Mowls, D. S., Brame, L. S., Martinez, S. A., & Beebe, L. A. (2016). Lifestyle behaviors among US cancer survivors. *Journal of Cancer Survivorship, 10*, 692–698.

Neff, K. (2003). Self-compassion: An alternative conceptualization of a healthy attitude toward oneself. *Self Identity, 2*, 85–101.

Neff, K. D., Kirkpatrick, K. L., & Rude, S. S. (2007). Self-compassion and adaptive psy-chological functioning. *Journal of Research in Personality, 41*, 139–154.

Nelson, S. H., Marinac, C. R., Patterson, R. E., Nechuta, S. J., Flatt, S. W., Caan, B. J., Kwan, M. L., Poole, E. M., Chen, W. Y., Shu, X.-O., & Pierce, J. P. (2016). Impact of very low physical activity, BMI, and comorbidities on mortality among breast cancer survivors. *Breast Cancer Research and Treatment, 155*, 551–557.

Nicklas, B. J., Gaukstern, J. E., Beavers, K. M., Newman, J. C., Leng, X., & Rejeski, W. J. (2014). Self-monitoring of spontaneous physical activity and sedentary behavior to prevent weight regain in older adults. *Obesity (Silver Spring), 22*, 1406–1412.

Phillips, S. M., Dodd, K. W., Steeves, J., McClain, J., Alfano, C. M., & McAuley, E. (2015). Physical activity and sedentary behavior in breast cancer survivors: New insight into activity patterns and potential intervention targets. *Gynecologic Oncol-ogy, 138*, 398–404.

Piet, J., Wurtzen, H., & Zachariae, R. (2012). The effect of mindfulness-based therapy on symptoms of anxiety and depression in adult cancer patients and survivors: A systematic review and meta-analysis. *Journal of Consulting and Clinical Psychology, 80*, 1007–1020.

Porges, S. W. (2007). The polyvagal perspective. *Biological Psychology, 74,* 116–143.

Porges, S. W. (2015). Play as neural exercise: Insights from the Polyvagal Theory. In D. Pearce-McCall (Ed.), *The power of play for mind-brain health* (pp. 3–7) [ebook]. MindGAINS.

Rejeski, W. J., Brawley, L. R., Ambrosius, W. T., Brubaker, P. H., Focht, B. C., Foy, C. G., & Fox, L. D. (2003). Older adults with chronic disease: Benefits of group-mediated counseling in the promotion of physically active lifestyles. *Health Psychology, 22,* 414–423.

Rejeski, W. J., Brubaker, P. H., Goff, D. C., Bearon, L. B., McClelland, J. W., Perri, M. G., & Ambrosius, W. A. (2011). Translating weight loss and physical activity programs into the community to preserve mobility in older, obese adults in poor cardiovascular health. *Archives of Internal Medicine, 171,* 880–886.

Rejeski, W. J., & Gauvin, L. (2013). The embodied and relational nature of the mind: Implications for clinical interventions in aging individuals and populations. *Clinical Interventions in Aging, 8,* 657–665.

Rejeski, W. J., Marsh, A. P., Chmelo, E., Prescott, A. J., Dobrosielski, M., Walkup, M. P., Espeland, M., Miller, M. E., & Kritchevsky, S. (2009). The Lifestyle Interventions and Independence for Elders Pilot (LIFE-P): 2-year follow-up. *Journal of Gerontology A: Biological Science and Medical Science, 64,* 462–467.

Rejeski, W. J., Spring, B., Domanchuk, K., Tao, H., Tian, L., Zhao, L., & McDermott, M. M. (2014). A group-mediated, home-based physical activity intervention for patients with peripheral artery disease: Effects on social and psychological function. *Journal of Translational Medicine, 12,* 29.

Rothman, A. J. (2000). Toward a theory-based analysis of behavioral maintenance. *Health Psychology, 19*(1, Suppl.), 64–69.

Santos, D. A., Silva, A. M., Baptista, F., Santos, R., Vale, S., Mota, J., & Sardinha, L. B. (2012). Sedentary behavior and physical activity are independently related to functional fitness in older adults. *Experimental Gerontology, 47,* 908–912.

Sapolsky, R. M., Krey, L. C., & McEwen, B. S. (1985). Prolonged glucocorticoid exposure reduces hippocampal neuron number: Implications for aging. *Journal of Neuroscience, 5,* 1222–1227.

Schmitz, K. H., Holtzman, J., Courneya, K. S., Masse, L. C., Duval, S., & Kane, R. (2005). Controlled physical activity trials in cancer survivors: A systematic review and meta-analysis. *Cancer Epidemiology, Biomarkers and Prevention, 14,* 1588–1595.

Segal, R. J., Reid, R. D., Courneya, K. S., Malone, S. C., Parliament, M. B., Scott, C. G., Venner, P. M., Quinney, H. A., Jones, L. W., Slovinec D'Angelo, M. E., & Wells, G. A. (2003). Resistance exercise in men receiving androgen deprivation therapy for prostate cancer. *Journal of Clinical Oncology, 21,* 1653–1659.

Seguin, R., Lamonte, M., Tinker, L., Woods, N., Michael, Y. L., Bushnell, C., & LaCroix, A. Z. (2012). Sedentary behavior and physical function decline in older women: Findings from the women's health initiative. *Journal of Aging Research, 2012,* 271589.

Shennan, C., Payne, S., & Fenlon, D. (2011). What is the evidence for the use of mindfulness-based interventions in cancer care? A review. *Psycho-oncology, 20,* 681–697.

Siegel, D. (2007). *The mindful brain.* New York: Norton.

Siegel, D. (2010). *Mindsight*. New York: Bantam.

Smith, J. E., Richardson, J., Hoffman, C., & Pilkington, K. (2005). Mindfulness-based stress reduction as supportive therapy in cancer care: Systematic review. *Journal of Advanced Nursing, 52,* 315–327.

Speck, R. M., Courneya, K. S., Masse, L. C., Duval, S., & Schmitz, K. H. (2010). An update of controlled physical activity trials in cancer survivors: A systematic review and meta-analysis. *Journal of Cancer Survivorship, 4,* 87–100.

Tang, Y. Y., Ma, Y., Fan, Y., Feng, H., Wang, J., Feng, S., Lu, Q., Hu, B., Lin, Y., Li, J., Zhang, Y., Wang, Y., Zhou, L., & Fan, M. (2009). Central and autonomic nervous system interaction is altered by short-term meditation. *Proceedings of the National Academy of Sciences USA, 106,* 8865–8870.

Tugade, M. M., Fredrickson, B. L., & Barrett, L. F. (2004). Psychological resilience and positive emotional granularity: Examining the benefits of positive emotions on coping and health. *Journal of Personality Assessment, 72,* 1161–1190.

Wilmot, E. G., Edwardson, C. L., Achana, F. A., Davies, M. J., Gorely, T., Gray, L. J., Khunti, K., Yates, T., & Biddle, S. J. H. (2012). Sedentary time in adults and the association with diabetes, cardiovascular disease and death: Systematic review and meta-analysis. *Diabetologia, 55,* 2895–2905.

Winningham, M. L., & MacVicar, M. G. (1988). The effect of aerobic exercise on patient reports of nausea. *Oncology Nursing Forum, 15,* 447–450.

Winningham, M. L., MacVicar, M. G., Bondoc, M., Anderson, J. I., Minton, J. P. (1989). Effect of aerobic exercise on body weight and composition in patients with breast cancer on adjuvant chemotherapy. *Oncology Nursing Forum, 16,* 683–689.

Wu, S. D., & Lo, P. C. (2008). Inward-attention meditation increases parasympathetic activity: A study based on heart rate variability. *Biomedical Research, 29,* 245–250.

Zainal, N. Z., Booth, S., & Huppert, F. A. (2013). The efficacy of mindfulness-based stress reduction on mental health of breast cancer patients: A meta-analysis. *Psycho-oncology, 22,* 1457–1465.

CHAPTER 7

Group Psychotherapy
as a Neural Exercise
Bridging Polyvagal Theory
and Attachment Theory

Philip J. Flores and Stephen W. Porges

While Bowlby's (1988) attachment theory has had a tremendous impact on the world of child development and adult psychotherapy during the past 25 years, it has gained added legitimacy from the neurosciences (Porges, 2011; Schore, 2003; Siegel, 1999). Since many features of attachment theory are implicitly dependent on the neurophysiological mechanisms described in Polyvagal Theory, the infusion of Polyvagal Theory helps shift the perspective of attachment from a strictly psychological theory to a more integrated biobehavioral theory. Further, Polyvagal Theory provides a conceptual bridge between basic scientific inquiry and practical clinical application by offering a new paradigm to explain the biobehavioral intricacies of social behaviors that occur during child development and are expressed as adult attachment. The theory offers a unique perspective that not only describes the neural mechanisms involved in attachment, but also provides a clinical model to guide more effective treatment. The theory informs intervention strategies that exercise the neural circuits involved in the social engagement system, a system that optimizes secure attachment.

Secure attachment not only translates into a greater capacity for emotional regulation and resilience, it also influences our bias to react to challenges through a process known as neuroception. Neuroception, as elaborated in Polyvagal Theory, is the capacity of the nervous system to evaluate risk in the environment without conscious awareness. Polyvagal Theory elaborates on this process, helping shift the description of attachment to include dynamic interactions between social engagement systems. This process involves neural exercises promoting enhanced physiological and behavioral state regulation. The product of these exercises provides a more resilient neural substrate for the regulation of affect and interpersonal behaviors that can be used outside of therapy. While it is important for attachment to occur, the neural exercises regulating physiological state via neural (vagal) mechanisms provide the biobehavioral flexibility necessary to promote resilient and adaptable behavioral and emotional regulation.

Within the context of translating Polyvagal Theory into clinical application, a neurophysiological perspective is introduced to help explain the importance of safety in psychotherapy and all prosocial human encounters. The theory introduces a novel process, neuroception, to describe how the nervous system evaluates risk in a situation or a person. This process is not learned, nor are we aware of the cues that trigger our feelings of safety, danger, or life threat. The process is neural and was refined through evolution. If safety is detected, a bias toward social engagement behaviors is potentiated. However, in an absence of cues of safety, a bias toward defensive mobilization (fight-flight) or defensive immobilization (becoming inanimate) is primed for activation. Turning off or preventing the triggering of the autonomic nervous system into states of defense is necessary before a strategy occurs, with the benefits of restoring healthy homeostasis and optimizing social interactions.

Polyvagal Theory informs us that, as social mammals, we must not forget our phylogenetic heritage and emphasizes that evolution equipped us with an innate ability to maintain and regulate our autonomic nervous system to support homeostasis through the reciprocity and synchronization of face-to-face social interactions. Thus, a neural link between our physiological state and the expressions of our face and the intonation of our voice evolved into an integrated social engagement system. This social engagement system, which operates predominantly through the cranial nerves regulating the muscles of the face and head, enables our social interactions to effortlessly regulate our physiological state.

POLYVAGAL THEORY: AN INTRODUCTION

Polyvagal Theory changes the theme of how the relation between our bodily processes and our psychological experiences is conceptualized. The theory accomplishes this by presenting an innovative explanation of the relationship between behavior and the state of the autonomic nervous system that is paradigm changing. Historically, the autonomic system has been described as having two branches, the sympathetic and the parasympathetic. Previous explanations of autonomic nervous system functioning had ignored the important role of sensory feedback from the visceral organs on brain processes and the hierarchical nature of autonomic reactivity to environmental challenges.

The theory articulates two defense systems: (1) the commonly known fight-or-flight system that is associated with activation of the sympathetic nervous system, and (2) a less-known system of immobilization and dissociation that is associated with activation of a phylogenetically more ancient vagal pathway. The theory emphasizes a hierarchical relation among components of the autonomic nervous system that evolved to support adaptive behaviors in response to the particular environmental challenges of safety, danger, and life threat (Porges, 2011). There are two vagal circuits: an evolutionarily ancient vagal circuit associated with immobilization defense and a phylogenetically newer circuit emerging with mammals related to calm states and spontaneous social behavior in safe environments. This innovation expands on a previous and more limited model that assumed the autonomic nervous system (i.e., through the sympathetic nervous system) supported only one defense strategy: fight-flight behaviors. The old model did not provide an explanation of the autonomic state that would support dissociation, freeze, collapse, shutdown, or death feigning, which many individuals experience, especially when faced with a life threat like rape, physical assault, or war.

The Quest for Safety as a Biological Imperative

The ability to differentially respond to safe and dangerous environments has been built into our evolutionary heritage. To survive, humans, as well as other mammals, needed to identify danger and rapidly determine which situations were safe or dangerous. Thus, the human nervous system evolved to be sensitive not only to the physical features in the environment, but also to the intentionality of movements and social interactions that may either trigger or dampen defensive physiological reactivity. In a safe environment, when the nervous system is no longer vigilant in anticipation of danger cues, there is a qualitative shift in physiological state that has a profound impact on psychological states like depression, anger, and anxiety. A physiological safe state is better able to function as a neural platform capable of facilitating circuits involved in optimizing mental and physical health. Without the appropriate contextual cues of safety and without the body shifting into a physiological state of calmness, attempts to support health will be challenging and often ineffective.

Physiological States Limit the Range of Psychological States

Our psychological processes are constrained by our physiological states, and these states are influenced by our responses to threat, safety, and uncertainty in our relationships and in our environment. Polyvagal Theory, by offering a biobehavioral translation of these bidirectional processes, contributes to a better understanding of the neural basis of attachment, emotional disorders, and affect regulation. The theory can also help us understand how to leverage this knowledge into the development of a more effective model of group treatment. Missing from more traditional approaches to group therapy has been a cogent articulation of the implicit neural mechanisms involved in explaining how and why interpersonal emotional engagement plays such a crucial part in all forms of treatment.

Group Psychotherapy, Attachment, and Polyvagal Theory

At first glance, translating the implications of Polyvagal Theory for guiding the application of clinical interventions in group therapy may appear to be an arduous task. However, if Polyvagal Theory is carefully examined, one will ultimately discover a natural complementary synergy between the basic tenets underlying the theory's explanation of the evolutionarily determined relationship between autonomic state and behavior and the theoretical foundations that guide not only attachment theory but all psychodynamic, interpersonal, and relationally oriented models of group psychotherapy (Flores, 2010; Grossmark & Wright, 2015; Ormont, 1992; Rutan et al., 2014; Yalom & Leszcz, 2005). Because the relational models of group therapy inherently provide a social environment that requires its members to emotionally engage each other interpersonally in recurring face-to-face social interactions, it naturally promotes many of the most crucial elements necessary for the promotion of the neural substrates required for attachment and affect regulation.

This chapter offers an explanation of how a properly constructed group therapy model, represented by an interpersonal perspective and the relational models of psychodynamic theory, can provide a theoretical foundation that is complementary and accommodating to the principles of Polyvagal Theory. An approach to group treatment based on these psychotherapy models also provides an ideal neural exercise regimen that is inherently suited to provide opportunities for strengthening the social engagement system that will improve our social communication, neuroception, and affect regulation. This continuing opportunity for exercising neural circuits that dampen sympathetic tone (fight-flight defenses), while simultaneously enhancing the detection of cues of safety in the face and voice of another, is essential for fostering prosocial behavior, affect regulation, and well-being, both psychologically and physiologically.

UTILIZING THE SOCIAL ENGAGEMENT SYSTEM: A CASE EXAMPLE OF PROMOTING AFFECT REGULATION IN GROUPS

Interpersonal emotion regulation and the establishment of coregulatory relationships are central features of our psychological lives and a barometer of our physical and psychological health. Despite assumptions to the contrary, the crucial importance of the capacity for affect regulation is not biologically guaranteed or innately hardwired into our nervous system at birth. The new discoveries of epigenetics, neuroplasticity, and neurogenesis have provided evidence for the ongoing need for continual practice and exercising of the essential neural platforms that evolution designed as crucial to keeping our social engagement system operating efficiently throughout our life span.

The following vignette illustrates the principles behind the employment of group psychotherapy as a neural exercise. Notice how the themes of safety, social engagement, emotional communication, and the recruitment of neuroception to facilitate implicit nonverbal communication are incorporated into this therapy group.

After studying nonstop for months for the oral defense of her dissertation, Sarah learns from her dissertation chair that the scheduled meeting for her defense has been postponed because of concerns about her data analysis. Frightened, confused, and distraught, Sarah arrives later that afternoon at a therapy group she has been attending weekly for the past eight months. Sarah sits quietly, noticeably distracted during the first 45 minutes of the meeting. When there is a brief pause, Betty, another member of the group, leans forward in her chair, looks at Sarah, and asks softly, "Sarah, are you okay?" Sarah immediately bursts into tears. A quiet, respectful hush settles over the group as all eyes turn toward her. The group waits for Sarah's crying to ease before Charley, another member, gently asks, "What's wrong? Has something happened?" Sarah proceeds to explain the events of the morning, expressing doubts about her competence and her ability to salvage her dissertation. The group presses for more details before Carl, a vividly outspoken member of the group, eventually erupts in anger. "What bullshit! I am so furious at your dissertation chair. Why wait to the last minute to give you this kind of feedback?" Sarah's eyes open wide. She clenches her fists, smiles cautiously, and nods vigorously in agreement. A chorus of group members joins Carl in his anger about her chairperson's callousness.

The group leader watches Sarah's reactions to Carl's anger carefully. The leader observes that the group is providing Sarah a shared experience of healthy protest, the kind that is required when someone feels violated or treated unfairly. Carl and the other group members are amplifying Sarah's experience of an emotion she lacks access to at the time—a healthy aggression needed for self-protection and the pursuit of fair treatment in relationships. Her absence of boldness also contributes to the erosion of self-confidence, reflecting an internal self-representation experienced as weak while others are perceived as powerful. Sarah's deficiency in assertiveness was demonstrated even at the beginning of the group, when she had to be recruited by another member to speak even though it was obvious that she was troubled and in a great deal of emotional discomfort when she first sat down. Sarah's restrained smile and clenched fist are implicitly conveying a new emerging comfort and pleasure with a previously forbidden emotion. The group is facilitating a newly emerging internal representation of herself and others.

Robert, another member of the group and a faculty professor at a local university, smiles softly at Sarah and proceeds to tenderly describe a similar struggle he had completing his dissertation nearly a decade before. Robert has typically been one of the more stoic, intellectual members of the group, and a tear in the corner of his eye and the gentleness in his voice have a calming influence on the entire group, deepening the intensity of the feelings within the room. Two other group members commiserate with Sarah about the terror organic chemistry is known to inspire, and to offer her assurances that they have confidence in her ability to salvage her dissertation. Another member hands her a box of tissues. Sarah wipes away her tears and manages a fragile smile in response to their support. Carl returns to his anger at the injustice of Sarah's treatment by her advisor and, with a twinkle in his eye, growls, "I think we all ought to storm his office and demonstrate our outrage." To everyone's surprise, Sally, who is usually quiet and timid, uncharacteristically raises her fist and spontaneously shouts, "Power to the people!" The group, including Sarah, erupts into laughter and begins cheering and chanting, "Power to Sarah! Power to Sarah!" After a few moments, the group settles into a quietly satisfied shared presence with Sarah.

At this point, the group leader takes the opportunity to ask Sarah to look around the group and encourages her to make eye contact with everyone. "What do you see and what do you feel at this moment as you look at people's faces in the group?" Sarah's look of defeat and apprehension has been replaced by confidence and conviction. Sarah scans the faces of the other group members, stopping briefly to look into Robert's eyes; they nod and smile at each other. "I see a lot of people that care and believe in me." Sarah sits up straight in her chair. She nods her head assertively. "I can make the changes that are necessary for me to salvage this dissertation."

It is clear in this clinical example that the group leader is not interested in focusing on diagnostic categories or hurling interpretations at Sarah's lack of assertiveness or Carl's excessive anger or suggesting that the group is in flight with their laughter and cheering. The group leader knows that playfulness, especially spontaneously induced adult play, is about transitions and reflects a lived shared experience that can occur only when group members feel safe and connected with each other. Play and the exploration of differences provide an important element of shared consideration, attention, and selflessness that aids in the development of the vagal brake—an increased flexibility in the autonomic nervous system essential for managing rapidly changing arousal states and the efficient, fluid shifting of emotional positions—a physiological capacity essential for managing all authentic relationships. The therapist focuses instead on the wide spectrum of shared emotional experiences in the group, the kind that preside in all authentic ongoing healthy relationships. The leader remains diligent in monitoring whether the group is able to experience the full range of emotions that are occurring in the group at this moment.

We see how important it is for the members to be empathic with one another as they share their experiences and take risks. Sarah is quiet for the first 45 minutes of the session and avoidant of expressing her needs or feelings in the group. A fellow group member reaches out to Sarah with curiosity and invites her to share her experience. This invitation triggers sadness, crying, and self-doubt. We detect evidence reflective of an insecure attachment style where Sarah blames herself and is fearful of conflict and her own anger. Her conditioned response is to be silent and then to turn on herself. During the group session, the other group members are not only sensitive to her sadness but are attuned to her underlying anger. The group's capacity to express a broader range of emotions is critical because it fosters Sarah's ability to protest and move from avoidance of these feelings to being able to tolerate emotions that usually are threatening to her. It is clear that the group is evoking a neuroception of safety for its members, who can now explore and experience feelings and thoughts that are typically forbidden or denied.

This is a group that's safe enough for members to reach out, take risks, and explore new behavior. While the group leader has been watching carefully how microviolations of neural expectancy and threat might be activating Sarah and the other members' psychological states, he is more interested in the implicit communication (prosody, facial expressions, eye contact, etc.) than their explicit verbal communication. The group leader recognizes that it is unlikely that Sarah will explicitly remember each group member's spoken words that were responsible for the shift in her emotional state; however, he is confident that the implicit communication of effort, kindness, and caring registered with her on an implicit level.

TASKS OF THE GROUP LEADER: THREE PRINCIPLES BASED ON POLYVAGAL THEORY

This section elaborates on how three polyvagal processes (i.e., neuroception, social engagement, and vagal brake) work during therapy to promote positive clinical outcomes. The group leader needs to understand these processes in order to integrate the recommendations put forth by Polyvagal Theory for increasing the effectiveness of group therapy:

1. Become familiar with the social and environmental features that bias neuroception and how this nonconscious neural process impacts a person's ability to discern between safety and threat.
2. Construct a group environment that utilizes environmental features to promote a neuroception of safety to downregulate defensiveness and

provide opportunities for the exercising of each group member's social
engagement system.
3. Exercise the vagal brake by providing repeated opportunities for group
    members to neutrally navigate through a sequence of states from calm, to
    vigilant, to startle, and back to calm.

If these principles of Polyvagal Theory are used to guide clinical interventions during group treatment, four essential outcomes will naturally emerge: (1)
improvement in both explicit and implicit affect regulation; (2) enhancement
of affect recognition and refining emotional literacy; (3) correction of faulty
neuroception; and (4) expansion of relational capacities by increasing acuity
in reading social cues and nonverbal implicit communication. Before we can
expect our group members to achieve any semblance of understanding what
their emotions and their body-based visceral feelings are communicating to
them and others, we must help them recognize and identify their emotions as
they are currently occurring in the group. We must assist them in becoming
aware of their visceral signals rather than avoiding them, by dissociating and
numbing them out, becoming frightened by their feelings, or acting them out.

UNDERSTANDING FAULTY NEUROCEPTION
AND THE BIOLOGICAL QUEST FOR SAFETY

Neuroception reflects our ability to evaluate the intentionality of biological
movement (bodily gestures, facial expressivity, and vocalization) in the service
of adapting to risk. Cues that trigger a neuroception of safety inhibit defensive
mobilization and enable the social engagement system to come online. Our
nervous system is on a constant quest to feel safe by finding people, situations,
and environments that are nonthreatening. We are constantly trying to negoti-
ate and navigate through a complex, stressful environment of challenges. These
challenges are manifested in the external environment that we are in, but also
through the emotional, visceral feedback of our internal physiological environment. Our body is constantly trying to interpret these signals and regulate our
physiological states.

Anytime a group therapist circles 8 to 10 chairs in a small room, he or she is
applying an intuitive understanding of neuroception, one of the essential processes of Polyvagal Theory. In order to develop a social bond, individuals have
to be in close proximity to each other. It also helps if the chairs are positioned
in a grouping that permits all members to have face-to-face contact with each
other via their social engagement systems. By optimizing opportunities for face-
to-face interactions, the muscles of the head producing gaze, facial expressions,
head movements, prosodic vocalizations, and enhanced listening via middle
ear muscles serve as expressive and receptive portals to neural circuits that acti-

vate the vagal system, shift neuroception, and stimulate the social engagement system. If the group leader provides safety and predictability, especially at the beginning of a new group, it will be virtually impossible for group members not to become attached to each other and for the group to become a secure base for its members. We involuntarily connect interpersonally when we experience safety, familiarity, and proximity with another safe person. Turning on a person's social engagement system makes it difficult for the defensive operations (fight-flight-freeze) of the autonomic nervous system to come online. Promoting a neuroception biased toward safety and implicit emotional communication, in contrast to a neuroception biased toward defense and explicit cognitive communication, will only help facilitate this process. For example, the simple act of encircling chairs in a way that promotes proximity and face-to-face interpersonal emotional engagement in a predictably safe environment starts the process of enhancing the neural mechanisms responsible for the emotional regulation of each group member's nervous system.

An important goal of group therapy involves attempts to expand group members' emotional awareness and to diffuse the disruptive effects of faulty neuroceptive reactions to stimuli that do not present a genuine threat. "Faulty neuroception" refers to situations that trigger defensive states that bias neuroception toward danger when there is no danger.

Polyvagal Theory informs us that the human nervous system provides two pathways for triggering the neural mechanisms capable of downregulating defense to enable states of calmness that support more accurate neuroception, learning, listening, understanding, health, spontaneous social behavior, and connectedness. There is a passive pathway and an active pathway to trigger mechanisms capable of downregulating defense to enable states of calmness by manipulating the clinical context in which group therapy is practiced. Physical features of the room that calm, soothe, and promote a feeling of safety through the process of neuroception are examples of the passive pathway. These features include a quiet setting, the circling of chairs, predictability, a peaceful environment, and starting and ending the group on time. The active pathway requires conscious voluntary behaviors that change the physiological state via the vagal brake and exercise the social engagement system by promoting face-to-face prosocial interactions, with an emphasis on emotional communication, synchronicity, reciprocity, compassion, congruence, and a keen sensitivity to the intentionality of biological movement (gestures, facial expressivity, prosody, and vocalization).

ACTIVATING THE SOCIAL ENGAGEMENT SYSTEM

When our neuroception appraises our environment as safe, defensive limbic structures are inhibited, enabling social engagement and calm visceral states to emerge. Providing continual opportunities for promoting face-to-face interpersonal interactions is the most crucial component of group psychotherapy for one very simple reason. As long as a person's social engagement system remains online, it will inhibit unnecessary activation of fight-flight and freeze defensive responses. From a Polyvagal Theory perspective, the active engagement of one person's social engagement system with another person's social engagement system lies at the heart of all psychotherapy, interpersonal learning, exploration, discovery, change, emotional regulation, and the maintenance of mutually gratifying relationships. Our social engagement systems work in tandem with neuroception to promote the development of a self at its best, which means a person is better able to read social cues, manage recurring coregulatory relationships, distinguish friend from foe, and develop a rich capacity for emotional literacy with self and others. A fuller range of access to empathy, compassion, playfulness, humor, and tolerance of differences is potentiated, resulting in a richer opportunity for lived experience and purpose in one's life. Self-awareness is also increased because an active social engagement system reduces and repairs distortions in faulty neuroception, inhibiting the unnecessary activation of the autonomic nervous system and the accompanying defensive operations of fight-flight or freeze.

During the evolutionary transition from reptiles to mammals, the neural regulation of the autonomic nervous system changed. Specifically, a branch of the vagus emerged from an area of the brainstem involved in the regulation of the muscles of the face and head, the components of the social engagement system. This new branch has myelinated motor fibers that function as an efficient and dynamically adjusting vagal brake (Porges et al., 1996). The vagal brake construct was introduced within Polyvagal Theory to describe the neurophysiological process through which rapid inhibition and disinhibition of cardiac vagal tone can quickly mobilize or calm an individual. Functionally and metaphorically, good cardiac vagal tone is similar to good muscle tone. Just as going to the gym to work out regularly improves muscle tone through doing push-ups and sit-ups, a good workout of the social engagement system in group strengthens the vagal brake, enabling it to efficiently modulate emotional arousal levels and visceral states. Ultimately, this improves a person's ability to rapidly engage and disengage with other individuals in the service of promoting self-soothing behaviors, cooperation, calm states, more accurate reading of social cues, and better reading of nonverbal social communication. The evidence is comprehensive and indisputable: A secure base is essential for healthy child development (Stern, 1995), a fulfilling satisfying marriage (Johnson, 2008), and successful psychotherapy treatment outcomes (Norcross, 2001). Evidence is equally robust documenting that enriched environments that provide optimal levels of arousal, excitement, and stimulation are essential for promoting neurogenesis, neuroplasticity, and general feelings of well-being, emotional stimulus, and happiness (Berns, 2005). This is also true for group psychotherapy. However, safety or a secure base in group therapy can often be misinterpreted as simply providing our group members with an environment or a relationship that is completely predictable and safe at all times. Not only is this unrealistic, it is not helpful. Safety is not a one-dimensional phenomenon. Safety or security is a more complex occurrence that prompts the experienced group leader to be constantly asking the question: Is it safe enough in this group for people to disagree, to hold opposing views, to challenge authority (the group leader), and to protest when they feel they are not being treated fairly or understood?

EXERCISING THE VAGAL BRAKE: A CLINICAL EXAMPLE

The next vignette illustrates how any approach to group psychotherapy that encourages spontaneous authentic interactions between group members will eventually result in an inevitable conflict between group members or with the group leader. Since interpersonal conflicts and disagreements are an integral part of all social interactions and close attachment relationships, relationally oriented group therapists welcome conflict since it presents the group with a valuable opportunity to experience and learn how the rupture, repair, and reunion processes can be some of the most beneficial components of successful treatment (Yalom & Leszcz, 2005). This is especially crucial since it is well documented that all dysfunctional relationships are marked by the absence of the repair process. This particular vignette draws on Polyvagal Theory's description of the vagal brake's role in regulating arousal states in the service of improving vagal tone, which potentiates the spontaneous reactivation of a person's social engagement system.

For over five years, Paul and Martha have been members of a psychotherapy group that meets weekly for an hour and a half. There are currently eight members in the group, five women and three men. At the start of this particular meeting, before anyone even had time to settle into their chairs, Martha immediately began the session by telling Angela that she went home from last week's meeting feeling "furious" at her. Angela was startled and surprised, as was the rest of the group, since nothing appeared to have happened in the last meeting that seemed unresolved. After Angela cautiously asked what she had done, Martha proceeded to lecture her about her "entitlement" as it related to Angela's description of a painful exchange she had had the week before with her demanding, narcissistic mother. Angela, as well as everyone else in the group, was initially taken aback by the strict harshness of the tone of Martha's voice and the stern, haughty look on Martha's face. After taking a few moments to recover from Martha's punishing judgment of her, Angela confessed that she could feel entitled at times and that Martha was correct in detecting this less-than-admirable quality she was ashamed to acknowledge. Angela's lack of defensiveness and forthcoming ownership of her entitlement did nothing to soften the look or tone of Martha's posture toward her. If anything, Martha's face took on an increased glare of self-righteous indignation. After a few moments, the group leader proceeded to ask how Martha felt about Angela's acknowledgment and nondefensive response to her confrontation. Martha shrugged indifferently before adding, "I still don't like it."

The group leader pushed the issue a little further. "Any idea of what feelings might be behind your intolerance of Angela's entitlement?" Martha quickly shook her head. "No, none at all!" Martha then glared at the group leader. "Listen, you aren't going to turn this around and make this about me!"

At this point, Paul, sitting across the room, erupted at Martha. "What do you mean entitlement? I have never seen any entitlement in Angela." The two of them proceeded to squabble with each other for a few minutes. While Martha's responses remained judgmental, stern, and steadfast, she kept control of the tone in her voice despite glaring at Paul with a look of utter contempt and a smirk on her face. Paul's anger steadily escalated into a tirade of shouting and swearing. "If you are not willing to look at your part in this, you ought to get the f–k out of the group!" The intensity of Paul's responses became alarming to the entire group, and although some of the members agreed with him, they felt that his shouting, cursing, and swearing at Martha was out of line. Paul refused to be persuaded by their concerns and continued with his bellowing, even though Martha had noticeably retreated from their exchange, stating, "This is going nowhere and you're frightening me."

Observing that the group was at an impasse, the group leader, guided by Polyvagal Theory, intervened. The leader tilted his head, leaned forward toward Paul, and spoke gently but firmly to shift Paul's attention away from Martha. Knowing that it is impossible for our nervous system to ignore head and upper body movement as well as facial expressions, the group leader took advantage of the fact that body movements always convey intentionality, naturally evoking a person's attention. Utilizing prosody to convey an absence of threat or arousal, the group leader made a calm request: "Paul, could you look at me for a second?" The group leader also knew that a person can listen and process verbal information more efficiently when there is eye contact because both processes require neural pathways involved in the social engagement system.

Conveying as much compassion as he could with his eyes, the group leader said gently and tenderly, "Paul, this is obviously stirring some very strong feelings in you. Can I ask you to stop shouting long enough for you to hear me?" Paul, breathing heavily, struggled to gain control of bodily responses. His sympathetic nervous system was clearly hyperaroused, and his vagal brake was offline. With concerted effort and because Paul had a long, trusting relationship with the group leader, he slowly nodded his head in agreement to the request. Because Paul's breathing was still labored, the group leader asked him to take a few slower, deep breaths because he knew that slow, steady exhalations activate the vagal brake, dampening the intensity of the fight-flight response.

The group therapist knew at this point that he was going to have to find a way to interrupt the emotional entanglement that Paul had with Martha and reach the part of Paul that their history together had provided as a safe haven. Eye contact and prosody were the two vehicles the group leader knew he needed to utilize at this point in order to reduce the level of Paul's arousal system. Paul was in full fight-flight mode. It took a few moments as Paul and the group leader maintained their engagement without involving the rest of the group. Paul's breathing gradually became less labored. At this point, the group leader asked if Paul would be willing to sit quietly for a few moments while he checked in with the rest of the group, assuring Paul that he would come back to him and Martha in a few minutes. The group leader knew it would take some time before Paul's arousal level could return to baseline, allowing him to feel calm enough to listen to feedback. Paul nodded yes, and Martha, looking noticeably relieved, quickly agreed.

The group leader knew he had to get the rest of the group involved and not allow the conflict to be contained by just two group members. The group leader spoke firmly, but softly. "What is the rest of the group feeling at this moment?" He allowed a brief pause before continuing, "I think we, as a group, have an opportunity to understand something important about ourselves as long as we don't allow Paul and Martha to carry this conflict for the entire group. This isn't just about them. This is about the group." The group proceeded to address how the exchange had impacted them, sometimes referring to similar events that had occurred in their own lives. Paul sat quietly, detached from the group, but with a distinct contemplative look on his face. After assessing that everyone in the group had managed to bring their social engagement system back online, the leader asked how Martha and Paul were doing.

Martha quickly replied, "I'm keeping quiet. I don't want to be attacked again." Paul responded to her. Speaking softly, with heartfelt earnestness, Paul proceeded to explain himself and apologize to her. "Martha, I don't want you to feel afraid of me or worry about me or anyone else in the group attacking you."

Maintaining eye contact with her, Paul gave her a reassuring smile. "And I definitely don't want you to leave the group. We've been through so much together in the five years we've been in group together. I don't want to lose you." Paul then explained to the entire group what he had been reflecting on for the last hour. He explained how the look of contempt and the smirk on Martha's face had triggered a series of old attachment wounds and past painful humiliations. Martha and the group had become intimately aware during their five years together of Paul's history with his mother, who had serially sexually abused him and his two brothers when they were children. "When you kept insisting that you saw Angela as entitled and I didn't, it triggered me. My mother would always try to tell me that what I saw or what she was doing wasn't really happening, and threatening her was the only way I could fight back to keep her from forcing herself and her version of reality down my throat. And when I or my brothers would ask her to look at the part she played in all the chaos, she always refused, saying it was all our fault." Martha's face softened immediately. Perceiving her to be in a moment of receptivity, the group leader asked if Paul's revelation had prompted any awareness in her. Martha swallowed and gave a knowing smile. "Oh, I realize a couple things for sure. Angela had become my brother, who was always my mother's entitled, favorite child, and I had become my critical, judgmental mother, who always expected her children to be perfect."

Not all ruptures are as dramatic as this clinical example. Most violations remain out of our conscious awareness. However, violations of neural expectancies are always recognized by the visceral response system wired into neuroception. Even though violations may sometimes be subtle, they remain encoded as a vague, uncomfortable experience of unknown origin or trigger. We are bombarded by violations throughout the day by a myriad of social interactions in a busy, stressful world. A passerby's friendly smile and greeting or a clerk's harsh scolding, "You have to wait your turn," leave a cumulative impact on whether we are having a good or a bad day. Evolution chose not to trust the detection of risk, danger, or safety to the slow track of conscious awareness to ensure survival. It is another variation of van der Kolk's maxim: "The body always keeps the score" (van der Kolk, 2014).

Disengaging from an individual whose social engagement system is primed to anticipate reciprocal and synchronous interactions with the cues of safety and trust violates a neural expectancy of safety and triggers a neuroception of defense, with the associated bodily reactions of fight-flight-freeze. Even minor disengagements can often elicit massive reactions in some individuals. The absence of a response (blank face, no eye contact, etc.) or even an indifferent, uninterested, or poorly emotionally attuned response (missing prosody, discounting of the emotional vulnerability or openness of the other person, totally intellectual and ignoring the emotional content of the engagement, etc.) can affect our mood or feelings about ourselves. Social experiences are associated with reciprocal and synchronous interactions that provide a neural expectancy of reciprocal and synchronous social engagement behaviors.

Group provides opportunities for experiences associated with a violation of the neural expectancy of reciprocal and synchronous interactions. The violation of this neural expectancy via neuroception immediately shifts the bodily state of the individual to a physiological state that supports defense—usually sympathetic activation to support flight-flight behaviors. Group also provides an opportunity to repair the consequences of the violation by completing the neural exercise of downregulating the defense reaction with the positive cues from the social engagement system of other group members. The neural exercise takes transitory defense reactions and diffuses them with a neural expectancy of safety and trust via prosodic voice, comforting gesture, and warm facial expressions. This is similar to a child playing peek-a-boo (Porges, 2015, Chapter 3). This shift from regulated social engagement (during which there is a neural expectancy for reciprocal social engagement cues), to disruptions in state due to violation of neural expectancy (neuroception of danger and triggers of visceral state that support defense strategies), to repairs of the disrupted system by a reengagement of the disrupted individual's social engagement system with cues of safety and trust constitutes the framework for group being conceptualized as a neural exercise that builds resilience. The ability to repair and be receptive to the repair emphasizes the dynamic nature and resilience of neural expectancy.

CONCLUSION

The notion of defining group psychotherapy as a neural exercise carries with it an implied conviction that there are advantages associated with approaching attachment theory and group treatment with a perspective that honors the neurophysiological contribution to behavioral and emotional difficulties. This shift in perspective reflects Polyvagal Theory's emphasis on the relationship between feelings and rational thought and the linking of nervous system regulation of biobehavioral state to mental and physical health while also understanding how nonverbal communication occurs at a level that is below conscious awareness.

Polyvagal Theory originally emerged from an understanding of the bidirectional relationship between our physiology (i.e., body) and our brain (i.e., mind). This conceptualization not only provided an understanding of brain-body interactions, but also incorporated an understanding of how social behavior is necessary for physical and mental health. At the core of Polyvagal Theory is the concept of how individuals coregulate their biobehavioral state. Mental health issues and behavioral problems are universally linked to an inability to coregulate, which is manifested in poor social relationships and emotional dysregulation. From a polyvagal perspective, group therapy is especially suited to provide the neural exercises required for promotion of the neural circuits involved in coregulation and emotional regulation.

Polyvagal Theory also expands our notion of what constitutes the mind by increasing our understanding of the concept of "embodied cognition" (Bargh, 2014) or "embodied brain" (Fonagy et al., 2002), helping shift psychodynamic theory from a theory of affect to a theory of affect regulation. Polyvagal Theory offers convincing evidence confirming the crucial importance that recurring authentic face-to-face social interactions will have for strengthening the functioning of vagal pathways, thus improving emotional communication, the accuracy of neuroception, and the dampening of sympathetic tone (unnecessary fight-flight defensive reactions that distort psychological experience). Polyvagal Theory provides a unique perspective that not only explains the neural mechanisms involved in attachment, but also offers a clinical model to guide more effective treatment. The theory accomplishes this by outlining strategies for exercising the neural circuits (i.e., social engagement system, neuroception, and regulation of affect via the vagal brake) that promote secure attachment and provide a more accurate explanation of how the mind and body influence each other.

REFERENCES

Bargh, J. A. (2014). Our unconscious mind: Unconscious impulses and desires impel what we think and do in ways Freud never dreamed of. *Scientific American, 310*(1), 32–39.

Berns, G. (2005). *Satisfaction: The science of finding true fulfillment.* New York: Henry Holt.

Bowlby, J. (1988). *A secure base: Clinical applications of attachment theory.* London: Routledge.

Flores, P. (2010). Group psychotherapy and neuroplasticity: An attachment theory perspective. *International Journal of Group Psychotherapy, 60,* 546–570.

Fonagy, P., Gergely, G., Jurist, E. L., & Target, M. (2002). *Affect regulation, mentalization and the development of the self.* New York: Other Press.

Grossmark, R., & Wright, F. (2015). *The one and the many: Relational approaches to group psychotherapy.* New York: Routledge.

Johnson, S. (2008). *Hold me tight: Seven conversations for a lifetime of love.* Boston: Little, Brown.

Norcross, J. C. (2001). *Psychotherapy relationships that work: Therapists' contributions and responsiveness to patients.* New York: Oxford University Press.

Ormont, L. (1992). *The group therapy experience.* New York: St. Martin's.

Porges, S. W. (1995). Orienting in a defensive world: Mammalian modifications of our evolutionary heritage. A Polyvagal Theory. *Psychophysiology, 32*(4), 301–318.

Porges, S. W. (2007). The polyvagal perspective. *Biological Psychology, 74*(2), 116–143.

Porges, S. W. (2011). *The Polyvagal Theory: Neurophysiological foundations of emotions, attachment, communication, and self-regulation.* Norton Series on Interpersonal Neurobiology. New York: Norton.

Porges, S. W. (2015). Play as neural exercise: Insights from the Polyvagal Theory. In D. Pearce-McCall (Ed.), *The power of play for mind-brain health* (pp. 3–7) [ebook]. MindGAINS.

Porges, S. W., Doussard-Roosevelt, J. A., Portales, A. L., & Greenspan, S. I. (1996). Infant regulation of the vagal "brake" predicts child behavior problems: A psychobiological model of social behavior. *Developmental Psychobiology, 29*(8), 697–712.

Rutan, J. S., Stone, W. N., & Shay, J. (2014). *Psychodynamic group psychotherapy* (5th ed.). New York: Guilford.

Schore, A. N. (2003). *Affect regulation and the repair of the self.* New York: Norton.

Siegel, D. L. (1999). *The developing mind: Toward a neurobiology of interpersonal experience.* New York: Guilford.

Stern, D. N. (1995). *The motherhood constellation.* New York: Basic Books.

van der Kolk, B. (2014). *The body keeps the score: Brain, mind, and body in the healing of trauma.* New York: Penguin Random House.

Yalom, I. D., & Leszcz, M. (2005). *The theory and practice of group psychotherapy* (5th ed.). New York: Basic Books.

CHAPTER 8

Neural Mechanisms Underlying Human–Animal Interaction
An Evolutionary Perspective

C. Sue Carter and Stephen W. Porges

Social support and positive social interactions can protect and heal (Cacioppo & Patrick, 2008). Thus, the biological causes and consequences of social behavior are important in many fields of science, including neuroscience and medicine. Social interactions have particular value in the face of challenge, especially when the benefits of living socially outweigh those of living alone. Although social behaviors typically involve within-species interactions, these also may be directed toward other species, creating interspecies relationships that are mutually beneficial or symbiotic.

This chapter considers—in the context of evolution—neuroendocrine and autonomic mechanisms underlying the biological consequences of positive social interactions. The neurobiological systems that are implicated in social behavior may help to explain the reported health benefits of human-animal interaction (HAI; e.g., Headey & Grabka, 2007; Headey et al., 2008). Animal-assisted therapies (AATs), built on HAIs, are increasingly common. Both HAIs and AATs are grounded in the same neural systems that are used to explain the general benefits of social support. Identifying these systems can offer insight into naturally occurring processes through which perceived social support protects or restores human health.

Companion animals can elicit positive emotions and may allow humans to experience a sense of safety, which in turn improves the capacity to regulate both emotional and physiological states. This improved regulation is manifest in better mental and physical health and is often observed as a greater resilience to stressors (Handlin et al., 2011). The behaviors intrinsic to human emotion include dynamic sensations, psychological feelings, and autonomic responses. Social support is most effective when bidirectional and is typically defined by selective social behaviors and social bonds (Carter, 1998), both given and received.

Here we focus primarily on the neurobiology of HAIs under conditions in which these relationships are reciprocal and positive, and thus mutually capable of regulating behavior. However, HAIs present behavioral challenges as well as benefits. Large animals may threaten or harm humans. The coexistence of overlapping neural systems for affiliative support and defensive aggression creates behavioral complexity for the HAI. Thus, awareness of the autonomic and neuroendocrine bases of defensive behaviors can provide insights into situations in which danger or aggression may arise.

BIOLOGICAL PROTOTYPES FOR THE PHYSIOLOGY OF SOCIALITY

The physiological elements that support mammalian maternal behavior are shared with those that underlie social behaviors in general (Carter, 1998, 2014; Carter et al., 2008). Research with rats revealed that social interactions between the mother and infant are facilitated by oxytocin (Pedersen & Prange, 1979), a hormone released during birth and lactation (Brunton & Russell, 2008). Maternal behavior involves huddling over an infant, which requires social engagement, followed by immobility. In addition, in male prairie voles, the presence of an infant quickly releases oxytocin, which in turn may facilitate or reinforce additional social engagement (Kenkel et al., 2012). In species with selective social behaviors, such as sheep (Keverne, 2006) and socially monogamous prairie voles (Williams et al., 1994), oxytocin is a component of the mechanisms that forge social bonds.

However, oxytocin is not the only hormone that can facilitate sociality, nor is its release at birth a requirement for the expression of parental behavior. Mice mutant for the oxytocin gene are capable of birth and some components of maternal behavior; the biochemical systems necessary for birth and maternal behavior are probably redundant (Russell et al., 2003). Adoptive parents and alloparents can show high levels of parental behavior. Oxytocin released during these circumstances may be a kind of hormonal insurance directing maternal or parental attention toward newborns. Many other molecules are candidates for the regulation of the causes and consequences of social behavior. As one example, the effects of oxytocin and vasopressin depend on the actions of dopamine, which may help to explain the rewarding effects of maternal behavior (Barrett & Fleming, 2011) and the development of social bonds (Aragona & Wang, 2009).

NEUROENDOCRINOLOGY AND SOCIAL BEHAVIOR

The neural systems responsible for mammalian social cognition and emotion can be influenced by the actions of oxytocin and vasopressin. Both are composed of nine amino acids, and thus are termed peptides. The peptide hormones found in mammals evolved from ancient precursors that created the template for modern oxytocin and vasopressin; they may have originated as cellular factors regulating water balance, immune processes, or other defensive mechanisms, which in multicellular organisms are synthesized in particularly high concentrations in the nervous system (sometimes called neuropeptides) and have developed the additional capacity to serve as hormones.

The actions of oxytocin and related neuropeptides depend on their capacity to bind to larger protein molecules (receptors), generally located on cell membranes. In mammals, peptides and their receptors function together to create a coordinated system, with activities throughout the body (e.g., oxytocin acts on receptors in the brain, peripheral nervous system, uterus, breast, gonads, heart, kidney, and thymus). Oxytocin serves both as a hormone and a neuromodulator (Landgraf & Neumann, 2004). As a hormone, it is synthesized in the hypothalamus and released into the bloodstream at the pituitary, acting on various target organs. As a neuromodulator, it may reach oxytocin receptors throughout the brain by diffusion through the nervous system. Oxytocin can serve as a signaling molecule that influences both behavior and physiology. Through neural pathways in the brainstem, it regulates the autonomic nervous system (ANS), with profound effects on both peripheral organs and emotional states and feelings.

Vasopressin is genetically and structurally related to oxytocin. Research in the socially monogamous prairie vole has implicated oxytocin and vasopressin in sociality, including social contact and pair-bonding, and either can facilitate social engagement with familiar partners. However, selective social behaviors, such as those necessary for pair-bonding (Cho et al., 1999) and responses to infants (Bales et al., 2004, 2007), appear to require both oxytocin and vasopressin. Because of their structural similarities, these peptides can affect each other's receptors. Untangling the functions of oxytocin and vasopressin has been difficult, but there is compelling evidence that their behavioral actions are not identical (Carter, 2007).

Centrally active vasopressin may be especially critical for the dramatic increase in defensive aggression that supports male pair-bonding (Winslow et al., 1993) or the paternal defense of offspring (Bosch & Neumann, 2012; Kenkel et al., 2012). Vasopressin (known for increasing blood pressure) also supports physical and probably emotional mobilization (Carter, 1998), as well as other active adaptive and defensive behaviors (Ferris, 2008). It is associated with hyperarousal, vigilance, and aggressive behaviors. As discussed in the following section, knowledge of its functions may be useful in explaining within- and between-species differences in domestication, the defensive aggression that can arise in HAIs, and the negative symptoms, such as depression and anxiety, that emerge when social bonds are disrupted.

EVOLUTION OF MAMMALIAN SOCIAL BEHAVIORS AND HAI

It is likely that the beneficial effects of HAI, as well as other forms of social support, are based in part on older neural systems that emerged before the modern neocortex. This can most easily be understood through an awareness of the evolution of the mammalian nervous system. The nervous system is hierarchically organized. Older neural pathways supporting survival are powerful and can override the more recently evolved cognitive systems. As with other animals, it can be difficult for humans to cortically regulate or understand their visceral reactions and emotional states. The bottom-up design of the mammalian nervous system helps to explain the impact of the comparatively fundamental experiences and feelings that, taken together, can characterize HAI.

The evolved nature of the human central and autonomic nervous systems also helps us understand the origins of mammalian social communication. For example, humans are highly sensitive to the appearance of and vocalizations produced by companion animals; emotional states in both humans and companion animals may, in turn, be regulated by these social signals. A kitten's purring or a dog's barking are common examples of cues that are difficult to ignore, and the evocative visual characteristics of companion animals can elicit emotional feelings in most healthy humans.

In the process of evolution, modern mammals acquired an increasingly sophisticated anatomical and neural capacity to produce and receive complex social cues, including acoustic signals. Among these signals is prosody (pitch, rhythm, and tempo), which is fundamental to human language but is also central to social communication in other mammals (Porges, 2011). Prosody can be recognized in domestic animals. Social communication in mammals is based in part on these systems (e.g., some dogs produce sounds that mimic elements of human language). Humans and companion species can be reciprocally sensitive to the types of sounds made by each other and can often use these signals to judge emotional intent and to regulate emotions.

AUTONOMIC NERVOUS SYSTEM, SOCIAL BEHAVIOR, AND EMOTION REGULATION

Of particular importance to social and emotional states is the autonomic core of the mammalian nervous system that manages involuntary functions (e.g., heart, lungs, digestive, and immune systems) that emerged long before the modern neocortex. The mammalian ANS also arose as a function of an evolutionary process. Among the evolved functions of the ANS are hierarchical processes that support the high levels of sociality and social communication seen in mammals.

The ANS is functionally divided into sympathetic and parasympathetic components. The sympathetic branches include spinal nerves capable of supporting states of mobilization and some aspects of social engagement but also flight or fight behaviors. As identified by the Polyvagal Theory (Porges, 2011), the parasympathetic nervous system contains two vagal pathways. An older unmyelinated branch of the vagus primarily innervates subdiaphragmatic (i.e., below the diaphragm) organs, with effects associated with conservation of energy and reductions in metabolism. In addition, the unmyelinated branch of the vagus slows the heart.

The more recently evolved myelinated vagal system is primarily supradiaphragmatic; it supports oxygenation of the neocortex as well as health, growth, and restoration and is necessary for social engagement. At the level of the mammalian heart, the myelinated vagus is associated with protective neural cardiac rhythms (respiratory sinus arrhythmia), which have been repeatedly associated with health, restoration, and positive social behaviors (Porges, 2011).

ANS AS A NEURAL SUBSTRATE FOR BEHAVIORAL EFFECTS OF OXYTOCIN AND VASOPRESSIN

Peptide hormones, including oxytocin and vasopressin, modulate the functions of the ANS. Oxytocin has complex effects on the autonomic nervous system that are not well studied, although the acute sympathetic effects of oxytocin may include actions permissive for active social engagement, including play. The chronic actions of oxytocin are more likely to include reductions in sympathetic activation, which over time allow less reactive social interactions such as parenting, at least in comparison to flight or fight reactions (Kenkel et al., 2013). Oxytocin also has actions on the myelinated ventral vagus in humans (Norman et al., 2011) and other social mammals (Grippo et al., 2009). The myelinated ventral vagus protects the heart, ensuring adequate oxygenation of the neocortex, which in turn is necessary for social interactions and cognition (Porges, 1998). Oxytocin also may directly co-opt the unmyelinated dorsal vagus, allowing animals to experience social contact, safely slowing the heart and permitting the immobility without fear that characterizes maternal and sexual behaviors, or sitting quietly with a pet. In contrast, immobility with fear, including freezing or death feigning, is not associated with positive social interactions. Shutdown reactions can leave mammals vulnerable to cardiac failure or even death. Oxytocin pathways are protective against a number of these adverse events, including cardiac arrhythmias.

BENEFICIAL EFFECTS OF OXYTOCIN

As described earlier, neuropeptides serve as signaling molecules capable of influencing a variety of neurophysiological functions and at the same time creating coordinated processes associated with growth, health, and restoration. For example, in highly social mammals, such as humans and dogs, oxytocin may bias autonomic reactions and the interpretation of feelings and visceral experiences, allowing emotional states, including those described as a sense of safety. Alternatively, in the face of perceived threat or danger, a rapid shift in state may facilitate protection of oneself or a companion.

Social behavior is critically intertwined with stress management. The capacity of companionship and animal assisted therapy (AAT) to protect in the face of physical and emotional challenge appears to rely on the biological and molecular substrates that permit the formation of social bonds. Oxytocin may help ensure that nonreproductive mammals have access to others in the face of danger. Social bonds can form in response to extreme stressors, especially when survival depends on the presence of another individual; under intense stress, oxytocin is released, leading to the formation of social bonds (Carter, 1998).

Social engagement and support, with an accompanying sense of safety, may be of particular importance to mental health in highly social species (e.g., humans, dogs, prairie voles). In rodents and other social mammals, chronic social isolation is associated with increases in measures of depression, anxiety, and physiological arousal, including changes in basal heart rate and reductions in parasympathetic activity (Grippo et al., 2009). Isolation or other forms of chronic stress also may reduce gene expression for the oxytocin receptor (Pournajafi-Nazarloo et al., 2013), possibly creating insensitivity to the beneficial effects of oxytocin. Concurrently, in female prairie voles, isolation is accompanied by an increase in blood levels of oxytocin (Grippo et al., 2009). The autonomic components of voles' responses to chronic isolation are prevented or reversed by chronic treatment with exogenous oxytocin, further implicating oxytocin in social support. Thus in the prairie vole model, isolation-associated elevations in endogenous oxytocin are not sufficient to protect against the autonomic and behavioral consequences of living alone. Whether comparable changes occur in humans remains to be determined, but the presence of a companion, via functional increases in oxytocin or its receptor, could potentially reverse some effects of chronic stress.

As explained, oxytocin can regulate behavioral and emotional reactivity to stress and may help regulate the behavioral and autonomic distress that typically follows separation (Carter, 1998). For example, oxytocin may protect mammals from the "reptile-like" freezing pattern (Porges, 2011). Brainstem regions that influence the ANS have receptors for oxytocin and vasopressin. These same peptides are activated by stressors, and there is increasing evidence that some behavioral consequences of oxytocin and vasopressin are due to their effects on the ANS. Thus conditions that favor activation of oxytocin-regulated processes may enhance resilience in the face of stressful experiences.

BENEFICIAL CONSEQUENCES OF COMPANIONSHIP

Wellness is more than the absence of illness or stress. Social engagement buffers the stress of life. Individuals who have a perceived sense of social support are more resilient in the face of stressors and disease, living longer than those who feel isolated or lonely (Cacioppo & Patrick, 2008). Lesions in various bodily tissues, including the brain, heal more quickly in animals that are living socially versus in isolation (Karelina & DeVries, 2011). Remarkably, the same hormones and brain areas that serve the body's survival demands also permit adaptation to an ever-changing social and physical environment. The protective effects of positive sociality appear to rely on a concoction of naturally occurring molecules with diverse actions throughout the body.

As one example, oxytocin may literally heal a damaged heart, promoting growth and restoration. Oxytocin receptors are expressed in the heart, and precursors for the oxytocin peptide appear to be critical to the development of the fetal heart (Danalache et al., 2010). Oxytocin has protective effects in part through the capacity to convert undifferentiated stem cells into cardiomyocytes and may facilitate adult neurogenesis, especially after a stressful experience. It also has direct anti-inflammatory and antioxidant properties that can be detected in in vitro models of atherosclerosis (Szeto et al., 2008).

Oxytocin, in conjunction with vasopressin, plays a dynamic role in the regulation of the ANS (Grippo et al., 2009; Porges, 2011). Oxytocin and vasopressin receptors also are found in brainstem regions that regulate heart rate. Both peptides modulate the sympathetic system, but it is probably oxytocin that normally restrains the overreactivity of the cardiovascular system in the face of extreme or chronic stress, as it has direct actions on the parasympathetic component of the ANS, permitting and promoting some of the benefits of social engagement.

IS OXYTOCIN AN ANTISTRESS HORMONE?

Initial research on the social consequences of oxytocin emphasized its capacity to downregulate the hypothalamic-pituitary-adrenal (HPA) axis (Carter, 1998). As data have accumulated, these overly simplistic perspectives have been replaced by more sophisticated views of the mechanisms through which oxytocin or social support can play an adaptive role in the response to a challenge. In addition, we have become increasingly aware of the importance of the ANS in the regulation of responses to challenge (Porges, 2011). As described earlier, the behavioral and autonomic consequences of exposure to oxytocin, vasopressin, or other hormones of the HPA axis are time and context dependent. Positive experiences may in some cases release oxytocin but are not the only mechanisms for stimulating oxytocin's release. Among the most reliable methods to release oxytocin are intense stressors, including birth. Under conditions of high arousal, the most immediate effects of exposure to oxytocin may be a transient activation of the HPA axis and sympathetic nervous system. Thus, interpretations of blood levels of hormones are not simple. High levels of oxytocin may be detected following both positive and negative experiences. The biological consequences of oxytocin levels may be best understood in the context of the status of the oxytocin (and vasopressin) receptors, but at present functional measures of receptors are not easily assessed, and we are limited to estimations of receptor activity based on measures of genetic and epigenetic markers.

Timing of hormone measurements and knowledge of individual differences and context are critical. Oxytocin has complex, dynamic effects on the HPA axis and the ANS, with potentially compensatory consequences for coping with challenge. Under some conditions, oxytocin can inhibit the release of glucocorticoids (a class of steroid hormones; cortisol is the most important human glucocorticoid). As with oxytocin, the effects of glucocorticoids also are time dependent. People given cortisol-like drugs are initially euphoric, although chronic exposure to glucocorticoids is associated with fatigue and depression (Judd et al., 2014).

BETWEEN- AND WITHIN-SPECIES VARIATIONS IN SOCIAL BEHAVIOR

Over the millennia, biological substrates emerged that permitted the expression of modern mammalian social engagement and permitted the experiences that humans call emotions (Donaldson & Young, 2008). Of particular relevance to HAIs are mechanisms for positive sociality and social bonds. These neural and anatomical systems are the underpinnings for contemporary social behaviors, including those observed in humans and most of their preferred companion animals. The evolved traits that allow a species to become a domestic species include the capacity to interact with humans over an extended period of time and in some cases to form selective social bonds.

Domestic animals have been bred to serve humans as companions, pets, and guards. The ancestors of species that could be domesticated were presumably also social to some extent. For example, modern dogs are believed to have arisen from wolves; both share with humans the capacity to develop social bonds. It is likely that shared physiological traits and habitats allowed the development of particularly strong ties between humans and dogs. Dogs also may serve to alert or protect against intruders, culminating with their well-established designation as "man's best friend" (Olmert, 2009).

SOCIAL ENGAGEMENT CAN ALLOW A SENSE OF
SAFETY AND IMPROVE STATE REGULATION

The capacity to socially engage, giving and receiving high levels of social behavior and especially selective social relationships, is of particular relevance to HAI. Humans, who may experience an enhanced sense of safety in the presence of human companions, can experience a similar sense of emotional safety with companion animals or pets. In fact, the affection of a pet may seem more unconditional and may be less complex to experience and return than that of human companions.

There is increasing evidence for health benefits of social support, especially in the face of extreme challenges or trauma (Olff, 2012). The neurophysiological consequences of social behavior can be profound, probably translating into a sense of biological and emotional safety. The benefits of social support are most readily detected when absent: Involuntary separation from a loved one, isolation, or a perceived sense of loneliness are associated with a host of negative consequences, including increases in depression and vulnerability to various diseases (Cacioppo & Patrick, 2008). Death of a pet can create a similar sense of loss. As with other positive influences on physiology and behavior, the benefits of HAI may be most easily detected when a need state exists, including in the face of external stress. Companion animals also can be of particular value during stressful periods, including bereavement or emotional loss.

ANIMAL-ASSISTED THERAPIES

Systematic efforts to access the value of AAT, most often using dogs, cats, or birds, have been reported in dozens of studies and across the life span (reviewed in Beetz et al., 2012). Among the commonly measured physiological changes described as a function of HAIs are reductions in heart rate, blood pressure, cortisol, and catecholamines. These changes can appear in healthy humans but may be most obvious in individuals faced with acute or chronic stressors or illness; benefits of HAIs have been reported for cardiovascular diseases, cancer, dementias, and various mental illnesses, including depression, schizophrenia, and autism. The diversity of diseases that gain benefit from AAT suggests that their biology is based on fundamental physiological processes with wide consequences.

CHALLENGES IN STUDYING OXYTOCIN
AND VASOPRESSIN IN HAI

The neurobiological processes through which HAIs are beneficial to either humans or their animal companions deserve further study. Clues to the underlying mechanisms are emerging from other behavioral models (e.g., maternal behavior) and from studies of socially monogamous rodents, which like humans and dogs have the capacity to show high levels of sociality and form long-lasting pair-bonds (Carter et al., 1995). These studies have repeatedly implicated oxytocin and vasopressin in social behavior, both during early life and in adulthood (Carter et al., 2009; Feldman, 2012; Meyer-Lindenberg et al., 2011).

Studies examining the specific neural mechanisms associated with HAIs have begun to focus on peptides implicated in social behavior (e.g., endocrine changes as a function of interactions with dogs include increases in oxytocin; Handlin et al., 2011; Nagasawa et al., 2009; Odendaal & Meintjes, 2003). Among the challenges in studying possible changes associated with exposure to an animal companion is the fact that changes may be small or transient; both sensitive measures and frequent sampling are required. The status of the oxytocin receptor may alter the consequences of exposure to either endogenous or exogenous hormones, although at present this can only be estimated by measures of genetic and epigenetic markers.

Differences are to be expected among individuals, species, and breeds but at present are not well understood. Paradigms that can be used for studies of HAI depend on the strength of the relationship between the companion and human (Rehn et al., 2014). Depending on the circumstance or individuals involved, changes may occur in one or both members of the dyad. In one study, levels of urinary oxytocin were measured as a function of human-pet interactions (Nagasawa et al., 2009). In comparing owners whose dog showed long versus short gaze toward the owner, only those owners with long-gaze dogs showed increases in oxytocin following an interaction with their pets (see Figure 8.1). In another study, repeated dog and human blood samples were taken immediately following interactions; changes were apparent within 1 to 3 minutes, and although increases in oxytocin were statistically significant in humans, it was dogs that showed the most marked increase (Handlin et al., 2011). In addition, the nature of the interaction between a dog and its partner can affect the oxytocin response. Physical (versus nonphysical) contact with a familiar partner has been associated with a longer-lasting increase in oxytocin in dogs (Rehn et al., 2014). Finally, there is evidence that exogenous oxytocin, given to dogs as an intranasal spray, can influence social behavior. Oxytocin-treated animals were more likely to show positive social interactions toward both their owners and other dogs (Romero et al., 2014).

Additional evidence for the power of companion animals to influence humans comes from studies showing that exogenous oxytocin given to a dog not only increased gazing by the dog toward its owner, but also was associated with a release of oxytocin in the owner (see Figure 8.1; Nagasawa et al., 2015). It is interesting to note that these effects were not seen in interactions between domesticated wolves and their owners. Results from these studies also have been used to support the argument that bonds between humans and dogs represent an example of "coevolution" (Nagasawa et al., 2015) or "evolutionary con-

FIGURE 8.1. Oxytocin (urinary) in pet owners increased between before (pre) and after (post) typical interactions with their dogs when the dogs were long-gaze-toward-owner dogs. Nagasawa, M., Kikusui, T., Onaka, T., & Ohta, M. (2009). "Dog's gaze at its owner increases owner's urinary oxytocin during social interaction." *Hormones and Behavior, 55*, 438. Copyright © 2008 by Elsevier, Inc. Adapted with permission.

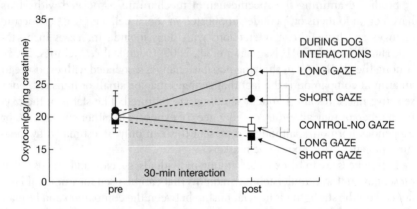

vergence" in which mechanisms typically used for within-species attachment are "hijacked," permitting the emergence of cross-species bonds (Maclean & Hare, 2015).

Taken together, these studies suggest that under some conditions, HAIs may release oxytocin. The release of oxytocin by social behaviors can be transitory or long lasting and can be affected by the relationship between dogs and their social partners. Furthermore, the capacity of oxytocin to elicit social behavior has been documented using exogenous oxytocin. Although changes have been measured in a variety of other chemicals during HAIs, the degree to which these are specific to social interactions, rather than reflecting more general changes associated with the testing conditions, have not been fully addressed (e.g., circumstances experienced as arousing may be either negative or positive). Thus, at present the strongest available evidence comes from dogs and supports the hypothesis that oxytocin may play a central role in the benefits of human-dog interaction.

SOCIAL BEHAVIORS, BREED DIFFERENCES, AND PEPTIDES

Dog breeds have been carefully sculpted by selective breeding. In some cases the breeding objective was to create an animal that would protect people or assist in hunting game, whereas in others, animals were bred as companions to help humans regulate their emotions. It is plausible that breed differences are related to differences in oxytocin and vasopressin. For example, highly social breeds, especially those that maintain puppy-like behavioral and physical features into adulthood (neoteny), may be expressing oxytocin-dependent traits.

A major issue in HAIs is understanding conditions under which either animals or their human caretakers may express aggression toward each other. The hormones that support guarding of a partner in particular are part of a delicately balanced system. Aggression is most often expressed in the face of challenge and toward perceived intruders but can misfire, appearing in unintended contexts or with undesired consequences. Other animals, or even friends and family, may become the object of aggression. The vasopressin system can support mobilization, defensive aggression, and anxiety (Ferris, 2008; Zhang et al., 2012). Breeds of dogs that show guarding behaviors may have been inadvertently bred for high levels of central vasopressin. A strong and selective social bond might be associated with a tendency to show defensive aggression, usually toward strangers, by some companion dogs.

To our knowledge, the relationships between oxytocin or ANS features and species and breed differences in sociality have not been systematically examined. However, knowledge of the role of the ANS and neuropeptides, such as oxytocin and vasopressin and their receptors, in the social behavior of pets or other domestic species could be useful to the creation of breeds of companion or domestic animals with a desired behavioral profile conducive to social bonding. Such knowledge might also be useful in selecting rescued animals with the highest chance of being successfully adopted.

SUMMARY

Evolution is thrifty, resculpting and repurposing molecules and neural systems. The modern nervous system evolved using chemicals with multiple sites of action, many of which were retained as additional functions emerged. They are components of integrated neural networks, coordinating sociality with other bodily processes. As with birth, social engagement is so critical that the systems regulating it may be redundant. It is likely that the neural systems and molecules that have been identified as underpinnings of social behaviors in rodents and humans are also critical to HAI. Domestic animals were derived from social ancestors and rely on neural pathways similar to those in humans. It would be possible, taking advantage of existing within-species or breed differences, to examine whether artificial selection and domestication act indirectly through manipulations of peptides. Oxytocin might be associated with a general tendency toward sociality and possibly neoteny. Both oxytocin and vasopressin, probably acting via the myelinated ventral vagus, may be necessary to produce animals showing strong selective social bonds, including toward human caretakers. However, vasopressin, which within the central nervous system is androgen dependent (Carter, 2007), is more likely to be associated with defensive or protective traits, expected to arise in adulthood, and to be context and gender dependent. Finally, the growing literature on HAI offers a novel opportunity to gain a deeper understanding of the evolutionary and neurobiological basis of mammalian sociality.

REFERENCES

Aragona, B. J., & Wang, Z. (2009). Dopamine regulation of social choice in a monogamous rodent species. *Frontiers in Behavioral Neuroscience, 3*, 15. http://dx.doi.org/10.3389/neuro.08.015.2009

Bales, K. L., Kim, A. J., Lewis-Reese, A. D., & Carter, C. S. (2004). Both oxytocin and vasopressin may influence alloparental behavior in male prairie voles. *Hormones and Behavior, 45*, 354–361. http://dx.doi.org/10.1016/j.yhbeh.2004.01.004

Bales, K. L., van Westerhuyzen, J. A., Lewis-Reese, A. D., Grotte, N. D., Lanter, J. A., & Carter, C. S. (2007). Oxytocin has dose-dependent developmental effects on pair-bonding and alloparental care in female prairie voles. *Hormones and Behavior, 52*, 274–279. http://dx.doi.org/10.1016/j.yhbeh.2007.05.004

Barrett, J., & Fleming, A. S. (2011). All mothers are not created equal: Neural and psychobiological perspective on mothering and the importance of individual differences. *Journal of Child Psychology and Psychiatry, 52*, 368–397. http://dx.doi.org/10.1111/j.1469-7610.2010.02306.x

Beetz, A., Uvnäs-Moberg, K., Julius, H., & Kotrschal, K. (2012). Psychosocial and psychophysiological effects of human-animal interactions: The possible role of oxytocin. *Frontiers in Psychology, 3*, 234. http://dx.doi.org/10.3389/fpsyg.2012.00234

Bosch, O. J., & Neumann, I. D. (2012). Both oxytocin and vasopressin are mediators of maternal care and aggression in rodents: From central release to sites of action. *Hormones and Behavior, 61*, 293–303. http://dx.doi.org/10.1016/j.yhbeh.2011.11.002

Brunton, P. J., & Russell, J. A. (2008). The expectant brain: Adapting for motherhood. *Nature Reviews Neuroscience, 9*, 11–25. http://dx.doi.org/10.1038/nrn2280

Cacioppo, J. T., & Patrick, W. (2008). *Loneliness: Human nature and the need for social connection.* New York: Norton.

Carter, C. S. (1998). Neuroendocrine perspectives on social attachment and love. *Psychoneuroendocrinology, 23*, 779–818. http://dx.doi.org/10.1016/s0306-4530(98)00055-9

Carter, C. S. (2007). Sex differences in oxytocin and vasopressin: Implications for autism spectrum disorders? *Behavioural Brain Research, 176*, 170–186. http://dx.doi.org/10.1016/j.bbr.2006.08.025

Carter, C. S. (2014). Oxytocin pathways and the evolution of human behavior. *Annual Review of Psychology, 65*, 17–39. http://dx.doi.org/10.1146/annurevpsych-010213-115110

Carter, C. S., Boone, E. M., Pournajafi-Nazarloo, H., & Bales, K. L. (2009). Consequences of early experiences and exposure to oxytocin and vasopressin are sexually dimorphic. *Developmental Neuroscience, 31*, 332–341. http://dx.doi.org/10.1159/000216544

Carter, C. S., DeVries, A. C., & Getz, L. L. (1995). Physiological substrates of mammalian monogamy: The prairie vole model. *Neuroscience and Biobehavioral Reviews, 19*, 303–314. http://dx.doi.org/10.1016/0149-7634(94)00070-H

Carter, C. S., Grippo, A. J., Pournajafi-Nazarloo, H., Ruscio, M. G., & Porges, S. W. (2008). Oxytocin, vasopressin and sociality. *Progress in Brain Research, 170,* 331–336. http://dx.doi.org/10.1016/s0079-6123(08)00427-5

Cho, M. M., DeVries, A. C., Williams, J. R., & Carter, C. S. (1999). The effects of oxytocin and vasopressin on partner preferences in male and female prairie voles (Microtus ochrogaster). *Behavioral Neuroscience, 113,* 1071–1079. http://dx.doi.org/10.1037/0735-7044.113.5.1071

Danalache, B. A., Gutkowska, J., Slusarz, M. J., Berezowska, I., & Jankowski, M. (2010). Oxytocin-gly-lys-Arg: A novel cardiomyogenic peptide. *PLoS ONE, 5*(10), e13643. http://dx.doi.org/10.1371/journal.pone.0013643

Donaldson, Z. R., & Young, L. J. (2008). Oxytocin, vasopressin, and the neurogenetics of sociality. *Science, 322,* 900–904. http://dx.doi.org/10.1126/science.1158668

Feldman, R. (2012). Oxytocin and social affiliation in humans. *Hormones and Behavior, 61,* 380–391. http://dx.doi.org/10.1016/j.yhbeh.2012.01.008

Ferris, C. F. (2008). Functional magnetic resonance imaging and the neurobiology of vasopressin and oxytocin. *Progress in Brain Research, 170,* 305–320. http://dx.doi.org/10.1016/s0079-6123(08)00425-1

Grippo, A. J., Trahanas, D. M., Zimmerman, R. R., II, Porges, S. W., & Carter, C. S. (2009). Oxytocin protects against negative behavioral and autonomic consequences of long-term social isolation. *Psychoneuroendocrinology, 34,* 1542–1553. http://dx.doi.org/10.1016/j.psyneuen.2009.05.017

Handlin, L., Hydbring-Sandberg, E., Nilsson, A., Ejdebäck, M., Jansson, A., & Uvnäs-Moberg, K. (2011). Short-term interaction between dogs and their owners—effects on oxytocin, cortisol, insulin and heart rate—an exploratory study. *Anthrozoös, 24,* 301–315. http://dx.doi.org/10.2752/175303711X13045914865385

Headey, B., & Grabka, M. M. (2007). Pets and human health in Germany and Australia: National longitudinal results. *Social Indicators Research, 80,* 297–311. http://dx.doi.org/10.1007/s11205-005-5072-z

Headey, B., Na, F., & Zheng, R. (2008). Pet dogs benefit owners' health: A "natural experiment" in China. *Social Indicators Research, 87,* 481–493. http://dx.doi.org/10.1007/s11205-007-9142-2

Judd, L. L., Schettler, P. J., Brown, E. S., Wolkowitz, O. M., Sternberg, E. M., Bender, B. G., Bulloch, K., Cidlowski, J. A., de Kloet, E. R., Fardet, L., Joëls, M., Leung, D. Y. M., McEwen, B. S., Roozendaal, B., Van Rossum, E. F. C., Ahn, J., Brown, D. W., Plitt, A., & Singh, G. (2014). Adverse consequences of glucocorticoid medication: Psychological, cognitive, and behavioral effects. *American Journal of Psychiatry, 171,* 1045–1051. http://dx.doi.org/10.1176/appi.ajp.2014.13091264

Karelina, K., & DeVries, A. C. (2011). Modeling social influences on human health. *Psychosomatic Medicine, 73,* 67–74. http://dx.doi.org/10.1097/psy.0b013e3182002116

Kenkel, W. M., Paredes, J., Lewis, G. F., Yee, J. R., Pournajafi-Nazarloo, H., Grippo, A. J., Porges, S. W., & Carter, C. S. (2013). Autonomic substrates of the response to pups in male prairie voles. *PLoS ONE, 8*(8), e69965. http://dx.doi.org/10.1371/journal.pone.0069965

Kenkel, W. M., Paredes, J., Yee, J. R., Pournajafi-Nazarloo, H., Bales, K. L., & Carter, C. S. (2012). Neuroendocrine and behavioural responses to exposure to an infant in male prairie voles. *Journal of Neuroendocrinology, 24,* 874–886. http://dx.doi.org/10.1111/j.1365-2826.2012.02301.x

Keverne, E. B. (2006). Neurobiological and molecular approaches to attachment and bonding. In C. S. Carter, L. Ahnert, K. E. Grossman, S. B. Hrdy, M. E. Lamb, S. W. Porges, & N. Saschser (Eds.), *Attachment and bonding: A new synthesis* (pp. 101–118). Cambridge, MA: MIT Press.

Landgraf, R., & Neumann, I. D. (2004). Vasopressin and oxytocin release within the brain: A dynamic concept of multiple and variable modes of neuropeptide communication. *Frontiers in Neuroendocrinology, 25,* 150–176. http://dx.doi.org/10.1016/j.yfrne.2004.05.001

Maclean, E. L., & Hare, B. (2015). Dogs hijack the human bonding pathway. *Science, 348,* 280–281. http://dx.doi.org/10.1126/science.aab1200

Meyer-Lindenberg, A., Domes, G., Kirsch, P., & Heinrichs, M. (2011). Oxytocin and vasopressin in the human brain: Social neuropeptides for translational medicine. *Nature Reviews Neuroscience, 12,* 524–538. http://dx.doi.org/10.1038/nrn3044

Nagasawa, M., Kikusui, T., Onaka, T., & Ohta, M. (2009). Dog's gaze at its owner increases owner's urinary oxytocin during social interaction. *Hormones and Behavior, 55,* 434–441. http://dx.doi.org/10.1016/j.yhbeh.2008.12.002

Nagasawa, M., Mitsui, S., En, S., Ohtani, N., Ohta, M., Sakuma, Y., Onaka, T., Mogi, K., & Kikusui, T. (2015). Oxytocin-gaze positive loop and the coevolution of human-dog bonds. *Science, 348,* 333–336. http://dx.doi.org/10.1126/science.1261022

Norman, G. J., Cacioppo, J. T., Morris, J. S., Malarkey, W. B., Berntson, G. G., & Devries, A. C. (2011). Oxytocin increases autonomic cardiac control: Moderation by loneliness. *Biological Psychology, 86,* 174–180. http://dx.doi.org/10.1016/j.biopsycho.2010.11.006

Odendaal, J. S., & Meintjes, R. A. (2003). Neurophysiological correlates of affiliative behaviour between humans and dogs. *Veterinary Journal, 165,* 296–301. http://dx.doi.org/10.1016/s1090-0233(02)00237-X

Olff, M. (2012). Bonding after trauma: On the role of social support and the oxytocin system in traumatic stress. *European Journal of Psychotraumatology, 3.* http://dx.doi.org/10.3402/ejpt.v3i0.18597

Olmert, M. D. (2009). *Made for each other: The biology of the human-animal bond.* Cambridge, MA: Da Capo.

Pedersen, C. A., & Prange, A. J., Jr. (1979). Induction of maternal behavior in virgin rats after intracerebroventricular administration of oxytocin. *Proceedings of the National Academy of Sciences, USA, 76,* 6661–6665. http://dx.doi.org/10.1073/pnas.76.12.6661

Porges, S. W. (1998). Love: An emergent property of the mammalian autonomic nervous system. *Psychoneuroendocrinology, 23,* 837–861. http://dx.doi.org/10.1016/s0306-4530(98)00057-2

Porges, S. W. (2011). *The Polyvagal Theory: Neurophysiological foundations of emotions, attachment, communication and self-regulation.* New York: Norton.

Pournajafi-Nazarloo, H., Kenkel, W., Mohsenpour, S. R., Sanzenbacher, L., Saadat, H., Partoo, L., Yee, J., Azizi, F., & Carter, C. S. (2013). Exposure to chronic isolation modulates receptors mrNAs for oxytocin and vasopressin in the hypothalamus and heart. *Peptides, 43,* 20–26. http://dx.doi.org/10.1016/j.peptides.2013.02.007

Rehn, T., Handlin, L., Uvnäs-Moberg, K., & Keeling, L. J. (2014). Dogs' endocrine and behavioural responses at reunion are affected by how the human initiates contact. *Physiology and Behavior, 124,* 45–53. http://dx.doi.org/10.1016/j.physbeh.2013.10.009

Romero, T., Nagasawa, M., Mogi, K., Hasegawa, T., & Kikusui, T. (2014). Oxytocin promotes social bonding in dogs. *Proceedings of the National Academy of Sciences, USA, 111,* 9085–9090. http://dx.doi.org/10.1073/pnas.1322868111

Russell, J. A., Leng, G., & Douglas, A. J. (2003). The magnocellular oxytocin system, the fount of maternity: Adaptations in pregnancy. *Frontiers in Neuroendocrinology, 24,* 27–61. http://dx.doi.org/10.1016/s0091-3022(02)00104-8

Szeto, A., Nation, D. A., Mendez, A. J., Dominguez-Bendala, J., Brooks, L. G., Schneiderman, N., & McCabe, P. M. (2008). Oxytocin attenuates NADPH-dependent superoxide activity and IL-6 secretion in macrophages and vascular cells. *American Journal of Physiology, Endocrinology and Metabolism, 295,* e1495–e1501. http://dx.doi.org/10.1152/ajpendo.90718.2008

Williams, J. R., Insel, T. R., Harbaugh, C. R., & Carter, C. S. (1994). Oxytocin administered centrally facilitates formation of a partner preference in female prairie voles (Microtus ochrogaster). *Journal of Neuroendocrinology, 6,* 247–250. http://dx.doi.org/10.1111/j.1365-2826.1994.tb00579.x

Winslow, J. T., Hastings, N., Carter, C. S., Harbaugh, C. R., & Insel, T. R. (1993). A role for central vasopressin in pair bonding in monogamous prairie voles. *Nature, 365,* 545–548. http://dx.doi.org/10.1038/365545a0

Zhang, L., Hernández, V. S., Liu, B., Medina, M. P., Nava-Kopp, A. T., Irles, C., & Morales, M. (2012). Hypothalamic vasopressin system regulation by maternal separation: Its impact on anxiety in rats. *Neuroscience, 215,* 135–148. http://dx.doi.org/10.1016/j.neuroscience.2012.03.046

CHAPTER 9

Therapeutic Presence
Neurophysiological Mechanisms Mediating Feeling Safe in Therapeutic Relationships

Shari M. Geller and Stephen W. Porges

Effective therapeutic work is only possible when the client feels safe and secure in the therapy setting. Research has demonstrated that the therapeutic relationship is central to positive change for clients in psychotherapy and that differential therapeutic outcomes may only be minimally attributed to specific techniques (Duncan & Moynihan, 1994; Lambert & Ogles, 2004; Lambert & Simon, 2008; Martin et al., 2000; Norcross, 2002, 2011; Orlinsky et al., 1994). These observations guided psychotherapy researchers to consider common factors of therapy that are central to client improvement (Norcross, 2011). Current research has suggested therapeutic presence may be a core therapeutic stance that contributes to the development of a positive therapeutic relationship (Geller et al., 2010; Geller & Greenberg, 2012; Hayes & Vinca, 2011; Pos et al., 2011).

Feelings of safety and security for the client often emerge through therapists' ability to be fully present and engaged, which is core to the development of a healthy therapeutic relationship (Geller & Greenberg, 2012; Lambert & Simon, 2008; Mearns, 1997; Rogers, 1957, 1980; Siegel, 2007, 2010). While clinical observations affirm that presence elicits feelings of safety in the client through the development of a positive therapeutic relationship, it is less clear how or why therapists' presence leads to clients' safety and, hence, effective therapeutic work. This chapter explores this question through the lens of neuroscience and biobehavioral mechanisms, as suggested by the well-researched and established Polyvagal Theory (Porges, 1995, 1998, 2007, 2011).

Contemporary neuroscience offers the field of psychotherapy a valid physiological framework for understanding how, through the operation of specific neurophysiological mechanisms, therapists' presence activates clients' feelings of safety (Porges, 2011; Schore, 2003, 2012; Siegel, 2007, 2010). The Polyvagal Theory is one such perspective that provides the clinician with a neurophysiological explanation of core autonomic mechanisms that support safety through presence in relationship (Cozolino, 2006; Porges, 1995, 1998, 2007, 2011; Siegel, 2007; Schore, 1994, 2003, 2012).

The Polyvagal Theory emphasizes that there are strong links between the autonomic nervous system and behavior and explains that when a client feels safe with the therapist, the client's physiological state can provide optimal conditions for both client and therapist to engage in effective therapeutic work. According to the Polyvagal Theory (Porges, 2003, 2007, 2011), this optimal therapeutic state spontaneously emerges when the nervous system detects features of safety. Once features of safety are detected, the client's physiology shifts to a state that downregulates their defenses and promotes spontaneous social engagement behaviors. During these periods of shared feelings of safety, the therapeutic relationship is strengthened, and the therapeutic process can efficiently progress. In addition to safety promoting optimal engagement between therapist and client, research suggests that a safe therapeutic environment facilitates the development of new neural pathways for the client, which in turn contributes to the repair of attachment injuries and provides the positive social interactions that are essential for health and neural growth for the client (Allison & Rossouw, 2013; Rossouw, 2013).

In this chapter, we (a) articulate the value of therapists' presence in creating client safety and deepening clients' therapeutic relationships with their therapists, and (b) present the Polyvagal Theory to explain how presence supports neural processes that enable feelings of safety, a fundamental component of healing. First, we provide a definition and description of therapeutic presence, followed by a presentation of the Polyvagal Theory. We then discuss how therapeutic presence contributes to clients' neuroception of safety. Following this, the therapeutic presence theory of change is described in the context of the Polyvagal Theory so that a neurophysiological description of how therapeutic presence results in the process of change can be illuminated. A clinical vignette is then presented. Finally, a suggestion for training in therapeutic presence is offered—one that is supported by neuroscience research, which argues for the integral value of creating a sense of safety with and for the client.

WHAT IS THERAPEUTIC PRESENCE?

Therapeutic presence involves therapists being fully in the moment on several concurrently occurring dimensions, including physical, emotional, cognitive, and relational (Dunn et al., 2013; Geller, 2009, 2013a, 2013b; Geller & Greenberg, 2002, 2012; Geller et al., 2010, 2012; McCollum & Gehart, 2010). Therapeutic presence begins with the therapist cultivating presence prior to a session and meeting the client from this state of presence. Expert therapists have reported that the experience of therapeutic presence involves concurrently (a) being grounded and in contact with one's integrated and healthy self; (b) being open, receptive to, and immersed in what is poignant in the moment; and (c) having a larger sense of spaciousness and expansion of awareness and perception. This grounded, immersed, and expanded awareness also occurs with (d) the intention of being with and for the client in service of their healing process. By being grounded, immersed, and spacious, with the intention of being with and for the other, the therapist invites the client into a deeper and shared state of relational therapeutic presence. An empirically validated model of therapeutic presence is described more fully in other publications (see Geller, 2013a, 2013b; Geller & Greenberg, 2002, 2012). It is our opinion that therapists' presence invites the client to feel met and understood, as well as safe enough to become present within their own experience, and in relationship with their therapist, allowing for deeper therapeutic work to occur.

We believe that therapists' present contact with self provides the preliminary mechanism by which therapist-attuned responsiveness to the client can occur (Geller & Greenberg, 2012). To be therapeutically present requires therapists to be first grounded, centered, and steady, as well as open and receptive to the whole of the client's experience. In moments of present-centered engagement, therapists are simultaneously in direct contact with themselves, the client, and the relationship between them. Effective therapists' responsiveness and use of intervention or technique emerge from this attuned in-the-moment connection and resonance with the client's experience (Geller & Greenberg, 2012; Germer et al., 2005; Goldfried & Davila, 2005; Greenberg et al., 1993; Lambert & Simon, 2008).

Research on Therapeutic Presence

A growing body of research is contributing to an understanding of therapeutic presence (Geller, 2001; Geller & Greenberg, 2002; Geller et al., 2010; Hayes & Vinca, 2011; Pos et al., 2011). A qualitative study in which therapists were interviewed about their experiences of presence resulted in a model of therapeutic presence that consists of three overarching categories (i.e., preparation, or the preliminary intention and practice therapists engage in to facilitate their being present; process, or what therapists are doing when they are being present; and experience, or what therapists' in-body experience of presence feels like; see Geller, 2001; Geller & Greenberg, 2002, 2012). A later study involved development of a measure of therapeutic presence, the Therapeutic Presence Inventory (TPI), which was based on the model noted above (Geller, 2001; Geller et al., 2010). Two versions of the TPI were created and studied, one from the therapist's perspective (TPI-T) and the second from clients' perception of their therapists' presence (TPI-C). The TPI-T can also be used as a self-audit tool for therapists to reflect on their degree of presence with a client (Geller, 2013b). Research demonstrated that both versions of the TPI were reliable and valid (Geller et al., 2010).

Emerging research using the TPI suggests that clients' reports of their therapists' therapeutic presence is predictive of the therapeutic relationship (Geller et al., 2010) and the therapeutic alliance (Pos et al., 2011). These findings support the propositions that presence provides a necessary foundation to develop a positive working therapeutic relationship and for empathic responding (Geller et al., 2010; Hayes & Vinca, 2011; Pos et al., 2011). The TPI-C has also been found to predict a positive therapeutic alliance across person-centered, process-experiential, and cognitive-behavioral therapies (Geller, 2001; Geller et al., 2010).

Clients' experience of their therapists' presence has also been found to relate to a positive session outcome (Geller et al., 2010) and symptom reduction (Hayes & Vinca, 2011). Further, a study indicates that therapists' preparation of presession presence relates to both their in-session presence and positive session outcome (Dunn et al., 2013).

A vast body of research indicates that the therapeutic alliance results in positive therapy outcome (Duncan & Moynihan, 1994; Lambert & Ogles, 2004; Lambert & Simon, 2008; Martin et al., 2000; Norcross, 2002, 2011; Orlinsky et al., 1994). Now, emerging studies suggest that presence is a precondition for a positive therapeutic relationship and alliance. These studies contribute to the validity of our theoretical assumptions that one possibility as to how presence contributes to effective therapy is by mediating and promoting a positive therapeutic alliance (Geller & Greenberg, 2012; Geller et al., 2012).

WHAT IS THE POLYVAGAL THEORY?

Polyvagal Theory is an innovative reconceptualization of how autonomic state and behavior interface. The theory emphasizes a hierarchical relation among three subsystems of the autonomic nervous system that evolved to support adaptive behaviors in response to the particular environmental features of safety, danger, and life threat (Porges, 2011). The theory has received significant interest from researchers and clinicians working with individuals, particularly those with a trauma history. This interest is based on how Polyvagal Theory articulates two defense systems: (a) the commonly known fight-or-flight system that is associated with activation of the sympathetic nervous system (fight or flight), and (b) a less-known system of immobilization and dissociation that is associated with activation of a phylogenetically more ancient vagal pathway. The theory is named "polyvagal" to emphasize that there are two vagal circuits. One is an ancient vagal circuit associated with defense. The second is a phylogenetically newer circuit, only observed in mammals, that is associated with physiological states related to feeling safe and spontaneous social behavior (Porges, 2012).

The theory has stimulated research across several disciplines (e.g., neonatology, obstetrics, bioengineering, pediatrics, psychiatry, psychology, exercise physiology, human factors, etc.) and has been used as a theoretical perspective to generate research questions and explain findings by numerous different research teams (e.g., Ardizzi et al., 2013; Beauchaine, 2001; Beauchaine et al., 2007; Egizio et al., 2008; Hastings et al., 2008; Perry et al., 2012; Schwerdtfeger & Friedrich-Mai, 2009; Travis & Wallace, 1997; Weinberg et al., 2009; Whitson & El-Sheikh, 2003). For example, the theory has been used as a core theoretical explanation to explain the biobehavioral shutting down that occurs following trauma (Bradshaw et al., 2011; Levine, 2010; Ogden et al., 2006; Quintana et al., 2012) and has also informed stress researchers of the important role the parasympathetic nervous system and its component vagal circuits play in neurophysiological mechanisms related to defensive strategies associated with reactivity, recovery, and resilience (Brown & Gerberg, 2005; Evans et al., 2013; Kim & Yosipovitch, 2013; Kogan et al., 2012; McEwen, 2002; Wolff et al., 2012). The Polyvagal Theory describes the neural mechanisms through which physiological states communicate the experience of safety and contribute to an individual's ability either to feel safe and spontaneously engage with others, or to feel threatened and recruit defensive strategies. The theory articulates how each of three phylogenetic stages in the development of the vertebrate autonomic nervous system is associated with a distinct and measurable autonomic subsystem, each of which remains active and is expressed in humans under certain conditions (Porges, 2009). These three involuntary autonomic subsystems are phylogenetically ordered and behaviorally linked to three global adaptive domains of behavior: (a) social communication (e.g., facial expression, vocalization, listening), (b) defensive strategies associated with mobilization (e.g., fight-or-flight behaviors), and (c) defensive immobilization (e.g., feigning death, vasovagal syncope, behavioral shutdown, and dissociation). Based on their phylogenetic emergence during the evolution of the vertebrate autonomic nervous system, these neuroanatomically based subsystems form a response hierarchy.

The hierarchical nature of the autonomic nervous system described in the Polyvagal Theory is consistent with the construct of dissolution proposed by John H. Jackson (1958), in which more recently evolved neural circuits inhibit the function of older circuits. Therefore, the newest autonomic circuit associated with social communication has the functional capacity to inhibit the older involuntary circuits involved in defense strategies of fight or flight or shutdown behaviors.

According to the Polyvagal Theory, effective social communication can only occur during states when we experience safety, because only then are the neurobiological defense strategies inhibited. Thus, we suggest that one of the keys to successful therapy is for the therapist to be present and to promote client safety so that the client's involuntary defensive subsystems are downregulated, and the client's newer social engagement system is potentiated. Functionally, during therapy, the repeated present-moment encounters provide a neural exercise of the social engagement system. As these neural exercises enhance the efficiency and reliability of the neural pathways inhibiting the defense systems, the client acquires a greater accessibility to feelings of safety, openness, and self-exploration.

The Polyvagal Theory emphasizes the distinct roles of two distinct vagal motor pathways identified in the mammalian autonomic nervous system. The vagus is a cranial nerve that exits the brainstem and provides bidirectional communication between the brain and several visceral organs. The vagus conveys (and monitors) the primary parasympathetic influence to the viscera. Most of the neural fibers in the vagus are sensory (i.e., approximately 80%). However, most interest has been directed to the motor fibers that regulate the visceral organs, including the heart and the gut. Of these motor fibers, only approximately 15% are myelinated. Myelin, a fatty coating over the neural fiber, is associated with faster and more tightly regulated neural control circuits.

Unlike other vertebrates, mammals have two functionally distinct vagal circuits. One vagal circuit is phylogenetically older and unmyelinated. It originates in a brainstem area called the dorsal motor nucleus of the vagus. The other vagal circuit is uniquely mammalian and myelinated. The mammalian myelinated vagal circuit originates in a brainstem area called the nucleus ambiguus. The phylogenetically older unmyelinated vagal motor pathways are shared with most vertebrates and, in mammals when not recruited as a defense system, function to support health, growth, and restoration via neural regulation of subdiaphragmatic organs (i.e., internal organs below the diaphragm). The newer myelinated vagal motor pathways originating in the source nucleus of the ventral vagus (nucleus ambiguus) are observed only in mammals, regulate the supradiaphragmatic organs (e.g., heart and lungs). This newer vagal circuit slows heart rate and supports states of calmness.

Through brainstem mechanisms, the phylogenetically newer vagal circuit is also neuroanatomically and neurophysiologically linked to the cranial nerves that regulate the striated muscles of the face and head, which are the primary structures involved in social engagement behaviors. This neuroanatomically based face-heart connection provides mammals with an integrated social engagement system through which vocal prosody and facial expression functionally convey an individual's present physiological state to others (Porges, 2011, 2012; Porges & Lewis, 2009; Stewart et al., 2013). When the newer mammalian vagus is optimally functioning in social interactions (i.e., inhibiting the sympathetic excitation that promotes fight-or-flight behaviors), emotions are well regulated, vocal prosody is rich, and the autonomic state supports calm, spontaneous social engagement behaviors. The face-heart system is bidirectional, with the newer myelinated ventral vagal circuit influencing social interactions and positive social interactions influencing vagal function to optimize health, dampen stress-related physiological states, and support growth and restoration.

According to the Polyvagal Theory, when the individual feels safe, two important features are expressed. First, bodily state is regulated in an efficient manner to promote growth and restoration (e.g., visceral homeostasis). Functionally, this is accomplished through an increase in the influence of myelinated ventral vagal motor pathways on the cardiac pacemaker to slow heart rate, inhibit the fight-or-flight mechanisms of the sympathetic nervous system, dampen the stress response system of the hypothalamic-pituitary-adrenal axis (e.g., cortisol), and reduce inflammation by modulating immune reactions (e.g., cytokines). Second, through the process of evolution, the brainstem nuclei that regulate the myelinated ventral vagus became integrated with the nuclei that regulate the muscles of the face and head. This integration of neuroanatomical structures in the brainstem provides the neural pathways for a functional social engagement system characterized by a bidirectional coupling between bodily states and the spontaneous social engagement behaviors expressed in facial expressions and prosodic vocalizations. Thus, the behavioral manifestation of this integrated social engagement system observed in mammals emerged specifically as a consequence of the neural pathways regulating visceral states (via the myelinated ventral vagus), becoming neuroanatomically and neurophysiologically linked with the neural pathways regulating the muscles (via special visceral efferent pathways) controlling gaze, facial expression, head gesture, listening, and prosody (see Porges, 2001, 2007, 2009).

NEUROCEPTION

Within the context of therapeutic presence, the Polyvagal Theory provides a neurophysiological perspective that can explain how bodily feelings and emotions potentially can be influenced by the presence of others. Not only is there bidirectional communication between brain (i.e., central nervous system) and body, but also there is bidirectional communication between the nervous systems of the people who constitute our social environment (Cozolino, 2006; Porges, 2011; Siegel, 2007, 2010). Often, this bidirectional communication operates outside the realm of awareness, and we are left with a gut (visceral) feeling that alerts us to discomfort within a social interaction. This process of automatic evaluation of risk in the environment without awareness has been labeled neuroception (Porges, 2003, 2007).

Neuroception is posited to take place in the brain, most likely involving areas of the prefrontal and temporal cortices with projections to the amygdala and the periaqueductal gray (Porges, 2003). As a process influencing our autonomic nervous system, neuroception is viewed as an adaptive mechanism that can either turn off defenses to engage others or prepare us for defensive strategies associated with either fight-or-flight behaviors or shutdown. Moreover, as this process shifts autonomic state, it may also bias perception of others in the negative direction during states supporting fight or flight or in a positive direction during states supporting social engagement. If our physiological state shifts toward behavioral shutdown and dissociation (i.e., mediated by the unmyelinated dorsal vagal pathways), we lose contact with the environment and others.

Our nervous system continuously monitors and evaluates risk in the environment. When features of safety, danger, or life threat are detected, areas of the brainstem are activated that regulate autonomic structures. When features of safety are detected, autonomic reactions promote open receptivity with others, but when features of threat are detected, autonomic reactions promote a closed state, limiting the awareness of others (Porges, 2003, 2007). For example, in the presence of someone with whom an individual feels safe, a person experiences the sequelae of positive social engagement behaviors consistent with a neuroception of safety. Our physiology calms, and our defenses are inhibited. Defensive strategies are then replaced with gestures associated with feeling safe, and with this state of safety there is a perceptional bias toward the positive. Appropriately executed prosocial spontaneous interactions reduce psychological and physical distance. Thus, activating a sense of safety through being present with and for the client can downregulate the client's defenses and promote positive growth and change.

The Polyvagal Theory (Porges, 2011) explicitly describes the mechanisms of bidirectional communication between the brain and the visceral organs in our body that occur during stress responses. This bidirectional influence between our brain and visceral organs explains how the therapist's social and emotional responses to the client can potentially, by influencing the physiological state of the client, mediate either an expansion or restriction of the client's range and valence of socioemotional responding. Similarly, the client's socioemotional responses can impact the therapist's physiological state and potentially bias the therapist's interpretations of the client's responses from support to reactive. Recent neuroscience theory has suggested that this bidirectional communication between areas in the right hemisphere promote adaptive interpersonal functioning between therapist and client (Allison & Rossouw, 2013; Schore, 2012; Siegel, 2012). This right-hemispheric bias in behavioral state regulation is consistent with the profound impact of the right myelinated vagus in the regulation of physiological state (see Porges et al., 1994).

The attachment literature documents that trauma and early lack of attunement (i.e., a caregiver not attuned to the needs of the child) result in emotional dysregulation (Schore, 1994, 2003; van der Kolk, 1994, 2011). When one experiences lack of attachment to one's primary caregivers, one can perceive oneself to be chronically in danger. As such, a person with a trauma background may have an autonomic nervous system that chronically maintains a reaction to danger that precludes the downregulation of defense strategies. Perpetuation of these early experiences may then also result in challenges in the social world of these clients, to which they may respond defensively even when there is no risk. This profoundly impacts the individual's social world by removing them from naturally occurring reciprocal positive reinforcement implicit in supportive social interactions. Instead, a feedback loop is created, as others socially disengage from the reactive trauma survivor, further heightening the trauma individual's sense of isolation. Such disengagements may be as subtle as the lack of a contingent facial expression, or speaking with a flat vocal tone, or as blatant as using a dominating voice or overtly turning away (e.g., to repeatedly look at the clock in a therapy session or to answer the phone in a session).

Consistent with the Polyvagal Theory, these potent regulators of our physiological state that mediate emotional expression are embedded in relationships (Cozolino, 2006; Siegel, 2012). Myron Hofer (1994) employed a similar concept to explain the role of mother-infant interactions in facilitating the health and growth of infants. The core of the social engagement system in mammals is reflected in the bidirectional neural communication between the face and the heart (Porges, 2012). Through reciprocal interactions, via facial expressivity, gesture, and prosodic vocalizations, attunement occurs between the social engagement systems of two individuals. This attunement, consistent with Hofer's insights, regulates behavioral states (i.e., emotional regulation) and simultaneously promotes health, growth, and restoration.

While a lack of attunement in early relationships may be the cause of current emotional dysregulation, attunement and connection in current relationships can heal or, at minimum, exercise the neural circuits (i.e., the social engagement system) that support feelings of safety (Allison & Rossouw, 2013; Grawe, 2007; Porges, 2011; Siegel, 2010). From this perspective, physiological activation and/or emotional dysregulation can be stabilized through social interactions, which would include, as described below, warm facial expression, open body posture, vocal tone, and prosody (intonation and rhythm of vocalizations).

THERAPEUTIC PRESENCE AND THE NEUROCEPTION OF SAFETY

Polyvagal Theory helps us understand how therapeutic presence can contribute to effective therapy by strengthening the therapeutic relationship and enhancing clients' sense of safety. The theory posits a functional "neural love code," which reflects the evolutionary and biological quest for safety in relationship with others (Porges, 2012). From this view, potent cues of safety or danger that are detected by cortical areas and shift physiological states are communicated interpersonally from movements of the upper part of the face, eye contact, prosody of voice, and body posture. These profound changes in physiological state are mediated by features in the social interaction that are, in general, outside the realm of our awareness. As such, an interaction with another (i.e., with client or therapist) can trigger a broad range of bodily changes that we can and do interpret. For example, when seeing or talking to another, there may be feelings in the pit of the stomach, a sense of urgency to get away, or a desire to engage. Although reminiscent of the James-Lange theory of emotion (Cannon, 1927; James, 1884), Polyvagal Theory, with its constructs of neuroception and the social engagement system, emphasizes that there are both top-down (i.e., brain to body) and bottom-up (body to brain) signals regulating our physiological state. However, because both top-down and bottom-up pathways can trigger similar physiological states and psychological experiences, the theory provides plausible mechanisms to understand the physiological states that form substrates for a variety of emotions and affective states. Relevant to the clinical setting, the theory also provides an understanding of how to impact physiological states via central pathways involved in neuroception of safety or via behaviors that signal safety. The occurrence of neuroception of safety is detectable by physiological markers (e.g., open posture, soft facial features, and breathing). We posit that these emergent markers of safe reciprocal social interaction can reflect successful therapist offering and client receiving of therapist presence.

An understanding of how automatic physiological states are hierarchically regulated also informs clinicians of the potential of therapeutic presence to therapeutically benefit the client: by recruiting myelinated vagal circuits in the client through nondefensive social engagement. Furthermore, the neural mechanisms of the newer vagal system offer an opportunity through which therapist presence can exercise neural circuits in the client. By supporting the client's capacity for nondefensive social engagement, a client's reactiveness can be transformed over time. In the presence of someone perceived as safe, the client's experience of safety will result both in their defenses being inhibited and in their expressing nonverbal markers of feeling safe. Over time, this would result in additional helpful clinical features such as bodily softening and opening that support client self-awareness. Hence, it is therapeutically beneficial for therapists to communicate with their clients using these nonverbal markers of their own opening and softening, as these will help turn off client defenses and communicate therapists' neuroception of safety as well. Through therapists' warmth and prosody of voice, soft eye contact, open body posture, and receptive and accepting stance, the client experiences a calm and safe therapist and further opens in the therapy encounter. The therapeutic environment and clients' growth is thus profoundly facilitated.

It is for this reason that offering the client a consistent presence that is open, grounded, and spacious, and shows the intent of being with and for the client, is essential to the development of a positive therapeutic relationship. By allowing clients to develop feelings of safety over time through providing consistent presence, the therapist relationally regulates the client's nervous system stress responses. This, in turn, facilitates self-exploration through social contact, heal-ing, and deepened self-understanding. Therapeutic presence also allows the therapist to attune to and recognize (e.g., in the facial expression of the client) when the client is not feeling safe as well as to recognize and regulate their own reactivity to maintain authentic consistency with their client.

The Face and Voice

According to the Polyvagal Theory, the face and voice are powerful conduits through which safety is communicated to another. This is consistent with the clinical notion that the face is where presence is communicated to the client (Geller & Greenberg, 2012). In the view of Levinas (1985), faces are information centers that offer encounters with the other that are direct and profound. Look-ing at the face of the other and listening to voice are central to human relating, dialogue, and presence (Geller & Greenberg, 2012).

The importance of facial connection and prosody of speech is affirmed in the Polyvagal Theory. From this perspective, the neural connection between face (and voice) and heart provides a portal through which neural regulation of physiological states can be exercised through social engagement. In offering therapeutic presence, the therapist's warm facial connection, receptive posture, open heart, and listening presence help the client to feel safe and further precip-itates neural regulation of the client's physiology. Over time, consistently offered present-centered encounters with the therapist can strengthen the client's emo-tional regulation. This occurs as the client's physiology begins to entrain with the therapist's presence. Consistent therapist presence shifts the client to more frequently experience safety in social interactions. Hence, effective therapy requires repeated present engagement by the therapist, which would include the therapist being able to self-regulate, and to be open and available in the face of the client's defense and pain.

THERAPEUTIC PRESENCE THEORY OF RELATIONSHIP

From the perspective of the Polyvagal Theory and therapeutic presence theory of relationship, a present-centered therapist activates an experience of safety in the client through a warm facial expression and a prosodic voice (Porges, 2007, 2009, 2011). The client's neural assessment of safety then provokes a shift in physiological regulation that enables an inhibition of defense and supports the responses that reflect calm, openness, and trust. Therefore, we suggest that feel-ing met and heard by a present therapist capable of being attuned and respon-sive to clients' experience and physiology allows clients to drop their defenses and to themselves feel open and present. We assert that this shared biobehav-ioral state is not only healing in and of itself, but allows for the possibility of deeper therapeutic work conducted in the safety of the relationship.

The therapeutic presence theory of relationship proposes that therapeutic presence is an essential component underlying any effective therapeutic relationship. Regardless of theoretical orientation or type of therapeutic approach, presence promotes good session process and outcome, as well as enhancing the therapeutic alliance (Geller, 2013a, 2013b; Geller & Greenberg, 2012; Geller et al., 2012). This theory suggests therapists' presence provides the therapy relationship with the type of depth and connection needed to help clients feel safe enough to access their deepest feelings, meanings, concerns, and needs, and to share these with the therapist. Therapeutic presence provides the type of environment in which these feelings and needs can be most effectively attended to, explored, shared, and transformed.

From this perspective, present-centered engagement with the client also originates in the therapist through an internal preparation and intention for presence. This preparation includes the therapist's cultivation of a capacity for presence, both in life and prior to meeting the patient (Geller & Greenberg, 2002, 2012). Therapist presence with self or internal attunement facilitates a sense of calm and safety within the therapist as he or she prepares to meet the client (Siegel, 2010). There is evidence that attuning to one's self and one's "felt sense" (Gendlin, 1978) of another, as therapeutic presence entails, is the basis for attuning to and understanding the other (Siegel, 2007, 2010). We posit that this experienced attunement, the client "feeling felt" by the therapist (Siegel, 2007), impacts the client's physiology through the calming feelings of safety that are evoked when one feels met and understood.

The theory of therapeutic relating based on presence also suggests that although the experience of presence by the therapist and its communication to the client is important, it is healing only if the client experiences the therapist as being fully there in the moment (Geller & Greenberg, 2012). This is based on research suggesting that it is the client's experience of the therapist's presence, not the therapist's experience, which promotes positive therapeutic process and change as well as a strong therapeutic alliance (Geller et al., 2010; Pos et al., 2011). There are also reciprocal relationships among the therapist's felt and communicated presence, the client receiving and feeling the therapist as present with them, and both parties developing greater presence within and between each other. This presence growing within and between therapist and client contributes to the development of relational presence. Relational presence provides the conditions for an "I-thou" encounter, and, ultimately, this mutual relational presence also promotes relational depth, safety, and therapeutic change (Buber, 1958; Cooper, 2005; Geller, 2013a; Geller & Greenberg, 2012).

Emerging theories from several scientific disciplines, including neuroscience research, invites us to recognize our inherent relational nature (Cozolino, 2006; Porges, 2011; Siegel, 2007, 2010). Through relational attuning, what has been termed "brain-to-brain coupling" may occur (Hasson et al., 2012), which results in a resonance from one brain to another. We believe that as the therapist is self-attuned and approaches the client with a calm and engaged presence, an entrainment process ensues that invites the client's brain to regulate into a safe presence-centered state.

We propose that the cultivation of safety through the emergence of a relational presence promotes therapeutic effectiveness and a client's positive growth and change through three mechanisms. Relational presence facilitates (a) clients' openness to engage in therapeutic work, (b) strengthening of the therapeutic relationship, and (c) therapists' being more attuned to the readiness of the client and more able to optimally offer effective and attuned interventions or responses (see Chart 9.1). Further, over time, from the perspective of the Polyvagal Theory, the client's capacity for neuroception of safety is encouraged through repeated encounters in the presence of a safe, present therapist.

In summary, a relationship theory based on therapeutic presence suggests that therapeutic presence will lead to the development of a synergistic relationship in which the client develops greater presence, while the deepening of relational presence between therapist and client occurs simultaneously. This has been articulated through the lens of the Polyvagal Theory. As the client, via neuroception, reacts (without cognitive awareness) to the present-centered therapist as safe, the client's physiology becomes regulated and calm, allowing for more openness and presence in the client. As such, we believe that presence is a relational stance fundamental to evoking a sense of safety in the therapist, in the client, and in the relational therapeutic environment. This sense of safety in turn can further promote a positive therapeutic alliance and effective clinical work across different therapeutic approaches.

CLINICAL VIGNETTES

Present-moment awareness and self-regulation are helpful for therapists not only to maintain presence in session, but also to notice when either they or their clients close down. Through present, in-the-moment awareness, the therapist has an opportunity to shift his or her own and the client's engagement. Following are two examples depicting two types of therapeutic interaction: (a) nonpresence, and (b) a return to therapeutic presence. The example of nonpresence reflects how when the therapist shuts down in a therapeutic moment, the client begins to feel unsafe and therefore pulls away. The example of returned presence reflects how a therapist used awareness of their own internal barriers to their own presence in the moment in order to reconnect to both the moment and the client to reestablish safety in the therapeutic encounter. Possible neurophysiological signs of connection and disconnection that the therapist might learn to attend to are suggested in parentheses to illustrate what happens concurrently in the brain and the body when the therapist is not present and when he or she is fully with and attuned to the client.

CHART 9.1.   How does therapeutic presence promote safety and therapy effectiveness?

Therapist's Attunement to Self →
Therapist Attunement to Client →
Client feeling felt, calming, becoming present within (safety) →
(a) and (b) and (c)*

(a) Client feeling safe to open and engage in therapeutic work
(b) Strengthening of therapeutic relationship
(c) Therapist responses and interventions attuned to the optimal moment for
     client to receive

*Repeated engagement and presence of the therapist also exercises neural regulation of the muscles involved in the client's experience of safety in self and in relationship.

Nonpresence: Vignette Reflecting the Barriers to Presence

Michael cried as he talked about the guilt he felt since his wife, Sally, had died. He described a fight he had with Sally a few weeks before her death, when he walked out of the house in an angry huff. When he returned that evening, her health had taken a turn for the worse, and her speech was now permanently compromised from a stroke. He cried with remorse, wondering if the stress from their fight and his leaving had caused her health to decline. As I was listening to him, I began to feel anxious and overwhelmed, doubting my ability to help him with his complicated grief (beginning of disconnection and therapist withdrawal). My anxiety grew as I began to hear my own internal voice say, "You can't help him. . . . You fought with your own mother before she died and you still feel guilty. . . . Who do you think you are?" (Therapist's sympathetic nervous system is activated and a relational disconnection is occurring.) My responses to him were concrete and flat, and my facial features tightened as I battled with my own critical voices. (Loss of myelinated ventral vagal tone was reflected in a loss of neuromuscular tone to upper part of the face, resulting in a flat face—voice would also lose prosody, and likely muscle tone of the lower face would increase as part of a more hardened, aggressive stance. Also, as neuromuscular tone of the upper face is reduced, there is a parallel reduction of neuromuscular tone to the middle ear muscles, and the therapist starts to lose contact with the syntactic and affective content of the client's vocalizations.) Michael went silent and his tears stopped (neuroception of a loss of safety as the client automatically perceived the therapist's withdrawal), while he shifted the conversation to the demands at his work and all the tasks he had to com-

plete. I felt the disconnection between us and did not know how to proceed (therapist's accurate perception of loss of safety and connection).

The disconnection and loss of safety in this example is a result of the emergence of the therapist's own barriers (self-doubt and unresolved issues from her mother's death).

Therapeutic Presence: Vignette Reflecting a Return to the Moment

Therapeutic presence is not just about being fully in the moment with a client, but also having a moment-to-moment awareness of the barriers to being present and being able to bring one's full awareness back to the client when these barriers emerge. The following example reflects the therapist's awareness of both self-doubt and subsequent disconnection. This awareness of nonpresence within herself and between herself and her client helped her to bring her attention back to the moment. This therapist continues:

> *As I became aware of the disconnection and my anxiousness, I took a few deep breaths to help regulate my emotions and bring my attention back to the room. (Exhaling slowly potentiated the myelinated ventral vagal brake on the heart, resulting in greater calm.) As I started to talk to Michael, I could feel my facial expression soften (as a result of the calmer physiological state in the therapist, the upper part of therapist's face provided warm cues to the client), my voice was rich with prosody, and I sensed our connection as he calmed and spontaneously engaged me by leaning forward with a facial expression that I experienced as open and feeling understood. My prior practice in presence primed me to silently imagine putting my doubts and unresolved issues with my mother aside for the moment. I noticed how Michael's distance and shutdown reflected my own internal distancing. I invited my attention back to the moment and was able to return with my full awareness to my client. As I looked in Michael's eyes, I reflected in a soft and warm voice, "The pain is so deep . . . pain and regret at wishing it could have been different." Michael's tears began to well up again as he looked at me and said, "Yes, I feel deep sadness. I miss her so much."*
>
> *I shared with Michael the sense of helplessness in the face of grief, and this open and compassionate sharing not only allowed him to open and express his layers of grief and despair, but also deepened the bond between us. (As long as the therapist's social engagement system was online, she was present and could support Michael with the appropriate cues to trigger in his nervous system a neuroception of safety that would enable him to process his profound grief.)*

The therapist's present-moment awareness served to notice the disconnection while her prior presence practice allowed her to self-regulate (through deep breathing and awareness), put aside self-doubt and unresolved issues, and return with full open presence to the client. In this example, the therapist's inward attending and contact with her experience, which is a part of the practice of therapeutic presence, allowed her to notice her own barriers and her distancing from the client. She was then able to return her attention to the client and open to the difficult feelings that he was experiencing, both of which allowed for a repair in the relational disconnection. This reconnection invited the client back to a place of safety with the therapist, where he could then grieve fully the loss of his wife.

FINAL REMARKS

Using empirical neurophysiological support provided by the Polyvagal Theory, it appears that feeling safe is a necessary prerequisite to establishing strong social bonds (i.e., a therapeutic relationship) that are potentially helpful or healing for a client. We propose that through present-centered relating that includes eye contact, softening and warmth in voice, vocal prosody, emotional attunement, and in-the-moment engagement, the client perceives safety. This experience of neuroception of safety eventually shuts down the client's defenses, which is healing in and of itself and also helps therapist and client engage in therapeutic work. Further, the capacity of the brain to develop new neural connections leading to calmer and healthier emotional states is facilitated when a safe therapeutic environment is promoted through the cultivation and expression of the therapist's presence (Allison & Rossouw, 2013; Cozolino, 2006; Geller & Greenberg, 2012; Porges, 2011). In this vein, we view therapeutic presence and the creation of safety that it supports as a transtheoretically important therapeutic process (Geller et al., 2012). Powerful in and of itself, therapeutic presence can also promote the greatest efficacy when accompanied with modality-specific techniques (Geller, 2013b; Geller & Greenberg, 2012). If, instead, a scripted and nonreflective response or intervention is provided to clients without present awareness of the client's in-the-moment experience, by a therapist who is detached from the humanism of the person-to-person encounter that psychotherapy entails, the client may feel defended, and the intervention will be limited in its efficacy. Alternatively, offering the intervention in a way that is infused with therapeutic presence and attuned to the readiness of the client promotes the client's safety and optimizes the window through which effective therapeutic work can occur.

We propose that cultivating presence and understanding the neurophysiological underpinnings of creating safety needs to be an essential component in therapist training programs across modalities. Psychotherapy training typically focuses on intervention and techniques without attention to how the therapist can cultivate the state of being present to support the client's neuroception of safety. We have argued here that therapeutic presence is foundational to promoting client safety, a core prerequisite for effective therapeutic work regardless of the therapeutic approach. As such, we also argue that understanding and cultivating therapeutic presence should be viewed as an essential foundation in psychotherapy training. It is important for therapists to maintain a calm presence in the face of pain or struggle. Hence, training can include ways of supporting this state through attention to bodily and emotional regulation as well as barriers to positive relating. Findings from neuroscience that reflect the neural correlates between the therapist's presence and the client's experience of safety can help therapists understand how to promote greater therapeutic attunement.

The therapist's cultivation of presence can also contribute to a necessary part of the therapist's ongoing self-care. Clients also may benefit in and out of session from neural exercises that promote experiences of inner safety. Such neural exercises that promote the neuroception of safety for both therapist and client can include slow exhalations following deep abdominal breathing (i.e., the influence of the myelinated ventral vagus on the heart is optimized during exhalation), social play (e.g., team sports, group drumming), improvisational music, being in nature, yoga, meditation, or programs such as Therapeutic Rhythm and Mindfulness (see http://www.rhythmandmindfulness.com/; Geller & Greenberg, 2012), specifically designed to promote therapeutic presence. Promoting the capacity to be present in session can also benefit the therapist, the client, and their relationship. For example, beginning a session with deep breathing or a mindfulness exercise may help both parties be more in the moment, soften their defenses, and promote deeper engagement.

In summary, the cultivation of therapeutic and relational presence that evokes a safe therapeutic encounter both in and out of session is imperative in order to promote the social engagement that leads to real and lasting change. The Polyvagal Theory provides us with deep understanding of the bidirectional neural feedback circuits within the brain and body that link human beings in relationship. This knowledge can help us appreciate the importance of approaching the therapeutic encounter in ways that cultivate and communicate being present with and for the client in order to promote clients' optimal health and well-being.

We hope that this chapter offers an impetus for future research in therapeutic presence and the neurophysiological mechanisms and structures involved in experiences related to presence, attunement, and creating safety. Many research avenues are possible. For example, observing the upper part of the face, vocal quality, posture, and patterns of breathing in both the therapist and client, in moments of presence and nonpresence, may help to illuminate how therapists optimally communicate presence in psychotherapy. Also, tracking clients' expressions of safety in relation to provided therapeutic presence may be an important focus. In addition, monitoring changes in visceral components of the social engagement system during sessions (e.g., vagal regulation of the heart by quantifying the respiratory sinus arrhythmia component of heart rate variability) as clients receive therapists' presence may help to illuminate the neurophysiological regulation and healing that present-centered therapeutic relating can evoke.

REFERENCES

Allison, K. L., & Rossouw, P. J. (2013). The therapeutic alliance: Exploring the concept of "safety" from a neuropsychotherapeutic perspective. *International Journal of Neuropsychotherapy, 1*, 21–29.

Ardizzi, M., Martini, F., Umilta, M. A., Sestito, M., Ravera, R., & Gallese, V. (2013). When early experiences build a wall to others' emotions: An electrophysiological and autonomic study. *PLoS One, 8*, e61004. doi:10.1371/journal.pone.0061004

Beauchaine, T. P. (2001). Vagal tone, development, and Gray's motivational theory: Toward an integrated model of autonomic nervous system functioning in psychopathology. *Development and Psychopathology, 13*, 183–214. doi:10.1017/S0954579401002012

Beauchaine, T. P., Gatzke-Kopp, L., & Mead, H. K. (2007). Polyvagal Theory and developmental psychopathology: Emotion dysregulation and conduct problems from preschool to adolescence. *Biological Psychology, 74*, 174–184. doi:10.1016/j.biopsycho.2005.08.008

Bradshaw, R. A., Cook, A., & McDonald, M. J. (2011). Observed and experiential integration (OEI): Discovery and development of a new set of trauma therapy techniques. *Journal of Psychotherapy Integration, 21*, 104–171. doi:10.1037/a0023966

Brown, R. P., & Gerbarg, P. L. (2005). Sudarshan kriya yogic breathing in the treatment of stress, anxiety, and depression: Part I—neurophysiologic model. *Journal of Alternative and Complementary Medicine, 11*, 189–201. doi:10.1089/acm.2005.11.189

Buber, M. (1958). *I and thou* (2nd ed.). New York: Charles Scribner's Sons.

Cannon, W. C. (1927). The James-Lange theory of emotions: A critical examination and an alternative theory. *American Journal of Psychiatry, 39*, 106–124.

Cooper, M. (2005). Therapists' experiences of relational depth: A qualitative interview study. *Counselling and Psychotherapy Research, 5*, 87–95.

Cozolino, L. J. (2006). *The neuroscience of relationships: Attachment and the developing social brain*. New York: Norton.

Duncan, B. L., & Moynihan, D. W. (1994). Applying outcome research: Intentional utilization of the client's frame of reference. *Psychotherapy: Theory, Research, Practice, Training, 31*, 294–301. doi:10.1037/h0090215

Dunn, R., Callahan, J. L., Swift, J. K., & Ivanovic, M. (2013). Effects of pre-session centering for therapists on session presence and effectiveness. *Psychotherapy Research, 23*, 78– 85. doi:10.1080/10503307.2012.731713

Egizio, V. B., Jennings, J. R., Christie, I. C., Sheu, L. K., Matthews, K. A., & Gianaros, P. J. (2008). Cardiac vagal activity during psychological stress varies with social functioning in older women. *Psychophysiology, 45*, 1046–1054. doi:10.1111/j.1469-8986.2008.00698.x

Evans, B. E., Greaves-Lord, K., Euser, A. S., Tulen, J. H. M., Franken, I. H. A., & Huizink, A. C. (2013). Determinants of physiological and perceived physiological stress reactivity in children and adolescents. *PLoS One, 8*, e61724. doi:10.1371/journal.pone.0061724

Geller, S. M. (2001). *Therapeutic presence: The development of a model and a measure* [Unpublished doctoral dissertation]. York University, Toronto, Canada.

Geller, S. M. (2009). Cultivation of therapeutic presence: Therapeutic drumming and mindfulness practices. *Dutch Tijdschrift Clientgerichte Psychotherapie* [Journal for Client-Centered Psychotherapy], 47, 273–287.

Geller, S. M. (2013a). Therapeutic presence as a foundation for relational depth. In R. Knox, D. Murphy, S. Wiggins, & M. Cooper (Eds.), *Relational depth: Contemporary perspectives* (pp. 175–184). Basingstoke, UK: Palgrave.

Geller, S. M. (2013b). Therapeutic presence: An essential way of being. In M. Cooper, P. F. Schmid, M. O'Hara, & A. C. Bohart (Eds.), *The handbook of person-centred psychotherapy and counselling* (2nd ed., pp. 209–222). Basingstoke, UK: Palgrave.

Geller, S. M., & Greenberg, L. S. (2002). Therapeutic presence: Therapists' experience of presence in the psychotherapeutic encounter. *Person-Centered and Experiential Psychotherapies, 1,* 71–86. doi:10.1080/14779757.2002.9688279

Geller, S. M., & Greenberg, L. S. (2012). *Therapeutic presence: A mindful approach to effective therapy.* Washington, DC: American Psychological Association.

Geller, S. M., Greenberg, L. S., & Watson, J. C. (2010). Therapist and client perceptions of therapeutic presence: The development of a measure. *Psychotherapy Research, 20,* 599– 610. doi:10.1080/10503307.2010.495957

Geller, S. M., Pos, A. W., & Colosimo, K. (2012). Therapeutic presence: A common factor in the provision of effective psychotherapy. *Society for Psychotherapy Integration, 47,* 6 –13.

Gendlin, E. (1978). *Focusing.* New York: Everest House.

Germer, C. K., Siegel, R. D., & Fulton, P. R. (2005). *Mindfulness and psychotherapy.* New York: Guilford.

Goldfried, M. R., & Davila, J. (2005). The role of relationship and technique in therapeutic change. *Psychotherapy: Theory, Research, Practice, Training, 42,* 421–430. doi:10.1037/0033-3204.42.4.421

Grawe, K. (2007). *Neuropsychotherapy: How neurosciences inform effective psychotherapy.* New York: Taylor and Francis.

Greenberg, L. S., Rice, L., & Elliott, R. (1993). *Facilitating emotional change: The moment-by-moment process.* New York: Guilford.

Hasson, U., Ghazanfar, A. A., Galantucci, B., Garrod, S., & Keysers, C. (2012). Brain to brain coupling: A mechanism for creating and sharing a social world. *Trends in Cognitive Sciences, 16,* 114–121. doi:10.1016/j.tics.2011.12.007

Hastings, P. D., Nuselovici, J. N., Utendale, W. T., Coutya, J., McShane, K. E., & Sullivan, C. (2008). Applying the Polyvagal Theory to children's emotion regulation: Social context, socialization, and adjustment. *Biological Psychology, 79,* 299–306. doi:10.1016/j.biopsycho.2008.07.005

Hayes, J., & Vinca, J. (2011). *Therapist presence and its relationship to empathy, session, depth, and symptom reduction.* Paper presented to the Society for Psychotherapy Research, Bern, Switzerland.

Hofer, M. A. (1994). Hidden regulators in attachment, separation, and loss. *Monographs of the Society for Research in Child Development, 59,* 192–207. doi:10.1111/j.1540-5834.1994.tb01285.x

Jackson, J. H. (1958). Evolution and dissolution of the nervous system. In J. Taylor (Ed.), *Selected Writings of John Hughlings Jackson* (pp. 45–118). London: Staples.

James, W. (1884). What is an emotion? *Mind, 9*, 188–205. doi:10.1093/mind/os-IX.34.188

Kim, H. S., & Yosipovitch, G. (2013). An aberrant parasympathetic response: A new perspective linking chronic stress and itch. *Experimental Dermatology, 22*, 239–244. doi:10.1111/exd.12070

Kogan, A. V., Allen, J. J. B., & Weihs, K. L. (2012). Cardiac vagal control as a prospective predictor of anxiety in women diagnosed with breast cancer. *Biological Psychology, 90*, 105–111. doi:10.1016/j.biopsycho.2012.02.019

Lambert, M. J., & Ogles, B. M. (2004). The efficacy and effectiveness of psychotherapy. In M. J. Lambert (Ed.), *Bergin and Garfield's handbook of psychotherapy and behavior change* (5th ed., pp. 139–193). New York: Wiley.

Lambert, M. J., & Simon, W. (2008). The therapeutic relationship: Central and essential in psychotherapy outcome. In S. F. Hick & T. Bien (Eds.), *Mindfulness and the therapeutic relationship* (pp. 19–33). New York: Guilford.

Levinas, E. (1985). *Ethics and infinity, conversations with Philippe Nemo* (R. A. Cohen, Trans., pp. 86–87). Pittsburgh, PA: Duquesne University Press.

Levine, P. A. (2010). *In an unspoken voice: How the body releases trauma and restores goodness.* Berkeley, CA: North Atlantic.

Martin, D. J., Garske, J. P., & Davis, M. K. (2000). Relation of the therapeutic alliance with outcome and other variables: A meta-analytic review. *Journal of Consulting and Clinical Psychology, 68*, 438–450. doi:10.1037/0022-006X.68.3.438

McCollum, E. E., & Gehart, D. R. (2010). Using mindfulness meditation to teach beginning therapists therapeutic presence: A qualitative study. *Journal of Marital and Family Therapy, 36*, 347–360.

McEwen, B. (2002). *The end of stress as we know it.* Washington, DC: John Henry Press.

Mearns, D. (1997). *Person-centred counselling training.* London: Sage.

Norcross, J. C. (2002). *Psychotherapy relationships that work: Therapists' contributions and responsiveness to patients.* New York: Oxford University Press.

Norcross, J. C. (2011). *Psychotherapy relationships that work: Evidence-based responsiveness* (2nd ed.). New York: Oxford University Press. doi:10.1093/acprof:oso/9780199737208.001.0001

Ogden, P., Minton, K., & Pain, C. (2006). *Trauma and the body: A sensorimotor approach to psychotherapy.* New York: Norton.

Orlinsky, D. E., Grawe, K., & Parks, B. K. (1994). Process and outcome in psychotherapy—noch einmal. In A. E. Bergen & S. Garfield (Eds.), *Handbook of psychotherapy and behavior change* (pp. 270–376). New York: Wiley.

Perry, N. B., Calkins, S. D., Nelson, J. A., Leerkes, E. M., & Marcovitch, S. (2012). Mothers' responses to children's negative emotions and child emotion regulation: The moderating role of vagal suppression. *Developmental Psychobiology, 54*, 503–513. doi:10.1002/dev.20608

Porges, S. W. (1995). Orienting in a defensive world: Mammalian modifications of our evolutionary heritage: A Polyvagal Theory. *Psychophysiology, 32*, 301–318. doi:10.1111/j.1469-8986.1995.tb01213.x

Porges, S. W. (1998). Love: An emergent property of the mammalian autonomic nervous system. *Psychoneuroendocrinology, 23*, 837–861. doi:10.1016/S0306-4530(98)00057-2

Porges, S. W. (2001). The Polyvagal Theory: Phylogenetic substrates of a social nervous system. *International Journal of Psychophysiology, 42*, 123–146. doi:10.1016/S0167-8760(01)00162-3

Porges, S. W. (2003). Social engagement and attachment: A phylogenetic perspective. Roots of Mental Illness in Children. *Annals of the New York Academy of Sciences, 1008,* 31–47. doi:10.1196/annals.1301.004

Porges, S. W. (2007). The polyvagal perspective. *Biological Psychology, 74,* 116–143. doi:10.1016/j.biopsycho.2006.06.009

Porges, S. W. (2009). The Polyvagal Theory: New insights into adaptive reactions of the autonomic nervous system. *Cleveland Clinic Journal of Medicine, 76,* S86–S90. doi:10.3949/ccjm.76.s2.17

Porges, S. W. (2011). *The Polyvagal Theory: Neurophysiological foundations of emotions, attachment, communication, self-regulation.* New York: Norton.

Porges, S. W. (2012). *What therapists need to know about the Polyvagal Theory.* Presentation at Leading Edge Seminars, Toronto, Ontario.

Porges, S. W., Doussard-Roosevelt, J. A., & Maiti, A. K. (1994). Vagal tone and the physiological regulation of emotion. *Monographs of the Society for Research in Child Development, 59,* 167–186.

Porges, S. W., & Lewis, G. F. (2009). The polyvagal hypothesis: Common mechanisms mediating autonomic regulation, vocalizations, and listening. In S. M. Brudzynski (Ed.), *Handbook of mammalian vocalizations: An integrative neuroscience approach* (pp. 255–264). Amsterdam: Academic Press.

Pos, A., Geller, S., & Oghene, J. (2011). *Therapist presence, empathy, and the working alliance in experiential treatment for depression.* Paper presented at the meeting of the Society for Psychotherapy Research, Bern, Switzerland.

Quintana, D. S., Guastella, A. J., Outhred, T., Hickie, I. B., & Kemp, A. H. (2012). Heart rate variability is associated with emotion recognition: Direct evidence for a relationship between the autonomic nervous system and social cognition. *International Journal of Psychophysiology, 86,* 168–172. doi:10.1016/j.ijpsycho.2012.08.012

Rogers, C. R. (1957). The necessary and sufficient conditions of therapeutic personality change. *Journal of Consulting Psychology, 21,* 95–103. doi:10.1037/h0045357

Rogers, C. R. (1980). *A way of being.* Boston: Houghton Mifflin.

Rossouw, P. J. (2013, January). The end of the medical model: Recent findings in neuroscience regarding antidepressant medication and the implications for neuropsychotherapy [Departmental article]. *Neuropsychotherapist.* http://www.neuropsychotherapist.com/the-end-of-the-medicalmodel/

Schore, A. N. (1994). *Affect regulation and the origin of the self: The neurobiology of emotional development.* Hillsdale, NJ: Erlbaum.

Schore, A. N. (2003). *Affect dysregulation and disorders of the self.* New York: Norton.

Schore, A. N. (2012). *The science and art of psychotherapy.* New York: Norton.

Schwerdtfeger, A., & Friedrich-Mai, P. (2009). Social interaction moderates the relationship between depressive mood and heart rate variability: Evidence from an ambulatory monitoring study. *Health Psychology, 28,* 501–509. doi:10.1037/a0014664

Siegel, D. J. (2007). *The mindful brain: Reflection and attunement in the cultivation of well-being.* New York: Norton.

Siegel, D. J. (2010). *Mindsight: The new science of personal transformation.* New York: Bantam.

Siegel, D. J. (2012). *The developing mind: How relationships and the brain interact to shape who we are* (2nd ed.). New York: Guilford.

Stewart, A. M., Lewis, G. F., Heilman, K. J., Davila, M. I., Coleman, D. D., Aylward, S. A., & Porges, S. W. (2013). The covariation of acoustic features of infant cries and autonomic state. *Physiology and Behavior, 120,* 203–210. doi:10.1016/j.physbeh.2013.07.003

Travis, F., & Wallace, R. K. (1997). Autonomic patterns during respiratory suspensions: Possible markers of transcendental consciousness. *Psychophysiology, 34,* 39–46. doi:10.1111/j.1469-8986.1997.tb02414.x

van der Kolk, B. A. (1994). The body keeps the score: Memory and the evolving psychobiology of posttraumatic stress. *Harvard Review of Psychiatry, 1,* 253–265. doi:10.3109/10673229409017088

van der Kolk, B. (2011). Foreword. In S. W. Porges, *The Polyvagal Theory: Neurophysiological foundations of emotions, attachment, communication, self-regulation.* New York: Norton.

Weinberg, A., Klonsky, E. D., & Hajcak, G. (2009). Autonomic impairment in borderline personality disorder: A laboratory investigation. *Brain and Cognition, 71,* 279–286. doi:10.1016/j.bandc.2009.07.014

Whitson, S., & El-Sheikh, M. (2003). Marital conflict and health: Processes and protective factors. *Aggression and Violent Behavior, 8,* 283–312. doi:10.1016/S1359-1789(01)00067-2

Wolff, B. C., Wadsworth, M. E., Wilhelm, F. H., & Mauss, I. B. (2012). Children's vagal regulatory capacity predicts attenuated sympathetic stress reactivity in a socially supportive context: Evidence for a protective effect of the vagal system. *Development and Psychopathology, 24,* 677–689. doi:10.1017/S0954579412000247

Play and the Dynamics of Treating Pediatric Medical Trauma
Insights From Polyvagal Theory

Stephen W. Porges and Stuart Daniel

KAL AND HIS POLAR BEAR

Kal was curled in the far corner of his hospital bed. His body was emaciated. He was six years old and suffering from every aspect of an especially nasty cancer. A few days earlier, Kal had received an injection as part of a particular treatment procedure. Crying and fighting, Kal had been physically restrained by his mother and two nurses. Since that procedure, Kal had refused to talk, make eye contact with anyone, or eat. His blood count was dangerously low.

Clare, the oncology psychologist, sat near Kal as he lay in bed. She introduced herself in a gentle voice and then sat quietly with Kal for a while. Clare tried a few playful initiations and, when Kal displayed a lack of interest, she used her melodic storyteller's voice to acknowledge this and lightheartedly tell herself off. Kal smiled a tiny smile. Clare then told a little story out loud of what Kal might be feeling. She used large emotional gestures, sighs, and her rhythmic voice to accompany the words of this story. Kal was actively listening now.

"Hey Kal, I've brought something with me today. Have a look at these. . . ."

Clare took out a box containing a range of play figures and set it down on the hospital-bed tray.

"I wonder if you could choose one."

Kal said nothing. But he looked at Clare for the first time, his eyes a little interested, a little hopeful. "How's about I start . . . ," Clare said, "maybe this one, and maybe right here in the middle. . . ."

Clare placed a tiny knight in the center of the tray. She looked at Kal. Kal was now shaking his head vigorously. He was half sitting up from his prone position.

Clare admonished herself mockingly, "Oh, I've got it wrong [big sigh]. . . . You know, I think I left my brain at home today. . . . Kal, can you knock on my head to see if my brain is in there?"

Kal did.

They both laughed and Clare continued, "Yep, no brain . . . I am really going to need you to help me."

Kal swapped the tiny knight for a huge polar bear. From this point on, Kal started to talk. He talked about what he was doing as he developed a complex play configuration with many characters. From these moments of shared emotional state, Kal moved into a powerful therapy process. Kal continued to speak, and eat, from that day on.

SYSTEMS OF SAFETY: INTRODUCING THE POLYVAGAL THEORY

This chapter introduces the Polyvagal Theory (Porges 1995, 2001, 2007, 2009, 2011), an innovative model that explores how human evolution has linked social behavior and health to the mechanisms that mediate our feelings of safety or danger. The Polyvagal Theory will be outlined and then used in an exploration of human connection, safety, trauma, and the potential healing power of play. Polyvagal Theory helps us understand how cues of risk and safety, which are continuously monitored by our nervous system, influence our physiological and behavioral states. The theory emphasizes that humans are on a quest to calm neural defense systems by detecting features of safety. This quest is initiated at birth when an infant's need to be soothed is dependent on the caregiver. This quest forms the motivation to develop social relationships that enable individuals to effectively coregulate each other. The quest continues throughout the life span with emerging needs for trusting friendships and loving partnerships.

Polyvagal Theory describes a three-tiered hierarchy of survival-oriented adaptive strategies: the social engagement system, the mobilization system, and the immobilization system.

We look first at the social engagement system. Without cognitive awareness, our nervous system continuously scans the environment for features of danger or safety. This reflexive process we refer to as neuroception. The term "neuroception" is used to contrast with classical notions of perception, which, due to requiring cognitive awareness, results in a slower appraisal of risk. When there is a neuroception of safety, two important features are expressed. First, bodily state is regulated in an efficient manner to promote health, growth, and restoration (visceral homeostasis). This occurs when the influence of mammalian myelinated ventral vagal motor pathways on the cardiac pacemaker increases. Increasing the influence of these vagal pathways slows heart rate, inhibits the fight-flight mechanisms of the sympathetic nervous system, dampens the stress response system of the hypothalamic-pituitary-adrenal (HPA) axis (e.g., cortisol), and reduces inflammatory reaction (e.g., cytokines). Second, through evolutionary processes, the brainstem nuclei that regulate the myelinated vagus are integrated with the nuclei that regulate the striated muscles of the face and head. This link enables a bidirectional coupling between spontaneous social engagement behaviors and bodily states. Thus, as mammals evolved, an integrated social engagement system emerged that not only expressed physiological state in facial expression and vocalizations, but also enabled social behavior to regulate physiological state. These concepts are developed below (see the next section).

The human nervous system, similar to that of other mammals, evolved not solely for life in a safe environment but also to survive in dangerous and life-threatening contexts. On neuroception of risk, or when the social engagement system is compromised, the two more primitive neural circuits regulating physiological state may be recruited to support defensive strategies. The first of these is the mobilization system, which orchestrates fight-flight behaviors, and the second is the evolutionarily ancient immobilization system (involving death-feigning behaviors).

Central to the Polyvagal Theory is the conceptualization that these three survival-oriented strategies are dependent on a parallel hierarchy in the function of the three neural circuits in the autonomic nervous system. This hierarchical perspective is a defining feature of the Polyvagal Theory and is in contrast with the traditional perspective of the autonomic nervous system as a paired-antagonist system: a model in which two subsystems, the sympathetic and parasympathetic nervous systems, have antagonistic functions (i.e., either activating or calming) on the same organ. In the polyvagal hierarchy of adaptive responses, the newest circuit (which supports the social engagement system) is recruited first; if that circuit fails to provide safety, the older circuits are recruited sequentially to orchestrate defense responses (mobilization, then immobilization). It is important to note that when these defense systems are recruited, the autonomic nervous system supports these survival-related behaviors at the expense of health, growth, and restoration; social behavior, social communication, and visceral homeostasis are all incompatible with the neurophysiological states and behaviors promoted by the two defense systems.

THE FACE-HEART CONNECTION

In vertebrates, which are the phylogenetic ancestors of mammals, the vagus originates in a brainstem area known as the dorsal nucleus of the vagus. During the evolutionary transition from primitive ancient reptiles to mammals, a second vagal motor pathway emerged that originated in the nucleus ambiguus, a brainstem area ventral to the dorsal nucleus of the vagus. Although the vagal pathways originating in the nucleus ambiguus are the primary motor pathways regulating the heart, the nucleus ambiguus is also part of a brainstem column that regulates the striated muscles of the face and head. This evolutionary boot-strapping process allowed for integration between the myelinated ventral vagus and the nuclei that regulate muscular control of the face and head: specifically the muscles controling facial expression, listening, and prosodic vocalizations. These emergent changes in neuroanatomy gave rise to a phylogenetically novel face-heart connection. The face-heart connection provided mammals with an ability to convey physiological state via facial expression and prosody (intona-tion of voice). This gave mammals, and subsequently humans, the potential to use social interactions to calm physiological state in others, through the facial expressions and vocalizations that form the core of social interactions. The face-heart connection enables humans to detect whether someone is in a calm phys-iological state and safe to approach, or is in a highly mobilized and reactive physiological state, during which engagement would be dangerous. The con-nection concurrently enables an individual to signal safety through patterns of facial expression and vocal intonation, and potentially calm an agitated other to form a social relationship.

The face-heart connection is the crucial element of our social engagement system. The system detects and communicates bodily states and the inten-tions of behaviors. Social engagement behaviors by an adult are potentially capable of calming, eliciting spontaneous social behaviors, and downregu-lating the stress responses (immediate and/or chronic) inherent in the two defense systems for a child.

The social engagement system is first expressed at birth when it is used to signal states of comfort and distress and to detect features of safety. For example, a mother's voice has the capacity to soothe her infant. As the infant listens to the mother's melodic vocalizations, feature detectors in the infant's brain inter-pret the voice as reflecting the mother's state as calm and her presence as safe and supportive. This sequence is not learned, but an evolved adaptive process that enables social signals to regulate biobehavioral state. The sounds of the mother's vocalization signal safety, which is detected by higher brain structures. The higher brain structures dampen defense systems and facilitate the calming effect on the heart by ventral vagal influences. In parallel to this calming effect, the regulation of the muscles of the face and head are enhanced to enable recip-rocal interactions between mother and infant. The reciprocal interactions func-tion as a neural exercise between their social engagement systems. The result is an infant-mother dyad that efficiently uses social communication to coregulate, with both participants feeling calm and bonded. This neural exercise builds capacity for the infant to develop relations with others and to deal with state regulation challenges and disruptions through the life span. In all cultures, the presentation of prosodic acoustic stimulation, whether vocal or instrumental, is an effective strategy for signaling safety and calming infants. In our example above, Clare's use of melodic intonation was crucial for Kal to feel safe in relationship; her voice functioned to contain Kal's emotional state.

The type of mutually modulated coregulation of emotion described in the mother's voice example occurs throughout all examples of healthy play; it is a defining feature of a healthy, playful relationship (Porges, 2015, Chapter 3; Stern, 2004; Trevarthen, 2001). Early play, within the infant-adult dyad, is a functional dialogue of coregulation experienced over time. It is a story of shared rhythm (the pulse of play) and of the experience of traveling through energetic and emotional contours together (Malloch & Trevarthen, 2009; Stern, 2010). The rhythms of reciprocity of play are defined primarily by synchronous changes in facial expression, quality of eye contact, touch (changing patterns of position, intention, and intensity of the body), and vocalization (changing patterns of rhythm, timbre, pitch, and volume in voice) (Malloch & Trevarthen, 2009). Play is a flowing series of face-heart connections defined by essentially musical parameters.

MEDICAL TRAUMA AND PATTERNS OF IMMOBILIZATION

The dynamics of childhood medical trauma may be described by two qualities: overwhelming fear and inescapability (either physical or perceived). Posttraumatic stress disorder (PTSD) is an increasingly recognized childhood response to the experience of cancer and cancer treatment (Phipps et al., 2005; Taïeb et al., 2003). Research by Graf, Bergstraesser, and Landolt (2013) on the prevalence of childhood PTSD (onset in preschool) in cancer survivors showed that 18.8% of subjects met the age-appropriate criteria for full PTSD proposed by Scheeringa and Zeanah (2005) and 41.7% met the criteria for partial PTSD.

What are the experiences, unfortunately common within the story of cancer and cancer treatment, that disrupt a child's ability to regulate physiological state? Primarily, these include any frightening procedure that involves being physically restrained, and/or intense and immobilizing toxic/physical shock, but also potentially MRI scans with anesthetic restraint (not including a general anesthetic). Sadly, despite many intelligent child-friendly hospital protocols, physical restraint continues to be used on a daily basis in most pediatric oncology wards. Studies by Diseth (2005) illustrate that children forced to undergo medical procedures, particularly in the context of their families holding them down, presented with significantly more dissociation than children treated less invasively. In our example above, Kal was repeatedly physically restrained for frightening procedures. It was one such experience that pushed him into what could have easily become a chronic trauma pattern. The following quote is from a mother I (SD) worked with, Angie, describing her son's early experiences on an oncology ward:

Initially Kieran appeared unaware of hospital visits, other than the effect my own stress would undoubtedly have had on him. He first started to show recognition around five or six months old—he was very scared of strangers and would openly react to a blue nurse's uniform, becoming very distressed and anxious. Kieran was eight months old when I first witnessed his complete shutting down. At the time he was a happy, chatty, lively little boy who was cruising round the furniture and didn't stay still for more than a few moments. We arrived at clinic at 10 a.m., and the instant we walked through the doors, Kieran stopped moving. He kept his head dropped, making no eye contact or sounds at all. He stayed this way for about five hours until he went in for his examination under anesthetic, literally not moving or reacting to myself or his grandma in any way. It was completely heartbreaking to see my son so broken.

The behavioral shutdown that Angie describes above, the psychological and social dissociation described by Diseth (2005), and Kal's almost total withdrawal from interaction in our initial example can be explained by the triggering of the immobilization system. The immobilization defense system is our body's phylogenetically ancient response to the detection of an inevitable and significant threat to physical integrity and/or imminent death. It is triggered by the co-occurrence of two factors: fear and inescapability, both registered preconsciously via neuroception. The immobilization defense system recruits the unmyelinated vagal motor pathways to the heart to produce an immediate and massive slowing of heart rate (i.e., bradycardia) and often the cessation of breathing (i.e., apnea), and is often associated with vasovagal syncope (i.e., fainting). This massive shift in metabolic resources results in the organism appearing to be inanimate. This defense pattern is a primary defense strategy for many reptiles. Not moving and appearing inanimate is an adaptive response of reptiles to avoid detection by a predator. This reaction is metabolically conservative, rapidly withdrawing resources from the highly oxygen-dependent central nervous system. Once activated, the immobilization defense system may involve feigning death, behavioral shutdown, and dissociation. As mentioned above, once the immobilization defense system is triggered, it produces a physiological state that is incompatible with a functioning social engagement system. Once the immobilization system is reflexively employed, the social engagement system is temporarily disabled, which immediately shuts down all coordinated regulation of prosocial behavior. A child being bombarded with shutdown cues will not perceive the environment as safe and will not have the ability to produce or accurately detect features of social communication.

For some children, the initial immobilization experience becomes a chronic pattern. The process through which this occurs is not fully understood. Many of these unfortunate children develop partial or full childhood PTSD. Drell and colleagues (1993) provide a clinical outline of the developmental progression of early PTSD signatures (summarized in Table 10.1).

TABLE 10.1. Symptoms of PTSD in Children 0 to 36 Months, Based on Drell, Siegel, and Gaensbauer (1993)

	0–6 months	6–12 months	12–18 months	18–24 months	24–36 months
Withdrawal and/or hypervigilance, exaggerated startle response, irritability, physiologic deregulation	*	*	*	*	*
Increased anxiety in strange situations, angry reactions, sleep disorders, active avoidance of specific situations		*	*	*	*
Clinginess to caretaker, over/ under use of words related to the trauma			*	*	*
Nightmares, verbal preoccupation with symbols of trauma				*	*
PTSD symptoms seen in older children, as defined in the DSM-IV					*

PLAY AND COREGULATION: INSIGHTS FROM POLYVAGAL THEORY

From the perspective of the Polyvagal Theory, play can be seen functionally as a neural exercise in which social cues of safety and danger are alternately expressed and explored (Porges, 2015, Chapter 3). The ability to safely transition dangerous states of disconnection—breaks in flowing emotional containment—is crucial to the development and internalization of a child's robust sense of self (Hughes, 2004; Porges, 2015, Chapter 3; Schore, 1994). During play, risks are taken, dangers are survived, and connections are repaired through coregulation. As an example, we can think of the simple game of peek-a-boo that a mother may play with her infant. By hiding her face and removing the cues of safety normally generated by the social engagement system (prosodic voice, facial expressions), the mother is creating a state of uncertainty in the infant. This state of uncertainty is followed by the mother startling the infant by showing her face and saying "peek-a-boo!" The sequence of the peek-a-boo game is ended when the mother uses a prosodic voice with warm facial expressions to calm the startled infant.

Deconstructing the behavioral sequence involved in peek-a-boo, we see the neural exercise embedded in this play behavior. First, the initial hiding of the mother's face elicits a state of uncertainty and vigilance. This state is associated with a depression of the infant's social engagement system, including a withdrawal of the myelinated ventral vagal pathways to the heart. This puts the infant in a vulnerable state in which a startle stimulus could easily recruit sympathetic activity to support mobilization (i.e., fight-flight behaviors). The mother provides the startle stimulus by showing her face and saying "boo" in a relatively loud and monotonic voice. The acoustic features of the mother's vocalizations support the unpredictable presentation of the mother's face, since the vocalizations of "boo" have acoustic features that are associated with danger and lack the prosodic features that would be calming. The cues of this sequence trigger a detection of danger, which recruits increased sympathetic activation. The next step in the sequence of this game provides the opportunity for a neural exercise that will promote resilience and enhance the infant's ability to calm.

After the infant is motorically and autonomically activated by the "boo," the mother needs to calm the infant with her social engagement system using a prosodic voice with warm facial expressions. Her prosodic voice and warm facial expressions trigger a detection of safety. The infant calms as the social engagement system comes back online, and the myelinated ventral vagal pathways downregulate the sympathetic activity. When effectively implemented, peek-a-boo provides opportunities for the infant to neurally navigate through a sequence of states (i.e., from calm, to vigilant, to startle, and back to calm). Repeating this game provides opportunities for the social engagement system to efficiently downregulate, via social interactions, sympathetic activation. The child will need this neural skill to adapt throughout every aspect of life.

BUILDING CONNECTIONS WITH TRAUMATIZED CHILDREN: POLYVAGAL THEORY INFORMS THERAPEUTIC PLAY

Tyler, who was nine years old at the time, was referred for play therapy with the following profile: social withdrawal punctuated by episodes of extreme anger and violence, hypervigilance, difficulty sleeping, difficulty making friends, and problems at school and home. When Tyler was four, he had been through an 18-month treatment for leukemia. Like Kal, Tyler had been regularly physically restrained for certain medical procedures.

In his first session, Tyler made it into the playroom. He sat on a little wooden chair near the window, doing tricks with his finger board (a mini-skateboard he brought with him) on the windowsill. He did this for an hour. The Polyvagal Theory provides a lens to understand Tyler's withdrawal behavior. At this point, Tyler was likely to be experiencing one of two defensive states—immobilization or mobilization—or fluctuating between periods of both. Tyler could have a sense of generalized anxiety while also feeling disconnected from his emotional surroundings, experiencing dissociation. In this immobilized state, his senses would be numbed, his thoughts ambiguous, his ability to detect and engage in a flowing interaction highly limited, and his motivation to socially interact would be nonexistent. Or Tyler could be feeling highly mobilized, with the necessary energy to flee or fight. Behaviorally, he might be easily triggered into anger and possibly violence. Although seemingly turned inward, Tyler might be scanning every aspect and moment of his environment for cues of risk and danger. Internally, his heart rate might be elevated, his breathing shallow and rapid, his viscera, blood vessels, and muscle tone constricted, ready for action. In this hypervigilant and mobilized state, Tyler would be likely to perceive almost everything as a threat. The Polyvagal Theory explores why this might be the case. In the process of risk detection, external cues are not the only source of information. Afferent feedback from the viscera provides a major mediator of the accessibility of prosocial circuits associated with social engagement behaviors. Polyvagal Theory predicts that states of mobilization compromise the ability to detect positive social cues. Functionally, visceral states distort or color our perception of other people. Thus, the features of a person engaging another may result in a range of outcomes, depending on the physiological state of the target individual. If the person being engaged is in a state in which the social engagement system is easily accessible, a reciprocal prosocial interaction is likely to occur with the calming benefits of coregulation. However, if the individual is in a state of mobilization, the same engaging response might be responded to with asocial features of withdrawal or aggression.

Sean, Tyler's play therapist, worked with the basic principles of nondirective play therapy as a foundation: acceptance, nonjudgment, empathy, and emotional honesty (Landreth, 2012). In that first session, Sean sometimes used whole-body gestures and empathic sighs to accompany reflections like, "Just not sure what it's all about in here" and "Feeling kind of weird—what am I doing in here . . . ?" After a while Tyler seemed to relax a little. His muscle tone dropped slightly, and his play with the miniboard became a little less intense. Sean intuitively understood that the musicality—the rhythmic pulse, the contours of volume, and in particular the quality of intonation—in his voice was a crucial factor in helping Tyler feel safe and to stimulate Tyler's social engagement system. If in a state of partial immobilization, Tyler would probably respond to very little, but he would need the background tone to be playful, peaceful, and musical (never a monotone) to give him the best chance of engagement. If Tyler was in a mobilized state, hypervigilant to risk factors and prone to interpreting any stimulus as a threat, Sean would need to keep his voice melodic and avoid projecting low vocal frequencies; according to the Polyvagal Theory, deep-sounding voices are signals of a predator and might trigger defense. If successful, Tyler's sympathetic nervous system would be downregulated. In this safe state, Tyler's innate prosocial ability would have an opportunity to be expressed in recipro-cal and synchronous interactions, promoting mutual feelings of connectedness between Tyler and Sean.

The ability to detect contour shifts in sound, especially in prosodic vocaliza-tion, is usually central to human connectedness through the healthy engage-ment of our social engagement systems. But there are children for whom hearing is not accessible (profoundly deaf children) and children who have inherent difficulties with the particular emotional quality of human voices (e.g., children with autism and related disorders). Likewise, the visual exchange of information involving eye contact, facial expression, and hand gestures is usually central to play. These features functionally provide the pathways for coregulation of physiological state, which optimize prosocial behavior and child development. Understanding the face-heart connection allows us to appreciate just how significant the human face is for coregulation of emotion and biobe-havioral states in support of psychological health. But there are many children for whom visual-facial information is not readily accessible; for instance, blind children and children with tendencies to avert their gaze, such as those with autism or related disorders. Somehow, we need to find ways to enable these children with experiences of safety, of flowing human connection, of healthy coregulation within exploratory play. We need to do this without recourse to the regular sensory pathways of sight and sound that evolution efficiently selected to trigger our social engagement system.

CONCLUSION

By deconstructing the play of mammals, whether we are observing kittens, dogs, or children on the playground, we see a common dynamic in social behavior—features of fight-flight are continually stimulated and actively inhib-ited by social engagement behaviors (e.g., facial expressions, gestures, prosodic vocalizations). Play is a natural and powerful therapeutic tool. From the poly-vagal perspective, play can be conceptualized as an efficient neural exercise that uses social engagement to actively inhibit fight-flight behaviors. A sensitive adult can attune herself to a way of communicating that recruits a child's social engagement system and downregulates defense. Therapists who work actively through playful modes consciously leverage this process. As illustrated in the clinical descriptions above, it is crucial that the therapist engenders a feeling of safety for the child via sensitive attunement. The experience of safety increases, in the child, the frequency of spontaneous reciprocal interactions. It is through these interactions that there is a resetting of the neuroceptive threshold from a defensive baseline to a robust sense of safety.

Frequently, children referred for therapy are in neurophysiological states that support mobilization, withdrawal, and shutdown. In these states, cognitive pro-cesses are greatly compromised, and there is a loss of awareness of the emotional states of others. Polyvagal Theory informs clinical practice that there is a neural circuit that can rapidly downregulate mobilization behaviors to foster the calm states that optimize social behavior. Although play is frequently characterized by movement and often recruits many of the neural circuits involved in fight-flight behaviors, it may be operationally distinguished from defense, since during play mobilization is easily downregulated by the social engagement system. However, the effectiveness and efficiency of the social engagement system to downregulate fight-flight behaviors requires practice. Although this practice usually starts early in a child's development through play, trauma may disrupt the child's ability to feel safe and to exhibit spontaneous social engagement behaviors. Given this situation, similar to the clinical examples provided above, clinicians need to provide the child with unambiguous biological signals of safety through intonation of voice, facial expressions, and gestures. Moreover, once these signals effectively trigger a spontaneous engagement by the child, the intuitive therapist must be ready to respond with reciprocity. Reciprocal exchange of cues of safety, between therapist and child, function as playful neural exercise of the social engagement system: the mechanism that shifts mobilization from defense to play and trust. From a polyvagal perspective, this is the central objective of therapy.

REFERENCES

Craig, A. D. (2002). How do you feel? Interoception: The sense of the physiological condition of the body. *Nature Reviews Neuroscience, 3*(8), 655–666.

Diseth, T. H. (2005). Dissociation in children and adolescents as reaction to trauma: An overview of conceptual issues and neurobiological factors. *Nordic Journal of Psychiatry, 59,* 79–91.

Drell, M. J., Siegel, C., & Gaensbauer, T. J. (1993). Posttraumatic stress disorder. In C. H. Zeanah (Ed.), *Handbook of infant mental health.* New York: Guilford.

Graf, A., Bergstraesser, E., & Landolt, M. A. (2013). Posttraumatic stress in infants and preschoolers with cancer. *Psycho-oncology, 22*(7), 1543–1548.

Hughes, D. (2004). An attachment-based treatment of maltreated children and young people. *Attachment and Human Development, 3*(6), 263–278.

Landreth, G. L. (2012). *Play therapy: The art of the relationship.* New York: Routledge.

Malloch, S., & Trevarthen, C. (2009). Musicality: Communicating the vitality and interests of life. In S. Malloch & C. Trevarthen (Eds.), *Communicative musicality: Exploring the basis of human companionship.* Oxford: Oxford University Press.

Phipps, S., Long, A., Hudson, M., & Rai, S. N. (2005). Symptoms of post-traumatic stress in children with cancer and their parents: Effects of informant and time from diagnosis. *Pediatric Blood and Cancer, 45,* 952–959.

Porges, S. W. (1993). The infant's sixth sense: Awareness and regulation of bodily processes. *Zero to Three, 14,* 12–16.

Porges, S. W. (1995). Orienting in a defensive world: Mammalian modifications of our evolutionary heritage. A Polyvagal Theory. *Psychophysiology, 32,* 301–318.

Porges, S. W. (2001). The Polyvagal Theory: Phylogenetic substrates of a social nervous system. *International Journal of Psychophysiology, 42*, 123–146.

Porges, S. W. (2007). The polyvagal perspective. *Biological Psychology, 74*, 116–143.

Porges, S. W. (2009). The Polyvagal Theory: New insights into adaptive reactions of the autonomic nervous system. *Cleveland Clinic Journal of Medicine, 76*, 86–90.

Porges, S. W. (2011). *The Polyvagal Theory: Neurophysiological foundations of emotions, attachment, communication, and self-regulation*. New York: Norton.

Porges, S. W. (2015). Play as neural exercise: Insights from the Polyvagal Theory. In D. Pearce-McCall (Ed.), *The power of play for mind-brain health* (pp. 3–7) [ebook]. MindGAINS. http://mindgains.org.

Scheeringa, M. S., & Zeanah, C. H. (2005). *PTSD semi-structured interview and observational record for infants and young children*. New Orleans: Department of Psychiatry and Neurology, Tulane University Health Sciences Center. (Note: Contains diagnostic algorithms since incorporated in the *DSM-5*).

Schore, A. N. (1994). *Affect regulation and the origin of the self*. Hillsdale, NJ: Lawrence Erlbaum.

Stern, D. N. (2004). *The first relationship: Infant and mother*. Cambridge, MA: Harvard University Press.

Stern, D. N. (2010). *Forms of vitality: Exploring dynamic experience in psychology, the arts, psychotherapy, and development*. Oxford: Oxford University Press.

Taïeb, O., Moro, M. R., Baubet, T., Revah-Lévy, A., & Flament, M. F. (2003). Post-traumatic stress symptoms after childhood cancer. *European Child and Adolescent Psychiatry, 12*, 255–264.

Trevarthen, C. (2001). Intrinsic motives for companionship in understanding: Their origin, development and significance for infant mental health. *Journal of Infant Mental Health, 22*, 95–131.

CHAPTER 11

Brain–Body Connection May Ease Autistic People's Social Problems

Stephen W. Porges

For more than five decades, I have studied how our physiology influences mental processes and behavior. During this period, I have studied people—including children with autism—who have trouble regulating their behavior and emotions. Based on my research, I have developed the Polyvagal Theory, a theory that emphasizes that the neural regulation of our bodily organs influences our emotional responses and behavior toward others and our environment.

Many people with autism have difficulty regulating their behavior and emotions. Their initial reaction to threat is often anger, irritability, or aggression that may be expressed as an uncontrollable tantrum. These responses constitute a fight-or-flight reaction that can be difficult to manage.

My research has documented parallels between the autonomic nervous system—the system that controls the fight-or-flight system and the functioning of our organs—and difficulties with learning and socializing (Porges, 2005). Essentially, if we cannot regulate our physiological state, we cannot socialize and connect with others. Based on this, my team and I have developed an auditory therapy that can help autistic people feel safe enough to engage with the world.

Over the years, I have listened to parents and teachers of autistic children and have heard a consistent message: a passionate wish to help the children improve behavioral regulation and avoid difficulties associated with experiencing anxiety, oppositional behavior, uncontrolled anger or frustration, tantrums or meltdowns, hypersensitivity, dissociation, and attentional problems.

However, the scientific community has provided little help. The primary treatments for autism involve drugs developed for anxiety or attention-deficit hyperactivity disorder that can ease difficult behavior. Unfortunately, these drugs may also suppress spontaneous social interactions. Behavioral therapies for autism may help children develop skills, but they are limited in their ability to teach the children to regulate their emotions or behavioral state.

We scientists have often treated autistic people as though they merely do not want to listen or control their behavior, rather than as though they are unable to do so. This bias assumes that treatments that apply rewards and punishments will help autistic people. But these reinforcement models are relatively ineffective at fostering spontaneous social interactions and controlling emotions.

My hope is to provide new tools to adjust autistic people's autonomic state, thereby enhancing their ability to regulate their emotions, engage in spontaneous social behavior, and learn and improve their cognitive function.

POLYVAGAL THEORY

The autonomic nervous system controls unconscious bodily functions such as heart rate, breathing, and urination—and the fight-or-flight response. Based on my research, I hypothesize that the autonomic nervous system functions as a neurophysiological platform that can facilitate or suppress various types of behavior, from spontaneous social interactions to aggressive and oppositional behavior and complete shutdown.

My hypothesis is based on the Polyvagal Theory, which I developed and named because it focuses on two vagal pathways—that is, a collection of neural fibers—that regulate the autonomic nervous system. These fibers are embedded in a large cranial nerve known as the vagus, which influences the functions of major organs and modulates the bidirectional relationship between these organs and the brain. The theory offers an explanation for some of autism's core features, from social difficulties to gut dysfunction and sensory sensitivity. It also proposes strategies that can ease the severity of these features. It is based on the idea that evolution has had a major influence on how our brains respond to threat.

The autonomic nervous system common to more evolutionarily primitive vertebrates such as reptiles has circuits that enable two types of defensive behaviors: mobilizing to support fight-or-flight responses, or immobilizing—freezing or involuntarily playing dead, with a loss of consciousness and muscle tone—to minimize detection. With the evolution of mammals, brainstem areas regulating a branch of the vagus became integrated with neural pathways that control the muscles of the face and head. This new branch of the vagus has a remarkable attribute that enables the control and regulation of the other two, more primitive, systems – the sympathetic nervous system and the other branch of the vagus that primarily regulates organs below the diaphragm. Functionally, this new circuit, by informing the more primitive circuits, evolved into an enabler of prosocial behavior. It can also regulate these older mechanisms to enable movement in a safe social context, such as play. Or it can shift the immobilization response away from fearful defense and toward a calm moment of intimacy— feeling safe and secure in another person's arms. This newest circuit is most relevant to a polyvagal understanding of autism.

The vagal pathways involved in the new system emerge from a part of the brainstem that helps control muscles of the face and head, including muscles involved in facial expression, ingestion, speaking, and listening. This system evolved in mammals to cue members of the same species, via vocalizations and facial expressions, that it is safe to approach and engage in social behavior.

Functionally, the system can turn off defensive responses and foster feelings of safety and trust; it can slow heart rate, tamp down the fight-or-flight response, and cue the enteric nervous system to support digestion (Kolacz & Porges, 2018). Turning down this system results in many traits associated with autism, including a lack of facial affect, poor vocal intonation and rhythm, hypersensitivity to sound, selective eating, gut problems, and a propensity to remain in a defensive state.

Because we are social animals, we often look to partners or trusted caregivers for safety cues, but autistic people may not be able to recognize or respond to these cues. Their social engagement system may be depressed: Their body detects cues of danger and not cues of safety in social engagement. This state of chronic defense can also disrupt the function of visceral organs—possibly explaining why gut and cardiovascular problems are common among autistic people.

MUSIC TO THE EARS

During the past 20 years, we have developed and tested an acoustic intervention, commercially available as the Safe and Sound Protocol, that is designed to enhance the social engagement system. Using computer processing, we modified vocal music to amplify the shifts in intonation that people typically detect as cues of safety. The result sounds something like a mother's lullaby. The Safe and Sound Protocol is available to professionals only through Integrated Listening Systems (https://integratedlistening.com/porges/).

In a 2013 study, we showed that listening to this audio for one hour on five sequential days normalizes auditory processing and increases the vagal regulation of the heart (Porges et al., 2013). Then, in a randomized trial in 2014 (see Chapter 12), we showed that the method decreases auditory hypersensitivity and improves spontaneous speech, behavioral organization, and emotional control (Porges et al., 2014). I was recently awarded a patent for the technology embedded in the intervention. The patent includes a claim for an acoustic vagal nerve stimulator.

My team is continuing to test the effectiveness of this approach in people with autism, but also in those with conditions such as Prader-Willi syndrome. Preliminary data from these ongoing studies are consistent with our earlier findings.

Through a better understanding of how the autonomic nervous system responds to cues of safety and threat, we plan to design cost-effective and efficient therapies that retune autonomic function and optimize social engagement in people on the spectrum.

REFERENCES

Kolacz, J., & Porges, S. W. (2018). Chronic diffuse pain and functional gastrointestinal disorders after traumatic stress: pathophysiology through a polyvagal perspective. *Frontiers in Medicine, 5*, 145.

Porges, S. W. (2005). The vagus: A mediator of behavioral and visceral features associated with autism. In M. L. Bauman & T. L. Kemper (Eds.), *The neurobiology of autism* (pp. 65–78). Baltimore: Johns Hopkins University Press.

Porges, S. W., Bazhenova, O. V., Bal, E., Carlson, N., Sorokin, Y., Heilman, K. J., Cook, E. H., Lewis, G. F. (2014). Reducing auditory hypersensitivities in autistic spectrum disorder: Preliminary findings evaluating the listening project protocol. *Frontiers in Pediatrics, 2*, 80.

Porges, S. W., Macellaio, M., Stanfill, S. D., McCue, K., Lewis, G. F., Harden, E. R., Handelman, M., Denver, J., Bazhenova, O. V., & Heilman, K. J. (2013). Respiratory sinus arrhythmia and auditory processing in autism: Modifiable deficits of an integrated social engagement system? *International Journal of Psychophysiology, 88*, 261–270.

CHAPTER 12

Reducing Auditory Hypersensitivities in Autistic Spectrum Disorder
Preliminary Findings Evaluating the Listening Project Protocol

Stephen W. Porges, Olga V. Bazhenova, Elgiz Bal, Nancy Carlson,
Yevgeniya Sorokin, Keri J. Heilman, Edwin H. Cook, and Gregory F. Lewis

INTRODUCTION

Frequently accompanying a diagnosis of autism spectrum disorder (ASD) are speech and language delays, difficulties in extracting human voices from background sounds, auditory hypersensitivities, and a general compromise in social communication skills (Coleman & Gillberg, 1985; Dissanayake & Sigman, 2001; Frith & Baron-Cohen, 1987; Hayes & Gordon, 1977; Klin, 1992; Lockyer & Rutter, 1969; Mundy, 1995; Rosenhall et al., 1999). In contrast to the prevalent reports of auditory processing deficits, most individuals with ASD, even those with noticeable auditory perceptual disorders, have normal hearing when tested on a standard audiogram (Ceponiene et al., 2003).

Several mechanisms have been proposed as contributing to frequently reported deficits in auditory processing, including damage or dysfunction to peripheral structures (i.e., middle ear and inner ear), neural pathways (e.g., auditory nerve), and central structures (e.g., brainstem nuclei and cortical areas) (e.g., Dawson, 1988; Gage et al., 2003; Gervais et al., 2004; Khalfa et al., 2004; Maziade et al., 2000; Smith et al., 1988; Tecchio et al., 2003; Thivierge et al.,

---

* The Safe and Sound Protocol is available to professionals only through Integrated Listening Systems (https://integratedlistening.com/porges/).

1990). A review suggests that although atypical auditory processing and both hypo- and hyperreactivity to auditory signals are frequently observed in autism, these atypical reactions cannot reliably be attributed to specific neural pathways (Marco et al., 2011). Thus, subjective methods remain the sole indicators of auditory hypersensitivities (Khalfa et al., 2002).

PHYSIOLOGY OF THE MIDDLE EAR

Borg and Counter (1989) described a role of middle ear muscles in facilitating the extraction of human speech by dampening the transmission of low-frequency noise from the external environment to the inner ear. The Borg and Counter model suggests that atypical neural regulation of middle ear muscles may contribute to the frequently observed auditory hypersensitivities and auditory processing deficits in ASD. Deconstructing the path through which sound is processed illustrates the role middle ear structures have in auditory processing and how atypical neural regulation of the middle ear muscles may contribute to auditory hypersensitivities and atypical auditory processing.

Sound enters the outer ear and travels through the external auditory canal to the eardrum, where it is transduced by the structures of the middle ear (i.e., small bones composing the ossicular chain), which connects the eardrum with the cochlea. The rigidity of the ossicular chain determines the stiffness of the eardrum. The middle ear muscles, via cranial nerves, regulate the position of the ossicles and stiffen or loosen the eardrum. When the eardrum is tightened, higher frequencies are absorbed and transmitted to the inner ear, and the energy of lower frequencies is attenuated (i.e., reflected) before being encoded by the inner ear (cochlea) and transmitted via the auditory nerve (cranial nerve VIII) to the cortex. Complementing the ascending pathways are descending pathways that regulate the middle ear muscles, which functionally determine the energy (i.e., attenuate, pass, or amplify) of specific frequencies that reach the inner ear. The features describing the transformation of sound intensity from outer to inner ear define the middle ear transfer function. If the acoustic information in the frequency band associated with speech is distorted by an atypical middle ear transfer function, the information being coded by the inner ear and subsequently being transmitted to the cortex will not be sufficient to enable accurate detection of speech sounds. In addition, there are descending pathways that regulate the hair cells in the cochlea to fine-tune auditory perception, which is especially important in the development of language skills. If the acoustic information related to human speech that reaches the cortex via ascending pathways is distorted, then the descending pathways to the cochlea may also be atypical and will further distort the individual's ability to process speech and to produce language.

As proposed by Borg and Counter (1989), atypical central regulation of peripheral middle ear structures may pass low-frequency sounds that dominate the acoustic spectrum in our mechanized society (e.g., ventilation systems, traffic, airplanes, vacuum cleaners, and other appliances), resulting in both a hypersensitivity to sounds and distorting or masking the frequency components associated with human speech reaching the brain. This emphasis on the functional role of the middle ear muscles in the dampening of background noise and the extraction of voice is based on a literature documenting two points: (1) The neural regulation of the middle ear muscles modulates the transfer function of the middle ear (Liberman & Guinan, 1988; Zwislocki, 2002), and (2) the transfer function of the middle ear determines the acoustic energy from low frequencies that reach the inner ear (Porges & Lewis, 2009). Thus, an atypical middle ear transfer function would be a potentially parsimonious explanation of both the auditory hypersensitivities and the difficulties in auditory processing frequently associated with autism.

DESIGNING THE LISTENING PROJECT PROTOCOL

The listening project protocol (LPP) is a theoretical departure from the disciplines frequently involved in the treatment of auditory processing disorders, which emphasize the role of central structures in the processing of speech (see Marco et al., 2011, for a review). The LPP was theoretically designed to reduce auditory hypersensitivities by recruiting the antimasking functions of the middle ear muscles to optimize the transfer function of the middle ear for the processing of human speech. The LPP is based on an exercise model that uses computer-altered acoustic stimulation to modulate the frequency band passed to the participant. The frequency characteristics of the acoustic stimulation were theoretically selected based on the documented frequency band and weights associated with the index of articulation (Kryter, 1962) and speech intelligibility index (American National Standards Institute, 1997). These indices emphasize the relative importance of specific frequencies in conveying the information embedded in human speech. During normal listening to human speech, via descending central mechanisms, the middle ear muscles contract and stiffen the ossicular chain. This process functionally removes most of the masking low-frequency background sounds from the acoustic environment and allows human voices to be more effectively processed by higher brain structures. Modulation of the acoustic energy within the frequencies of the human voice, similar to exaggerated vocal prosody, is hypothesized to recruit and modulate the neural regulation of the middle ear muscles and to functionally reduce auditory hypersensitivities (see Porges & Lewis, 2010).

The features of the intervention, including the context, the duration of stimulation, and frequency band selected, were theoretically determined and based on the following neurophysiological principles: (a) the transfer function of the middle ear serves as an antimasking mechanism to dampen low-frequency sounds and to facilitate extraction of the human voice from background sounds (Borg & Counter, 1989); (b) acoustic energy is readily transmitted across middle ear structures, regardless of the neural tone, to the middle ear muscles, at a resonance frequency in children between 800 and 1200 Hz (Hanks & Rose, 1993); (c) middle ear muscles are primarily composed of fast-twitch muscles and are vulnerable to rapid fatigue (Schiaffino & Reggiani, 2011); and (d) the phylogenetic convergence in mammals of a brainstem area involved in the neural regulation of striated muscles of the face and head, including the middle ear muscles (see Porges, 2005, 2007; Porges & Lewis, 2010). Principles (a) and (b) were used to design the acoustic stimuli, principle (c) informed decisions related to the duration of each session, and principle (d) provided the basis for the social support provided during the intervention (i.e., autonomic state is calmed and the neural regulation of the middle ear muscles is optimized in a safe context).

The LPP applies computer-altered vocal music (i.e., filtered music) designed to exaggerate the features of human prosody and hypothetically to exercise the neural regulation of the middle ear muscles. By modulating the frequency band associated with human vocalizations, it was hypothesized that the ascending pathways would be providing dynamically changing information that would feed back on the descending pathways regulating the middle ear muscles. Metaphorically, the procedure could be conceptualized as a treadmill exercise for the middle ear muscles, during which the demands to listen and process the acoustic features of the intervention stimuli were dynamically changing. To test the primary hypothesis that the filtered music condition would reduce hearing sensitivities in children with ASD, two trials were conducted. Trial I contrasted a filtered music group to a headphones-only group, and Trial II contrasted a filtered music group to an unfiltered music group.

The intervention consisted of five daily sessions of approximately 45 minutes during which the participant passively listened to the acoustic stimulation through headphones in a quiet room, while researchers provided social support to ensure that the participants remained calm. The frequency bands were temporally modulated within each session and, independent of amplitude, the band of frequencies that were modulated progressively increased across the five sessions. Theoretically, the changing frequency bands were presented to increase the neural regulation of middle ear structures to dampen the perception of background low-frequency sounds and to potentiate the extraction of the human voice. Although middle ear muscle regulation could not be assessed, the Borg and Counter (1989) model provided the scientific basis to hypothesize that the exercises embedded in the LPP would reduce auditory hypersensitivities. The Safe and Sound Protocol is an updated version of the LLP that is currently available to therapists. More information can be obtained from Integrated Listening Systems (https://integratedlistening.com/porges/).

METHODS: TRIAL I AND TRIAL II

Participants

Potential participants contacted the laboratory for initial inclusion screening. Participants were informed about the research project by clinicians, parents who previously participated in our research program, and via professional presentations and/or newsletters. Individuals with a suspected diagnosis of ASD, who did not have a history of seizures, were scheduled for a diagnostic assessment that consisted of the Autism Diagnostic Interview–Revised (ADI-R; Lord et al., 1994). The ADI-R provides a diagnostic algorithm consistent with the Diagnostic and Statistical Manual of Mental Disorders, Fourth Edition (DSM-IV; American Psychiatric Association, 1994) and International Classification of Diseases, 10th Edition (ICD-10; World Health Organization, 1992). Informed consent was obtained from parents. The institutional review boards at the University of Maryland, the University of Illinois at Chicago, and the University of North Carolina approved the project. The protocols are excluded from the requirement to be registered (e.g., ClinicalTrials.gov), since enrollment was initiated before January 1, 2001, and data collection was completed before December 26, 2007.

Parents of 178 children contacted the laboratory to participate in the research. Based on the ADI-R criteria, 146 children met the full criteria for autism. Of the children who did not meet full criteria, 29 exceeded the ADI-R cutoff on at least the qualitative impairments in reciprocal social interaction and/or communication scales. Three children who did not meet the cutoff on scales of either qualitative impairments in reciprocal social interaction or communication, were excluded from participating in the research.

Based on presentation at the laboratory, the first 73 children were assigned to Trial I. In Trial I, data from nine children (two in the filtered music and seven in the headphone-only groups) were lost due to technical problems. In Trial I, questionnaire data were scored for 36 children in the filtered music group and 28 children in the headphones-only group. Following the completion of Trial I, 102 children who had not participated in Trial I were enrolled in Trial II. In Trial II, due to scheduling difficulties, families of six children withdrew before participating in the trial, and one family withdrew after the second day of the intervention. In Trial II, data from one child who was diagnosed with Fragile X were excluded from the data analyses. In addition, data from 12 children in the filtered music group were lost due to parents not returning the questionnaires, or returning the questionnaires late, or health issues. Data are not available for documenting the specific causes for lack of compliance. Questionnaire data in Trial II were available from 50 participants in the filtered music group and 32 participants in the unfiltered music group. Descriptive statistics of demographic features of the subjects from Trial I and Trial II with questionnaire data are reported in Table 12.1.

TABLE 12.1. Demographic Information for Subjects, With Complete Data by Group Assignment and Sex

	Trial I		Trial II	
	Filtered music Mean age (SD)[b]	Headphones only condition Mean age (SD)[b]	Filtered music Mean age (SD)[b]	Unfiltered music Mean age (SD)[b]
Met at least partial criteria on ADI-R[a]				
Male	58.24 (10.14), n = 25	49.46 (10.96), n = 23	54.89 (14.83), n = 44	56.20 (9.36), n = 27
Female[c]	48.67 (11.99), n = 11	61.00 (7.91), n = 5	44 (20.66), n = 6	60.33 (9.29), n = 5
Total	55.37 (11.42), n = 36	52.67 (11.30), n = 28	53.33 (15.95), n = 50	56.74 (9.25), n = 32

[a] Exceeded the ADI-R cut off on at least the qualitative impairments in reciprocal social interaction and/or communication scales.
[b] Mean age and standard deviation in months.
[c] Females in Trial I were significantly older in the headphone only group.

Trial I and Trial II included 86 participants in the filtered music condition, 32 participants in the unfiltered music condition, and 28 participants in the headphones only condition (see Table 12.1). Although mental age of the participants was not formally assessed, all participants either had speech (at least five words apart from "mama" and "dada," used spontaneously and meaningfully) or followed verbal instructions. Approximately 80% of the participants were Caucasian, and the remaining 20% included children from African American, Latino, and Asian parents.

EXPERIMENTAL DESIGN

The intervention research was conducted as two sequential randomized controlled trials with parallel control groups. All participants were randomly assigned sequentially by presentation at the laboratory to either the filtered music group or a control condition group. No clinical or behavioral feature was used to determine group assignment. Trial I participants were randomly assigned to either a filtered music or a headphones-only group, which consisted of children wearing headphones without music.

Trial I was initiated to evaluate whether the intervention had an effect beyond the contextual variables of supportive play and low-intensity social interactions that characterized the experimental environment for both groups. Since data analyses of parent questionnaires indicated a treatment effect on auditory hypersensitivities, Trial II was conducted to evaluate whether the filtering of the music uniquely determined intervention effects. Trial II participants were randomly assigned to either a filtered music group or an unfiltered music group. To ensure a sample size sufficient to test hypotheses related to auditory hypersensitivities, twice as many participants were assigned to the filtered music group.

Parents were not informed about their child's group assignment until the follow-up sessions were completed. Nor were parents informed about the features of the intervention (i.e., filtered music) or the control condition within each trial (i.e., headphones only in Trial I and unfiltered music in Trial II). Circumaural headphones were used, since they provide excellent sound quality, are comfortable to wear, and have excellent external noise rejection. The features of the headphone in combination with low-intensity auditory stimuli precluded the parents from detecting whether their child was receiving the filtered music condition or a control condition. Based on our interactions with parents, it appeared that parents were not informed about the group assignment of their children. After the completion of the follow-up assessment sessions, the children in the unfiltered and the headphones-only conditions were given the opportunity to receive the filtered music. Since knowing group assignment might bias parental perceptions of the child's behavior, data from the children, who received the filtered music after participating in either the headphones-only or unfiltered music conditions, were not included in the data analyses.

One week following the intervention, parent reports were obtained for all participants in both trials. None of the children who participated in Trial I participated in Trial II. In addition to the parent questionnaire, semistructured play-based behavioral assessment sessions were conducted with the children and videotaped before and after the intervention.

CONDITIONS AND PROCEDURE

Each condition (i.e., the filtered music, unfiltered music, and headphones-only conditions) consisted of approximately 45-minute sessions conducted during five consecutive days. During the intervention, regardless of group assignment, each child wore headphones in the same laboratory environment. The same vocal music selections were used for both the filtered music and the unfiltered music conditions. In the filtered music condition, the vocal music was computer processed based on a proprietary algorithm developed to remove low and high frequencies and to modulate the width of the frequency band associated with the human voice. The intervention stimuli were stored on compact discs and played via high-quality compact disc player (Marantz CC-4000) to high-quality over-the-ear headphones (Beyerdynamic DT831). Maximum loudness was calibrated at a peak of 75 decibels before the intervention started. During the headphones-only condition, no auditory stimulation was provided through the headphones, although the context was identical to the filtered music and unfiltered music conditions. The low volume of the intervention stimuli and the use of over-the-ear headphones ensured that the intervention stimuli could not be distinguished from the ambient background sounds in the test room by the parents.

The sessions were conducted in a research room with toys (e.g., books, dollhouse and accessories, parking garage and cars, pretend kitchen and accessories, stuffed animals, coloring books, and crayons). During the intervention, the children were able to freely play with the toys. One experimenter stayed in the room during the intervention to assist the child with the headphones when needed.

Parents were also allowed to be in the room with their child. The experimenter and the parents were instructed to be quiet and to interact with the child only to maintain and to support a calm behavioral state. Due to the nature of the study (e.g., checking the integrity of the headphones), the experimenter who conducted the intervention session was not always blind to the child's group assignment. In Trial I, since the headphones-only group received headphones without sound, the experimenter was frequently aware of the child's group assignment. However, since only the experimenter adjusted the headphones, the parents remained blind. In Trial II, since acoustic stimulation was being presented to both groups, the experimenter and the parent were unaware of the child's group assignment. Accordingly, to avoid the possibility of rating bias, the experimenter who conducted the intervention sessions did not participate in the play-based assessments during which sharing behaviors were coded.

BEHAVIORAL ASSESSMENT

Parent Questionnaire

Following the intervention and the play-based assessments, parents were given a structured questionnaire developed in our laboratory, targeting specific categories of their child's developmental and behavioral problems including auditory hypersensitivities. The parents of children in all groups were instructed to complete and to return the questionnaire to the laboratory in a week. The questionnaire focused on whether the child had difficulties in a specific behavioral area and whether there were any changes in this area following participation in the research. For each behavioral category, parents were required to document changes, if any, following the intervention by providing specific examples of observed new behaviors. The structured questionnaire focused on the behavioral domains listed in Table 12.2.

Questionnaire Scoring

Each of the 10 items representing the behavioral domains described in Table 12.2 was scored as a 1, 0, or −1. A score of 1 was assigned if the parents indicated that their child had a problem in the area of interest before participation in the project and provided an example of a new behavior that could be considered an improvement in this area. An item received a score of 0 if the parents indicated that their child had a problem in the area of interest, but provided no example of a change. Nonspecific parental responses (e.g., "somewhat better" and "a lot better") that were not supported by concrete examples of the new behaviors also were conservatively scored as 0. An item received a score of −1 if the parent indicated that the behavior became worse after participating in the research and provided an example of the new worsened behavior. If the parent did not indicate a problem in the area of interest, the item did not receive a score. Each

TABLE 12.2. Behavioral Domains and Explanations for the
Structured Parent Questionnaire

	Definitions
Hearing sensitivity	Exaggerated negative responses (e.g., crying or placing hands over the ears) to common noises (e.g., vacuum cleaner, garbage disposal, baby crying, and air conditioning)
Spontaneous speech	Unprompted use of words and sentences to communicate thoughts and ideas
Receptive speech	Ability to understand instructions and phrases
Spontaneity	Unprompted behaviors initiated by the child
Behavioral organization	Ability to occupy oneself (when left alone) in a productive and nonstereotypical way
Emotional control	Ability to calm quickly when upset, to respond to unexpected changes without getting upset, and to tolerate objections and contradictions of other people
Affection	Behaviors reflective of warm emotional state expressed by the child toward familiar people (e.g., hugging, kissing, and saying "I love you" to the parent)
Listening	Ability to focus on human speech without visual or contextual cues, to understand spoken words, and to follow verbal requests
Eye contact	Making and maintaining eye contact during social interactions
Relatedness	Unprompted social behaviors that reflect understanding of a joint partnership in interactions and sharing the same goals during social interactions (e.g., looking at a partner, showing toys, sharing an idea or a thought, and directing emotions to the partner)

questionnaire was scored by two researchers, at least one of whom was blind to the child's group assignment. Only when both scorers agreed that the example provided by the parent constituted a new and relevant behavior was a score of 1 given. Scores of −1 were rare and did not occur on any of the behaviors coded in Trial I and only three times in Trial II. Thus, separate analyses for scores of −1 were not conducted.

Social Interaction Coding Scale

Prior to and following their participation in the intervention project, all children participated in a 10-minute semistructured play-based observational assessment of social engagement skills with the Social Interaction Coding Scale (SICS; Bazhenova et al., n.d.). The SICS provides information regarding the child's social engagement activity. Similar to the Autism Diagnostic Observational Scale (ADOS; Lord et al., 2000) and Early Social Communication Coding Scales (ESCS; Seibert et al., 1982), the SICS requires a semistructured presentation of standard tasks. Each task provides an opportunity for social engagement by requiring the child to engage in a joint activity. In the current study, the number of spontaneous sharing behaviors was quantified.

Coding the Social Interaction Coding Scale

The frequency of sharing behaviors was coded from videotapes by trained coders. Coders obtained reliability with each other on training tapes before using the scale for research (i.e., 80% agreement on individual items, mean kappa > 0.60 for three consecutive joint scorings). Each tape was coded by two trained coders independently and compared for agreement. At least one of the coders was not aware of the participant's group assignment when coding. Consensus was used to establish the final code. If raters disagreed on the same item, the code of the unbiased coder was recorded. If coders were uncertain about the final code, the opinion of the third trained coder was requested, and the code that received the consensus of at least two coders was recorded. If all three coders disagreed on the final code, the behavior was not coded.

DATA ANALYSES

Analyses of variance and nonparametric χ^2 analyses were used to evaluate group differences within each trial on each of the behavioral domains. Since both analysis strategies identified the same group differences within each trial, only the analyses of variance are presented. A Bonferroni correction adjusted significance levels for multiple comparisons.

RESULTS: QUESTIONNAIRE DATA

Global Evaluation of Problems

Confirming the effectiveness of the randomization procedures, there were no group differences in the representation of the behavioral problems reported via the parental questionnaire within each trial or across trials (see Table 12.3). For example, the representation of hearing hypersensitivities across the four groups

TABLE 12.3. Distribution of Initial Behavioral Problems (%) Within Each Trial[a]

	Trial I		Trial II	
	Filtered music (%)	**Headphones only group (%)**	**Filtered music (%)**	**Unfiltered music (%)**
Hearing sensitivity	50	43	46	50
Affect	44	61	64	59
Eye contact	75	61	60	63
Behavioral organization	53	57	56	53
Emotional control	50	43	66	59
Spontaneous speech	75	82	82	78
Receptive speech	72	82	90	81
Listening	81	86	74	66
Spontaneity	69	71	44	44
Relatedness	83	82	64	66
At least 1 problem	92	96	98	97
At least 2 problems	92	93	98	94
At least 3 problems	89	89	96	91
At least 4 problems	83	79	94	88
At least 5 problems	81	75	92	78

[a]No significant differences were found among the groups on any behavioral dimension.

across both trials ranged from 43% to 50%. When the number of problem dimensions was summed for each participant, more than 95% of the parents reported that their child had at least one behavioral problem. The percentage of parents reporting multiple behavioral problems decreased as the number of domains increased, with approximately 80% of the parents reporting problems in at least five behavioral domains.

Trial I: Global and Specific Evaluation of Improvement

To evaluate the effectiveness of the filtered music treatment, group differences were evaluated with analyses of variance for each of the 10 behavioral dimen-

FIGURE 12.1. Behavioral improvements at the 1-week post treatment assessment in Trial I. The data are reported as the percent of participants with a specific behavioral problem who improved.

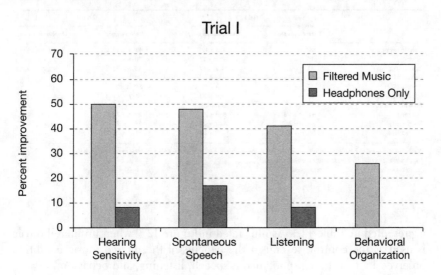

sions included in the questionnaire. As illustrated in Figure 12.1, significant improvements, relative to the headphones-only group, were noted in the filtered music group in hearing sensitivity, $F(1, 29) = 6.46$, $p = 0.017$; spontaneous speech, $F(1, 49) = 5.61$, $p = 0.022$; listening, $F(1, 52) = 8.25$, $p = 0.006$; and behavioral organization, $F(1, 34) = 5.39$, $p = 0.027$. The percentage of the participants improving, who had a problem within each domain, is presented in Table 12.4. At one week postintervention, analysis of variance confirmed that the filtered music group exhibited significantly more improvements summed across domains than the headphones-only group (i.e., 2.36 versus 0.81), $F(1, 62) = 7.76$, $p = 0.007$.

Trial II: Global and Specific Evaluation of Improvement

Since the relative benefits observed during Trial I could be attributed to listening to music, independent of the computer modulation of the acoustic features, Trial II was conducted, contrasting the filtered music condition to the same music in an unfiltered form. The unfiltered music condition was similar to the structured listening condition described by Bettison (1996). As illustrated in Figure 12.2, significant improvements in the filtered music condition relative to the unfiltered music condition were observed in both hearing sensitivity, $F(1, 28) = 4.53$, $p = 0.040$, and emotional control, $F(1, 49) = 5.84$, $p = 0.019$. The percentage of the participants improving, who had a problem within each domain,

TABLE 12.4.   Percentage[a] Improving Who Had a Problem Within Each Behavioral Domain at the One-Week Follow-Up

	Trial I		Trial II	
	Filtered music	Headphones only	Filtered music	Unfiltered music
Hearing sensitivity	**50**[b], n = 18	8, n = 12	**43**[c], n = 23	13, n = 15
Affect	19, n = 16	18, n = 17	25, n = 32	21, n = 19
Eye contact	41, n = 27	24, n = 17	33, n = 30	40, n = 20
Behavioral organization	**26**[b], n = 19	0, n = 16	29, n = 28	18, n = 17
Emotional control	17, n = 18	0, n = 12	**24**[c], n = 33	0, n = 19
Spontaneous speech	**48**[b], n = 27	17, n = 23	51, n = 41	44, n = 25
Receptive speech	31, n = 25	9, n = 23	9, n = 45	15, n = 25
Listening	**41**[b], n = 29	8, n = 24	30, n = 37	29, n = 21
Spontaneity	43, n = 25	20, n = 20	36, n = 22	36, n = 14
Relatedness	30, n = 30	13, n = 23	34, n = 32	29, n = 21

[a]*Defined by the number of individuals who improved devided by the number of individuals with problems (o) within the behavioral domain.*
[b]*Significant improvement relative to headphones only in Trial I.*
[c]*Significan improvement relative to unfiltered music in Trial II.*

is presented in Table 12.4. As illustrated in Figure 12.3, when unfiltered music is used as the control, several of the benefits of the filtered music condition observed in Trial I (i.e., spontaneous speech, listening, and behavioral organization) appear to be due to listening to music (i.e., unfiltered music) and not to the algorithm used to filter the music. Consistent with this interpretation, there was no significant difference in the sum of improvements for the filtered music group (1.98) when contrasted with the unfiltered music group (1.53). These data suggest that a unique benefit of the filtered music is a significant reduction in hearing sensitivity.

Contrasts Between Trial I and Trial II

Analyses of variance confirmed the similarity between the filtered music condition in Trial I and Trial II. The percentage of participants improving on each domain was similar for the filtered music groups within Trial I and Trial II (see Table 12.4). Similarly, the number of problem domains was similar for all groups on entry into the protocol (see Table 12.3).

Sharing Behaviors

Video data from a random subsample of children in the filtered music condition (n = 61) were coded. The subsample was partitioned into three groups: children who had no hearing sensitivity at the start of the study (n = 34), children who showed improvements on hearing sensitivity following the intervention (n = 14), and children who had no improvements on hearing sensitivity following the intervention (n = 13). A repeated-measures analysis of variance identified a

FIGURE 12.2. Behavioral improvements at the 1-week post treatment assessment in Trial II. The data are reported as the percent of participants with a specific behavioral problem who improved.

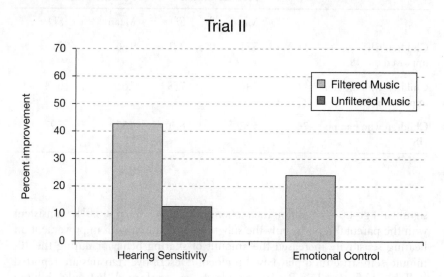

FIGURE 12.3. Combined data from Trial I and Trial II illustrating significant behavioral improvements at the 1-week post treatment assessment. The data are reported as the percent of participants with specific behavioral problems who improved.

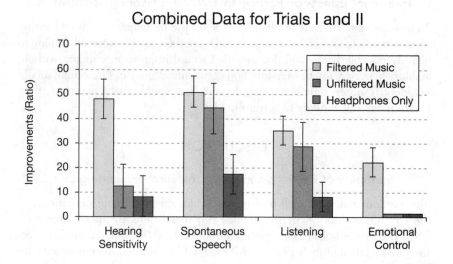

TABLE 12.5.   Hearing Sensitivity (HS) and Total Number
of Shares (N, mean, and SD)

	N	Preintervention		Postintervention	
		Mean	SD	Mean	SD
Children who improved on HS	14	5.71	7.31	9.86	10.53
Children who did not improve on HS	13	7.46	7.33	7.62	6.74
Children who had no HS	34	5.82	8.50	6.32	7.97

significant group × condition interaction, $F(2, 58) = 4.88$, $p < 0.011$. Consistent with the parental reports, only the subgroup of children with improvement on hearing sensitivity increased the amount of sharing behavior during the 10-minute semistructured play-based protocol. Descriptive statistics are reported in Table 12.5. Post hoc Bonferroni adjustment confirmed that only children who were reported to improve on hearing sensitivity increased the amount of sharing behavior during the 10-minute semistructured play-based observational assessment of social engagement skills with the Social Interaction Coding Scale (SICS; Bazhenova et al., n.d.).

Treatment Effects on Participants Without Hearing Sensitivities

To investigate the effects of filtered music on the participants without hearing sensitivities, analyses of variance were calculated on each behavioral domain to identify possible behavioral domains that would improve in children without auditory hypersensitivities as a function of the filtered music. These analyses did not identify any specific behavioral domain that would reliably improve in the children without auditory hypersensitivities.

DISCUSSION

Summary of Findings and Other Research Evaluating LPP

Two randomized controlled trials were conducted to evaluate the efficacy of the LPP on auditory hypersensitivities and social behavior in children with ASD. Data from both trials confirmed that the LPP (i.e., filtered music) selectively reduced auditory hypersensitivities. Trial I contrasted filtered music with a headphones-only condition. The results of Trial I led to a more stringent Trial II in which filtered music was contrasted with an unfiltered music condition. In both trials, the LPP selectively reduced auditory hypersensitivities. In addition, within the filtered music groups the children with auditory hypersensitivities who improved following LPP significantly increased their spontaneous sharing behaviors. These findings, consistent with the Polyvagal Theory, support the hypothetical basis for designing the LPP as a neural exercise of pathways involved in regulating behavioral state, listening, looking, and other social engagement behaviors such as spontaneous sharing.

The current findings are consistent with a previous study (Porges et al., 2013) evaluating the LPP with a more diverse sample of ASD children. In the previous study, the effectiveness of the LPP was objectively assessed by evaluating auditory processing (assumed to be a function of the transfer function of the middle ear structures) and autonomic state (assumed to mediate behavioral state regulation). The study demonstrated that the LPP significantly increased vagal regulation of the heart (i.e., increased amplitude of respiratory sinus arrhythmia) and normalized auditory processing on the filtered words and competing words subtests from the SCAN test for auditory processing disorder (Keith, 1986, 2000). Collectively, the data from the current trials and Porges et al. (2013) provide convergent preliminary support that the LPP enhances function of the polyvagal social engagement system manifested in improved auditory processing, reduced auditory hypersensitivities, increased vagal regulation of the heart, and increased spontaneous social behaviors (e.g., sharing).

Contrasts With Traditional Auditory Intervention Therapies

Since the LPP delivers computer-altered acoustic stimuli through headphones, it shares some of the features of auditory intervention therapies (i.e., AIT). However, although the LPP is a sound therapy, at the time this research was conducted it was not clinically available and differs from other available forms of AIT (e.g., Berard, 1993; Tomatis, 1991) in method and theory. First, the LPP is based on the Polyvagal Theory and reflects a strategic attempt to engage neural regulation of specific structures involved in the social engagement system (Porges, 2005). Second, the LPP focuses on auditory hypersensitivities that may be expressed by individuals with and without clinical diagnoses. Third, the effectiveness of the LPP can be measured through well-defined behavioral and physiological features of the social engagement system. Fourth, the LPP was designed with several unique features to engage and to exercise the neural regulation of the middle ear muscles, including an understanding of the transfer function of the middle ear structures and the vulnerability of the fast-twitch middle ear muscles to fatigue. Fifth, the duration of the LPP is shorter (i.e., approximately 5 hours) than most forms of AIT. Therefore, the effects of the LPP described in this study should not be generalized to any other form of auditory intervention.

There are several problems related to the evaluation of traditional AITs. First, since the interventions have evolved from clinical observations and insights, the neurophysiological theory underlying the interventions is often not well developed or tested. Second, research has been frequently structured to ask questions of efficacy instead of developing protocols to test theoretically relevant components of the treatment in order to understand the mechanisms and to refine the methodology. Third, since auditory interventions are applied within a clinical setting, several experimental design parameters are difficult to control, including (1) a constant protocol, (2) limiting concurrent treatments including medication, (3) randomization of participants into conditions, and (4) the selection of outcome variables that are theoretically relevant to the intervention model. Perhaps the greatest limiting factor is the broad range of domains that auditory interventions are proposed to improve without a description of a causal link through which the intervention would result in functional changes in behavior. Due, in part, to the above limitations, the literature documenting efficacy for the clinically available forms of AIT has been difficult to interpret.

Some studies evaluating the effectiveness of the AIT report improvements (Edelson et al., 1999; Rimland & Edelson, 1995) and others do not (Bettison, 1996; Gillbert et al., 1997; Kershner et al., 1990; Mudford et al., 2000; Zollweg et al., 1997). However, some of the above studies that do not support unique effects of AIT, document positive effects. For example, Bettison (1996) reports positive effects in both the experimental group (received auditory training) and the control group (listened to the same unmodified music under the same conditions). Bettison suggests, consistent with our findings, that features in the AIT shared with listening to selected unmodified music may have beneficial effects on children with autism. Moreover, as our data suggest, if participants do not have auditory hypersensitivities, then the effects of the LPP may be mediated through different biobehavioral pathways with unpredictable (i.e., nonspecific) positive outcomes, which are not consistent with the middle ear transfer function model. Perhaps, similar to the outcomes with children without auditory hypersensitivities in the LPP trials, observed positive effects of AIT may be recruiting pathways outside of the middle ear model via the potential therapeutic calming effects of music and social support by clinicians.

Gilmor (1999) conducted a meta-analysis based on several studies conducted in the 1980s with the Tomatis method involving 231 children. Gilmor clustered the outcome measures into five behavioral domains and identified small effects for linguistic, psychomotor, personal and social adjustment, and cognitive domains. Interestingly, he found no reliable effect in the auditory domain. These findings should be cautiously interpreted because the studies were limited by small sample sizes, issues related to defining control conditions, and limited use of random assignment. Regardless of these limitations, parents and clinicians of children with ASD have reported that forms of auditory intervention therapy have been helpful.

LIMITATIONS OF THE CURRENT STUDY

The data from the current study need to be cautiously interpreted for the reasons outlined below.

1. The major findings were dependent on the subjective reports of parents.
2. Some of the hypotheses tested were dependent on the small sizes of critical subgroups (e.g., individuals with or without auditory hypersensitivities who did or did not show improvements partitioned by the various treatment conditions).
3. The participants were receiving other treatments during the intervention and assessment period. Several participants were receiving daily interventions using behavioral approaches and other therapies, which may have enhanced or dampened the effects of the LPP.
4. Frequent contact of parents with therapists might bias parental reports and compromise the validity of the parents as objective informants. These factors could obfuscate the real effects of the intervention and inaccurately identify changes. Alternatively, features that might have improved could have been neglected. Possibly the hearing sensitivity domain on the parent questionnaire is less vulnerable to clinician-parent bias. Based on our experience, the therapists and parents appear to be less interested in this dimension, although it was the focal point of our study.
5. Improvements were observed in the groups not receiving the filtered music. Approximately 40% of the parents of children not receiving the filtered music reported improvements on at least one behavioral feature. These positive reactions might be due to nonspecific features of the protocol, such as a relaxed intervention environment fostering social engagement and spontaneous play, as well as a positive expectation bias and the effects of familiarity with staff and context as the child progressed through the five laboratory sessions. However, the groups receiving filtered music diverged from the control groups when parents reported improvements in hearing sensitivity.
6. Standardized assessments of cognitive function and developmental landmarks were not evaluated. The lack of this information precluded confirmation of matching on these variables, although, based on the sample size, random assignment should have led to a reasonable expectation of matched samples. The randomization of participants, with regard to the evaluated parameters, was effective, and there were no group differences in their representation. Standardized assessments of cognitive function and development would provide data to investigate two questions: (1) Are auditory hypersensitivities related to cognitive function and developmental landmarks? (2) Is the effectiveness of the LPP related to individual differences in cognitive function?

7. Our participants were young and on the severe end of the autism spectrum, and the findings may not generalize to older or less severe ASD.
8. The studies precluded an opportunity to confirm the specific neural pathways responsible for the observed behavioral improvements. The methods employed could not confirm whether auditory hypersensitivity was due to a compromise in functional neural regulation of the middle ear muscles (as proposed by the Polyvagal Theory) and remediated through an exercise model.
9. The studies did not provide information necessary to distinguish among alternative pathways leading to or remediating auditory hypersensitivities, such as the potential influence of the intervention on damaged neural pathways (e.g., auditory or facial nerve), on damaged peripheral structures (e.g., middle ear and inner ear), or central structures involved in processing the acoustic signal or in cortical representation.
10. The hypothesized link between the middle ear transfer function and auditory hypersensitivities could be limited. Hypersensitivities, especially to high-frequency sounds, might be due not to the neural regulation of the middle ear muscles but to the olivary cochlear reflexes. Tests of inner ear function and the degree of auditory hypersensitivity to high-frequency sounds need to be evaluated to rule out this possibility.
11. The general improvements in behavior observed following a reduction in hearing sensitivity might not be related to the proposed integrative social engagement system. Rather, the enhanced behavior might be naturally occurring when sounds are welcoming and functionally increase ventral vagal tone, while calming the autonomic nervous system.

FUTURE DIRECTIONS

A measure of the hypothesized intervening mechanism, the middle ear transfer function, has been missing from the formal experiments evaluating effectiveness of the LPP. At the time the participants were tested, no commercial clinical or research device was available to monitor the middle ear transfer function. Without a sensitive measure of the middle ear transfer function, the only method to demonstrate efficacy was to quantify physiology, auditory processing, and measures of behavior and to infer that the LPP normalized an atypical middle ear transfer function. We have developed a Middle Ear Sound Absorption System (MESAS) to measure the middle ear transfer function (Lewis & Porges, 2012). MESAS provides an objective measure of the potential mediating role that middle ear muscles play in experiencing auditory hypersensitivities (see Porges & Lewis, 2013).

By providing an objective measure of the middle ear transfer function, future research with MESAS will enable a selective test of the efficacy of the LPP in normalizing the middle ear transfer function. If confirmed, the LPP could be applied to individuals with atypical middle ear function, including rehabilitation following otitis media. In addition, MESAS will enable future research to evaluate the behavioral and psychological consequences of an atypical middle ear transfer function, provide data to validate a quantitatively scaled measure of auditory hypersensitivities independent of subjective reports, and contribute to the improvement of interventions (e.g., LPP) that may function as efficient neural exercises to normalize the middle ear transfer function.

REFERENCES

American National Standards Institute. (1997). ANSI S3.5-1997: *Methods for calculation of the Speech Intelligibility Index*. New York: Acoustical Society of America.

American Psychiatric Association. (1994). *Diagnostic and statistical manual of mental disorders* (4th ed.). Washington, DC: American Psychiatric Association.

Bazhenova, O. V., Sorokin, Y., Bal, E., Carlson, N., Heilman, K. J., Denver, J. W., et al. n.d. The Social Interaction Coding Scale (SICS) [Unpublished manuscript].

Berard, G. (1993). *Hearing equals behavior*. New Canaan, CT: Keats.

Bettison, S. (1996). The long-term effects of auditory training on children with autism. *Journal of Autism and Developmental Disorders, 26*, 361–374. doi:10.1007/BF02172480

Borg, E., & Counter, S. A. (1989). The middle-ear muscles. *Scientific American, 261*, 74–80. doi:10.1038/scientificamerican0889-74

Ceponiene, R., Lepistö, T., Shestakova, A., Vanhala, A., Alku, P., Näätänen, R., & Yaguchi, K. (2003). Speech-sound selective auditory impairment in children with autism: They can perceive but do not attend. *Proceedings of the National Academy of Sciences USA, 100*, 5567–5572. doi:10.1073/pnas.0835631100

Coleman, M., & Gillberg, C. (1985). *The biology of the autistic syndromes*. New York: Praeger.

Dawson, G. (1988). Cerebral lateralization in autism: Clues to its role in language and affective development. In D. L. Molfese & S. J. Segalowitz (Eds.), *Brain lateralization in children: Developmental implications* (pp. 437–461). New York: Guilford.

Dissanayake, C., & Sigman, M. (2001). Attachment and emotional responsiveness in children with autism (pp. 239–266). In G. L. Masters (Ed.), *International review of research in mental retardation: Autism*. San Diego, CA: Academic Press.

Edelson, S. M., Arin, D., Bauman, M., Lukas, S. E., Rudy, J. H., Sholar, M., & Rimland, B. (1999). Auditory integration training: A double blind study of behavioral and electrophysiological effects in people with autism. *Focus on Autism and Other Developmental Disabilities, 14*, 73–81. doi:10.1177/108835769901400202

Frith, U., & Baron-Cohen, S. (1987). Perception in autistic children. In D. J. Cohen, A. M. Donnellan, & R. Paul (Eds.), *Handbook of autism and pervasive developmental disorders* (pp. 85–102). New York: Wiley.

Gage, N. M., Siegel, B., & Roberts, T. P. L. (2003). Cortical auditory system maturational abnormalities in children with autism disorder: An MEG investigation. *Developmental Brain Research, 144*, 201–209. doi:10.1016/S0165-3806(03)00172-X

Gervais, H., Belin, P., Boddaert, N., Leboyer, M., Coez, A., Sfaello, I., Barthélémy, C., Brunelle, F., Samson, Y., & Zilbovicius, M. (2004). Abnormal cortical voice processing in autism. *Nature Neuroscience, 7*, 801–802. doi:10.1038/nn1291

Gillberg, C., Johansson, M., Steffenberg, S., & Berlin, O. (1997). Auditory integration training in children with autism: Brief report of an open pilot study. *Autism, 1,* 97–100. doi:10.1177/1362361397011009

Gilmor, T. (1999). The efficacy of the Tomatis method for children with learning and communication disorders: A meta-analysis. *International Journal of Listening, 13,* 12–23. doi:10.1080/10904018.1999.10499024

Hanks, W. D., & Rose, K. J. (1993). Middle ear resonance and acoustic immittance measures in children. *Journal of Speech and Hearing Research, 36,* 218–222.

Hayes, R., & Gordon, A. (1977). Auditory abnormalities in autistic children. *Lancet, 2,* 767. doi:10.1016/S0140-6736(77)90278-1

Keith, R. W. (1986). *SCAN: A screening test for auditory processing disorders.* San Antonio, TX: Harcourt Brace Jovanovich.

Keith, R. W. (2000). *SCAN: A screening test for auditory processing disorders in children—revised.* San Antonio, TX: Harcourt Brace Jovanovich.

Kershner, J. R., Cummings, R. L., Clarke, K. A., Hadfield, A. J., & Kershner, B. A. (1990). Two-year evaluation of the Tomatis listening training program with learning disabled children. *Learning Disability Quarterly, 13,* 43–53. doi:10.2307/1510391

Khalfa, S., Bruneau, N., Roge, B., Georgieff, N., Veuillet, E., Adrien, J. L., Barthélémy, C., & Collet, L. (2004). Increased perception of loudness in autism. *Hearing Research, 198,* 87–92. doi:10.1016/j.heares.2004.07.006

Khalfa, S., Dubal, S., Veuillet, E., Perez-Diaz, F., Jouvent, R., & Collet, L. (2002). Psychometric normalization of a hyperacusis questionnaire. *ORL: Journal of Oto-rhino-laryngology and Related Specialties, 64,* 436–442. doi:10.1159/000067570

Klin, A. (1992). Listening preferences in regard to speech in 4 children with developmental disabilities. *Journal of Child Psychology and Psychiatry, 33,* 763–769. doi:10.1111/j.14697610.1992.tb00911.x

Kryter, K. D. (1962). Methods for the calculation and use of the articulation index. *Journal of the Acoustic Society of America, 34,* 1689–1697. doi:10.1121/1.1909096

Lewis, G. F., & Porges, S. W. (2012). U.S. Patent Application No. WO2012082721 A2. Washington, DC: U.S. Patent and Trademark Office.

Liberman, C. M., & Guinan, J. J. (1988). Feedback control of the auditory periphery: Antimasking effects of middle ear muscles vs. olivocochlear efferents. *Journal of Community Disorders, 31,* 471–483. doi:10.1016/S0021-9924(98)00019-7

Lockyer, L., & Rutter, M. (1969). A five-to-fifteen-year follow-up study of infantile psychosis: III. Psychological aspects. *British Journal of Psychiatry, 115,* 865–882. doi:10.1192/bjp.115.525.865

Lord, C., Risi, S., Lambrecht, L., Cook, E. H., Leventhal, B. L., DiLavore, P. C., Pickles, A., & Rutter, M. (2000). The autism diagnostic observation schedule–generic: A standard measure of social and communication deficits associated with the spectrum of autism. *Journal of Autism and Developmental Disorders, 30*(3), 205–223. doi:10.1023/A:1005592401947

Lord, C., Rutter, M., & Le Couteur, A. (1994). Autism diagnostic interview–revised: A revised version of a diagnostic interview for caregivers of individuals with possible pervasive developmental disorders. *Journal of Autism and Developmental Disorders, 24,* 659–685. doi:10.1007/BF02172145

Marco, J. E., Hinkley, L. B. N., Hill, S. S., & Nagarajan, S. S. (2011). Sensory processing in autism: A review of neurophysiologic findings. *Pediatric Research, 69*, 48–54. doi:10.1203/PDR.0b013e3182130c54

Maziade, M., Merette, C., Cayer, M., Roy, M. A., Szatmari, P., Cote, R., & Thivierge, J. (2000). Prolongation of brainstem auditory-evoked responses in autistic probands and their unaffected relatives. *Archives of General Psychiatry, 57*, 1077–1083. doi:10.1001/archpsyc.57.11.1077

Mudford, O. C., Cross, B. A., Breen, S., Cullen, C., Reeves, D., Gould, J., & Douglas, J. (2000). Auditory integration training for children with autism: No behavioral benefits detected. *American Journal of Mental Retardation, 105*, 118–129. doi:10.1352/0895-8017(2000)105<0118:AITFCW>2.0.CO;2

Mundy, P. (1995). Joint attention and social-emotional approach behavior in children with autism. *Developmental Psychopathology, 7*, 63–82. doi:10.1017/S0954579400006349

Porges, S. W. (2005). The vagus: A mediator of behavioral and visceral features associated with autism. In M. L. Bauman & T. L. Kemper (Eds.), *The neurobiology of autism* (pp. 65–78). Baltimore: Johns Hopkins University Press.

Porges, S. W. (2007). The polyvagal perspective. *Biological Psychology, 74*, 116–143. doi:10.1016/j.biopsycho.2006.06.009

Porges, S. W., & Lewis, G. F. (2010). The polyvagal hypothesis: Common mechanisms mediating autonomic regulation, vocalizations and listening. In S. M. Brudzynski (Ed.), *Handbook of mammalian vocalization: An integrative neuroscience approach* (pp. 255–264). Amsterdam: Academic Press.

Porges, S. W., & Lewis, G. F. (2013). U.S. Patent Application No. 13/992,450. Washington, DC: U.S. Patent and Trademark Office.

Porges, S. W., Macellaio, M., Stanfill, S. D., McCue, K., Lewis, G. F., Harden, E. R., Handelman, M., Denver, J., Bazhenova, O. V., & Heilman, K. J. (2013). Respiratory sinus arrhythmia and auditory processing in autism: Modifiable deficits of an integrated social engagement system? *International Journal of Psychophysiology, 88*, 261–270. doi:10.1016/j.ijpsycho.2012.11.009

Rimland, B., & Edelson, S. M. (1995). Brief report: A pilot study of auditory integration training in autism. *Journal of Autism and Developmental Disorders, 25*, 61–70. doi:10.1007/BF02178168

Rosenhall, U., Nordin, V., Sandström, M., Ahlsén, G., & Gillberg, C. (1999). Autism and hearing loss. *Journal of Autism and Developmental Disorders, 29*, 349–357. doi:10.1023/A:1023022709710

Schiaffino, S., & Reggiani, C. (2011). Fiber types in mammalian skeletal muscles. *Physiology Review, 91*, 1447–1531. doi:10.1152/physrev.00031.2010

Seibert, J. M., Hogan, A. E., & Mundy, P. C. (1982). Assessing interactional competencies: The early social-communication scales. *Infant Mental Health Journal, 3*, 244–258. doi:10.1002/1097-0355(198224)3:4<244::AID-IMHJ2280030406>3.0.CO;2-R

Smith, D. E., Miller, S. D., Stewart, M., Walter, T. L., & McConnell, J. V. (1988). Conductive hearing loss in autistic, learning disabled, and normal children. *Journal of Autism and Developmental Disorders, 18*, 53–65. doi:10.1007/BF02211818

Tecchio, F., Benassi, F., Zappasodi, F., Gialloreti, L. E., Palermo, M., Seri, S., & Rossini, P. M. (2003). Auditory sensory processing in autism: A magnetoencephalographic study. *Biological Psychiatry, 54*, 647–654. doi:10.1016/S0006-3223(03)00295-6

Thivierge, J., Bedard, C., Cote, R., & Maziade M. (1990). Brainstem auditory evoked response and subcortical abnormalities in autism. *American Journal of Psychiatry, 147,* 1609–1613.

Tomatis, A. A. (1991). *The conscious ear: My life of transformation through listening.* Barrytown, NY: Station Hill.

World Health Organization. (1992). *International classification of diseases* (10th ed.). Geneva: World Health Organization.

Zollweg, W., Palm, D., & Vance, V. (1997). The efficacy of auditory integration training: A double blind study. *American Journal of Audiology, 6,* 39.

Zwislocki, J. J. (2002). Auditory system: Peripheral nonlinearity and central additivity, as revealed in the human stapedius-muscle reflex. *Proceedings of the National Academy of Sciences USA, 99,* 14601–14606. doi:10.1073/pnas.222543199

CHAPTER 13

The Significance of Stillness

A Dialogue with Stephen W. Porges and Denise Winn

WINN: Professor Porges, you first formulated Polyvagal Theory in 1994 and, as you say at the beginning of The Pocket Guide to Polyvagal Theory, its major impact has been to provide "plausible neurophysiological explanations for several of the experiences described by individuals who have experienced trauma." In the guide, you show how, from a polyvagal perspective, not feeling safe is the core behavioral feature that leads to mental and physical illness. The Human Givens psychotherapeutic approach holds that when essential emotional needs are not sufficiently well met, or when the innate resources we have to help us meet them are damaged or misused, that is when mental ill health occurs—and security is certainly one of our essential emotional needs. So, I'm really interested to hear more about your findings in this respect, and about the related role of what you term social engagement. But let's begin at the beginning, which was that, in graduate school, you were attracted to a new interdisciplinary area called psychophysiology. What is that?

PORGES: Psychophysiology was a new discipline that focused on how physiological processes were related to psychological experiences. Basically, it provided a science to infer mental processes through the monitoring of physiological variables. I thought it was an extremely interesting discipline with exciting applications. It fit my personal interests. At that time, I was in my early 20s, and I was curious about what we could learn about a person by monitoring physiology without requiring them to make verbal or written responses. I realized that what people say or write frequently represented a confabulated narrative that was generated to fit specific needs. There was a disconnect between intentions and what was actually being said.

WINN: When you say, "to fit specific needs," what do you mean?

PORGES: Their sense of self and who they were. Let me give you an example. Let's say a person was brought up with certain very strong religious beliefs, and they don't think it is appropriate to make negative statements about another person, regardless of what they might feel. They would have facial expressions and vocal intonations that didn't match the intentions of the words they were speaking. To me, the idea of being able to monitor heart rate, pulse, and skin conductance was really thrilling and exciting as a way of seeing what was going on beneath the skin.

WINN: And did that set you off on the road to developing Polyvagal Theory?

PORGES: Well, not immediately. In the late 1960s and early 1970s I first conceptualized how to quantify heart rate variability, and how it changed during psychological and physical challenges. In fact, I was the first scientist to quantify heart rate variability (see Porges, 1969), which is the variation in the time between heartbeats. The heart doesn't beat with a constant rhythm; embedded in the beat-to-beat heart rate pattern are modulated rhythms that are due to neural influences. In my early research, I documented that individuals with greater variations in the time between heartbeats appeared to have a greater capacity to pay attention, had faster reaction times, and were more resilient. These observations led me into studying the neurophysiology of heart rate variability and started me on an intellectual journey that resulted in Polyvagal Theory (Porges, 1995).

WINN: Before we go further into that, can we just say a bit more about the vagus, which you describe as the major nerve of the parasympathetic nervous system, functionally connecting our brains to our bodies?

PORGES: The vagus, first of all, is a cranial nerve and, as you say, it is the major component of the parasympathetic nervous system. We have a sympathetic nervous system that, in general, supports mobilization and energetic activities, including pumping blood. Most people conceptualize the sympathetic nervous system as a fight-and-flight system. However, although it supports the fight-and-flight responses, it has other more prosocial functions and supports energetic activities. Without a well-functioning sympathetic nervous system, we would be lethargic. Our exuberance and upbeat movements and feelings are dependent on the sympathetic nervous system as an energy source, whereas, in general, the parasympathetic nervous system is about repose and support of health, growth, and restoration.

WINN: And, prior to Polyvagal Theory, it wasn't recognized that the parasympathetic nervous system had two vagal branches.

PORGES: That's right—or, more accurately, that the vagus, the major component of the parasympathetic nervous system, had two functional pathways that originated in different areas of the brainstem where the vagal motor fibers originate and then travel down the vagus to visceral organs. The traditional view of the autonomic nervous system put the emphasis on the antagonistic influence of the motor pathways of the sympathetic and parasympathetic nervous systems regulating internal organs. The bidirectionality of the system was minimized, especially the bidirectionality of vagal pathways between the visceral organs in the body and the brainstem areas in which the motor pathways originated and the sensory pathways terminated. In fact, about 80% of vagal fibers are sensory fibers, informing brain structures of the status of visceral organs. This provides a plausible explanation of how gut problems influence how you feel and how the rate your heart is beating at can influence how you perceive the world.

In the early 1900s, physiologists had already identified the specific fibers in the vagus that were cardioinhibitory and could slow the heart when stimulated. My aim was to develop a better measure to quantify this vagal influence on the heart. After almost two decades, in 1985, I received a patent for procedures to dynamically monitor vagal influences on the heart. The methodology was embodied in a device that I called the "vagal tone monitor." With a standardized methdodology, I started to apply the technology in clinical settings and measured patients with various mental and physical health diagnoses and challenges.

WINN: We have long been familiar with the fight-or-flight explanation for emotional arousal, which is all about activating the sympathetic nervous system and readying us for action when we are under threat. But your work on the vagus identified another even older defense system, connected with the parasympathetic nervous system—more usually, as you say, associated with repose. This second defense system is about immobilization, shutdown, and dissociation from a threatening event. I believe you came to these understandings through your research on preterm babies.

PORGES: Yes. In the early 1990s, I was conducting research with preterm infants. At that time the literature informally described vagal pathways and the entire parasympathetic nervous system as a health, growth, and restoration system. There was no qualification that a part of the parasympathetic nervous system, a vagal circuit, could be recruited as a defense system in response to cues of threat to life. It was as if this fact about the vagus was expunged from the common understanding of the parasympathetic nervous system. It wasn't that people didn't know that the heart rate could slow to extremes that could result in brain damage and death; they just couldn't conceptualize the neural mechanisms that mediated it. Without an appreciation of a vagal mechanism that could be lethal, the vagus could be described as a wonderful health-providing resource, and the sympathetic nervous system became synonymous with stress and became the mortal enemy.

WINN: So, the vagus was seen as all good, despite clear evidence to the contrary. It was a neonatologist that alerted you to the contradiction, wasn't it?

PORGES: Yes. It occurred during a period of my research when I was working with high-risk preterm babies. I had already developed the measure for cardiac vagal tone. I wanted to apply it to identify clinical risk and to use it in assessments to provide helpful feedback to clinicians. My work was based on the assumption that, if a preterm infant had more vagal regulation of the heart, the infant would be more resilient, more likely to survive and have a positive outcome; conversely, if the infant was very premature, the vagal system wouldn't be working sufficiently, and the infant would be at greater risk.

In 1992, I wrote a paper, published in a major pediatrics journal (Porges, 1992), in which I described the important protective value of cardiac vagal tone, which could be monitored in the preterm infant by quantifying the respiratory component of heart rate variability. After its publication, I received a letter from a neonatologist who said that, in medical school, he had learned that bradycardia (slow heart rate) could kill you and that bradycardia was caused by the vagus. What stuck in my mind was that he wrote, "Perhaps too much of a good thing is bad?"

Intellectually that didn't make any sense to me. I thought about what I had learned over the years from my research in neonatal intensive care units and what I had observed in my laboratory. From my observations, I inferred that the respiratory rhythm in the beat-to-beat heart rate variability has a protective function and, when that respiratory rhythm wasn't observable, the infant was vulnerable to bradycardia and could die. I later documented this phenomenon (see Reed et al., 1999). But how could I reconcile that the vagus was responsible for both lethal bradycardia and protective heart rate variability? I called this contradiction the vagal paradox.

WINN: Is this what led you to discoveries about the unmyelinated and myelinated vagal pathways?

PORGES: Yes. I often say that the whole unfolding of what became Polyvagal Theory was right in front of my eyes in the neonatal intensive care unit, where the observant scientist can actually see the vagal system develop.

My research showed me that humans and other mammals have both unmyelinated and myelinated vagal pathways. Myelin is an insulating layer around the nerve that facilitates faster and more efficient neural transmission. These two vagal pathways originate in two different areas of the brainstem. An extremely preterm infant born at less than 30 weeks' gestational age doesn't have a functioning myelinated vagus. The process of myelination of vagal motor fibers, the vagal fibers with a respiratory rhythm, only begin to develop at 30 to 32 weeks of gestation. Through scientific publications describing vagal fibers in preterm infants who had died, I was able to find studies that provided sufficient information for me to generate a hypothetical developmental curve of the myelination of the vagal motor fibers going to the heart, and map what I had observed in my research onto that curve (see Porges & Furman, 2011).

It was an "aha!" moment for me, because I could monitor the shift in the neural regulation of the heart that was now paralleling the vulnerabilities experienced by the high-risk infant. The major vulnerabilities of a preterm baby are apnea (cessation of breathing) and bradycardia, during which heart rate slows to a degree that the brain is not receiving sufficient oxygenated blood. If we transpose these developmental observations into an evolutionary context, we can interpret the preterm's reactions of apnea and bradycardia from a reptilian perspective. For example, reptiles, which have only unmyelinated vagal motor fibers, hold stop breathing (they can survive several hours without breathing) and slow their heart rate to appear to be inanimate. It is a primary defense strategy for them, and it serves reptiles well, since they have small brains and are not as oxygen dependent as mammals. Mammals with their large brains require a continuous source of oxygen.

WINN: In effect, you recognized that babies born before 32 weeks have an autonomic nervous system with features more akin to that of a reptile than a mammal.

PORGES: Yes. Primitive extinct reptiles are the ancestors from which both modern reptiles and mammals evolved. Through these common ancestors, we evolved with a functional common core in our brainstem, which changes during embryological development, as the brainstem structures and emerging cranial nerves change and shift in function. In mammals, the primary role of the unmyelinated vagal fibers is to regulate organs below the diaphragm. Only mammals have a myelinated vagus that is linked in the brainstem to circuits regulating the striated muscles of the face and head. In mammals this vagal pathway is the primary regulator of organs above the diaphragm. So, bradycardia and apnea are due to an ancient defense system that is still available in the preterm baby and then, as we get older, becomes less accessible, although some unmyelinated fibers remain connected to the heart's pacemaker.

WINN: Does the mammalian nervous system, or the myelinated vagus, ever develop in severely preterm babies?

PORGES: The environment in which preterm babies survive is not as supportive as the intrauterine environment, in terms of that type of development. Once the preterm infant leaves the womb, the infant is bombarded with challenges from all the senses, and its nervous system is reacting and defending. At times these reactions may occur merely to being touched. When the system is protected in utero, it doesn't have those challenges, but when the baby leaves the womb, the body has to react with what tools it has, which are the defense reactions similar to a reptile.

WINN: Let me make sure I have this clear. All this development happens in utero and, by the time the baby is born, if it is full term, the mammalian system is functioning? But not so for the preterm baby?

PORGES: Yes. It is during the last five to eight weeks of gestation that the mammalian myelinated vagus comes online. The origin of these myelinated fibers are a product of a neural migration from one area of the brainstem to another, functionally developing into two distinct vagal pathways.

WINN: So, does that mean that those preterm babies, if they survive, are more at risk of using that older defense system if under any kind of severe stress?

PORGES: The answer is a qualified yes, but there are other features associated with this disruption in maturation of the myelinated vagus. A major landmark of health in preterm infants is the proper coordination in sucking, swallowing, and breathing, which involves the use of the cranial nerves controlling the striated muscles of the face and head. In the brainstem, structures regulating the cranial nerves that control these muscles communicate with the brainstem structure regulating the activity of the myelinated vagus. This provides the mechanisms for social behaviors such as facial expressions and vocalizations, as well as ingesting food, to regulate physiological state.

In our biological quest for safety, we have an implicit biological imperative to connect and coregulate our physiological state with another. Even how we look at each other is critical in this capacity to connect. For the preterm infant, these systems are challenged and poorly coordinated. In the time since I have been lecturing to groups involved in treating survivors of trauma, I've learned much more from parents about the outcomes of children born severely preterm. Whenever I asked about cognitive ability, usually their child would be doing well. But when I asked, "How is your child in social interactions and relationships?" they would say, "Clueless." Now I only ask about relationships.

WINN: Very interesting! Because when we talk about the potential developmental risks for children that were born preterm, we don't tend to think of that one.

PORGES: No, we don't. Advances in medical treatment have reduced risks for mental retardation and motor development. It appears that the major issue is about coregulation, which occurs naturally with most infants who are born full term. When a mother calms her baby with cooing and smiles and loving gestures, the baby relaxes, and that in turn calms the mother—coregulation. Neurophysiologically, coregulation is primarily about reciprocal facial expressions, gestures, and vocalizations between mother and infant via the striated muscles of the face and head. The preterm baby doesn't have the neural resources for behaviors that would enable coregulation. Those systems are blunted. But I'm an optimist. I believe that these systems can still be recruited and remapped or retuned.

WINN: From what I understand of Polyvagal Theory, we don't make conscious decisions about which defense system to use when under threat. Interestingly, you give the example of people highly fearful of public speaking feeling terrified that they are about to pass out. People having panic attacks often fear the same. From a fight-or-flight-response perspective, fainting wouldn't make sense, as blood pressure increases rather than falls. But are people who respond in that way actually going into this earlier defense mode instead?

PORGES: I think you are asking how the circuits are triggered. Let's look at the sequence of how the autonomic nervous system evolved in vertebrates. Ancient vertebrates started with a very simple autonomic nervous system, and the first neural component was the unmyelinated vagus. When it was functioning, it helped support physiological homoeostasis, but it could also react in defense. And when it reacted in defense, the animal defecated, stopped breathing, and reduced its metabolic output. Through evolutionary processes, some vertebrates developed a spinal sympathetic nervous system that fostered rapid movement. As evolution progressed, mammals evolved with a vagal circuit that was linked in brainstem structures to the neural regulation of the muscles of the face and head, forming an integrated social engagement system. Although I understood this sequence of evolutionary changes in the autonomic nervous system, I was missing a concept that explained how the different circuits could be triggered or buffered.

To answer this question, I first had to conceptualize what I knew about the autonomic nervous system into an evolutionary order or hierarchy. The hierarchy provided a rule determining the order in which the circuits could be recruited; newer circuits inhibit older circuits. This doctrine was based on the work of John Hughlings Jackson, an important English neurologist of the late 1800s. Jackson described how damage to parts of the human brain through illness or injury disinhibit older circuits. He used the word "dissolution," meaning evolution in reverse, to describe the process. When I read about dissolution, I realized that dissolution was the perfect construct to describe the sequence of autonomic reactions to challenges. When we face severe challenges, we adaptively respond by triggering evolutionarily older systems as we attempt to survive.

WINN: Do you mean when we face severe challenges where we perceive ourselves as unable to escape? In other words, where triggering the fight-or-flight system wouldn't work?

PORGES: These responses are reflexive and not planned. In fact, I developed the concept of neuroception to explain how we react without awareness to cues of safety, danger, or life threat—whether accurate or not. Neuroception is distinct from perception, since it occurs reflexively long before we actually perceive and interpret the risk in the environment. You are a therapist?

WINN: Yes.

PORGES: Actually, you don't even have to be a therapist, just a social human being, to notice what I am going to describe. Imagine you are talking to someone and you accidentally say something that is a trigger to that person, and suddenly their physiological state alters: their facial expression becomes evaluative or aggressive; their muscle tone becomes tight, and their hands clench. When these shifts in physiological state occur, their whole perspective of you changes, and they may lash out with aggressive words or behavior. Have you ever had that happen?

WINN: Yes.

PORGES: Because from your perspective your intentions were admirable, you don't understand what is going on, and you feel that you are a victim. But the person who lashed out at you is in a physiological state that shifts their perspective, and they will structure a narrative to justify their behavior. So there is a shift from a socially connected state to a state that has survival as its only priority. The beauty of being a human or any other social mammal is that, if we reflexively shift into defense, we also have the opportunity to be calmed and soothed as we reengage our social engagement system with another person. If we are exposed to cues of safety, trust, and love, through social engagement behaviors that may include a soft voice and appropriate gestures, we calm. This state of calmness spontaneously occurs in response to supportive social engagement behaviors and not in response to being lectured.

The link between physiological state and the circuits that produce facial expressions and prosodic vocalizations is unique to mammals. These integrated behavioral features are dependent on a neural circuit that also includes myelinated vagal pathways that calm the heart and downregulate the sympathetic nervous system. As mammals evolved, they maintained neural structures to be defensive, while developing unique neural pathways to downregulate defense by being comforted by another. Thus, the ability to rapidly move back and forth between social and defensive states is deeply wired into our nervous system. As mammals evolved, they had to be acutely aware of and reactive to cues of danger, but they also had to seek safety and comfort in the presence of others.

This sequence of dissolution, moving from social engagement to defense and then inhibiting defense through reengagement, works beautifully in most mammals. But what happens when you experience severe trauma or have certain disease states? We lose the accessibility of the facial muscles and the intonation of voice. Now, as the body is stuck in a state of defense, the cues of safety may be distorted and less effective in calming and soothing. Do you remember the singer Johnny Mathis?

WINN: Yes. He had a wonderfully smooth voice.

PORGES: When Johnny Mathis recordings were played, it enabled adolescents to feel safe—basically, for their bodies to feel safe in close proximity to each other. This type of vocal music may communicate cues of safety, via neuroception, that there is no danger and your body doesn't need to be protected. In other words, Johnny Mathis's voice enabled couples to feel physically close. When I lecture, I frequently use the metaphor that our nervous system is waiting for Johnny Mathis, because there are certain inflections and intonations of voice that our nervous system is primed to respond to and can't block. We are wired to respond to prosodic vocalizations. Mothers intuitively know this. Fathers often know how to employ prosodic vocalizations with their dogs, but not so much with their kids. That is because fathers tend to speak in a low-pitched, monotonic voice, which functions to create a boundary or constraint for a child, whereas the child's nervous system just wants to be safe and is waiting for a voice that is composed of frequencies similar to a mother's lullaby.

Since our nervous system is seeking Johnny Mathis, intonation of voice provides a portal through which we can reach people who have had traumatic experiences.

WINN: And calm them down.

PORGES: But feeling calm is double edged! When a person with a severe trauma history starts to calm down, their body may be triggered to go into defense, if the cues of calmness and immobilization are associated with a violation of trust and abuse. Functionally, as the body gives up defense, it becomes vulnerable and may trigger an implicit memory associated with an event during which trust had been violated.

WINN: That is what Human Givens therapists would call pattern matching.

PORGES: So now the body is unable to trust and move out of a state of defense. For some people with a trauma history, giving up defense triggers panic. They don't know why they are reacting in that way but, as they start to calm down, they may attempt to communicate their feelings, saying, "I'm not feeling good"; "I've got a bad feeling in my gut"; "I'm feeling angry." They are trying to figure it out. But what has actually happened is that their body has gone into a state of vulnerability.

Hypothetically, being calm and trusting another should not create vulnerability. But for many with trauma histories it does trigger feelings of vulnerability. I have been working on a methodology to shift individuals out of feeling vulnerable in this physiological state. I thought I could do it with computer-altered vocalizations. I developed acoustic stimuli that processed vocals to exaggerate prosody. This worked extremely well with children, and many autistic children became spontaneously engaged, after a few listening sessions; even their facial muscles changed.

WINN: Is this the Listening Project Protocol?

PORGES: Yes, it started out as that. But it is now commercially available and marketed as the Safe and Sound Protocol (see https://integratedlistening. com/porges/). Many trauma therapists have started to use it, and what I have found out since it was released is that some of their clients were triggered into states of vulnerability and became anxious and mobilized. At a workshop in London, I played a computer-altered version of a song sung by Judy Collins. I played only six minutes of the altered music, yet many of the participants had reactions ranging from feelings of slight anxiety to strong feelings of dysregulation. Several needed supportive engagement with others to help them feel comfortable again. This demonstrated to me, as well as the participants, that stimuli as simple as listening to computer-altered music could trigger anxiety and gut pains in some, while others experienced the same stimuli as blissful—or criticized what I had done to the music! Surprisingly, the range of reactions was great.

WINN: That is quite telling.

PORGES: These surprising observations led me to think about the mechanisms that would trigger these diverse reactions. Cues of safety were no longer functioning as cues of safety, but were transformed into cues that would anticipate being immobilized or restrained and becoming vulnerable. So I started to inquire how stillness was perceived. For instance, did a person perceive a state of stillness as a wonderful moment when time expanded, when they could be at peace within themselves, or did they experience stillness with fear of losing boundary and falling into the void? If you start talking about stillness to people with trauma, you immediately learn that it is frightening to many of them.

Let's imagine a woman or child living in a climate of domestic abuse—what does their body do? The old understanding of our autonomic nervous system was that we activated the sympathetic nervous system to support fight-and-flight behaviors. But, frequently, clients provide a totally different narrative that focuses on immobilization, restraint, and dissociation, which functionally enables the individual mentally to be in a safe place. But the narrative could also include passing out, defecating, or urinating in their clothing. When this immobilization defense circuit is triggered, it doesn't seem to be easy to regulate back to a calm state or to reengage with others and coregulate. After experiencing this type of shutdown defense, how do individuals protect themselves from going into that immobilized state in the future?

WINN: You mean because the extreme defensive reaction has become their default position?

PORGES: Yes. What they frequently do, to stop going into an immobilized state of defense, is to keep mobilized, keep moving. This would follow the evolutionary hierarchy of the autonomic nervous system, with newer circuits inhibiting older circuits. The adaptive strategy would be to maintain muscle tension and appear to be highly anxious and have a very low threshold for reacting with aggressive behavior. These individuals might be prone to experience panic. Panic has an adaptive function; it is mobilization and keeps them from shutting down.

To understand the origin of panic disorders and vulnerability to panic, we need to understand a person's clinical history, and it is not necessary for the clinical history to include documented emotional trauma through abuse. It could be triggered by memories of a medical procedure that was frightening. It could be related to a history of being restrained when the child was very young. Even if the intentions of the individual doing the restraint were good, the body of a young infant doesn't discriminate between the intentions to do good or to do harm. As a society, we need to have an appreciation of the body's reaction to the event or behavior, independent of the intention or motivation leading up to the behavior.

WINN: I'd like to come back to what you said earlier about trauma seeming to affect the way people express themselves, through the looks on their faces and their tone of voice. You describe in your books the way that this is often manifested in certain psychiatric disorders, such as schizophrenia. What is happening there, physiologically, to cause the emotional flatness that you often see in schizophrenia, the lack of tonal variation and so on?

PORGES: Let's throw away diagnoses for a moment. There are certain core features in several diagnostic categories, and these core features can be clustered into the functions disrupted by the loss of neural regulation of the striatal muscles of the face and head. When these functions are lost, it changes the autonomic state, and vagal regulation of the heart is depressed. Such individuals will have flat affect, lack prosodic vocalizations, and have difficulty extracting the human voice in background voices and sounds. They will have an autonomic nervous system that isn't calm and resilient, but instantaneously reacts to minor events and is literally ready to react and defend. Thus, the social engagement system is retracted to facilitate the opportunity to defend. We talk about all these clinical disorders, but we are actually talking about a physiological state that is easily triggered to become defensive; the neural circuit for coregulation, connectedness, and resilience is turned off.

WINN: So this is what trauma therapists who are working with your ideas are trying to reverse?

PORGES: Yes. First, I think these ideas have been helpful to trauma therapists by reframing their perspective in interpreting the reactions of their clients: Clients' limited repertoire of expressive behaviors can be categorized not as good or bad but as adaptive reactions of the nervous system that are triggered to protect the individual. When clients start to understand the adaptive nature of their behaviors, their personal narrative changes, and much shame and blame is reduced; they can even feel heroic. This new prosocial understanding allows them to start to shift away from being defensive toward the therapist and to expand their world.

WINN: You have explained that the neural circuits supporting social behavior and effective emotional regulation are available only when our nervous system deems the environment to be safe. The social engagement system seems to chime with Human Givens understandings about the vital need for social connection and for using innate resources to help us achieve it. Could you say a bit more about how social engagement works, from the polyvagal perspective?

PORGES: Sure. In part, many human behaviors involved in our interactions are attempts to recruit the social engagement system to downregulate defensive reactions. We often use facial expressions, voices, listening, and hand gestures to regulate our behavioral state. As a therapist, you will see people making various movements—ingesting, sucking, chewing their nails—and these are desperate attempts to utilize the social engagement system to trigger the calming effects of the vagus and our autonomic function.

WINN: Could you explain that a bit more?

PORGES: We can see this more easily in young infants. When infants are agitated, fussy, or crying, how are they calmed? Usually, by feeding. But as they rapidly mature and reach the age of about six months, social interaction becomes more potent than food in regulating their behavioral state. This is illustrated in Ed Tronick's famous "still face" experiment (Tronick et al., 1978). In this experimental paradigm, the mother or experimenter looks at the young infant, who is about nine months old, with a flat facial expression. The infant's responses follow a predictable sequence. First the infant will try to engage the mother or experimenter with facial expressions that may be supplemented with arm gestures. As the mother or experimenter goes on maintaining a still face, the frustrated infant will disengage and look away or else may go into a tantrum.

We forget that adults do this as well. If we have colleagues or bosses or spouses with whom there is a disruption in reciprocal interaction, we lose self-control and react.

Also, as a therapist, you will have clients with various dysfunctions or difficulties, and they often have physical ailments as well, such as irritable bowel, fibromyalgia, hypertension, and hypotension. The apparent comorbidities are due to the compromised function of the autonomic nervous system that occurs when the social engagement system is depressed. Functionally, the social engagement system needs to be switched on to support homoeostatic functions. Once the social engagement system is downregulated, the autonomic nervous system is vulnerable for defense.

WINN: So when the social engagement system isn't working, the whole body is thrown out of kilter?

PORGES: Yes. Without an adequately functioning social engagement system, the autonomic nervous system is incapable of supporting processes associated with health, growth, and restoration.

WINN: That is really significant. You say play is important as a means of helping us learn to downregulate stress responses and feel safe with others.

PORGES: Yes, play with others involves social interaction. Play allows us to mobilize, using the sympathetic nervous system along with the social engagement system. The social engagement system downregulates the sympathetic excitation to ensure that we don't move into fight or flight. We take our cues from the playful expressions and actions of those we are engaging with.

WINN: So we know that we are safe and it is not about aggression.

PORGES: Yes. We also have intimacy. When we are not face-to-face with individuals whom we trust, we can use gesture and voice as portals to the social engagement system. This coupling between the social engagement system and our evolutionary oldest component of the autonomic nervous system, the unmyelinated vagal circuit that enables reptiles to feign death, enables us to experience stillness as a positive state and to remain calm in the arms of another without triggering immobilization in defense. In these blendings of physiological states, we see the function of the social engagement system in coordinating or choreographing the entire autonomic nervous system. With an adequately functioning social engagement system, we can recruit all the attributes of the autonomic nervous system, and this optimizes health as well as social behavior.

WINN: For those who have suffered significant trauma, and particularly those who have never felt safe in their lives, you say, "feeling safe is the treatment." This has been taken on board by a lot of trauma specialists working with people who have often been diagnosed as having complex PTSD and commonly experience dissociation and emotional dysregulation. Is feeling safe really the treatment—or is it the initial first step in treatment?

PORGES: This leads to some new concepts. What I have been talking about, I call active and passive pathways. Feeling safe is the passive pathway—it enables physiological state to shift to one that supports more open and trusting behaviors. The active pathway consists of what I call neural exercises— these could, for instance, be reciprocal play or therapeutic interactions. Singing, especially in groups, is a good neural exercise. Neurophysiologically, since singing requires longer exhalations relative to inhalations, the calming impact of the myelinated vagus is potentiated. Singing also activates other aspects of the social engagement system by exercising the neural regulation of the muscles of the face, middle ear structures, and larynx and pharynx. Yes, safety is the treatment, but it also provides the substrate for other treatments.

WINN: It seems it isn't just safety within an individual's personal orbit that concerns you, however. I'm quoting from your book here: "Polyvagal Theory challenges the parameters that our educational, legal, political, religious and medical institutions use to define safety. By moving the defining features of 'safety' from a structural model of the environment, with fences, metal detectors and surveillance monitoring, to a visceral sensitivity model evaluating shifts in the neural regulation of autonomic state, the theory challenges our societal values regarding how people are treated. The theory forces us to question whether our society provides sufficient and appropriate opportunities to experience safe environments and trusting relationships. Once we recognize that the experiences within our social institutions, such as schools, hospitals and churches, are characterized by chronic evaluations that trigger feelings of danger and threat, we can see that these institutions can be as disruptive to health as political unrest, fiscal crisis and war."

Indeed, you even mention noticing treatment rooms in clinical settings that have a lot of low-frequency sound from ventilation systems, and this can be enough to disrupt feelings of safety. Do you think there is much we can do about all that?

PORGES: Scholars, educators, and scientists in disparate fields are becoming interested in Polyvagal Theory because the theory provides an understanding of how our nervous system responds to contextual and even historical challenges. We, as a species, were born without a manual. Polyvagal Theory identifies some critical indicators and processes that we need to incorporate into our manual. But importantly, we don't need to be safe all the time. We don't need to have reciprocal coregulation all the time. But we need to have access to safe environments and relationships.

There are two major points here. First, the removal of threat is not the equivalent of safety. This point is often missed by society. Second, we need to acknowledge that humans are a traumatized species. We should never have the expectation of a blissful life because our bodies also need novelty and challenge. We are wonderfully complex organisms, residing in a complex society. The irony is that those who are provided with the cues of safety and can utilize them are often the ones who become the most bold and creative. It is a paradox. If we have the feeling of being safe with others, we can do things that are extremely challenging. But if we forget the critical role of the antecedent state of safety and assume that we don't need a safe base from which to deal with challenges, the outcome is often tragic and limiting, with individuals living severely compromised lives.

WINN: I think that fits very well with understandings from developmental psychology about how infants whose emotional and physical needs are met are the ones that feel confident enough to want to explore and learn and take risks. What you have just said sort of answers what I was going to ask you next, about human resilience. Even if our environments are far from ideal, isn't it true that people are, in the main, able to cope and get by well enough? We do cope with trauma a lot of the time. Would you agree with that?

PORGES: Absolutely. And I think we have to celebrate our resilience and our ability to cope with challenges, because that is how the nervous system grows. Neural exercises are really transitory challenges to this system and how rapidly it can recover.

WINN: Lastly, and I think you have half answered this as well, now—you emphasize that the human organism needs to perceive itself as safe to survive and thrive, which means interacting safely with others. Does this mean you see this as the organism's goal? One of the most important emotional needs identified in the Human Givens approach is the need for meaning. Without it there is hopelessness, and the kind of depression that may lead to suicide. Is there a place for sense of meaning and purpose in your understandings about what makes a flourishing human being?

PORGES: Let me put it this way. We have a quest for safety, but it is not our sole goal. Safety is a facilitator of our internalized personal goals. Polyvagal Theory is actually moving toward some new ideas. I am working on the notion of purpose—purpose to live or purpose in life. We have learned from those who have experienced and survived severe trauma that the biggest impact of trauma is the loss of purpose in life. The concept of purpose is deeply rooted in our nature, and potentially biological. This process is now a focus as I expand Polyvagal Theory to further understand the consequences of reactions to life threat and our ability to thrive in spite of trauma-related disruptions.

WINN: Thank you, Professor Porges.

REFERENCES

Porges, S. W. (1992). Vagal tone: a physiologic marker of stress vulnerability. *Pediatrics*, 90(3 Pt 2), 498–504.

Porges, S. W. (1995). Orienting in a defensive world: Mammalian modifications of our evolutionary heritage. A polyvagal theory. *Psychophysiology*, 32(4), 301–318.

Porges, S. W. (2017). *The pocket guide to the polyvagal theory: The transformative power of feeling safe*. New York: Norton.

Porges, S. W., & Furman, S. A. (2011). The early development of the autonomic nervous system provides a neural platform for social behaviour: A polyvagal perspective. *Infant and child development*, 20(1), 106–118.

Porges, S. W., & Raskin, D. C. (1969). Respiratory and heart rate components of attention. *Journal of Experimental Psychology*, 81(3), 497–503.

Reed, S. F., Ohel, G., David, R., & Porges, S. W. (1999). A neural explanation of fetal heart rate patterns: a test of the polyvagal theory. Developmental Psychobiology: *The Journal of the International Society for Developmental Psychobiology*, 35(2), 108–118.

Tronick, E., Als, H., Adamson, L., Wise, S., & Brazelton, T. B. (1978). The infant's response to entrapment between contradictory messages in face-to-face interaction. *Journal of the American Academy of Child Psychiatry*, 17(1), 1–13.

CHAPTER 14

The COVID-19 Pandemic Is a Paradoxical Challenge to Our Nervous System
A Polyvagal Perspective

Stephen W. Porges

THE PANDEMIC IMPACTS ON OUR BIOLOGICAL IMPERATIVE TO CONNECT

As the COVID-19 crisis challenges the fabric of our society, we look to our science to understand how the crisis is influencing our mental and physical health, how we perceive the world, and the way we interact with others. Polyvagal Theory provides a neurobiological model to explain how the crisis elicits threat-related responses, disrupts our capacity to regulate our behavioral and emotional states, interferes with our optimism, and compromises our ability to trust and feel safe with one another.

Similar to several other mammals, humans are a social species. Being a social species explicitly emphasizes that human survival is dependent on coregulating our neurophysiological state via social interaction. The dependence of an infant on the mother is an archetypical example of this dependency and even illustrates the bidirectionality of the social interaction; the mother is not only regulating the infant, but the infant is reciprocally regulating the mother. The features of coregulation, reciprocity, connectedness, and trust resonate through the mammalian nervous system and optimize homeostatic function, providing a neurobiological link between our mental and physical health.

Theodosius Dobzhansky, a prominent evolutionary biologist, emphasized that connectedness rather than physical strength enabled the evolutionary success of mammals and redefined survival of the fittest by stating that "the fittest may also be the gentlest, because survival often requires mutual help and cooperation" (1962). According to Dobzhansky, it is this capacity to cooperate that enabled the earliest mammalian species to survive in a hostile world dominated by physically larger and potentially aggressive reptiles. Although I was unaware of Dobzhansky's major contributions when I formulated Polyvagal Theory, the title of the publication that introduced Polyvagal Theory was "Orienting in a Defensive World: Mammalian Modifications of Our Evolutionary Heritage. A Polyvagal Theory" (Porges, 1995). In retrospect, the title was a tribute to Dobzhansky's insightful statement that "nothing in biology makes sense except in the light of evolution" (1973).

A ONE-NERVOUS-SYSTEM MODEL HEIGHTENS AWARENESS OF BIDIRECTIONAL BRAIN-BODY COMMUNICATION

As we struggle with the pandemic, we need to reinterpret and reframe our reactions within an informed appreciation of our nervous system, acknowledging that our reactions to the pandemic will only make sense if informed by our understanding of evolution. This leads us to ask questions directed at our reactivity to threat and uncertainty and our needs to sufficiently coregulate our bodily state to move from feelings of fear and danger to feelings of safety and trust in others. In addition, we need update our understanding of brain-body communication. To understand how threat changes both psychological and physiological processes, we need to accept a one-nervous-system model (see below) rather than an antiquated model in which the central nervous system is separate from the autonomic nervous system. Functionally, the brain and visceral organs are connected by neural pathways that send signals from the brain to our visceral organs and from the visceral organs to the brain. Thus, threat reactions through definable and measurable pathways may have predictable effects on our mental and physical health.

The contemporary conceptualization of bidirectional communication between visceral organs and the brain is rooted in the work of Walter Hess. In 1949, Hess was awarded the Nobel Prize in Physiology or Medicine for his paradigm-shifting research on the central control of visceral organs. His Nobel lecture discussing brain control of visceral organs was titled "The Central Control of the Activity of Internal Organs" (Hess, 1949). The first sentence of his Nobel Prize speech is both prescient and historical, stating that "a recognized fact which goes back to the earliest times is that every living organism is not the sum of a multitude of unitary processes, but is, by virtue of interrelationships and of higher and lower levels of control, an unbroken unity." This brief statement provides the context upon which development, application, and acceptance of neuroautonomic disciplines, such as neurocardiology, have emerged.

This integrative one-nervous-system perspective encourages a better understanding of the dynamics of neural regulation of an integrated nervous system, while being constrained by the limited paradigms that are frequently used in the contemporary training of physicians.

A POLYVAGAL PERSPECTIVE

Consistent with Hess and Dobzhansky, our biological mandate of connectedness requires a functional social engagement system (Porges, 2009), which through common brainstem structures coordinates the striated muscles of the face and head with the vagal regulation of the viscera originating in a brainstem region known as the nucleus ambiguus. Thus, the optimally resilient individual has opportunities to coregulate physiological state with a safe and trusted other. Ideally, this other person projects positive cues regarding their autonomic state through prosodic voice, warm and welcoming facial expressions, and gestures of accessibility. From an evolutionary perspective, the integration of the neural regulation of the viscera with the regulations of the striated muscles of the face and head enable visceral state to be projected in vocalizations and facial expressions. This also allows vocalizations and facial expressions, modulated by autonomic states, to serve as cues of safety or threat to others. Together these pathways connect behavior to the nervous system and form the basis for social communication, cooperation, and connectedness.

Polyvagal Theory, by articulating an evolutionary hierarchy in the response of the autonomic nervous system to challenges, provides a map of the state of the autonomic nervous system during any challenge. By understanding the autonomic state of an individual, this map informs us of the emergent behavioral, emotional, and physiological reactivity that an individual may have in response to threat or alternatively to positive experiences.

From a polyvagal perspective, it will be helpful to investigate how the COVID-19 crisis moves us into physiological states of threat that would disrupt our connectedness and place our mental and physical health at risk. But, more relevant to both clients and personal survival, therapists need to identify and emphasize the innate resources they have available to mitigate the potentially devasting reactions to threat, which in turn can destabilize the autonomic nervous system, resulting in visceral organ dysfunction and compromised mental health. Awareness of the neural systems underlying Polyvagal Theory informs both therapists and clients regarding the threats to survival that can shift autonomic state, moving it through sequential neural platforms or states that mimic evolution in reverse, or dissolution (Jackson, 1884). Functionally, as we progress through this trajectory of dissolution, we first lose the competence of our social engagement system (a uniquely mammalian myelinated vagal pathway involving brainstem structures regulating vocal intonation and facial expressions) to connect with others and calm our physiology. Without these resources, we are vulnerable to move into adaptive defensive states.

Our defense repertoire is first expressed as chronic mobilization requiring activation of the sympathetic nervous system and then expressed as immobilization controlled by an evolutionarily older unmyelinated vagal pathway. In the absence of an active social engagement system, the mobilized state provides an efficient neural platform for fight and flight behaviors. For many individuals this state will reflect chronic anxiety or irritability. When mobilization does not successfully move the individual into a safe context, then there is the possibility that the nervous system will shift into an immobilized state with associated features of death feigning, syncope, dissociation, withdrawal, loss of purpose, social isolation, despair, and depression. Although both defensive strategies have adaptive values in protecting the individual, they are dependent on different neural pathways (i.e., high sympathetic tone or high dorsal vagal tone), both of which interfere with interpersonal interactions, coregulation, accessibility, trust, and feeling safe with another person. Thus, defensive states emerge from neural platforms that evolved to defend, while simultaneously compromising capacities to downregulate our defenses through coregulation with a safe and trusted individual. Basically, the theory emphasizes that in the presence of cues of predictable social interactions of support, our nervous system of safety, the mammalian social engagement system, can downregulate our innate reactions to threat, whether the threat is tangible and observable or invisible and imaginable.

PUBLIC HEALTH STRATEGIES COMPOUND FEELINGS OF THREAT

A polyvagal perspective provides clarity in understanding how our perceived vulnerability to the sarsCov2 virus and the mandated strategies of social distancing and self-quarantining impact on our nervous system. First the threat shifts our autonomic nervous system into states of defense, which interfere with the neurophysiological states needed to both co-regulate with others and to optimize homeostatic processes leading to health, growth, and restoration. Thus, our nervous system is simultaneously being challenged by incompatible demands demanding both avoidance of contact with the sarsCov2 virus and the fulfillment of our biological imperative of connecting with others to feel calm and safe. These paradoxical demands require different neurophysiological states. Avoiding being infected triggers a chronic mobilization strategy that downregulates our capacity to calm through social communication and connectedness. Although downregulating our capacity to socially engage, our nervous system intuitively is motivated to seek opportunities for social engagement in which our body would feel safe in the proximity of a safe and trusted person. However, opportunities to engage others, which throughout our evolutionary history have been an antidote to threat that moved us out of physiological states of defense and feelings of anxiety, now convey threat of infection. Thus, the resources of human contact that humans intuitively use to calm may now signal threat. This perspective places us in a quandary, since we now need to both avoid the virus and socially connect.

MITIGATING THREAT RESPONSES
THROUGH VIDEOCONFERENCING

There is no easy solution to this paradox. However, modern technologies provide us with tools that we can learn to use in a more mindful way. The upside of the current crisis is that although the pandemic is devastating to our nervous system, it is occurring during a unique time in history when we have tools that enable us to connect even when we are mandated to isolate. To reduce the burden on the nervous systems of those with whom we interact, we need to retrain ourselves in the use of the portals for social communication that we have available. This will mean that we are more present and less distractible, while providing cues of safety and connectedness through spontaneous reciprocal coregulatory facial expressions and vocal intonations.

For the many clinicians who are now doing therapy remotely through videoconferencing, there is a learning curve. This can be exhausting, as both therapist and client become more present while conducting online therapy sessions. Recognition of these challenges can be useful in coping. For example, we need to learn to share feelings and not just words through videoconferencing platforms. Our historic use of video technologies has been for entertainment, business, and education. We have become accustomed to video images as being personally distal, asymmetrical, asynchronous, and unrelated to our personal experiences. Thus, our neural sensitivity to video images is relatively numb through our historical adaptation to two-dimensional screens.

Given the current demands during the health crisis and potentially in the near future, while videoconferencing we will need to retune our nervous system to be more aware of facial expression, vocal intonation, and head gesture, although in the physical presence of another, while actively involved in spontaneous face-to-face interactions, our nervous system detects these cues intuitively and rapidly without involving conscious awareness. Polyvagal Theory labels this spontaneous process as neuroception (Porges, 2003, 2004).

We are used to multitasking while watching television and streaming movies. This disembodiment in a social interaction does not provide the nervous system with the required reciprocity to enable and optimize coregulation and connectedness. This distinction between the real and virtual worlds functioned well as long as our nervous systems had sufficient opportunities to coregulate in a physical face-to-face world with safe and trusted friends, parents, or partners. However, with the COVID-19 crisis, the world is different. We need to embrace the virtual world of communication with our knowledge of the cues that our nervous system craves. To accomplish this, we need to become more accomplished at sharing feeling moments and not just syntax while videoconferencing.

CONCEPTUALIZING AUTONOMIC STATE AS AN INTERVENING VARIABLE ENHANCES THE UNDERSTANDING OF RISK AND OPTIMIZES TREATMENT

Polyvagal Theory informs us that autonomic state functions as an intervening variable moving the individual from states of vulnerability in response to threat to states of accessibility when supported by cues of safety and appropriate social support. Thus, the physiological state of an individual provides a portal into understanding how they will respond to the pandemic. For example, if we are in an autonomic state of defense, the threat of illness will be compounded by the lack of opportunities to coregulate. Thus, the public health strategies to flatten the curve and slow the transmission of the disease by social distancing and self-quarantining will exacerbate the negative impact that the pandemic will have on us.

As we grapple with the current situation, it will be helpful to gather data on what therapists and their clients are experiencing. Within this context, we are currently conducting a survey study (Kolacz et al., 2020) in which we evaluate autonomic state using the Body Perception Questionnaire (Cabrera et al., 2018; Porges, 1993). The Body Perception Questionnaire is a survey tool that provides subjective responses of autonomic reactivity consistent with the autonomic circuits described in Polyvagal Theory to support mobilized (i.e., fight/flight) and immobilized (i.e., death feigning, dissociation, shutdown) defense reactions to threat. Our preliminary analyses of about 1,500 responders documented two important findings consistent with the Polyvagal Theory. First, the participants who experienced greater autonomic reactivity (i.e., their autonomic nervous system is more frequently reacting in defense) during the COVID-19 crisis also expressed greater amounts of worry about health and economic dangers and greater feelings of social isolation. In addition, if participants had a history of trauma, including childhood abuse, sexual assault, and physical assault, they reported higher levels of threat-related autonomic reactivity and active PTSD symptoms in response to the pandemic. Thus, using a perspective based on Polyvagal Theory, we gain a new respect for how an individual's nervous system is attempting to navigate through the threats and challenges of the pandemic. We also have a better understanding of the underlying mechanisms that determine thresholds of reactivity. Finally, these findings may help us develop strategies for using cues of safety and trust to the autonomic nervous system, moving both therapists and their clients into states that will support accessibility and coregulation.

REFERENCES

Cabrera, A., Kolacz, J., Pailhez, G., Bulbena-Cabre, A., Bulbena, A., & Porges, S. W. (2018). Assessing body awareness and autonomic reactivity: Factor structure and psychometric properties of the Body Perception Questionnaire–Short

Form (BPQ-SF). *International Journal of Methods in Psychiatric Research*, 27(2), e1596.

Dobzhansky, T. (1962). *Mankind evolving*. New Haven, CT: Yale University Press.

Dobzhansky, T. (1973). Nothing in biology makes sense except in the light of evolution. *American Biology Teacher*, 35(3), 125–129.

Hess, W. R. (1949). The central control of the activity of internal organs. *Nobel Lectures, Physiology or Medicine* (1942–1962). https://www.nobelprize.org/nobel_prizes/medicine/laureates/1949/hess-lecture.html

Jackson, J. H. (1884). The Croonian lectures on evolution and dissolution of the nervous system. *British Medical Journal*, 1(1215), 703.

Kolacz, J., Dale, L., Nix, E., Roath, O., Lewis, G., & Porges, S. (2020). Adversity History Predicts Self-Reported Autonomic Reactivity and Mental Health in US Residents During the COVID-19 Pandemic. *Frontiers in Psychiatry*, 11: 577728. doi: 10.3389/fpsyt.2020.577728. PMID: 33192715; PMCID: PMC7653174.

Porges, S. (1993). *Body perception questionnaire*. Laboratory of Developmental Assessment, University of Maryland.

Porges, S. W. (1995). Orienting in a defensive world: Mammalian modifications of our evolutionary heritage. A Polyvagal Theory. *Psychophysiology*, 32(4), 301–318.

Porges, S. W. (2003). Social engagement and attachment: A phylogenetic perspective. *Annals of the New York Academy of Sciences*, 1008(1), 31–47.

Porges, S. W. (2004). Neuroception: A subconscious system for detecting threats and safety. *Zero to Three (J)*, 24(5), 19–24.

Porges, S. W. (2007). The polyvagal perspective. *Biological Psychology*, 74(2), 116–143.

Porges, S. W. (2009). The Polyvagal Theory: New insights into adaptive reactions of the autonomic nervous system. *Cleveland Clinic Journal of Medicine*, 76(Suppl. 2), s86.

Polyvagal Theory
A Primer

Stephen W. Porges

OVERVIEW

This appendix provides an overview of the theory. Although it is dense and scientific, I hope that the appendix provides a source of information on the theory that the reader can efficiently access for clarifications of Polyvagal related constructions mentioned in the preceding chapters. To facilitate the generalizability of Polyvagal Theory to clinical application, the appendix is organized with headings identifying important constructs within the theory.

Polyvagal Theory describes an autonomic nervous system that is influenced by the central nervous system and responds to signals from both the environment and bodily organs. The theory emphasizes that the human autonomic nervous system has a predictable pattern of reactivity, which is dependent on neuroanatomical and neurophysiological changes that occurred during evolution. Specifically, the theory focuses on the phylogenetic changes in the neural regulation of bodily organs during the evolutionary transition from ancient extinct reptiles to the earliest mammals.

EVOLUTION OF THE VERTEBRATE
AUTONOMIC NERVOUS SYSTEM

As mammals evolved, their behaviors differentiated them from their primitive reptilian ancestors. Unlike the solitary behaviors and lack of nurturance of their vertebrate ancestors, mammals expressed a broad range of social behaviors, including caring for offspring and cooperation. These behaviors supported the survival of mammals. However, in order for these behaviors to occur, the mammalian nervous system had to selectively downregulate defensive reactions. This convergence was dependent on the coevolution of modifications in the neural regulation of the autonomic nervous system and the sociality that defines mammalian behavior.

To understand Polyvagal Theory, it is first necessary to understand three contingent points: first, the relationship between autonomic state and defensive behaviors; second, the changes that occurred during vertebrate evolution in the neural regulation of the autonomic nervous system; and third, the physiological state that enables bodily responses and feelings of safety to optimize social behavior while concurrently optimizing health, growth, and restoration.

In most vertebrates, the two primary defense systems are fight-or-flight and immobilization. Fight-or-flight behaviors enable the organism to flee or defend when threatened. These behaviors require the rapid accessibility of resources to mobilize through the activation of the metabolically costly sympathetic nervous system. Immobilization is a more ancient defense system, which is shared with virtually all vertebrates. In contrast to the metabolically costly mobilization strategy, immobilization is an adaptive attempt to reduce metabolic demands (e.g., reduced options for food and oxygen) and to appear inanimate (e.g., death feigning). Juxtaposed with the rapid activation of the sympathetic nervous system required to promote fight-or-flight behaviors, immobilization defense behaviors required a massive shutting down of autonomic function via a vagal pathway within the parasympathetic nervous system.

Over time, a second vagal pathway evolved that had the capacity to downregulate both forms of defense. This second vagal pathway is observed in mammals and not reptiles. In addition, the anatomical structures regulating this component of the vagus interacted in the brainstem with structures regulating the striated muscles of the face and head to provide an integrated social engagement system. This emergent social engagement system provided the mechanism for coregulation of physiological state, as mammals conveyed cues of safety and danger—via vocalizations, head gestures, and facial expressions—to conspecifics. The social engagement system enabled mammals to co-opt some of the features of the vertebrate defense systems to promote social interactions such as play and intimacy. These changes in the autonomic nervous system provided mammals with neural mechanisms to promote the biobehavioral states necessary for caring for offspring, reproducing, and cooperative behavior. In contrast, the adverse behavioral and psychological effects of trauma appear to target a disruption of the social engagement system, its management of defense reactions, and its contribution to coregulation and cooperative behaviors, including intimacy and play.

ORIGIN OF POLYVAGAL THEORY: THE VAGAL PARADOX

Polyvagal Theory emerged from research studying heart rate patterns in human fetuses and newborns. In obstetrics and neonatology, the massive slowing of heart rate known as bradycardia is a clinical index of risk and is assumed to be mediated by the vagus. During bradycardia, heart rate is so slow that it no longer provides sufficient oxygenated blood to the brain. This type of vagal influence on the fetal and neonatal heart could potentially be lethal. However, with the same clinical populations, a different index of vagal function was assumed to be a measure of resilience. This measure was beat-to-beat heart rate variability and was the focus of my research for several decades. Animal research demonstrated that both signals could be disrupted by severing the vagal pathways to the heart or via pharmacological blockade (i.e., atropine), interfering with the inhibitory action of the vagus on the sinoatrial node (for review, see Porges, 1995). These observations posed the paradox of how cardiac vagal tone could be both a positive indicator of health when monitored with heart rate variability and a negative indicator of health when it manifests as bradycardia.

The resolution to the paradox came from understanding how the neural regulation of the autonomic nervous system changed during evolution, especially through the transition from primitive extinct reptiles to mammals. During this transition, mammals evolved a second cardio-inibitory vagal motor pathway. This uniquely mammalian pathway is myelinated and conveys a respiratory rhythm to the heart's pacemaker, resulting in a rhythmic oscillation in heart rate at the frequency of spontaneous breathing known as respiratory sinus arrhythmia. Myelin is a fatty substance that surrounds the fiber. Myelin provides electrical insulation for the fiber, which enables the signal to be transmitted with greater specificity and speed. This branch of the vagus originates in an area of the brainstem known as the nucleus ambiguus, travels primarily to organs above the diaphragm, and interacts within the brainstem with structures regulating the striated muscles of the face and head. The other vagal motor pathway does not have a respiratory rhythm, is observed in virtually all vertebrates, is unmyelinated, travels primarily to organs below the diaphragm, and originates in an area of the brainstem known as the dorsal nucleus of the vagus.

PHYLOGENETIC SHIFTS IN VERTEBRATE
AUTONOMIC NERVOUS SYSTEMS

By tracking the evolutionary changes in the vertebrate autonomic nervous system, I identified a phylogenetic pattern consisting of three evolutionary stages. During the first stage, vertebrates relied on an unmyelinated vagus with motor pathways originating in an area of the brainstem resembling the dorsal vagal complex. During the second stage, an excitatory spinal sympathetic nervous system developed, which complemented the downregulation functions of the

FIGURE A.1. The social engagement system consists of a somatomotor component (solid blocks) and a visceromotor component (dashed blocks). The somatomotor component involves special visceral efferent pathways that regulate the striated muscles of the face and head, while the visceromotor component involves the myelinated vagus that regulates the heart and bronchi.

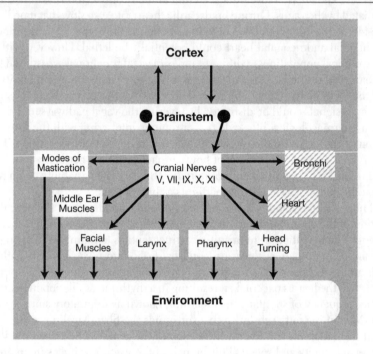

ancient vagal pathway. During the third stage, defined by the emergence of mammals, an additional vagal pathway evolved, during which cells of origin of the vagus migrated from the dorsal nucleus of the vagus to the nucleus ambiguus; many of the vagal motor fibers originating in the nucleus ambiguus became myelinated and integrated in the function of the brainstem regulation of a family of motor pathways (i.e., special visceral efferent pathways) that control the striated muscles of the face and head (see Figure A.1).

In mammals, the unmyelinated vagal pathways originating in the dorsal nucleus of the vagus primarily regulate the organs below the diaphragm, though some of these unmyelinated vagal fibers terminate on the heart's pacemaker (sinoatrial node). Polyvagal Theory hypothesizes that these unmyelinated vagal fibers primarily remain dormant until life threat, and they are probably potentiated during hypoxia and states in which the influence of the myelinated vagal input to the heart is depressed. This sequence is observable in human fetal heart rate, in which bradycardia is more likely to occur when the tonic influence of the myelinated vagal pathways, manifest in respiratory sinus arrhythmia, is low (Reed et al., 1999). This also may be the mechanism mediating trauma-elicited dissociation, defecation, and syncope (i.e., fainting).

In ancient vertebrates, an unmyelinated vagal pathway emerging from the brainstem was a critical component of the neural regulation of the entire viscera. This bidirectional system reduced metabolic output when resources were low, such as during times of reduced oxygen. The nervous systems of primitive vertebrates did not need much oxygen to survive and could lower heart rate and metabolic demands when oxygen levels dropped. Thus, this circuit provided a conservation system that in mammals was adapted as a primitive defense system manifested as death feigning and trauma-driven responses of syncope and dissociation. Since this defense system could be lethal in oxygen-demanding mammals, fortunately it functions as the last option for survival. The phylogenetically older unmyelinated vagal motor pathways are shared with most vertebrates and, in mammals, when not recruited as a defense system, function to support health, growth, and restoration via neural regulation of subdiaphragmatic organs (i.e., internal organs below the diaphragm).

The newer myelinated ventral vagal motor pathways regulate the supradiaphragmatic organs (e.g., heart and lungs) and are integrated in the brainstem with structures that regulate the striated muscles of the face and head via special visceral efferent pathways, resulting in a functional social engagement system. This newer vagal circuit slows heart rate and supports the states of calmness required for social interactions. The ventral vagal circuit, coupled with other autonomic circuits, supports social play (i.e., ventral vagal coupled with sympathetic activation) and safe intimacy (i.e., ventral vagal coupled with the dorsal vagal circuit). Thus, the mammalian vagus has properties that promote states that contain the range of responding of all components of the autonomic nervous system and functionally restrains the system from moving into states of defense.

THE EMERGENCE OF THE SOCIAL ENGAGEMENT SYSTEM

The integration of the myelinated cardiac vagal pathways with the neural regulation of the face and head gave rise to the mammalian social engagement system. As illustrated in Figure A.1, the outputs of the social engagement system consist of motor pathways regulating striated muscles of the face and head (i.e., somatomotor) and smooth and cardiac muscles of the heart and bronchi (i.e., visceromotor). The somatomotor component involves special visceral efferent pathways that regulate the striated muscles of the face and head. The visceromotor component involves the myelinated supradiaphragmatic vagal pathway that regulates the heart and bronchi. Functionally, the social engagement system emerges from a face-heart connection that coordinates the heart with the muscles of the face and head. The initial function of the system is to coordinate sucking, swallowing, breathing, and vocalizing. Atypical coordination of this system early in life is an indicator of subsequent difficulties in social behavior and emotional regulation.

When fully developed, two important biobehavioral features of this system are expressed. First, bodily state is regulated in an efficient manner to promote growth and restoration (e.g., visceral homeostasis). Functionally, this is accomplished through an increase in the influence of myelinated vagal motor pathways on the cardiac pacemaker to slow heart rate, inhibit the fight-or-flight mechanisms of the sympathetic nervous system, dampen the stress response system of the hypothalamic-pituitary-adrenal (HPA) axis (responsible for cortisol release), and reduce inflammation by modulating immune reactions (e.g., cytokines; for review, see Porges, 2007). Second, the phylogenetically mammalian face-heart connection functions to convey physiological state via facial expression and prosody (intonation of voice), as well as regulate the middle-ear muscles to optimize species-specific listening within the frequency band used for social communication (Kolacz et al., 2018; Porges, 2007, 2009, 2011; Porges & Lewis, 2010).

The brainstem source nuclei of the social engagement system are influenced by higher brain structures (i.e., top-down influences) and by sensory pathways from visceral organs (i.e., bottom-up influences). Direct pathways from cortex to brainstem (i.e., corticobulbar) reflect the influence of frontal areas of the cortex (i.e., upper motor neurons) on the medullary source nuclei of this system. Bottom-up influences occur via feedback through the sensory pathways of the vagus (e.g., tractus solitarius), conveying information from visceral organs to medullary areas (e.g., nucleus of the solitary tract) and influencing both the source nuclei of this system and the forebrain areas, via the insula, that are assumed to be involved in several psychiatric disorders, including depression and anxiety (Craig, 2005; Thayer & Lane, 2000, 2007). In addition, the anatomical structures involved in the social engagement system have neurophysiological interactions with the HPA axis, the social neuropeptides (e.g., oxytocin and vasopressin), and the immune system (Carter, 1998; Porges, 2001).

Sensory pathways from the target organs of the social engagement system, including the muscles of the face and head, also provide potent input to the source nuclei regulating both the visceral and somatic components of the social engagement system. The source nucleus of the facial nerve forms the border of nucleus ambiguus, and sensory pathways from both the facial and trigeminal nerves provide a primary sensory input to the nucleus ambiguus (see Porges, 1995, 2007). Thus, the ventral vagal complex, consisting of the nucleus ambiguus and the nuclei of the trigeminal and facial nerves, is functionally related to the expression and experience of affective states and emotions. Activation of the somatomotor component (e.g., listening, ingestion, vocalizations, facial expressions) could trigger visceral changes that would support social engagement, while modulation of visceral state, depending on whether there is an increase or decrease in the influence of the myelinated vagal motor fibers on the sinoatrial node (i.e., increasing or decreasing the influence of the vagal brake), would either promote or impede social engagement behaviors (Porges, 1995, 2007). For example, stimulation of visceral states that promote mobilization (i.e., fight-or-flight behaviors) would impede the ability to express social engagement behaviors.

The face-heart connection enabled mammals to detect whether a conspecific was in a calm physiological state and safe to approach, or in a highly mobilized and reactive physiological state during which engagement would be dangerous. The face-heart connection concurrently enables an individual to signal safety through patterns of facial expression and vocal intonation, and potentially calm an agitated conspecific to form a social relationship. When the newer mammalian vagus is optimally functioning in social interactions, emotions are well regulated, vocal prosody is rich, and the autonomic state supports calm, spontaneous social engagement behaviors. The face-heart system is bidirectional, with the newer myelinated vagal circuit influencing social interactions and positive social interactions influencing vagal function to optimize health, dampen stress-related physiological states, and support growth and restoration. Social communication and the ability to coregulate interactions, via reciprocal social engagement systems, lead to a sense of connectedness and are important defining features of the human experience.

VAGAL BRAKE

The vagal brake reflects the tonic inhibitory influence of the myelinated vagal pathways on the heart, which slows the intrinsic rate of the heart's pacemaker. The intrinsic heart rate of young, healthy adults is about 90 beats per minute. However, baseline heart rate is noticeably slower due to the influence of the vagus, which functions as a vagal brake. When the vagus decreases its influence on the heart (i.e., the vagal brake releases), heart rate spontaneously increases. This is not due to an increase in sympathetic excitation; rather, the release of the vagal brake allows the rate intrinsic in the pacemaker to be expressed. The vagal brake represents the actions of engaging and disengaging the vagal influences to the heart's pacemaker. In addition, the release of the vagal brake on the heart also enables tonic underlying sympathetic excitation to exert more influence on the autonomic nervous system. Polyvagal Theory specifically assumes that the vagal brake is mediated solely through the myelinated ventral vagus and can be quantified by the amplitude of respiratory sinus arrhythmia (see Chapter 2). The theory acknowledges other neural (e.g., dorsal vagal pathways) and neurochemical influences that can slow heart rate (e.g., clinical bradycardia), which are not included within the construct of the vagal brake.

DISSOLUTION

The human nervous system, similar to that of other mammals, evolved not solely to survive in safe environments, but also to promote survival in dangerous and life-threatening contexts. To accomplish this adaptive flexibility, the mammalian autonomic nervous system, in addition to the myelinated vagal pathway that is integrated into the social engagement system, retained two more primitive neural circuits to regulate defensive strategies (i.e., fight-or-flight and death-feigning behaviors). It is important to note that social behavior, social communication, and visceral homeostasis are incompatible with the neurophysiological states that support defense. Polyvagal response strategies to challenge are phylogenetically ordered, with the newest components of the autonomic nervous system responding first. This model of autonomic reactivity is consistent with John Hughlings Jackson's construct of dissolution, in which he proposed that "the higher nervous arrangements inhibit (or control) the lower, and thus, when the higher are suddenly rendered functionless, the lower rise in activity" (1882, p. 412). In this hierarchy of adaptive responses, the newest social engagement circuit is used first; if that circuit fails to provide safety, the older circuits are recruited sequentially.

NEUROCEPTION

Polyvagal Theory proposes that the neural evaluation of risk does not require conscious awareness and functions through neural circuits that are shared with our phylogenetic vertebrate ancestors. Thus, the term "neuroception" was introduced to emphasize a neural process, distinct from perception, capable of distinguishing environmental and visceral features that are safe, dangerous, or life-threatening (Porges, 2003, 2004). Although all vertebrates have a neuroception that responds to threat, only mammals have a neuroception that responds to cues of safety. In safe environments, a mammal's autonomic state is adaptively regulated to dampen sympathetic activation and to protect the oxygen-dependent central nervous system, especially the cortex, from the metabolically conservative reactions of the dorsal vagal complex (e.g., fainting).

Neuroception is proposed as a reflexive mechanism capable of instantaneously shifting physiological state. Feature detectors, located in areas of or near the temporal cortex, which are sensitive to the intentionality of biological movements including voices, faces, gestures, and hand movements, might be involved in the process of neuroception. Embedded in the construct of neuroception is the capacity of the nervous system to react to the intention of these movements. Neuroception functionally decodes and interprets the assumed goal of movements and sounds of inanimate and living objects. Thus, the neuroception of familiar individuals and individuals with appropriately prosodic voices and warm, expressive faces frequently translates into a positive social interaction, promoting a sense of safety. Although we are often unaware of the stimuli that trigger different neuroceptive responses, we are generally aware of our body's reactions.

AUTONOMIC STATE AS AN INTERVENING VARIABLE

Polyvagal Theory proposes that physiological state is a fundamental part, and not a correlate, of emotion or mood. According to the theory, autonomic state functions as an intervening variable biasing our detection and evaluation of environmental cues. Depending on physiological state, the same cues will be reflexively evaluated as neutral, positive, or threatening. Functionally, a change in state will shift access to different structures in the brain and support either social communication or the defensive behaviors of fight-or-flight or shutdown. Contemporary research on the impact of vagal nerve stimulation on cognitive function and emotion regulation supports this model (Groves & Brown, 2005). The theory emphasizes a bidirectional link between brain and viscera, which would explain how thoughts change physiology and physiological state influences thoughts. As individuals change their facial expressions, the intonation of their voices, the pattern in which they are breathing, and their posture, they are also changing their physiology through circuits involving myelinated vagal pathways to the heart.

THE ROLE OF SENSATIONS FROM BODILY ORGANS IN THE REGULATION OF AUTONOMIC STATE

The prevalent focus of research investigating the neural regulation of the heart has focused on motor pathways emerging from brainstem nuclei (i.e., vagal pathways) and the sympathetic nervous system. Limited research has been conducted on the influence of sensory feedback from bodily organs (i.e., visceral afferents) in the neural regulation of the autonomic nervous system, and how these influences are manifested in the heart and other visceral organs. This is, in part, due to a top-down bias in medical education that limits the conceptualization of the neural regulation of the heart and other bodily organs by emphasizing the role of motor fibers and minimizing the role of sensory fibers. However, this bias is rapidly changing due to research on the applications of vagal nerve stimulation, a bottom-up model that focuses on the vagus as a sensory nerve (approximately 80% of the vagal fibers are sensory). Interestingly, the side effects of vagal nerve stimulation are frequently due to the influence of vagal nerve stimulation on motor pathways. These side effects are primarily noted on features of the social engagement system, including changes in voice and difficulties swallowing (Ben-Menachem, 2001). However, in some cases, the stimulation has been manifested in subdiaphragmatic organs, resulting in diarrhea (Sanossian & Haut, 2002). As vagal nerve stimulation becomes more commonly applied to medical disorders, there is an emerging awareness of the influence of the sensory pathways of the vagus on neurophysiological function (e.g., epilepsy), emotional state (e.g., depression), and cognition (e.g., learning and attention; Howland, 2014).

According to Polyvagal Theory, the social engagement system is regulated by complex neural circuits, involving both sensory pathways from visceral organs (i.e., bottom-up) and higher brain structures (i.e., top-down) that influence the brainstem source nuclei controlling both the myelinated vagus and the striated muscles of the face and head. As the surveillance role of sensory pathways providing feedback from bodily organs to the brainstem is incorporated into an understanding of the autonomic nervous system, clinicians and researchers will begin to recognize manifestations in the vagal control of the heart in patients with a variety of disorders of peripheral organs. With that understanding, rather than interpreting the atypical neural regulation of the heart as a cardiovascular disease, comorbidities may be explained as manifestations of system dysfunction, consistent with the prescient views of Walter Hess (1949).

Several chronic diseases manifested in specific subdiaphragmatic organs (e.g., kidney, pancreas, liver, gut, genitals, etc.) have identifiable features that have led to treatments that target organs (e.g., medication, surgery). However, other disorders that have an impact on quality of life, such as irritable bowel syndrome and fibromyalgia, are defined by nonspecific symptoms. The literature links these nonspecific chronic disorders with atypical vagal regulation of the heart, reflected in diminished heart rate variability (Mazurak et al., 2012; Staud, 2008). Consistent with these findings, heart rate variability has been proposed as a biomarker for these disorders.

Polyvagal Theory proposes an alternative interpretation of this covariation. Consistent with the integrated model of the autonomic nervous system described in the theory, atypical heart rate variability is not interpreted as a biomarker of any specific disease. Rather, depressed heart rate variability is proposed as a neurophysiological marker of a diffuse retuning of the autonomic nervous system, indicating a withdrawal of the ventral vagal circuit following an adaptive complex autonomic reaction to threat. Compatible with this interpretation, there are strong links between the prevalence of a history of abuse, especially sexual abuse in women, and the manifestations of nonspecific clinical disorders such as irritable bowel syndrome and fibromyalgia. In addition, emotional stress intensifies symptoms and hinders positive treatment outcomes, and trauma may trigger or aggravate symptoms (Clauw, 2014; Whitehead et al., 2007). The initial adaptive neural response to threat, via sensory feedback from the visceral organs to the brainstem, may result in a chronic reorganization of the autonomic regulation observed in vagal regulation of the heart (i.e., depressed heart rate variability) in conjunction with altered subdiaphragmatic organ function and pain signaling.

A NEW PERSPECTIVE ON THE
AUTONOMIC NERVOUS SYSTEM

Polyvagal Theory uses an inclusive definition of the autonomic nervous system that includes sensory pathways and emphasizes the brainstem areas regulating autonomic function. The theory links the brainstem regulation of the ventral vagus to the regulation of the striated muscles of the face and head to produce an integrated social engagement system.

In contrast to the traditional model that focuses on tonic motor influences on visceral organs, Polyvagal Theory emphasizes autonomic reactivity. Polyvagal Theory accepts the traditional model of interpreting tonic autonomic influences on several visceral organs as the sum of a paired antagonism between vagal and sympathetic pathways. However, Polyvagal Theory proposes a phylogenetically ordered hierarchy in which autonomic subsystems react to challenges in the reverse of their evolutionary history, consistent with the principle of dissolution.

The theory postulates that when the ventral vagus and the associated social engagement system are optimally functioning, the autonomic nervous system supports health, growth, and restoration. During this ventral vagal state, there is an optimal autonomic balance between the sympathetic nervous system and the dorsal vagal pathways to subdiaphragmatic organs. When the function of the ventral vagus is dampened or withdrawn, the autonomic nervous system is optimized to support defense and not health. According to Polyvagal Theory, these defense reactions may be manifested as fight or flight or shutdown. In fight-or-flight defense, there is an increase in sympathetic activity to promote mobilization strategies while inhibiting digestion (and other dorsal vagal functions). In contrast, when manifested as shutdown, sympathetic activation is depressed, while there is a surge of the dorsal vagal influences that would promote fainting, defecation, and an inhibition of motor behavior often seen in mammals feigning death.

CUES OF SAFETY ARE THE TREATMENT

Polyvagal Theory proposes that cues of safety are an efficient and profound antidote for trauma. The theory emphasizes that safety is defined by feeling safe and not simply by the removal of threat. Feeling safe is dependent on three conditions: (1) The autonomic nervous system cannot be in a state that supports defense; (2) the social engagement system needs to be activated to downregulate sympathetic activation and functionally contain the sympathetic nervous system and the dorsal vagal circuit within an optimal range (homeostasis) that would support health, growth, and restoration; and (3) cues of safety (e.g., prosodic vocalizations, positive facial expressions and gestures) need to be available and detected via neuroception. In everyday situations, the cues of safety may initiate the sequence by triggering the social engagement system via the pro-cess of neuroception, which will contain autonomic state within a homeostatic range and restrict the autonomic nervous system from reacting in defense. This constrained range of autonomic state has been referred to as the window of tolerance (see Ogden et al., 2006; Siegel, 1999) and can be expanded through neural exercises embedded in therapy.

NEURAL EXERCISE AS INTERVENTION

Polyvagal Theory focuses on specific neural exercises that provide opportunities to optimize the regulation of physiological state. According to the theory, neural exercises consisting of transitory disruptions and repairs of physiological state through social interactions employing cues of safety would promote greater resilience. Play, such as peek-a-boo, is an example of a neural exercise that par-ents frequently employ with their children. Play provides an example of a thera-peutic model in which autonomic state is disrupted and then stabilized through the recruitment of the social engagement system. This model can be general-ized to the clinical setting, in which the client experiences disrupted changes in autonomic state, which are stabilized through the support of the therapist. Functionally, therapy becomes a platform to exercise the capacity to shift state by recruiting features of the social engagement system to keep the autonomic nervous system out of prolonged states of defense. This process is initialized through coregulation between the client and the therapist. Subsequently, when the client experiences reliable coregulation, the potency of transitory shifts in state as triggers of defense is reduced and self-regulation spontaneously emerges.

Through the metaphor of play, the social engagement system is coupled with the sympathetic nervous system. This coupling enables bodily cues of mobili-zation to be contained within a social setting and not to erupt into aggression. However, these eruptions or tantrums frequently occur in children and adults with behavioral problems and psychiatric disorders. Research documents a con-sistency of a downregulated social engagement system (e.g., lack of prosody, blunted facial expression, auditory hypersensitivities, poor eye gaze) in individ-uals with state regulation disorders (see Porges, 2011). Polyvagal Theory empha-sizes that the vulnerability to these disruptions is due to a physiological state shift characterized by sympathetic activation without the resource of efficient self-soothing or calming through the social engagement system.

The metaphor of play is also useful in deconstructing intimacy. Intimacy is a state-dependent behavior that involves coupling the social engagement sys-tem with the dorsal vagal circuit to enable immobilization without shutdown. Intimacy requires a state in which touch and proximity do not trigger defense. For mammals, immobilization is a vulnerable state. For intimacy to occur, neu-roception has to interpret proximity and contact as safe and shift the body into a state that is welcoming. This coupling of two bodies initially occurs through cues of safety, such as prosodic vocalizations and gentle contact. Intimacy is often associated with a form of play, foreplay. However, similar to the positive attributes of play, which functions as a neural exercise optimizing the ability of the social engagement system to regulate the sympathetic nervous system, foreplay and truly safe experiences of intimacy provide a neural exercise optimizing the ability of the social engagement system to regulate the dorsal vagal pathway. This form of neural exercise may have long-term beneficial effects on the regulation of bodily organs by supporting homeostasis. Moreover, safe foreplay and intimacy may also be a preparatory neural exercise for women that, by enabling immobilization without fear, would optimize the reproductive behaviors and processes, including facilitating childbirth.

LISTENING AS A NEURAL EXERCISE

Polyvagal Theory emphasizes how listening is a portal to the social engagement system. Based on Polyvagal Theory, the Listening Project Protocol is a listening intervention designed to reduce auditory hypersensitivities, improve auditory processing, calm physiological state, and support spontaneous social engagement. The intervention is currently known as the Safe and Sound Protocol and is available to professionals only through Integrated Listening Systems (https://integratedlistening.com/porges/).

The Safe and Sound Protocol is based on an exercise model that uses computer-altered acoustic stimulation to modulate the frequency band passed to the participant. The protocol was theoretically designed to calm the autonomic nervous system and to reduce auditory hypersensitivities by recruiting the antimasking functions of the middle ear muscles to optimize the transfer function of the middle ear for the processing of human speech. Modulation of the acoustic energy within the frequencies of the human voice, similar to exaggerated vocal prosody, is hypothesized to provide cues of safety to the client. Hypothetically, these cues are processed, via neuroception, and reflexively recruit and modulate the neural regulation of the middle ear muscles. Based on the theory, this process would functionally reduce auditory hypersensitivities, stimulate spontaneous social engagement, and calm physiological state by increasing the influence of ventral vagal pathways on the heart. The intervention stimuli are listened to on headphones. The protocol consists of 60 minutes of listening on five consecutive days in a quiet room without major distractors, while the clinician, parent, or researcher provides social support to ensure that the participant remains calm. The neurophysiological basis of the intervention is elaborated in other publications (see Porges, 2011; Porges & Lewis, 2010).

Since the late 1990s, my research group has been evaluating and refining the protocol. We have tested the protocol on several hundred children with a variety of disorders including children with autism spectrum disorders, speech/language delays, auditory hypersensitivities, and behavioral regulation disorders.

The outcomes have been positive, with noticeable increases in spontaneous social engagement behaviors, reduced sound sensitivities, improved auditory processing, improved organization of social behaviors and emotional state, improved verbal communication highlighted by more expressive voices, and increased vagal regulation. We have also conducted and published two peer-reviewed publications describing our findings (see Porges et al., 2013, 2014). During the past few years, we have organized several clinical trials, which are currently registered on ClinicalTrials.gov. These new clinical trials are evaluating the intervention with different populations including children with abuse histories, individuals with attention and concentration difficulties, and children with Prader-Willi syndrome.

Since the release of the Safe and Sound Protocol, we have received feedback from therapists that matches the positive behavioral changes in children that we observed in our research. During the 20 years that we have tested the Safe and Sound Protocol with children, we have not observed any major adverse effects. Occasionally, we have observed an initial tactile sensitivity to the headphones, which resolves rapidly. Also, perhaps due to previous unpleasant experiences with sounds and headphones, the combination of sounds and context might provoke minor anxiety in the child, which has rapidly resolved. This success is, in part, due to the safe context in which the intervention is delivered. For children, the safe context is efficiently structured by creating a safe clinical environment with a therapist who projects welcoming cues of warmth to the child. This sense of a safe container is supported by a safe and protective parent or caregiver accompanying the child, while the child experiences the Safe and Sound Protocol.

The Safe and Sound Protocol as an intervention has two components: first, structuring a safe context in which the intervention is delivered; and second, delivering the acoustic features of the sound presented during the intervention that serve as a neural exercise. The safe component is managed by the practitioner delivering the intervention. The sound component is embedded in the acoustic stimuli. It is important to acknowledge that successful implementation of the intervention requires both components. For the Safe and Sound Protocol to be effective, it is necessary to maintain the client's nervous system in a state of safety.

This state of safety is necessary for adults as well as children. This may be challenging, especially for adults with trauma histories, who frequently do not feel safe in the proximity of others. While children are usually provided with a safe clinical context and are supported by caring adults, adults frequently arrive at a clinic without a supportive partner. Suggesting that a trusted friend, who would be available for support and regulation, accompany the client would be helpful in maintaining the client in a state of safety. Vulnerability to state changes might be exacerbated if the adult comes alone to the clinic.

Emotional and physiological reactions to the intervention are a potent signal that the stimuli are effectively triggering neural circuits. However, for the stimuli to trigger and exercise neural circuits that promote spontaneous social communication, improved state regulation, and reduced auditory hypersensitivities, the nervous system has to be in a safe state. More accurately, the nervous system has to feel protected and sufficiently trusting not to move into states of self-protection, hypervigilance, and defense. This may require a titration of the acoustic stimuli, with the client temporarily pausing the intervention stimuli when the sounds elicit a strong emotional or visceral reaction. A client who feels discomfort should be empowered to pause the intervention to allow their nervous system to stabilize. Although the fixed protocol works extremely well with children, adults may have a complicated history and may have difficulties feeling safe. As we move into the treatment of adults, we continue to learn through detailed comments from therapists about variations in responses. This important feedback will allow us to modify the protocol to optimize the client's outcome.

PASSIVE AND ACTIVE PATHWAYS

The human nervous system provides two pathways to trigger neural mechanisms capable of downregulating defense and enabling states of calmness that support health, spontaneous social behavior, and connectedness. One pathway is passive and does not require conscious awareness (see neuroception), and the other is active and requires conscious voluntary behaviors to trigger specific neural mechanisms that change physiological state (see neural exercise).

Both the passive and active pathways regulate the social engagement system. The passive pathway recruits the social engagement system through cues of safety such as a quiet environment, positive and compassionate therapist-patient interactions, prosodic quality (e.g., melodic intonation) of the therapist's vocalizations, and music modulated across frequency bands that overlap with vocal signals of safety used by a mother to calm her infant. Successful therapists, regardless of their orientation, often intuitively manipulate the passive pathway in treatment. In contrast, the active pathway recruits the social engagement system when the patient engages in reciprocal dialogue and other practices, such as vocalizations, voluntarily controlled breathing, movements, or postures. Access to the client's active pathway is dependent on the passive pathway effectively triggering a state of safety in the client.

The passive pathway is an effective and efficient method to recruit the social engagement system to spontaneously transition the client into a ventral vagal state. The passive pathway provides the client with feelings of safety. The active pathway provides the neural exercises to empower the client to efficiently move into and out of a ventral vagal state. Through effective interventions, the client may have transitory experiences in states previously associated with defense and dominated by either the sympathetic nervous system or the dorsal vagus. The exercises enable the client to functionally contain previously disruptive autonomic states by accessing the social engagement system and the ventral vagus. The passive pathway provides the client with feelings of safety, while the active pathway challenges these feelings of safety by exercising the neural resources of the social engagement system. These sequential processes expand resilience and provide resources to calm, coregulate, and self-regulate when challenged.

POLYVAGAL THEORY: TRAUMA ONLY MAKES SENSE IN THE LIGHT OF EVOLUTION

At the core of the evolved features that define mammals is the role that social interaction plays in their survival. Functionally, the ability to establish feelings of safety within a social interaction underlies survival and acts as a prepotent biological imperative. This important attribute and refinement of the meaning of "survival of the fittest" was emphasized by the evolutionary biologist Dobzhansky (1962) when he stated that "the fittest may also be the gentlest, because survival often requires mutual help and cooperation." For the survivors of trauma, their lives reflect a loss of these mammalian qualities. As Polyvagal Theory has deconstructed several of the mechanisms through which trauma retunes the nervous system, an understanding of evolution and dissolution provides insights into physiological and psychological experiences and helps the client generate a plausible personal explanatory narrative. This emphasis on evolution in understanding trauma reactions is reminiscent of Dobzhansky's most famous quote, "Nothing in biology makes sense except in the light of evolution" (1973, p. 125). Consistent with Dobzhansky, a polyvagal perspective explicitly assumes that the response to trauma only makes sense in the light of evolution.

SYNTHESIS

Polyvagal Theory emphasizes that humans, similar to other mammals, consist of a collection of dynamic, adaptive, interactive, and interdependent physiological systems. From this perspective, it becomes apparent that the autonomic nervous system cannot be treated as functionally distinct from the central nervous system. Consistent with Polyvagal Theory, the heart and other organs are not floating in a visceral sea, but are metaphorically anchored to central structures by motor pathways and continuously signaling central regulatory structures via an abundance of sensory pathways. This dynamic, bidirectional communication between brain structures and bodily organs influences mental state, biases perception of the environment, and prepares the individual to be either welcoming or defensive toward others. These processes simultaneously support or disrupt health, growth, and restoration.

The theory provides a plausible explanation of how a response to life threat could retune the autonomic nervous system to lose resilience and to remain in defense states. This retuning might lead to disruptions in homeostatic function, with manifestations in visceral organs (e.g., heart disease, irritable bowel) or diffuse symptoms of dysregulation (e.g., fibromyalgia, dysautonomia), while simultaneously limiting access to the social engagement system that would compromise the ability to coregulate through social interactions. These common consequences of trauma are highlighted by difficulties in feeling connected and safe with others. Polyvagal Theory explains how both aspects of disruption (i.e., lack of safety with others and disorders of bodily organs) are manifestations of a retuned autonomic nervous system and offers insights into rehabilitation. Thus, Polyvagal Theory provides an optimistic strategy for therapy, which would be based on a retuning of the autonomic nervous system through portals of the social engagement system.

REFERENCES

Ben-Menachem, E. (2001). Vagus nerve stimulation, side effects, and long-term safety. *Journal of Clinical Neurophysiology, 18*(5), 415–418.

Carter, C. S. (1998). Neuroendocrine perspectives on social attachment and love. *Psychoneuroendocrinology, 23*(8), 779–818.

Clauw, D. J. (2014). Fibromyalgia: A clinical review. JAMA, *311*(15), 1547–1555.

Craig, A. D. (2005). Forebrain emotional asymmetry: A neuroanatomical basis? *Trends in Cognitive Sciences, 9*(12), 566–571.

Dobzhansky, T. G. (1962). Mankind evolving: The evolution of the human species. *Eugenics Review, 54*(3), 168–169.

Dobzhansky, T. G. (1973). Nothing in biology makes sense except in the light of evolution. *American Biology Teacher, 35*(3), 125–129.

Groves, D. A., & Brown, V. J. (2005). Vagal nerve stimulation: A review of its applications and potential mechanisms that mediate its clinical effects. *Neuroscience and Biobehavioral Reviews, 29*(3), 493–500.

Hess, W. (1949). The central control of the activity of internal organs. Nobel Lecture, December 12. Nobel Prize. https://www.nobelprize.org/nobel_prizes/medicine/ laureates/1949/hess-lecture.html

Howland, R. H. (2014). Vagus nerve stimulation. *Current Behavioral Neuroscience Reports, 1*(2), 64–73.

Jackson, J. H. (1882). On some implications of dissolution of the nervous system. *Medical Press and Circular, 2*, 411–414.

Kolacz, J. K., Lewis, G. F., & Porges, S. W. (2018). The integration of vocal communication and biobehavioral state regulation in mammals: A polyvagal hypothesis. In S. M. Brudzynski (Ed.), *Handbook of ultrasonic vocalization*. London: Elsevier.

Mazurak, N., Seredyuk, N., Sauer, H., Teufel, M., & Enck, P. (2012). Heart rate variability in the irritable bowel syndrome: A review of the literature. *Neurogastroenterology and Motility, 24*(3), 206–216.

Ogden, P., Minton, K., & Pain, C. (2006). *Trauma and the body: A sensorimotor approach to psychotherapy*. New York: Norton.

Porges, S. W. (1995). Orienting in a defensive world: Mammalian modifications of our evolutionary heritage. A Polyvagal Theory. *Psychophysiology, 32*(4), 301–318.

Porges, S. W. (2001). The Polyvagal Theory: Phylogenetic substrates of a social nervous system. *International Journal of Psychophysiology, 42*(2), 123–146.

Porges, S. W. (2003). Social engagement and attachment. *Annals of the New York Academy of Sciences, 1008*(1), 31–47.

Porges, S. W. (2004). Neuroception: A subconscious system for detecting threats and safety. *Zero to Three (J), 24*(5), 19–24.

Porges, S. W. (2007). The polyvagal perspective. *Biological Psychology, 74*(2), 116–143.

Porges, S. W. (2009). The Polyvagal Theory: New insights into adaptive reactions of the autonomic nervous system. *Cleveland Clinic Journal of Medicine,* 76 (Suppl.), S86.

Porges, S. W. (2011). *The Polyvagal Theory: Neurophysiological foundations of emotions, attachment, communication, and self-regulation.* Norton Series on Interpersonal Neurobiology. New York: Norton.

Porges, S. W., Bazhenova, O. V., Bal, E., Carlson, N., Sorokin, Y., Heilman, K. J., Cook, E. H., & Lewis, G. F. (2014). Reducing auditory hypersensitivities in autistic spectrum disorder: Preliminary findings evaluating the Listening Project Protocol. *Frontiers in Pediatrics, 2,* 80. doi:10.3389/fped.2014.00080

Porges, S. W., & Lewis, G. F. (2010). The polyvagal hypothesis: Common mechanisms mediating autonomic regulation, vocalizations and listening. *Handbook of Behavioral Neuroscience, 19,* 255–264.

Porges, S. W., Macellaio, M., Stanfill, S. D., McCue, K., Lewis, G. F., Harden, E. R., Handelman, M., Denver, J., Bazhenova, O. V., & Heilman, K. J. (2013). Respiratory sinus arrhythmia and auditory processing in autism: Modifiable deficits of an integrated social engagement system? *International Journal of Psychophysiology, 88*(3), 261–270.

Reed, S. F., Ohel, G., David, R., & Porges, S. W. (1999). A neural explanation of fetal heart rate patterns: A test of the Polyvagal Theory. *Developmental Psychobiology, 35*(2), 108–118.

Sanossian, N., & Haut, S. (2002). Chronic diarrhea associated with vagal nerve stimulation. *Neurology, 58*(2), 330–330.

Siegel, D. J. (1999). *The developing mind: How relationships and the brain interact to shape who we are.* New York: Guilford.

Staud, R. (2008). Heart rate variability as a biomarker of fibromyalgia syndrome. *Future Rheumatology, 3*(5), 475–483.

Thayer, J. F., & Lane, R. D. (2000). A model of neurovisceral integration in emotion regulation and dysregulation. *Journal of Affective Disorders, 61*(3), 201–216.

Thayer, J. F., & Lane, R. D. (2007). The role of vagal function in the risk for cardiovascular disease and mortality. *Biological Psychology, 74*(2), 224–242.

Whitehead, W. E., Palsson, O. S., Levy, R. R., Feld, A. D., Turner, M., & Von Korff, M. (2007). Comorbidity in irritable bowel syndrome. *American Journal of Gastroenterology, 102*(12), 2767–2776.

Credits

Chapter 1: Neurocardiology Through the Lens of the Polyvagal Theory

This article was published in *Neurocardiology: Pathophysiological Aspects and Clinical Implications* (ed. Ricardo J. Gelpi and Bruno Buchholz), Stephen W. Porges and Jacek Kolacz, Neurocardiology through the lens of polyvagal theory, 343–352, Copyright Elsevier 2018.

Chapter 4: Vagal Pathways: Portals to Compassion

Porges, S. W. (2017). Vagal pathways: Portals to compassion. E. M. Seppala, E. Simon-Thomas, S. L. Brown, M. C. Worline, C. D. Cameron, and J. R. Doty (Eds.), *Oxford handbook of compassion science* (pp. 189–202). Reprinted by permission of Oxford University Press.

Chapter 5: Yoga Therapy and Polyvagal Theory: The Convergence of Traditional Wisdom and Contemporary Neuroscience for Self-Regulation and Resilience

Copyright © 2018 Sullivan, M. B. Erb, M. Schmalzl, L. Moonaz, S. Noggle Taylor, J., and Porges, S. W. Reprinted by permission of Frontiers Media.

Chapter 6: Mindfulness-Based Movement: A Polyvagal Perspective

Lucas, A. R., Klepin, H. D., Porges, S. W., Rejeski, W. J. (2018). Mindfulness-based movement: A polyvagal perspective. *Integrative Cancer Therapies*, 17(1), 5–15. https://doi.org/10.1177/2F1534735416682087. Reprinted by permission of SAGE Publications.

Chapter 7: Group Psychotherapy as a Neural Exercise: Bridging Polyvagal Theory and Attachment Theory

Flores, P. J., Porges, S. W. (2017). Group psychotherapy as a neural exercise: Bridging polyvagal theory and attachment theory. *International Journal of Group Psychotherapy*, 67(2), 202–222. https://doi.org/10.1080/00207284.2016.1263544. Reprinted by permission of American Group Psychotherapy Association, www.agpa.org.

Chapter 8: Neural Mechanisms Underlying Human-Animal Interaction: An Evolutionary Perspective

Carter, C. S., Porges, S. W. (2016). Neural mechanisms underlying human-animal interactions: An evolutionary perspective. In L.S. Freund, S. McCune, L. Esposito, N.R. Gee, and P. McCardle (Eds.), *Social neuroscience of human-animal interaction* (pp. 89–105). Reprinted by permission of American Psychological Association.

Chapter 9: Therapeutic Presence: Neurophysiological Mechanisms Mediating Feeling Safe in Therapeutic Relationships

Geller, S. M., Porges, S. W. (2014). Therapeutic presence: Neurophysiological mechanisms mediating feeling safe in clinical interactions. *Journal of Psychotherapy Integration*, 24(3), 178–192. https://doi.apa.org/doi/10.1037/a0037511. Reprinted by permission of American Psychological Association.

Chapter 10: Play and the Dynamics of Treating Pediatric Medical Trauma: Insights From Polyvagal Theory

This chapter originally appeared in *Rhythms of Relating in Children's Therapies: Connecting Creatively with Vulnerable Children*, ed. by Stuart Daniel and Colwyn Trevarthen. © Jessica Kingsley Publishers 2017. Reproduced with permission of Jessica Kinglsey Publishers Limited through PLSClear.

Chapter 11: Brain–Body Connection May Ease Autistic People's Social Problems

This article originally appeared on spectrumnews.org at https://www.spectrumnews .org/opinion/viewpoint/brain-body-connection-may-ease-autistic-peoples-social -problems/. Reprinted by permission of spectrumnews.org.

Chapter 12: Reducing Auditory Hypersensitivities in Autistic Spectrum Disorder: Preliminary Findings Evaluating the Listening Project Protocol

Copyright © 2014 Porges, S. W., Bazhenova, O. V., Bal, E., Carlson, N., Sorokin, Y., Heilman, K. J., Cook, E. H., and Lewis, G. F. Reprinted by permission of Frontiers Media.

Chapter 13: The Significance of Stillness

Porges, S. W., Winn, D. (2017). The significance of stillness. *Human Givens Journal*, 24(2). Reprinted with permission of Human Givens Journal.

Chapter 14: The COVID-19 Pandemic Is a Paradoxical Challenge to Our Nervous System: A Polyvagal Perspective

Porges, S. W. (2020). The COVID-19 pandemic is a paradoxical challenge to our nervous system: A polyvagal perspective. *Clinical Neuropsychiatry*, 17(2), 135–138. doi .org/10.36131/CN20200220. Reprinted by permission of *Clinical Neuropsychiatry*.

Appendix: Polyvagal Theory: A Primer

From CLINICAL APPLICATIONS OF THE POLYVAGAL THEORY: THE EMERGENCE OF POLYVAGAL-INFORMED THERAPIES edited by Stephen W. Porges and Deb Dana. Copyright © 2018 by Stephen W. Porges. Used by permission of W. W. Norton & Company, Inc.

Index

Note: Italicized page locators refer to figures; tables are noted with t.

chants and chanting, 68,
69, 70
  contemplative practices,
    social engagement
    system, and, 78, 79
  Gregorian and Buddhist,
    82
  physiology of, 69*t*
  temple acoustics and
    harmonics of, 82–83
childhood medical trauma.
  see pediatric medical
  trauma
chronic diseases
  dissolution and symptoms
    related to, 27–29
  heart rate variability and,
    14
CIH. *see* complementary and
  integrative health care
  (CIH)
circumaural headphones,
  LPP trials and use of,
  214
classical composers of music,
  acoustic features for
  calming infants used by,
  83–84
*Clinical Applications of the
  Polyvagal Theory* (Porges
  & Dana), xxii, 22*t*
cochlea, 209
coevolution, human-dog
  bonds as example of,
  163
cognition, "embodied," 152
cognitive function, vagal
  nerve stimulation and,
  13
Collins, J., 238
colorectal cancer
  physical activity research
    on survivors of, 121
  sedentary behaviors and
    risk of mortality for
    survivors of, 122
comorbidities, 2
companion animals, 161
  bereavement periods and
    value of, 162
  defensive aggression and,
    165
  human sensitivity to vocal-
    izations of, 157
  oxytocin studies on, 163
  positive emotions, sense of
    safety, and, 154–55

companionship, beneficial
  consequences of, 160
compassion, 147
  antecedent states for, 80
  defining, 66
  healing, respect for individ-
    ual experience of pain,
    and, 68
  newer vagal circuit and, 74
  recruitment of social safety
    system and, 83
  safe state and, 70–71
  state differences between
    empathy and, 67–68
  steps to, 85*t*
  vagal pathways as portals
    to, 66–85
  yoga and, 104
compassion-focused therapy,
  83, 86
complementary and integrative health care (CIH),
  yoga therapy and, 97,
  112
computer-altered music
  Listening Project Protocol
    and, 211
  range of reactions to,
    238–39
conflict in group psycho-
  therapy, exercising the
  vagal brake (clinical
  example), 148–52
connectedness, COVID-19
  pandemic and impact
  on, 245–46
contemplative neuroscience
  assumption of directional
    causality and, 69, 70
  emergence of, as a disci-
    pline, 66
contemplative practices, 74
  downregulation of defense
    and promotion of calm-
    ness with, 70
  enhanced vagal regulation
    and, 70
  face-heart connection and,
    75–76
  neuroception and, 82
  optimizing effects of, multi-
    step sequential model
    for, 85–86
  physiological state and
    initiation of, 75–76
  rituals tied to, and states of
    calm and safety, 71

safe states and, 70, 78,
  79–80
social engagement system
  and, 78–80
vagal regulation of physiological state and, 76
vagal states intertwined
  within history of, 68–71
cooperation, survival of the
  fittest for mammals and,
  45, 247, 268
co-opting, 54
coregulation, xxi, 32, 236,
  249, 259
  COVID-19 pandemic and
    developing strategies
    for, 150
  functioning of the vagal
    brake and, xx
  of neurophysiological state
    via social interaction,
    246
  play and, 198–99, 264
  unique mammalian auto-
    nomic nervous system
    and, 54
coregulatory relationships,
  establishment of, 141
cortex, social engagement
  system and, 10, 77, 77,
  256
cortisol, xviii, 75, 161, 176,
  194
Counter, S. A., 209
Courneya, K. S., 120
COVID-19 pandemic
  conceptualizing autonomic
    state as an intervening
    variable during, 251
  impact of, on our bio-
    logical imperative to
    connect, 246–47
  mitigating threat responses
    through videoconferenc-
    ing during, 250
  one-nervous system model
    and awareness of
    bidirectional brain-body
    communication, 247–48
  as a paradoxical challenge
    to our nervous system,
    246–51
  polyvagal perspective on,
    248–49
  public health strategies and
    compounded feelings of
    threat during, 249–50

Other Polyvagal Theory Print Resources

*The Polyvagal Theory: Neurophysiological Foundations of
Emotions, Attachment, Communication, and Self-regulation*
Stephen W. Porges

*The Pocket Guide to Polyvagal Theory: The Transformative
Power of Feeling Safe*
Stephen W. Porges

*Clinical Applications of the Polyvagal Theory: The Emergence
of Polyvagal-Informed Therapies*
Edited by Stephen W. Porges and Deb Dana

*The Polyvagal Theory in Therapy: Engaging the Rhythm of
Regulation*
Deb Dana

*Polyvagal Exercises for Safety and Connection:
50 Client-Centered Practices*
Deb Dana

*Polyvagal Theory and the Developing Child: Systems of Care
for Strengthening Kids, Families, and Communities*
Marilyn R. Sanders and George S. Thompson

Polyvagal Flip Chart: Understanding the Science of Safety
Deb Dana

About the Author

Stephen W. Porges, Ph.D., is Distinguished University Scientist at Indiana University where he is the founding director of the Traumatic Stress Research Consortium in the Kinsey Institute. He is Professor of Psychiatry at the University of North Carolina, and Professor Emeritus at both the University of Illinois at Chicago and the University of Maryland. He served as president of the Society for Psychophysiological Research and the Federation of Associations in Behavioral and Brain Sciences, and is a former recipient of a National Institute of Mental Health Research Scientist Development Award. He has published more than 350 peer reviewed scientific papers across several disciplines including anesthesiology, biomedical engineering, critical care medicine, ergonomics, exercise physiology, gerontology, neurology, neuroscience, obstetrics, pediatrics, psychiatry, psychology, psychometrics, space medicine, and substance abuse.

Porges is the world's leading expert on the relationship between the autonomic nervous system, a neural system that oversees largely unconscious functions such as heart rate and digestion, and social behavior. He is the creator of the groundbreaking Polyvagal Theory, a theory that explains how social behavior is linked to our physiology. By describing the evolutionary journey from asocial reptiles to social mammals, the theory identifies the unique role that cues of safety play in our lives. The theory has transformed the conceptualization of trauma treatment and has been integrated in treatment strategies by clinicians around the world. The theory has provided exciting new insights for therapists and clients into the way our autonomic nervous system unconsciously mediates accessibility to treatment, social engagement, trust, and intimacy.

He holds several patents involved in monitoring and regulating autonomic state with applications in mental and physical health. He is the creator of a music-based intervention, the Safe and Sound Protocol ™ , which currently is used by more than 2,000 therapists to improve spontaneous social engagement, to reduce hearing sensitivities, and to improve language processing, state regulation, and spontaneous social engagement.